NATIONAL STANDARDS

FOR

WORLD HISTORY

EXPLORING PATHS TO THE PRESENT

Grades 5–12

Expanded Edition

Including Examples of Student Achievement

National Center for History in the Schools
University of California, Los Angeles

The development of the World History Standards was administered by the National Center for History in the Schools at the University of California, Los Angeles under the guidance of the National Council for History Standards. The standards were developed with funding from the National Endowment for the Humanities and the U.S. Department of Education. This publication does not necessarily represent positions or policies of the United States government, and no official endorsement should be inferred. With the exception of photographs and other visual materials, this publication may be freely reproduced and distributed for educational and research purposes.

Project Co-directors:	Charlotte Crabtree
	Gary B. Nash
Project Assistant Director:	Linda Symcox
Art Director:	Robin Weisz
Production planning:	Chris Coniglio
Production:	UCLA Publication Design Services
Document control:	Marta Hill
Photo Research:	David Vigilante
Copyright procurement:	Leticia Zermeno

First Printing 1994

Ordering Information
National Standards for World History: Exploring Paths to the Present
ISBN 0-9633218-2-X

Write to:

National Center for History in the Schools
University of California, Los Angeles
10880 Wilshire Blvd., Suite 761
Los Angeles, CA 90024-4108
FAX: (310) 825-4723

PREFACE

Publication of the *National Standards for World History: Exploring Paths to the Present* could not be more timely. These standards address one of the major goals for education reform contained in the landmark legislation, **Goals 2000: Educate America Act,** signed into law by President Bill Clinton in March 1994. This statute affirms that by the year 2000, "All students will leave grades 4, 8, and 12 having demonstrated competency over challenging subject matter" in the core academic subjects of the school curriculum, history among them. Heralding passage of this legislation by the Congress, Secretary of Education Richard W. Riley announced, "Final passage of the Goals 2000 legislation moves us one step closer to the day when we can assure every parent in America that their children . . . are receiving an education that is up to world class standards." It is a goal broadly supported by the American people, their state governors, their legislators in the United States Congress, and the two successive administrations of Presidents George Bush and Bill Clinton.

Support for the development of internationally competitive national standards of excellence for the nation's schools was first voiced in the National Education Goals adopted by the nation's fifty governors in their 1989 meeting in Charlottesville, Virginia. The third of the six education goals adopted in that meeting identified history as one of five school subjects for which challenging new national achievement standards should be established.

In October 1992 President Clinton reaffirmed his commitment to achieving these goals, including the "establishment of world class standards [specifically to include history] and development of a meaningful national examination system . . . to determine whether our students are meeting the standards . . . , to increase expectations, and to give schools incentives and structures to improve student performance." That same year, the importance of national standards in history was again affirmed in *Raising Standards for American Education,* the report to Congress of the National Council on Education Standards and Testing, appointed by the Congress to advise on these matters under the co-chairmanship of Governors Roy Romer (D-Colorado) and Carroll A. Campbell (R-South Carolina).

It was in this robust climate of education reform that the National History Standards Project was born. Funded in the spring of 1992 by the National Endowment for the Humanities and the Office of Educational Research and Improvement of the United States Department of Education, this Project sought to develop broad national consensus for what constitutes excellence in the teaching and learning of history in the nation's schools. Developed through a broad-based national consensus-building process, this task has involved working toward agreement both on the larger purposes of history in the school curriculum and on the more specific history understandings and thinking processes all students should have equal opportunity to acquire over twelve years of precollegiate education.

In undertaking this process, it was widely agreed that the History Standards, as finally drafted, would in fact mark a critical advance but not the final destination in what must be an ongoing, dynamic process of improvement and revision over the years to come. History is an extraordinarily dynamic field today, and standards drafted for the schools must be open to continuing development to keep pace with new refinements and revisions in this field.

This present publication, *National Standards for World History,* marks a major milestone in the development of standards of excellence for the nation's schools. It is the result of over two years of intensive work by hundreds of gifted classroom teachers of history; of supervisors, state social studies specialists, and chief state school officers responsible for history in the schools; of dozens of talented and active academic historians in the nation; and of representatives of a broad array of professional and scholarly organizations, civic and public interest groups, parents and individual citizens with a stake in the teaching of history in the schools.

The National Council for History Standards, the policy-setting body responsible for providing policy direction and oversight of the project, consisted of thirty members, including the present or immediate past presidents of such large-membership organizations directly responsible for the content and teaching of history as the Council of Chief State School Officers, the Association for Supervision and Curriculum Development, the Council of State Social Studies Specialists, the National Council for the Social Studies, the National Council for History Education, the Organization of American Historians, and the Organization of History Teachers. In addition, members included the director and associate director of the Social Studies Development Center at Indiana University, supervisory and curriculum development staff of county and city school districts, experienced classroom teachers, and distinguished historians in the fields of United States and world history. To foster correspondence in the development of the United States history standards with the work under development for the 1994 National Assessment of Educational Progress (NAEP) in United States History, several participants in the NAEP Planning and Steering Committees were included in the National Council for History Standards. For similar reasons two members of the congressionally mandated National Council for Education Standards and Testing also served on this Council. Finally, the two directors of the National Center for History in the Schools, responsible for administering this project, served as co-chairs of the Council.

The National Forum for History Standards was composed of representatives from major education, public interest, parent-teacher, and other organizations concerned with history in the schools. Advisory in its function, the Forum provided important counsel and feedback for this project as well as access to the larger public through the membership of the organizations represented in the Forum.

Nine Organizational Focus Groups of between fifteen and twenty-nine members each, chosen by the leadership of their respective organizations, were engaged to provide important advisory, review, and consulting services to the project. Organizations providing this special service included the Council of Chief State School Officers, the Association for Supervision and Curriculum Development, the American Historical Association, the World History Association, the National Council for the Social Studies, the Organization of American Historians, the National Council for History Education, the Council of State Social Studies Specialists, and the Organization of History Teachers.

Three Curriculum Task Forces were formed, totaling more than fifty members, with responsibility for developing the standards for students in grades K-4, and for students in grades 5-12 in the fields of United States and world history. Composed of veteran classroom teachers from throughout the United States who were recommended by the many organizations participating in this project, and of recognized scholars of United States and world history with deep commitments to history education in schools, these groups have worked for many months in grade-alike writing teams and in meetings of the whole to ensure continuity of standards across all levels of schooling, elementary through high school.

The drafting of the World History Standards required more than the usual collaborative effort that any standards project must mount. Acknowledgements and appreciation are therefore especially apt. The National Council for History Standards established an *ad hoc* World History Committee of experienced teachers and historians with expertise in various eras and areas of world history to draft a scaffolding for the writing of the standards. This devoted group, which met for three work sessions over a period of six months, was chaired by Michael Winston, Howard University and the Alfred Harcourt Foundation. The other members of the committee were: Joan Arno, George Washington High School, Philadelphia,

Pennsylvania; David Baumbach, Woolsair Elementary Gifted Center, Pittsburgh, Pennsylvania; Richard Bulliet, Columbia University; Ainslee T. Embree, Columbia University; Carol Gluck, Columbia University; Akira Iriye, Harvard University; Henry G. Kiernan, Director of Curriculum, West Morris Regional High School District, Chester, New Jersey; Colin Palmer, University of North Carolina, Chapel Hill; Richard Saller, University of Chicago; and Theodore Rabb, Princeton University.

Working from the Winston Committee's report was a group of experienced, knowledgeable, and dedicated classroom teachers and historians who have been in the forefront of efforts to teach and write a more balanced and inclusive world history. This group — the World History Curriculum Task Force — worked over two summers and in week-long sessions throughout these two academic years. They included: Joann Alberghini, Lake View Junior High School, Santa Maria, California; John Arevalo, Harlandale High School, San Antonio, Texas; Joan Arno, George Washington High School, Philadelphia, Pennsylvania; David Baumbach, Woolsair Elementary Gifted Center, Pittsburgh, Pennsylvania; Edward Berenson, University of California, Los Angeles; Margaret Binnaker, St. Andrews-Swanee School, St. Andrews, Tennessee; Jacqueline Brown-Frierson, Lemmel Middle School, Baltimore, Maryland; Richard Bulliet, Columbia University; Stanley Burstein, California State University, Los Angeles; Anne Chapman, Western Reserve Academy, Hudson, Ohio; Peter Cheoros, Lynwood High School, Lynwood, California; Sammy Crawford, Soldotna High School, Soldotna, Alaska; Ross Dunn, San Diego State University; Benjamin Elman, University of California, Los Angeles; Jean Fleet, Riverside University High School, Milwaukee, Wisconsin; Jana Flores, Pine Grove Elementary School, Santa Maria, California; Michele Forman, Middlebury High School, Middlebury, Vermont; Charles Frazee, California State University, Fullerton; Marilynn Jo Hitchens, Wheat Ridge High School, Wheat Ridge, Colorado; Jean Johnson, Friends Seminary, New York, New York; Henry G. Kiernan, West Morris Regional High School District, Chester, New Jersey; Carrie McIver, Santee Summit High School, Santee, California; Susan Meisler, Vernon Center Middle School, Vernon, Connecticut; Joe Palumbo, Long Beach Unified School District, Long Beach, California; Sue Rosenthal, High School for Creative and Performing Arts, Philadelphia, Pennsylvania; Heidi Roupp, Aspen High School, Aspen, Colorado; Irene Segade, San Diego High School, San Diego, California; Geoffrey Symcox, University of California, Los Angeles; David Vigilante, Gompers Secondary School, San Diego, California; Scott Waugh, University of California, Los Angeles; Julia Werner, Nicolet High School, Glendale, Wisconsin; and Donald Woodruff, Fredericksburg Academy, Fredericksburg, Virginia.

To all of these precollegiate and university members of the World History Curriculum Task Force we express great respect and admiration for their tireless efforts and good spirits in negotiating the choppy waters of world history. None of their efforts would have reached fruition without the very special involvement of Ross Dunn, who played a leading and indispensable role in coordinating the work of the World History Curriculum Task Force, led two of the drafting sessions, and acted as a gentle intellectual *padrone* in negotiating the many cross-currents that necessarily attend the writing of anything as ambitious as a framework for the study of humankind's entire history.

In the final drafting of *National Standards for World History: Exploring Paths to the Present*, a small group of people worked with Dunn in the summer and early fall of 1994: Joann Alberghini, Roger Beck, Anne Chapman, Jean Fleet, Jana Flores, Jean Johnson, Henry Kiernan, David Vigilante, and Donald Woodruff. The East Asian Curriculum Project at the East Asian Institute, Columbia University, and The Council on Islamic Education greatly assisted this group as they drafted grade-level materials. The co-directors of this project believe that only rarely in the history of

American education has such a group of good-spirited, gifted, and devoted teachers — from across the country and teaching at every level of education from elementary schools to baccalaureate institutions — accomplished so much for the teaching of history in the schools.

Our thanks go also to the many members of the National Council for History Standards, the National Forum for History Standards, and the Organizational Focus Groups who gave unfailingly and selflessly of their time and professional expertise during the more than two years of intensive work that went into the development of the standards. The Appendix presents the rosters of all these working groups. In particular, we salute those who read draft after draft under difficult deadlines throughout the spring and summer of 1994, and submitted substantive recommendations for revision that have contributed importantly to the completion of this volume.

Special appreciation is due also to the many school districts and administrators who time and again agreed to the release time that allowed the gifted teachers who served on the World History Curriculum Task Force to meet at UCLA for week-long working sessions throughout the school year in order to complete the development of the standards and of the grade-appropriate examples of student achievement of the standards.

As co-directors of this project, we express special appreciation, also, to the many thousands of teachers, curriculum leaders, assessment experts, historians, parents, textbook publishers, and others too numerous to mention who have sought review copies of the standards and turned out for public hearings and information sessions scheduled at regional and national conferences throughout these two years, and who have provided their independent assessments and recommendations for making these standards historically sound, workable in classrooms, and responsive to the needs and interests of students in the schools.

Finally, we note with appreciation the funding provided by the National Endowment for the Humanities and by the Office of Educational Research and Improvement of the United States Department of Education to conduct this complex and broadly inclusive enterprise.

In this most contentious field of the curriculum, there have been many who have wondered if a national consensus could be forged concerning what all students should have opportunity to learn about the history of the world and of the peoples of all racial, religious, ethnic, and national backgrounds who have been a part of that story. The responsiveness, enormous good will, and dogged determination of so many to meet this challenge has reinforced our confidence in the inherent strength and capabilities of this nation now to undertake the steps necessary for bringing to all students the benefits of this endeavor. The stakes are high. It is the challenge that must now be undertaken.

Charlotte Crabtree and Gary B. Nash
Co-directors

TABLE OF CONTENTS

"There is an old saying that

the course of course of civilization

is a race between catastrophe

and education. In a democracy

such as ours, we must make sure

that education wins the race"

John F. Kennedy

Developing Standards in World History for Students in Grades 5-12

Significance of History for the Educated Citizen

Setting standards for history in the schools requires a clear vision of the place and importance of history in the general education of all students. The widespread and growing support for more and better history in the schools, beginning in the early grades of elementary education, is one of the more encouraging signs of the decade. The reasons are many, but none are more important to a democratic society than this: *Knowledge of history is the precondition of political intelligence.* Without history, a society shares no common memory of where it has been, what its core values are, or what decisions of the past account for present circumstances. Without history, we cannot undertake any sensible inquiry into the political, social, or moral issues in society. And without historical knowledge and inquiry, we cannot achieve the informed, discriminating citizenship essential to effective participation in the democratic processes of governance and the fulfillment for all our citizens of the nation's democratic ideals.

Thomas Jefferson long ago prescribed history for all who would take part in self-government because it would enable them to prepare for things yet to come. The philosopher Etienne Gilson noted the special significance of the perspectives history affords. *"History,"* he remarked, *"is the only laboratory we have in which to test the consequences of thought."* History opens to students the great record of human experience, revealing the vast range of accommodations individuals and societies have made to the problems confronting them, and disclosing the consequences that have followed the various choices that have been made. By studying the choices and decisions of the past, students can confront today's problems and choices with a deeper awareness of the alternatives before them and the likely consequences of each.

Current problems, of course, do not duplicate those of the past. Essential to extrapolating knowledgeably from history to the issues of today requires yet a further skill, again dependent upon one's understanding of the past: differentiating between (1) relevant historical antecedents that properly inform analyses of current issues and (2) those antecedents that are clearly irrelevant. Students must be sufficiently grounded in historical understanding in order to bring sound historical analysis to the service of informed decision making.

What is required is mastery of what Nietzsche once termed "critical history" and what Gordon Craig has explained as the "ability, after painful inquiry and sober judgment, to determine what part of history [is] relevant to one's current problems and what [is] not," whether one is assessing a situation, forming an opinion, or taking an active position on the issue. In exploring these matters, students will soon discover that history is filled with the high costs of decisions reached on the basis of false analogies from the past as well as the high costs of actions taken with little or no understanding of the important lessons the past imparts.

These learnings directly contribute to the education of the *public citizen*, but they uniquely contribute to nurturing the *private individual* as well. Historical memory is the key to self-identity, to seeing one's place in the stream of time, and one's connectedness with all of humankind. We are part of an ancient chain, and the long hand of the past is upon us — for good and for ill — just as our hands will rest on our descendants for years to come. Denied knowledge of one's roots and of one's place in the great stream of human history, the individual is deprived of the fullest sense of self and of that sense of shared community on which one's fullest personal development as well as responsible citizenship depends. For these purposes, history and the humanities must occupy an indispensable role in the school curriculum.

Finally, history opens to students opportunities to develop a comprehensive understanding of the world and of the many societies whose traditions and values may in many ways be different from their own. From a balanced and inclusive world history students may gain an appreciation both of the world's many peoples and of their shared humanity and common problems. Students may also acquire the habit of seeing matters through others' eyes and come to realize that they can better understand themselves as they study others. Historical understanding based on such comparative studies in world history does not require approval or forgiveness for the tragedies either of one's own society or of others; nor does it negate the importance of critically examining alternative value systems and their effects in supporting or denying basic human rights and aspirations. Especially important, an understanding of world history can contribute to fostering the kind of mutual patience, respect, and civic courage required in our increasingly pluralistic society and interdependent world.

If students are to see ahead more clearly, and be ready to act with judgment and with respect for the shared humanity of all who may be touched by the decisions they as citizens make, then schools must attend to this critical field of the curriculum.

Definition of Standards

Standards in history make explicit the goals that all students should have opportunity to acquire, if the purposes just considered are to be achieved. In history, standards are of two types:

1. *Historical thinking skills* that enable students to evaluate evidence, develop comparative and causal analyses, interpret the historical record, and construct sound historical arguments and perspectives on which informed decisions in contemporary life can be based.

2. *Historical understandings* that define what students should *know* about the history of their nation and of the world. These understandings are drawn from the record of human aspirations, strivings, accomplishments, and failures in at least five spheres of human activity: the social, scientific/technological, economic, political, and philosophical/religious/aesthetic. They also provide students the historical perspectives required to analyze contemporary issues and problems confronting citizens today.

Historical thinking and understanding do not, of course, develop independently of one another. Higher levels of historical thinking depend upon and are linked to the attainment of higher levels of historical understanding. For these reasons, the standards presented in Chapter 3 of this volume provide an integration of historical thinking and understanding.

Criteria for the Development of Standards

The development of national standards in United States and world history presents a special challenge in deciding what, of the great storehouse of human history, is the most significant for all students to acquire. Perhaps less contentious but no less important is deciding what historical perspectives and what skills in historical reasoning, values analysis, and policy thinking are essential for all students to achieve.

The following criteria, developed and refined over the course of a broad-based national review and consensus process, were adopted by the National Council for History Standards in order to guide the development of history standards for grades kindergarten through 12.

1. Standards should be intellectually demanding, reflect the best historical scholarship, and promote active questioning and learning rather than passive absorption of facts, dates, and names.

2. Such standards should be equally expected of *all* students and all students should be provided equal access to the curricular opportunities necessary to achieving those standards.

3. Standards should reflect the ability of children from the earliest elementary school years to learn the meanings of history and the methods of historians.

4. Standards should be founded in chronology, an organizing approach that fosters appreciation of pattern and causation in history.

5. Standards should strike a balance between emphasizing broad themes in United States and world history and probing specific historical events, ideas, movements, persons, and documents.

6. All historical study involves selection and ordering of information in light of general ideas and values. Standards for history should reflect the principles of sound historical reasoning — careful evaluation of evidence, construction of causal relationships, balanced interpretation, and comparative analysis. The ability to detect and evaluate distortion and propaganda by omission, suppression, or invention of facts is essential.

7. Standards should include awareness of, appreciation for, and the ability to utilize a variety of sources of evidence from which historical knowledge is achieved, including written documents, oral tradition, popular culture, literature, artifacts, art and music, historical sites, photographs, and films.

8. Standards for United States history should reflect both the nation's diversity, exemplified by race, ethnicity, social and economic status, gender, region, politics, and religion, and the nation's commonalities. The contributions and struggles of specific groups and individuals should be included.

9. Standards in United States history should contribute to citizenship education through developing understanding of our common civic identity and shared civic values within the polity, through analyzing major policy issues in the nation's history and through developing mutual respect among its many peoples.

10. History Standards should emphasize the nature of civil society and its relationship to government and citizenship. Standards in United States history should address the historical origins of the nation's democratic political system and the continuing development of its ideals and institutions, its controversies, and the struggle to narrow the gap between its ideals and practices. Standards in world history should include different patterns of political institutions, ranging from varieties of democracy to varieties of authoritarianism, and ideas and aspirations developed by civilizations in all parts of the world.

11. Standards in United States and world history should be separately developed but interrelated in content and similar in format. Standards in United States history should reflect the global context in which the nation unfolded; and world history should treat United States history as one of its integral parts.

12. Standards should include appropriate coverage of recent events in United States and world history, including social and political developments and international relations of the post-World War II era.

13. Standards in U.S. history and world history should utilize regional and local history by exploring specific events and movements through case studies and historical research. Local and regional history should enhance the broader patterns of U.S. and world history.

14. Standards in U.S. and world history should integrate fundamental facets of human culture such as religion, science and technology, politics and government, economics, interactions with the environment, intellectual and social life, literature, and the arts.

15. Standards in world history should treat the history and values of diverse civilizations, including those of the West, and should especially address the interactions among them.

Developing Standards in World History

Approaching World History

These standards rest on the premise that our schools must teach a comprehensive history in which all students may share. That means a history that encompasses humanity. In writing the standards a primary task was to identify those developments in the past that involved and affected relatively large numbers of people and that had broad significance for later generations. Some of these developments pertain to particular civilizations or regions. Others involve patterns of human interconnection that extended across cultural and political boundaries. Within this framework students are encouraged to explore in depth particular cases of historical change that may have had only regional or local importance but that exemplify the drama and humane substance of the past.

These standards represent a forceful commitment to world-scale history. No attempt has been made, however, to address the histories of all identifiable peoples or cultural traditions. The aim rather is to encourage students to ask large and searching questions about the human past, to compare patterns of continuity and change in different parts of the world, and to examine the histories and achievements of particular peoples or civilizations with an eye to wider social, cultural, or economic contexts.

Periodization

Because the standards are organized chronologically, they must incorporate a system of historical periodization. Arranging the study of the past into distinct periods of time is one way of imposing a degree of order and coherence on the incessant, fragmented flow of events. Periodizing world history, that is, dividing it into distinct eras, is part of the process of making it intelligible. Historians have devised a variety of periodization designs for world history. Students should understand that every one of these designs is a creative construction reflecting the historian's particular aims, preferences, and cultural or social values.

A periodization of world history that encompasses the grand sweep of the human past can make sense only at a relatively high level of generalization. Historians have also worked out periodizations for particular civilizations, regions, and nations, and these have their own validity, their own benchmarks and turning points. The history of India, for example, would necessarily be periodized differently than would the history of China or Europe, since the major shifts in Indian history relate to the Gupta age, the Mughal empire, the post-independence era, and so on.

We believe that as teachers work toward a more integrated study of world history in their classrooms they will appreciate having a periodization design that encourages study of those broad developments that have involved large segments of the world's population and that have had lasting signficance. The standards are divided into eight eras of world history. The title of each era attempts to capture the very general character of that age. Note that the time periods of some of the eras overlap in order to incorporate both the closure of certain developments and the start of others. The beginning and ending dates should be viewed as approximations representing broad shifts in the human scene.

Era 1. The Beginnings of Human Society

Era 2. Early Civilizations to 1000 BCE

Era 3. Classical Traditions, Major Religions, and Giant Empires, 1000 BCE-300 CE

Era 4. Expanding Zones of Exchange and Encounter, 300-1000 CE

Era 5. Intensified Hemispheric Interactions, 1000-1500 CE

Era 6. Emergence of the First Global Age, 1450-1770

Era 7. The Age of Revolutions, 1750-1914

Era 8. The Twentieth Century

Historical Understanding

History is a broadly integrative field, recounting and analyzing human aspirations and strivings in various spheres of human activity: **social, political, scientific/technological, economic,** and **cultural.** Studying history — inquiring into families, communities, states, nations, and various peoples of the world — at once engages students in the lives, aspirations, struggles, accomplishments, and failures of real people, in all these aspects of their lives.

Through social history, students come to deeper understandings of society: of what it means to be human, of different and changing views of family structures, of men's and women's roles, of childhood and of children's roles, of various groups and classes in society, and of relationships among all these individuals and groups. This sphere considers how economic, religious, cultural, and political changes have affected social life, and it incorporates developments shaping the destiny of millions: the history of slavery; of class conflict; of mass migration and immigration; the human consequences of plague, war, and famine; and the longer life expectancy and rising living standards following upon medical, technological, and economic advances.

Through political history, students come to deeper understandings of the political sphere of activity as it has developed in their local community, their state, their nation, and in various societies of the world. Efforts to construct governments and institutions; the drive to seize and hold power over others; the struggle to achieve and preserve basic human rights, justice, equality, law, and order in societies; and the evolution of regional and world mechanisms to promote international law are all part of the central human drama to be explored and analyzed in the study of history.

Through history of science and technology, students come to deeper understandings of how the scientific quest to understand nature, the world we live in, and humanity itself is as old as recorded history. So, too, is the quest to improve ways of doing everything from producing food, to caring for the ill, and transporting goods, and advancing economic security and the well-being of the group. Understanding how scientific/technological developments have propelled change and how these changes have altered all other spheres of human activity is central to the study of history.

Through economic history students come to deeper understanding of the economic forces that have been crucial in determining the quality of people's lives, in structuring societies, and in influencing the course of events. Exchange relationships within and between cultures have had major impacts on society and politics, producing changing patterns of regional, hemispheric, and global economic dominance and permitting the emergence in the 20th century of a truly international economy, with far-reaching consequences for all other spheres of activity.

Through cultural history, students learn how ideas, beliefs, and values have profoundly influenced human actions throughout history. Religion, philosophy, art, and popular culture have all been central to the aspirations and achievements of all societies, and have been a mainspring of historical change from earliest times. Students' explorations of this sphere of human activity, through literature, sacred writings and oral traditions, political treatises, drama, art, architecture, music, and dance, deepen their understandings of the human experience.

Analyzing these five spheres of human activity requires considering them in the contexts both of *historical time* and *geographic place*. The historical record is inextricably linked to the geographic setting in which it developed. Population movements and settlements, scientific and economic activities, geopolitical agendas, and the distributions and spread of political, philosophical, religious, and aesthetic ideas are all related in some measure to geographic factors. The opportunities, limitations, and constraints with which people have addressed the issues and challenges of their time have, to a significant degree, been influenced by the environment in which they lived or to which they have had access, and by the traces on the landscape, malignant or benign, irrevocably left by those who came before.

Because these spheres are inextricably interwoven in the real lives of individuals and societies, essential understandings in world history often cut across these categories. Thus, to comprehend the forces leading to the Iberian Conquest of Mesoamerica in the 15th and 16th centuries, students must address the **economics** of the interregional trading system that linked peoples of Africa, Asia, and Europe on the eve of the European overseas voyages; the **political and religious** changes initiated with the rise of centralized monarchies of Spain and Portugal; and the major **technological** innovations that the Portuguese and Spanish made in shipbuilding, navigation, and naval warfare and the influence of northern Europe, Muslim, and Chinese maritime technology on these changes.

Similarly, understanding the consequences of the Iberian Conquest of Mesoamerica demonstrates how change in any one of these spheres of human activity often had impact on some or all of the others. The many consequences of the Iberian military victories included, for example, the founding of Spanish and Portuguese **colonial empires** in the Americas; the **worldwide exchange** of flora, fauna, and pathogens following the Columbian encounter, the **social changes** wrought by the subjugation and enslavement of the indigenous peoples of the Americas, the devastating **demographic effects** caused by the introduction of new disease microorganisms into the Americas, the **forced relocation and enslavement** of some 10 million Africans in the European colonies, the changes in **religious beliefs and practices** that followed the introduction of Christianity into the Americas, and the **economic and social effects** of the infusion into the European economies of the vast gold and silver resources of the Americas. These many effects demonstrate the complexity of historical events and the broadly integrative nature of history itself. They also affirm, once again, the unique power of history to deepen students' understanding of the past, and of how we are still affected by it.

Historical Thinking

Beyond defining what students should _know_ — that is, the understandings in world history that all students should acquire — it is essential to consider what students should be able to _do_ to demonstrate their understandings and to apply their knowledge in productive ways.

The study of history involves much more than the passive absorption of facts, dates, names, and places. Real historical understanding requires students to think through cause-and-effect relationships, to reach sound historical interpretations, and to conduct historical inquiries and research leading to the knowledge on which informed decisions in contemporary life can be based. These thinking skills are the processes of _active_ learning.

Properly taught, history develops capacities for analysis and judgment. It reveals the ambiguity of choice, and it promotes wariness about quick, facile solutions which have so often brought human suffering in their wake. History fosters understanding of paradox and a readiness to distinguish between that which is beyond and that which is within human control, between the inevitable and the contingent. It trains students to detect bias, to weigh evidence, and to evaluate arguments, thus preparing them to make sensible, independent judgments, to sniff out spurious appeals to history by partisan pleaders, and to distinguish between anecdote and analysis.

To acquire these capabilities, students must develop competence in the following five types of historical thinking:

Chronological thinking, developing a clear sense of historical time — past, present, and future — in order to identify the temporal sequence in which events occurred, measure calendar time, interpret and create time lines, and explain patterns of historical succession and duration, continuity and change.

Historical comprehension, including the ability to read historical narratives with understanding, to identify the basic elements of the narrative structure (the characters, situation, sequence of events, their causes, and their outcomes); to develop historical perspectives — that is, the ability to describe the past through the eyes and experiences of those who were there, as revealed through their literature, art, artifacts, and the like, and to avoid "present-mindedness," judging the past solely in terms of the norms and values of today.

Historical analysis and interpretation, including the ability to compare and contrast different experiences, beliefs, motives, traditions, hopes, and fears of people from various groups and backgrounds, and at various times in the past and present; to analyze how these differing motives, interests, beliefs, hopes and fears influenced people's behaviors; to consider multiple perspectives in the records of human experience and multiple causes in analyses of historical events; to challenge arguments of historical inevitability; and, to compare and evaluate competing historical explanations of the past.

Historical research capabilities, including the ability to formulate historical questions from encounters with historical documents, artifacts, photos, visits to historical sites, and eyewitness accounts; to determine the historical time and context in which the artifact, document, or other record was created; to judge its credibility and authority; and to construct a sound historical narrative or argument concerning it.

Historical issues-analysis and decision-making, including the ability to identify problems that confronted people in the past, to analyze the various interests and points of view of people caught up in these situations; to evaluate alternative proposals for dealing with the problem(s); to analyze whether the decisions reached or the actions taken were good ones and why; and, to bring historical perspectives to bear on informed decision-making in the present.

Integrating Standards in Historical Understanding and Thinking

Chapter 2 presents the standards in historical thinking, largely independent of historical content in order to specify the quality of thinking desired for each. None of these skills in historical thinking, however, can be developed or even expressed in a vacuum. Every one of them requires historical content in order to function — a relationship made explicit in Chapter 3, in which the standards integrating historical understanding and historical thinking are presented for all eight eras of world history for grades 5-12.

Figure 1 illustrates the approach taken to integrate historical thinking and historical understandings in the standards. The example is drawn from Era 3, *"Classical Traditions, Major Religions, and Giant Empires, 1000 BCE-300 CE."* As illustrated, the five skills in historical thinking (the left side of the diagram) and the three historical understandings students should acquire concerning Aegean civilization (the right side of the diagram) are integrated in the central area of overlap in the diagram in order to define (immediately below) Standard 2A: What students should be able to do to demonstrate their understanding of the achievements and limitations of the democratic institutions that developed in Athens.

Pages 10 and 11 provide a further illustration of this same standard, presented this time in the format in which the standards are stated (Chapter 3). The selection is again drawn from Era 3, *"Classical Traditions, Major Religions, and Giant Empires, 1000 BCE-300 CE."* As illustrated, the standard first presents a statement defining what students should understand: "The democratic institutions and cultural achievements of Aegean civilization and the interrelations that developed between Hellenism and the cultural traditions of Southwest Asia and Egypt, 600-200 BCE."

The standard next presents a statement (2A), identifying the first understanding contained in Standard 2. The five statements in the shaded box specify what students should be able to do to demonstrate their understanding of the achievements and limitations of the democratic institutions that developed in Athens. Each statement illustrates the integration of historical thinking and understanding by marrying a particular thinking skill (*e.g.,* comparing) to a specific historical understanding (*e.g.,* Athenian democracy and the military aristocracy of Sparta). The particular thinking skill is further emphasized in the bracketed words following the statement (*e.g.,* **Compare and contrast**). The particular thinking skill is not the only one that can be employed but is a particularly apt one. Finally, each component of Standard 2A is coded to indicate in which grades the standard can appropriately be developed.

> 5-12 indicates the standard is appropriate for grades 5-6, as well as for all higher levels, from grades 7-8 through grades 9-12.

> 7-12 indicates the standard is appropriate for grades 7-8 through grades 9-12.

> 9-12 indicates the standard is best reserved for students in grades 9-12.

Finally, the shaded box under the subhead "Students Shall Be Able to" is supplemented with examples of student achievement of Standard 2A appropriate for grades 5-6, 7-8, and 9-12.

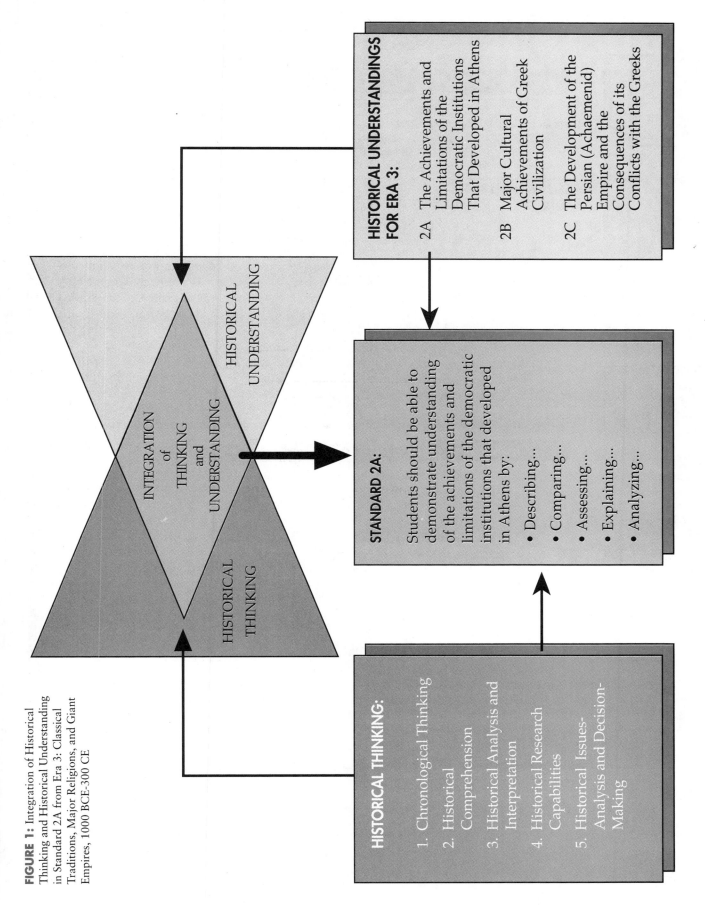

FIGURE 1: Integration of Historical Thinking and Historical Understanding in Standard 2A from Era 3: Classical Traditions, Major Religions, and Giant Empires, 1000 BCE-300 CE

HISTORICAL UNDERSTANDINGS FOR ERA 3:

2A   The Achievements and Limitations of the Democratic Institutions That Developed in Athens

2B   Major Cultural Achievements of Greek Civilization

2C   The Development of the Persian (Achaemenid) Empire and the Consequences of its Conflicts with the Greeks

HISTORICAL UNDERSTANDING

INTEGRATION of THINKING and UNDERSTANDING

HISTORICAL THINKING

STANDARD 2A:

Students should be able to demonstrate understanding of the achievements and limitations of the democratic institutions that developed in Athens by:

• Describing...

• Comparing...

• Assessing...

• Explaining...

• Analyzing...

HISTORICAL THINKING:

1. Chronological Thinking

2. Historical Comprehension

3. Historical Analysis and Interpretation

4. Historical Research Capabilities

5. Historical Issues-Analysis and Decision-Making

STANDARD 2

Statement of the historical understandings that students should acquire

Students Should Understand: *How Aegean civilization emerged and how interrelations developed among peoples of the eastern Mediterranean and Southwest Asia, 600-200 BCE.*

Students Should Be Able to:

Statement identifying the first understanding of Standard 2— The achievements and limitations of the democratic institutions that developed in Athens

2A Demonstrate understanding of the achievements and limitations of the democratic institutions that developed in Athens and other Aegean city-states by:

5-12 Comparing Athenian democracy with the military aristocracy of Sparta. [**Compare and contrast differing sets of ideas, values, and institutions**]

5-12 Explaining the class divisions of Greek society and the social and political roles of major classes, including slaves. [**Evidence historical perspectives**]

7-12 Describing the changing political institutions of Athens in the 6th and 5th centuries BCE and analyzing the influence of political thought on public life. [**Reconstruct patterns of historical succession and duration**]

7-12 Analyzing the place of women in Athenian society. [**Interrogate historical data**]

9-12 Assessing the importance of participatory government in Greek city-states for the development of Western political thought and institutions. [**Hypothesize the influence of the past**]

*Components of Standard 2A, demonstrating integration of historical understanding and **thinking***

Grades 5-6

Examples of student achievement of Standard 2A include:

Examples of student achievement of Standard 2A

♦ Assume the role of either a citizen, a merchant, a foreign resident, or a slave in both Athens and Sparta. Describe your life in each of these city-states. Compare the rights and responsibilities of a citizen in each city. After the class shares their findings, answer the question: *How did life differ depending on social class?*

♦ Construct a comparative chart that graphically depicts similarities and differences between Athenian democracy and the military aristocracy of Sparta.

♦ *If you were a woman in the 6th or 5th century BCE, would you rather have lived in Sparta or in Athens?* Give reasons based on historical evidence for your decision.

♦ Create a map of the Aegean area and depict each of the major Greek city-states. Delineate each city-state as to its form of government (democracy, oligarchy, tyranny, aristocracy, monarchy) by a symbol or color. *How many other Greek city-states followed the political lead of Athens or Sparta, and how many followed neither?*

78

ERA 3: CLASSICAL TRADITIONS, MAJOR RELIGIONS, AND GIANT EMPIRES, 1000 BCE-300 CE

Grades 7-8

Examples of student achievement of Standard 2A include:

- Prepare a chart listing the major political systems of Greek city-states in the 6th and 5th centuries BCE and explain the evolution of these governmental systems. *What are the advantages and disadvantages of each system?*

- Construct a chart showing the major changes in Athenian political organization from the initial monarchy to the forms under Solon and Cleisthenes. *What innovations did Cleisthenes make?*

- Describe the roles that women had in Athenian society and their rights under the law. Hypothesize why "democracy" was limited to males only.

- Analyze Pericles' *Funeral Oration* to discern Athenian values during the 5th century BCE. *Did daily life in classical Athens reflect these ideals?*

> *Examples of student achievement of Standard 2A*

Grades 9-12

Examples of student achievement of Standard 2A include:

- Describe the Greek concept of the "barbarian" as set forth in the works of Aristotle and other writers, and explain the position of "barbarians" in Greek city-states. *Could a "barbarian" become a Greek? How could the Greek concept of "barbarian" provide a foundation for greater communication between Greeks and outsiders? What is ethnocentrism? Are all modern societies and nations ethnocentric to some degree?*

- Analyze selections from *The Republic*. Prepare a report on how Plato's ideal polis has influenced political thought in the modern world.

- Develop a hypothesis to explain why the maturing of democratic institutions in Greece resulted in greater restrictions on the rights and freedoms of women. *What evidence can you give to support your hypothesis?*

- Explain the social strata in Athens and Sparta in the 5th century BCE. Choose one of the two, and compare its social structure to that of another Greek city-state such as Corinth or Thebes. *How would you account for similarities and differences?*

- Draw evidence from Thucydides' *Melian Dialogue* to examine the concepts of political freedom, national security, and justice. Appraise Pericles' "Funeral Oration" from the perspective of a Melian following the Athenian conquest.

- Support or refute the statement: "Athens was the laboratory of democracy and democratic law."

> *Examples of student achievement of Standard 2A*

Pericles
Library of Congress

79

As demonstrated above, Standard 2A is converted to appropriate achievement expectations for three levels of schooling: grades 5-6, grades 7-8, and grades 9-12. The point here is not to require the study of Era 3 in World history at all three levels of schooling. Rather, it is to provide teachers with examples of what is appropriate achievement for students in whatever grade (or grades) this era is studied in their local school curriculum.

Questions Concerning These Standards

Q: **Do these standards require that Era 3 be taught at all three levels, grades 5-6, 7-8, and 9-12?**

A: **No.** The local school curriculum will determine when Era 3 is to be taught, whether at grades 5-6, 7-8, and/or 9-12. Once that curriculum decision is made, teachers can enter these standards to determine which ones are appropriate for their students, and how the standards they select are related to others within a well-articulated curriculum in history, grades 5-12.

Q: **Are teachers expected to give equal time to all the standards (for example, standard 1A, 1B, and 1C) developed for each era?**

A: **No.** Priority should be given to the **Core Standards** in each era — that is, to those standards that most directly support students' understanding of the two to four major historical developments of the era, described in the introduction to each era in Chapter 3 under the title, "Giving Shape to World History." A second group of standards — the **Related Standards** — go beyond the core to expand, enhance, and enrich students' basic understandings of the era.

Figure 2 (on page 13) illustrates the relationships among the **Major Developments, Core Standards,** and the **Related Standards for Era 4.** The **Core Standards** identify the understandings that all students should have equal opportunity to investigate and acquire. The **Related Standards** offer teachers a range of important opportunities to deepen or extend students' understandings. For example, teachers can select from among these **Related Standards** to pursue a particular topic in greater depth (e.g., feudal Europe); to respond more fully to students' interests in a particular region of the world (e.g., Mesoamerica); or, to follow the narrative history of a particular region over successive eras, even though it may not be included among the **Core Standards** in a particular era of world history (e.g., Southeast Asia).

The designation of any standard as **Core** or **Related** is a reasoned judgment, reflecting the agreements broadly supported in the national consensus-building process through which the World History Standards were developed. Individual states and local school districts might choose to modify these particular recommendations when developing their curriculum frameworks.

Q: **Are high school teachers expected to teach all Core Standards identified as appropriate for grades 9-12?**

A: **No.** These standards assume that schools will devote three years of study to world history sometime between grades 5 and 12. Therefore, an era will probably be studied in some depth during at least one earlier school year (e.g,. grade 8). In that case, the more numerous standards deemed appropriate for grades 9-12 will, in part, have already been addressed in an earlier grade, and the emphasis can be turned in the high school world history course to those standards judged not to be appropriate for the earlier grades. Again, these are matters of well-designed, articulated curriculum planning within the jurisdiction of local schools.

Q: **Does the thinking skill incorporated in a particular standard limit teachers to that one skill?**

A: **No.** Within the shaded box, each standard highlights a particularly important thinking process. However, it is understood that good teaching will incorporate more than a single thinking skill to develop these understandings.

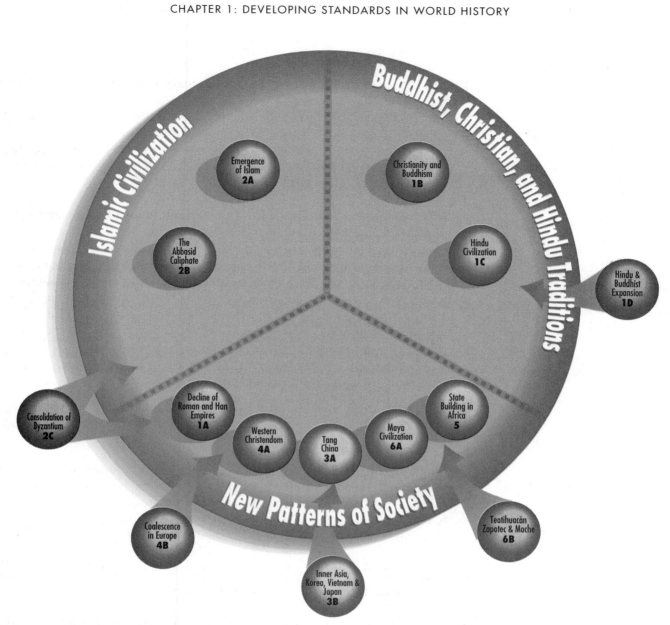

**Figure 2. Relationships Among Major Developments,
Core Standards, and Related Standards for Era 4**

In Figure 2, the three **Major Developments** of Era 4 are represented in the three sections of the larger circle: the rise and spread of Islamic civilization; the spread of the Buddhist, Christian, and Hindu traditions; and the development of new patterns of society in Europe, Asia, Africa, and the Americas.

The nine **Core Standards** of Era 4 are identified and located in the major development each exemplifies or illustrates: Core Standards 1A, 1B, 1C, 2A, 2B, 3A, 4A, 5 and 6A.

The five **Related Standards** appear outside the circle, each linked to the major development(s) it enhances or extends: i.e., the consolidation of Byzantium (2C), linked to the break-up of the Roman Empire (1A) and rise of Islam (2AB); expansion of Buddhism and Hinduism into SE Asia (1D), linked to their spread in India and China (1BC); and, the further development of societies in Europe, Asia, and the Americas (3B, 4B, 6B), linked to new patterns of society in these same regions (3A, 4A, 6A).

Q: Does the particular thinking skill identified in the standard limit the instructional approaches teachers might adopt to develop these outcomes with students?

A: No. To take one example, the third bulleted component of Standard 2A from Era 3 (page 10), "Describing the changing political institutions of Athens in the 6th and 5th centuries BCE, and analyzing the influence of political thought on public life," can be developed through any number of teaching approaches. For example, teachers might select one episode from the time of the Persian Wars when Athens faced invasion (480 BCE) and the Assembly voted upon a bill proposed by the Athenian general Themistocles for the defense of Athens. In this case, students might:

▶ Recount or create a flow chart of the procedure for passing a bill in 5th-century BCE Athens.

▶ Prepare a speech such as Themistocles might have delivered before the Athenian Assembly setting forth the plans for the evacuation and defense of Athens, and conduct a mock session of the Assembly to debate the proposal.

▶ Consider the roles of people from different classes in Athenian society such as women, children, the elders, landowning males under the age of 50, slaves, and those who had been ostracized or disenfranchised. Analyze who was allowed to participate in the democratic process under Athenian law at this time, and how each group would be affected by the Assembly's decision on the proposed evacuation.

In short, these standards are intended to open possibilities, not to limit teachers' options for engaging students in lively activities within what has been called the "thinking curriculum."

Q: Won't these bulleted standards each require a separate lesson or sequence of lessons, and doesn't the total teaching load therefore far exceed the total number of teaching days available, even over three years of instruction?

A: No. Good teaching, it should be emphasized, will often develop two or more of these bulleted standards in a single lesson or sequence of lessons. The standards appearing as individual statements in the shaded boxes are intended to signify desired *outcomes* of instruction and not to prescribe a particular teaching plan. Teachers will creatively design their own instructional plans, integrating related understandings in a variety of ways to accomplish these ends.

For example, in the teaching approaches just considered — creating a flow chart, conducting a mock meeting of the Athenian Assembly, and analyzing the political roles of people from different classes of Athenian society — the first and second activities contribute directly to achieving the first of the five bulleted standards and the third activity contributes directly to achieving three of them: the first (describing the changing political institutions of Athens and the influence of political thought on public life); the fourth (explaining class divisions of Greek society and the social and political roles of major classes); and the fifth (analyzing the place of women in Athenian society). Teachers seeking to make the most of their instructional time will therefore probably select the third activity over the least productive activity of creating a flow chart, and thereby snare the proverbial two — or three! — birds with a single stone.

Three Policy Issues

Ensuring Equity for All Students

The purposes of the national standards developed in this document are three-fold: (1) to establish high expectations for what all students should know and be able to do; (2) to clarify what constitutes successful achievement; and (3) *most significantly, to promote equity in the learning opportunities and resources to be provided all students in the nation's schools.*

Standards in and of themselves cannot ensure remediation of the pervasive inequalities in the educational opportunities currently available to students. The roots of these problems are deep and widely manifested in gross inequities in school financing, in resource allocations, and in practices of discriminatory "lower tracks" and "dumbed down" curricula that continue to deny large sectors of the nation's children equal educational opportunity.

What the national commitment to high achievement standards for all students *can* do is to serve as an engine of change: (1) defining for all students the goals essential to success in a rapidly changing global economy and in a society undergoing wrenching social, technological, and economic change; and (2) establishing the moral obligation to provide equity in the educational resources required to help all students attain these goals.

As for resources, if students are to achieve the understandings and thinking skills specified in the World History Standards, they must have equal access to well-prepared history teachers and to engaging, balanced, accurate, and challenging curricular materials. For these reasons the success of Goals 2000 and of the systemic educational reform program it has launched requires the provision of high quality professional development in world history and in pedagogy for teachers who are not prepared to teach the content or thinking skills presented in this document. Equally important, all students must be provided with the best available textbooks and other curricular materials in world history.

As Robert Hutchins said many years ago: "The best education for the best should be the best education for all." Every child is entitled to and must have equal access to excellence in the goals their teachers strive to help them achieve and in the instructional resources and opportunities required to reach those ends. Nothing less is acceptable in a democratic society; no commitment is more essential to meeting the challenges — economic, social, and ethical — confronting this nation in the years ahead.

Providing Adequate Instructional Time for History

In developing these standards, the National Council for History Standards kept in mind the purposes of Goals 2000, the national education reform program supported by President Clinton, the nation's governors, and the Congress. Developing the internationally competitive levels of student achievement called for in this reform movement clearly cannot be accomplished by limiting the study of world history to one year (or less) over the eight years of middle and high school education. Excellence in history requires the instructional time to pursue an era in some depth and to engage students' active learning through the higher processes of historical thinking.

For these reasons it is important that the schools devote no less than three years of instruction to world history over the eight years of students' middle and high school education, grades 5-12. Currently, fourteen states provide two or more years of world history and six of these states provide three years, though under a variety of curriculum plans. In formulating national standards for excellence, the Council argued, we should not be setting our sights lower than those states that have already committed three years of instruction to this field.

Accommodating Variability in State and Local Curriculum Plans

Because schools today vary widely as to when and how they offer their courses in world history, the Council sought a flexible approach to history standards which would accommodate local variability rather than impose a single national curriculum on the nation's schools. Already illustrated on pages 10-11 of this chapter, this approach required converting each standard to appropriate achievement expectations for students at three levels of schooling: grades 5-6, grades 7-8, and grades 9-12. **The purpose here is not to suggest that all eras in world history be taught at all three levels of schooling.** Rather, the purpose is to provide teachers, parents, and students with examples of appropriate achievement on standards for whatever historical eras their local school or school district has determined should be studied at that grade level. Deciding **when** these eight eras in world history should be studied, whether in grades 5-6, 7-8, or 9-12, is a **curriculum decision**, and should remain under local or state control.

Thus, under Florida's state course of study, world history is developed in relation to United States history over three successive high school years — grades 9 (birth of civilizations through the 18th-century democratic revolutions); grade 10 (through World War I); and grade 11 (from 1848 until today). In addition, Florida begins a three-year sequence in history with grade 3 in which students are engaged in humanities-enriched studies of significant developments of the ancient world, the middle ages, and the Renaissance. Teachers of grade 9 following this course of study will draw upon the world history standards developed for eras 1 through 6; teachers of grade 10 will draw upon the world history standards developed for era 7; and teachers of grade 11 will draw upon the world history standards developed for eras 7 and 8.

In California, by contrast, where the state framework suggests concentrating upon the study of the early eras 1-3 in world history in grade 6, eras 4-6 in grade 7, and eras 7-8 in grade 10, teachers following this plan will turn to the standards in a different way. Teachers of grade 6 will turn to the standards developed for the ancient world. Teachers of grade 7 will *selectively* draw upon these same standards in their initial review but will concentrate upon the standards developed for eras beginning with the fall of the Roman and Han empires and continuing through 18th-century world history. Teachers of grade 10 will again *selectively* draw upon the standards for the earlier eras in their initial reviews, but will concentrate upon the standards developed for the 19th and 20th centuries of world history. In all cases, teachers will focus within any of these eras upon the standards developed for their particular grade level, whether for grades 5-6, 7-8, or 9-12.

Standards in Historical Thinking

The study of history, as noted earlier, involves more than the passive absorption of facts, dates, names, and places. Real historical understanding requires students to engage in historical thinking: to raise questions and to marshal evidence in support of their answers; to go beyond the facts presented in their textbooks and examine the historical record for themselves; to consult documents, journals, diaries, artifacts, historic sites, and other evidence from the past, and to do so imaginatively — taking into account the historical context in which these records were created and comparing the multiple points of view of those on the scene at the time.

Real historical understanding requires that students have opportunity to create historical narratives and arguments of their own. Such narratives and arguments may take many forms — essays, debates, and editorials, for instance. They can be initiated in a variety of ways. None, however, more powerfully initiates historical thinking than those issues, past and present, that challenge students to enter knowledgeably into the historical record and to bring sound historical perspectives to bear in the analysis of a problem.

Historical understanding also requires that students thoughtfully read the historical narratives created by others. Well-written historical narratives are interpretative, revealing and explaining connections, change, and consequences. They are also analytical, combining lively storytelling and biography with conceptual analysis drawn from all relevant disciplines. Such narratives promote essential skills in historical thinking.

Reading such narratives thoughtfully requires that students analyze the assumptions — stated and unstated — from which the narrative was constructed and assess the strength of the evidence presented. It requires that students consider the significance of what the author included as well as chose to omit — the absence, for example, of the voices and experiences of other men and women who were also an important part of the history of their time. And, it requires that students examine the interpretative nature of history, comparing, for example, alternative historical narratives written by historians who have given different weight to the political, economic, social, and/or technological causes of events, and who have developed competing interpretations of the significance of those events.

Students engaged in activities of the kinds just considered will draw upon skills in the following five types of historical thinking:

1. Chronological Thinking
2. Historical Comprehension
3. Historical Analysis and Interpretation
4. Historical Research Capabilities
5. Historical Issues-Analysis and Decision-Making

These skills, while presented in five separate categories, are nonetheless interactive and mutually supportive. In conducting historical research or creating a historical argument of their own, for example, students must be able to draw upon skills in all five categories. Beyond the skills of conducting their research, students must, for example, be able to comprehend historical documents and records, analyze their relevance, develop interpretations of the document(s) they select, and demonstrate a sound grasp of the historical chronology and context in which the issue, problem, or events they are addressing developed.

In short, these five sets of skills, developed in the following pages as the five Standards in Historical Thinking, are statements of the **outcomes** we desire students to achieve. They are not mutually exclusive when put into practice, nor do they prescribe a particular teaching sequence to be followed. Teachers will draw upon all these Thinking Standards, as appropriate, to develop their teaching plans and to guide students through challenging programs of study in history.

Finally, it is important to point out that these five sets of Standards in Historical Thinking are defined in the following pages as though largely independent of historical content in order to specify the quality of thinking desired for each. It is essential to understand, however, that these skills do not develop, nor can they be practiced, in a vacuum. Every one of these skills requires historical content in order to function — a relationship that is made explicit in Chapter 3, which presents the standards integrating historical understandings and thinking for world history for grades 5-12.

Overview of Standards in Historical Thinking

Standard 1. Chronological Thinking

A. Distinguish between past, present, and future time.
B. Identify in historical narratives the temporal structure of a historical narrative or story.
C. Establish temporal order in constructing historical narratives of their own.
D. Measure and calculate calendar time.
E. Interpret data presented in time lines.
F. Reconstruct patterns of historical succession and duration.
G. Compare alternative models for periodization.

Standard 2. Historical Comprehension

A. Reconstruct the literal meaning of a historical passage.
B. Identify the central question(s) the historical narrative addresses.
C. Read historical narratives imaginatively.
D. Evidence historical perspectives.
E. Draw upon data in historical maps.
F. Utilize visual and mathematical data presented in charts, tables, pie and bar graphs, flow charts, Venn diagrams, and other graphic organizers.
G. Draw upon visual data, literary, and musical sources.

Standard 3. Historical Analysis and Interpretation

A. Identify the author or source of the historical document or narrative.
B. Compare and contrast differing sets of ideas, values, personalities, behaviors, and institutions.
C. Differentiate between historical facts and historical interpretations.
D. Consider multiple perspectives.
E. Analyze cause-and-effect relationships and multiple causation, including the importance of the individual, the influence of ideas, and the role of chance.
F. Challenge arguments of historical inevitability.
G. Compare competing historical narratives.
H. Hold interpretations of history as tentative.
I. Evaluate major debates among historians.
J. Hypothesize the influence of the past.

Standard 4. Historical Research Capabilities

A. Formulate historical questions.
B. Obtain historical data.
C. Interrogate historical data.
D. Identify the gaps in the available records, marshal contextual knowledge and perspectives of the time and place, and construct a sound historical interpretation.

Standard 5. Historical Issues-Analysis and Decision-Making

A. Identify issues and problems in the past.
B. Marshal evidence of antecedent circumstances and contemporary factors contributing to problems and alternative courses of action.
C. Identify relevant historical antecedents.
D. Evaluate alternative courses of action.
E. Formulate a position or course of action on an issue.
F. Evaluate the implementation of a decision.

Students examining history projects
Lakeview Junior High School
Santa Maria, CA

STANDARD 1

Chronological Thinking

Chronological thinking is at the heart of historical reasoning. Without a strong sense of chronology — of when events occurred and in what temporal order — it is impossible for students to examine relationships among those events or to explain historical causality. Chronology provides the mental scaffolding for organizing historical thought.

In developing students' chronological thinking, instructional time should be given to the use of well constructed **historical narratives**: literary narratives including biographies and historical literature, and well written narrative histories that have the quality of "stories well told." Well-crafted narratives such as these have the power to grip and hold students' attention. Thus engaged, the reader is able to focus on what the narrator discloses: the temporal structure of events unfolding over time, the actions and intentions of those who were there, the temporal connections between antecedents and their consequences.

In the middle and high school years, students should be able to use their mathematical skills to measure time by years, decades, centuries, and millennia; to calculate time from the fixed points of the calendar system (BC or BCE and AD or CE); and to interpret the data presented in time lines.

Students should be able to analyze *patterns of historical duration or continuity*. Such patterns are strikingly illustrated, for example, by the enduring character of the Chinese imperial system which was established by the Qin emperor Shi Huangdi in the second century BCE and continued, with few interruptions, over two millennia until the revolution of 1911.

Students should also be able to analyze *patterns of historical succession or change* illustrated, for example, in the development, over time, of ever larger systems of interaction, beginning with trade among settlements of the Neolithic world; continuing through the growth of the great land empires of Rome, Han China, the Islamic world, and the Mongols; expanding in the early modern era when Europeans crossed the Atlantic and Pacific, and established the first worldwide networks of trade and communication; and culminating with the global systems of trade and communication of the modern world.

Students Should Be Able to:

A. **Distinguish between past, present, and future time.**

B. **Identify in historical narratives the temporal structure of a historical narrative or story:** its beginning, middle, and end (the latter defined as the outcome of a particular beginning).

C. **Establish temporal order in constructing historical narratives of their own:** working *forward* from some beginning through its development, to some end or outcome; working *backward* from some issue, problem, or event to explain its origins and its development over time.

D. **Measure and calculate calendar time** by days, weeks, months, years, decades, centuries, and millennia, from fixed points of the calendar system: BC (before Christ) and AD (*Anno Domini,* "in the year of our Lord") in the Gregorian calendar and the contemporary secular designation for these same dates, BCE (before the Common Era) and CE (in the Common Era); and compare with the fixed points of other calendar systems such as the Roman (753 BC, the founding of the city of Rome) and the Muslim (622 AD, the Hegira).

E. **Interpret data presented in time lines** and create time lines by designating appropriate equidistant intervals of time and recording events according to the temporal order in which they occurred.

F. **Reconstruct patterns of historical succession and duration** in which historical developments have unfolded, and apply them to **explain historical continuity and change.**

G. **Compare alternative models for periodization** by identifying the organizing principles on which each is based.

Grades 5-6

Examples of student achievement include:

▶ Differentiate autobiographies, biographies, literary narratives, and historical narratives and explain or diagram the temporal structure of events in the story.

▶ Construct multiple-tier time lines, entering information on multiple themes developing over the same years: e.g., important social, economic, and political developments in the history of the thirteen English colonies between the years 1600 and 1800; or comparative developments in the English, Spanish, and French colonies in North America between 1500 and 1800.

▶ Group (periodize) events by broadly defined eras in the history of the nation or region they are studying.

▶ Calculate calendar time, determining the onset, duration, and ending dates of historical events or developments.

▶ Interpret data presented in time lines in order to determine when critical developments occurred and what else was occurring at the same time.

Grades 7-8

Examples of student achievement include:

▶ Measure time by millennia and calculate calendar time BC or BCE, and AD or CE.

▶ Explain patterns of historical continuity and change in the historical succession of related events unfolding over time.

◗ Impose temporal structure in developing historical narratives, including biographies, historical arguments, and stories by: working *forward* from some initiating event to follow its development and transformation to some outcome over time; working *backward* from some issue, problem, or event to explain its causes, arising from some beginning and developing through subsequent transformations over time.

Grades 9-12

Examples of student achievement include:

◗ Reconstruct the temporal order and connections disclosed in historical narratives and biographies and draw upon that information to construct sound interpretations of the text. (For standards in historical interpretation, see Standard 3, below.)

◗ Compare at least two alternative systems of recording calendar time, such as those based on a solar year (Egyptian, Indian, Roman, Gregorian, Mayan, Aztec, or Chinese calendars); a lunar year (the Muslim calendar); or a semilunar calendar, adjusting the lunar year to a solar year (the Jewish calendar). Demonstrate understanding of the astronomical system on which the calendar is based, its fixed points for measuring time, and its respective strengths and weaknesses.

◗ Demonstrate historical continuity and/or change with respect to a particular historical development or theme by reconstructing and analyzing the chronological succession and duration of events associated with it.

◗ Analyze a model for periodization (such as the one adopted in their history textbook) by identifying the organizing principles on which the particular sequence of historical eras was chosen, and comparing with at least one alternative model and the principles on which it is based.

Aztec Calendar,
Bettmann Archives

S T A N D A R D   2

Historical Comprehension

One of the defining features of historical narratives is their believable recounting of human events. Beyond that, historical narratives also have the power to disclose the intentions of the people involved, the difficulties they encountered, and the complex world in which such historical figures actually lived. To read historical stories, biographies, autobiographies, and narratives with comprehension, students must develop the ability to read imaginatively, to take into account what the narrative reveals of the humanity of the individuals involved — their motives and intentions, their hopes, doubts, fears, strengths, and weaknesses. Comprehending historical narratives requires, also, that students develop historical perspectives, the ability to describe the past on its own terms, through the eyes and experiences of those who were there. By studying the literature, diaries, letters, debates, arts, and artifacts of past peoples, students should learn to avoid "present-mindedness" by not judging the past solely in terms of the norms and values of today, but taking into account the historical context in which the events unfolded.

Acquiring these skills begins in the early years of childhood, through the use of superbly written biographies that capture children's imagination and provide them an important foundation for continuing historical study. As students move into middle grades and high school years, historical literature should continue to occupy an important place in the curriculum, capturing historical events with dramatic immediacy, engaging students' interests, and fostering deeper understanding of the times and cultural milieu in which events occurred.

Beyond these important outcomes, students should also develop the skills needed to comprehend "thick narratives" — historical narratives that *explain* as well as recount the course of events and that *analyze* relationships among the various forces that were present at the time and influenced the ways events unfolded. These skills include: (1) identifying the central question the historical narrative seeks to answer; (2) defining the purpose, perspective, or point of view from which the narrative has been constructed; (3) reading the historical explanation or analysis with meaning; and (4) recognizing the rhetorical cues that signal how the author has organized the text.

Comprehending historical narratives will also be facilitated if students are able to draw upon the data presented in historical maps, graphics, and a variety of visual sources such as historical photographs, political cartoons, paintings, and architecture in order to clarify, illustrate, or elaborate upon the information presented in the text.

Students Should Be Able to:

A. **Reconstruct the literal meaning of a historical passage** by identifying who was involved, what happened, where it happened, what events led to these developments, and what consequences or outcomes followed.

B. **Identify the central question(s)** the historical narrative addresses and the purpose, perspective, or point of view from which it has been constructed.

C. **Read historical narratives imaginatively,** taking into account (a) the historical context in which the event unfolded — the values, outlook, options, and contingencies of that time and place; and (b) what the narrative reveals of the humanity of the individuals involved — their probable motives, hopes, fears, strengths, and weaknesses.

D. **Evidence historical perspectives** — the ability (a) to describe the past on its own terms, through the eyes and experiences of those who were there, as revealed through their literature, diaries, letters, debates, arts, artifacts, and the like; and (b) to avoid "present-mindedness," judging the past solely in terms of present-day norms and values.

E. **Draw upon data in historical maps** in order to obtain or clarify information on the geographic setting in which the historical event occurred, its relative and absolute location, the distances and directions involved, the natural and man-made features of the place, and critical relationships in the spatial distributions of those features and the historical event occurring there.

F. **Utilize visual and mathematical data** presented in charts, tables, pie and bar graphs, flow charts, Venn diagrams, and other graphic organizers to clarify, illustrate, or elaborate upon information presented in the historical narrative.

G. **Draw upon visual, literary, and musical sources** including: (a) photographs, paintings, cartoons, and architectural drawings; (b) novels, poetry, and plays; and (c) folk, popular and classical music to clarify, illustrate, or elaborate upon information presented in the historical narrative.

Grades 5-6

Examples of student achievement include:

- Identify the central question(s) the historical narrative attempts to address and the purpose, perspective, or point of view from which it has been constructed.

- Demonstrate historical perspectives by taking into account the lives of individuals, their values, and outlooks within the historical context.

- Identify specific characteristics of the historical place and time that influenced why events or actions developed where and when they did.

- Read and interpret the data presented in two-way and three-way tables, classifications, and data retrieval charts.

- Read geographic symbols, map scales, and directional indicators in order to obtain and interpret such information from historical maps as: the geographical features of the setting in which events occurred, their absolute and relative locations, and the distances and directions involved.

- Read and interpret the visual and mathematical data presented in flow charts, pie graphs, and Venn diagrams.

- Read and interpret the visual data presented in historical photographs, paintings, and drawings of the people, places, and historical events under study.

Grades 7-8

Examples of student achievement include:

- ◗ Read and understand primary sources such as the United States Declaration of Independence, the French Declaration of the Rights of Man and Citizen, and Zapata's "Plan de Ayala." Students should recognize that understanding requires not only what the words say, but where such ideas arose and how they evolved from earlier ideas.

- ◗ Determine the causes and consequences of events and demonstrate understanding through various techniques such as peer-teaching, Socratic seminars, written analysis, and graphic organizers (flow charts, clustering, Venn diagrams).

- ◗ Draw upon documentary photographs, political cartoons and broadsides, art, and other visual data presented in historical narratives to clarify, elaborate upon, and understand the historical period. The critical examination of sources, such as caricatures of Louis Philippe or Andrew Jackson, photographs by Mathew Brady and by Lewis Hine, paintings of Pablo Picasso and Diego Rivera, and Maoist poster art, assists in understanding historical periods.

- ◗ Demonstrate the ability to draw warranted conclusions from data presented in political, physical, and demographic maps in appraising the importance of location, region, and movement in history.

- ◗ Examine historical records to take into account the context of the historical period in which they were written and to avoid "present-mindedness" (i.e., judging the past solely in terms of the norms and values of today).

Grades 9-12

Examples of student achievement include:

- ◗ Discern the significance of historical accounts and explain the writer's perceptions of movements and trends.

- ◗ Explain the ways in which historical literature reflects the attitudes, values, and passions of the era. For example, probe the motives of U.S. muckrakers such as Lincoln Steffens, Upton Sinclair, John Spargo, and Ida Tarbell; examine the impact of literary figures of the Harlem Renaissance such as Langston Hughes and Claude McKay; or examine the impact of antiwar novels such as Erich Maria Remarque's *All Quiet on the Western Front*.

- ◗ Draw upon statistical data presented in charts and graphs in order to elaborate on information presented in historical narratives.

STANDARD 3

Historical Analysis and Interpretation

One of the most common problems in helping students to become thoughtful readers of historical narrative is the compulsion students feel to find the one right answer, the one essential fact, the one authoritative interpretation. "Am I on the right track?" "Is this what you want?" they ask. Or, worse yet, they rush to closure, reporting back as self-evident truths the facts or conclusions presented in the document or text.

These problems are deeply rooted in the conventional ways in which textbooks have presented history: a succession of facts marching straight to a settled outcome. To overcome these problems requires the use of more than a single source: of history books other than textbooks and of a rich variety of historical documents and artifacts that present alternative voices, accounts, and interpretations or perspectives on the past.

Students need to realize that historians may differ on the facts they incorporate in the development of their narratives, and disagree as well on how those facts are to be interpreted. Thus, "history" is usually taken to mean what happened in the past; but *written* history is a dialogue among historians not only about what happened but about why and how it happened, how it affected other happenings, and how much importance it ought to be assigned. The study of history is not only remembering answers. It requires following and evaluating arguments and arriving at usable, even if tentative, conclusions based on the available evidence.

Well-written historical narrative has the power to promote students' analysis of historical causality — of how change occurs in society, of how human intentions matter, and how ends are influenced by the means of carrying them out, in what has been called the tangle of process and outcomes. Few challenges can be more fascinating to students than unraveling the often dramatic complications of cause. And nothing is more dangerous than a simple, monocausal explanation of past experiences and present problems.

Finally, well-written historical narratives can also alert students to the traps of *lineality and inevitability.* Students must understand the relevance of the past to their own times, but they need also to avoid the trap of lineality, of drawing straight lines between past and present, as though earlier movements were being propelled teleologically toward some rendezvous with destiny in the late 20th century.

A related trap is that of thinking that events have unfolded inevitably — that the way things are is the way they had to be, and thus that humankind lacks free will and the capacity for making choice. Unless students can conceive that history could have turned out differently, they may unconsciously accept the notion that the future is also inevitable or predetermined, and that human agency and individual action count for nothing. No attitude is more likely to feed civic apathy, cynicism, and resignation — precisely what we hope the study of history will fend off. Whether in dealing with the main narrative or with a topic in depth, we must always try, in one historian's words, to "restore to the past the options it once had."

Students Should Be Able to:

A. Identify the author or source of the historical document or narrative and assess its credibility.

B. Compare and contrast differing sets of ideas, values, personalities, behaviors, and institutions by identifying likenesses and differences.

C. Differentiate between historical facts and historical interpretations, but acknowledge also that the two are related: that the facts the historian reports are selected and reflect therefore the historian's judgment of what is most significant about the past.

D. Consider multiple perspectives of various peoples in the past by demonstrating their differing motives, beliefs, interests, hopes, and fears.

E. Analyze cause-and-effect relationships bearing in mind multiple causation including (a) the importance of the individual in history; (b) the influence of ideas, human interests, and beliefs; and (c) the role of chance, the accidental, and the irrational.

F. Challenge arguments of historical inevitability by formulating examples of historical contingency, of how different choices could have led to different consequences.

G. Compare competing historical narratives by contrasting different historians' choice of questions, and their use of sources reflecting different experiences, perspectives, beliefs, and points of view, and by demonstrating how an emphasis on different causes contributes to different interpretations.

H. Hold interpretations of history as tentative, subject to change as new information is uncovered, new voices heard, and new interpretations broached.

I. Evaluate major debates among historians concerning alternative interpretations of the past.

J. Hypothesize the influence of the past, including both the limitations and the opportunities made possible by past decisions.

Grades 5-6

Examples of student achievement include:

▶ Read historical narratives to identify the author's main points and the purpose or point of view from which the narrative has been written.

▶ Analyze historical narratives to identify the facts the author has provided and to evaluate the credibility of the generalization or interpretation the author has presented on the basis of the evidence he or she has assembled.

▶ Analyze or construct causal analyses taking into account two or more factors contributing to the historical event.

Grades 7-8

Examples of student achievement include:

▶ Determine an author's frame of reference in primary and secondary sources and form analytical questions to examine the data and to determine bias in documents and historical narratives.

▶ Consult multiple sources reflecting differing interpretations of a historic event or individual.

▶ Recognize that historical accounts are subject to change based on newly uncovered records and new interpretations. The publication of government documents and formerly suppressed records (e.g., release of secret treaties and "White Papers" in the post-World War I era and the revelations of Stalinist purges), or changing perspectives on movements, may alter previously accepted historical accounts.

▶ Assess the importance of the individual in history and the importance of individual choices. In assessing the importance of individual action and decision making, for example, students should consider the impact of humanitarian efforts of individuals such as Mother Teresa of Calcutta, or the social consciousness of persons such as Jane Addams, Martin Luther King Jr., or Raul Wallenberg. Students should be able to analyze sources to determine what they reveal about ordinary people as well as recognized leaders and historical events, movements, and trends.

▶ Critically evaluate the evidence presented in both primary and secondary sources and recognize the danger in drawing analogies without considering different circumstances presented by time and place.

Grades 9-12

Examples of student achievement include:

▶ Analyze the motives and interests expressed in both primary and secondary sources and distinguish between accepted historical facts and interpretations.

▶ Compare two or more historical interpretations, differentiate between fact and interpretation, and determine what facts are most significant in the historian's judgment and why. Students should be able to evaluate arguments and arrive at conclusions based on the evidence.

▶ Consider multiple perspectives in interpreting the past and explain how different motives, beliefs, interests, and perspectives influence interpretations of the past.

▶ Evaluate the validity and credibility of historical interpretations, including new or changing interpretations which have developed as new information about the past is uncovered, new voices heard, and new methodologies and interpretations are developed.

▶ Challenge prevailing attitudes of historical inevitability by examining how alternative choices could produce different consequences. Students should understand that options existed in the past and that history is contingent on human agency and individual choices.

▶ Recognize that historical events are the products of deliberate actions or spontaneous responses to given circumstances. Students should understand change and continuity and the dynamics of the interplay of individuals and groups promoting and resisting change.

S T A N D A R D   4

Historical Research Capabilities

Perhaps no aspect of historical thinking is as exciting to students or as productive of their growth in historical thinking as "doing history." Such inquiries can arise at critical turning points in the historical narrative presented in the text. They might be generated by encounters with historical documents, eyewitness accounts, letters, diaries, artifacts, photos, a visit to a historic site, a record of oral history, or other evidence of the past. Worthy inquiries are especially likely to develop if the documents students encounter are rich with the voices of people caught up in the event and sufficiently diverse to bring alive to students the interests, beliefs, and concerns of people with differing backgrounds and opposing viewpoints on the event.

Historical inquiry proceeds with the formulation of a problem or set of questions worth pursuing. In the most direct approach, students might be encouraged to analyze a document, record, or site itself. Who produced it, when, how, and why? What is the evidence of its authenticity, authority, and credibility? What does it tell them of the point of view, background, and interests of its author or creator? What else must they discover in order to construct a useful story, explanation, or narrative of the event of which this document or artifact is a part? What interpretation can they derive from their data, and what argument can they support in the historical narrative they create from the data?

In this process students' contextual knowledge of the historical period in which the document or artifact was created becomes critically important. Only a few records of the event will be available to students. Filling in the gaps, evaluating the records they have available, and imaginatively constructing a sound historical argument or narrative requires a larger context of meaning.

For these purposes, students' ongoing narrative study of history provides important support, revealing the larger context. But just as the ongoing narrative study, supported by but not limited to the textbook, provides a meaningful context in which students' inquiries can develop, it is these inquiries themselves that imbue the era with deeper meaning. Hence the importance of providing students documents or other records beyond materials included in the textbook, that will allow students to challenge textbook interpretations, to raise new questions about the event, to investigate the perspectives of those whose voices do not appear in the textbook accounts, or to plumb an issue that the textbook largely or in part bypassed.

Under these conditions, students will view their inquiries as creative contributions. They will better understand that written history is a human construction, that certain judgments about the past are tentative and arguable, and that historians regard their work as critical inquiry, pursued as ongoing explorations and debates with other historians. By their active engagement in historical inquiry, students will learn for themselves why historians are continuously reinterpreting the past, and why new interpretations emerge not only from uncovering new evidence but from rethinking old evidence in the light of new ideas springing up in our own times. Students then can also see why the good historian, like the good teacher, is interested not in manipulation or indoctrination but in acting as the honest messenger from the past — not interested in possessing students' minds but in presenting them with the power to possess their own.

Students Should Be Able to:

A. **Formulate historical questions** from encounters with historical documents, eyewitness accounts, letters, diaries, artifacts, photos, historical sites, art, architecture, and other records from the past.

B. **Obtain historical data** from a variety of sources, including: library and museum collections, historic sites, historical photos, journals, diaries, eyewitness accounts, newspapers, documentary films; and so on.

C. **Interrogate historical data** by uncovering the social, political, and economic context in which it was created; testing the data source for its credibility, authority, authenticity, internal consistency and completeness; and detecting and evaluating bias, distortion, and propaganda by omission, suppression, or invention of facts.

D. **Identify the gaps in the available records and marshal contextual knowledge and perspectives of the time and place** in order to elaborate imaginatively upon the evidence, fill in the gaps deductively, and construct a sound historical interpretation.

Grades 5-6

Examples of student achievement include:

▶ Studying historical documents to formulate significant questions such as: Who produced the document? When, how, and why? What does the document tell about the person(s) who created it? What do the students need to find out in order to "tell a story" about the document and the people and events connected with it?

Grades 7-8

Examples of student achievement include:

▶ Formulate questions to guide and focus research.

▶ Draw from a variety of primary and secondary sources, including diaries, letters, periodicals, literature, oral histories, artifacts, art, and documentary photographs and films in historical research.

▶ Interpret the data obtained from historical documents to analyze the historical context in which they were created, and develop a report about them.

▶ Examine historical accounts to determine what voices are missing from narratives; explain reasons for omissions, and challenge generalizations and interpretations in text accounts.

Grades 9-12

Examples of student achievement include:

▶ Consult bibliographical studies to help select appropriate source materials for the research of historical periods, events, or personalities. Encyclopedic endnotes, footnote references, recommended readings in texts and monographs, and bibliographies such as the *Harvard Guide to American History* should be used as an aid in gathering materials for research projects and papers.

◗ Use book reviews and critiques to make choices regarding historical sources and examine references to determine the context in which they were written. Students should, as a matter of habit, cross-reference sources and ask probing questions to determine the authenticity and credibility of references.

*Ramusio's "Navigationi el viaggi
Mexico City, 1557
Library of Congress*

STANDARD 5

Historical Issues-Analysis and Decision-Making

Issue-centered analysis and decision-making activities place students squarely at the center of historical dilemmas and problems faced at critical moments in the past and the near-present. Entering into such moments, confronting the issues or problems of the time, analyzing the alternatives available to those on the scene, evaluating the consequences that might have followed those options for action that were not chosen, and comparing with the consequences of those that were adopted, are activities that foster students' deep, personal involvement in these events.

If well chosen, these activities also promote capacities vital to a democratic citizenry: the capacity to identify and define public policy issues and ethical dilemmas; analyze the range of interests and values held by the many persons caught up in the situation and affected by its outcome; locate and organize the data required to assess the consequences of alternative approaches to resolving the dilemma; assess the ethical implications as well as the comparative costs and benefits of each approach; and evaluate a particular course of action in light of all of the above and, in the case of historical issues-analysis, in light also of its long-term consequences revealed in the historical record.

Because important historical issues are frequently value-laden, they also open opportunities to consider the moral convictions contributing to social actions taken. The point to be made is that teachers should not use critical events to hammer home a particular "moral lesson" or ethical teaching. Not only will many students reject that approach; it fails also to take into account the processes through which students acquire the complex skills of principled thinking and moral reasoning. The best approach is to open these issues to analysis grounded in historical evidence and allow a variety of perspectives on the problem to emerge.

Value-laden issues worthy of classroom analysis include not only those irredeemable events in human history from which students can most easily draw clear ethical judgment — the Holocaust, for example, or the Cambodian genocide under the Pol Pot regime. These analyses should also address situations of lasting consequence in which what is morally "right" and "wrong" may not be self-evident. Was it right, for example, for Lincoln, in his Emancipation Proclamation, to free only those slaves behind the Confederate lines? Because of the complicated way values act upon people confronted with the need to decide, the full moral situation in a past event is not always immediately clear. Students should understand, therefore, that their opinions should be held tentative and open to revision as they acquire new insight into these historical problems.

As the history course approaches the present era, such inquiries assume special relevance, confronting students with issues that resonate in today's headlines and invite their participation in lively debates, simulations, and Socratic seminars — settings in which they can confront alternative policy recommendations, judge their ethical implications, challenge one another's assessments, and acquire further skills in the public presentation and defense of positions. In these analyses, teachers have the special responsibility of helping students differentiate between (1) relevant historical antecedents and appropriate historical analogies, and (2) those that are clearly inappropriate and irrelevant. Students need to learn how to use their knowledge of history (or the past) to bring sound historical analysis to the service of informed decision making.

Students Should Be Able to:

A. **Identify issues and problems in the past** and analyze the interests, values, perspectives, and points of view of those involved in the situation.

B. **Marshal evidence of antecedent circumstances** and contemporary factors contributing to problems and alternative courses of action.

C. **Identify relevant historical antecedents** and differentiate from those that are inappropriate and irrelevant to contemporary issues.

D. **Evaluate alternative courses of action** in terms of ethical considerations, the interests of those affected by the decision, and the long- and short-term consequences of each.

E. **Formulate a position or course of action on an issue** by identifying the nature of the problem, analyzing the underlying factors contributing to the problem, and choosing a plausible solution from a choice of carefully evaluated options.

F. **Evaluate the implementation of a decision** by analyzing the interests it served; estimating the position, power, and priority of each player involved; assessing the ethical dimensions of the decision; and evaluating its costs and benefits from a variety of perspectives.

Grades 5-6

Examples of student achievement include:

▶ Examine proposals for resolving a problem, compare the possible consequences of two or more courses of action, and analyze their effects on various individuals and groups caught up in the situation.

▶ Identify the values and moral convictions of those on different sides of an issue and evaluate some of the long-term as well as immediate consequences of the decisions made.

▶ Apply these same skills to the analysis of a contemporary issue in the students' local community or state which has its roots in past decisions and requires resolution today.

Grades 7-8

Examples of student achievement include:

▶ Identify factors that led to a historical issue, define the problems involved in its resolution, and explain the motives, values, and varying perspectives surrounding the problem. For example, students might investigate background causes that led Alexander II to abolish serfdom in Russia and Lincoln to issue the Emancipation Proclamation. They should explore various attitudes regarding these policy decisions, the factors that led to their enactment, and form warranted value judgments regarding the timing and the scope of these decisions.

▶ Use primary source materials to assume the role of an individual and explain a policy issue from the perspective of that individual within the context of time and place.

▶ Analyze individual decisions and grapple with the personal dilemmas encountered in pursuing a course of action. Students should be able to examine choices such as Susan B. Anthony's decision to vote in the presidential election of 1872, Mohandas Gandhi's decision to organize the 1930 salt march, or Rosa Park's decision to confront Jim Crow laws in Montgomery, Alabama.

▶ Reach value judgments regarding the course of action taken by individuals in history by weighing the influence of attitudes, values, and alternative options of that particular time and place. For example, in analyzing whether delegates at the Philadelphia Convention of 1787 should have taken a firm stand against slavery, thereby confronting threats by South Carolina and Georgia to withdraw support for the Constitution, students should be able to identify the issues involved, compare the alternative perspectives and ethical considerations of the delegates on issues of slavery and union, and assess the compromises reached.

▶ Analyze the historical circumstances and reach warranted ethical judgments concerning such events as Hitler's "final solution" and Pol Pot's "killing fields."

| Grades 9-12 | **Examples of student achievement include:** |

▶ Analyze value-laden public policy issues by taking into account the social conditions, the interests of the players involved, the values that came into conflict in the situation, and the policies adopted on the issue.

▶ Analyze the decisions leading to events recognized as major turning points in history, compare alternative courses of action, and hypothesize, within the context of the historic period, other possible outcomes. For example, students may debate the alternative actions Britain and France could have taken at Munich given the political situation and diplomatic initiatives of September 1938. Students could focus on opposition to Prime Minister Chamberlain as expressed by Winston Churchill and Clement Attlee through debates in the British House of Commons.

▶ Assess the nonrational, irrational, and the accidental in history and human affairs. In appraising decisions, students should be cautious to avoid present-mindedness by asking whether circumstances evolving in later years necessarily made a decision irrational at the time it was made. (For example, was Woodrow Wilson's neglect of a youthful Ho Chi Minh's appeal to apply to the French colonies of Southeast Asia the same principle of self-determination that Wilson advocated at Versailles irrational at the time? What were the influences of prevailing early 20th-century attitudes regarding colonialism, diplomatic goals, and confrontation with allies over self-determination for colonies? Students should debate similar issues and assess reactions to given situations in the context of time.)

▶ Debate national and international policy issues and suggest alternative courses of action based on sound reasoning that employs historical analysis and interpretation.

▶ Differentiate appropriate from inappropriate historical analogies by critically assessing the parallels between the current situation and that of the past.

World History Standards for Grades 5-12

Overview

This chapter presents the Standards in world history for grades 5-12. An overview of the 39 historical understandings for eras 1-8 is presented below, followed by the standards integrating these understandings with the five standards in historical thinking for each era in world history.

Era 1: The Beginnings of Human Society

Standard 1: The biological and cultural processes that gave rise to the earliest human communities

Standard 2: The processes that led to the emergence of agricultural societies around the world

Era 2: Early Civilizations and the Rise of Pastoral Peoples, 4000-1000 BCE

Standard 1: The major characteristics of civilization and how civilizations emerged in Mesopotamia, Egypt, and the Indus valley

Standard 2: How agrarian societies spread and new states emerged in the third and second millennia BCE

Standard 3: The political, social, and cultural consequences of population movements and militarization in Eurasia in the second millennium BCE

Era 3: Classical Traditions, Major Religions, and Giant Empires, 1000 BCE–300 CE

Standard 1: Innovation and change from 1000–600 BCE: horses, ships, iron, and monotheistic faith

Standard 2: The emergence of Aegean civilization and how interrelations developed among peoples of the eastern Mediterranean and Southwest Asia, 600–200 BCE

Standard 3: How major religions and large-scale empires arose in the Mediterranean basin, China, and India, 500 BCE–300 CE

Standard 4: The development of early agrarian civilizations in Mesoamerica

Era 4: Expanding Zones of Exchange and Encounter, 300–1000 CE

Standard 1: Imperial crises and their aftermath, 300–700 CE

Standard 2: Causes and consequences of the rise of Islamic civilization in the 7th–10th centuries

Standard 3: Major developments in East Asia in the era of the Tang dynasty, 600–900 CE

Standard 4: The search for political, social, and cultural redefinition in Europe, 500–1000 CE

Standard 5: The spread of agrarian populations and rise of states in Africa south of the Sahara

Standard 6: The rise of centers of civilization in Mesoamerica and Andean South America in the first millennium CE

Era 5: Intensified Hemispheric Interactions, 1000–1500 CE

Standard 1: The maturing of an interregional system of communication, trade, and cultural exchange in an era of Chinese economic power and Islamic expansion

Standard 2: The redefining of European society and culture, 1000–1300 CE

Standard 3: The rise of the Mongol empire and its consequences for Eurasian peoples, 1200–1350

Standard 4: The growth of states, towns, and trade in Sub-Saharan Africa between the 11th and 15th centuries

Standard 5: Patterns of crisis and recovery in Afro-Eurasia, 1300–1450

Standard 6: The expansion of states and civilizations in the Americas, 1000–1500

Era 6: Global Expansion and Encounter, 1450-1770

Standard 1: How the transoceanic interlinking of all major regions of the world from 1450 to 1600 led to global transformations

Standard 2: How European society experienced political, economic, and cultural transformations in an age of global intercommunication, 1450-1750

Standard 3: How large territorial empires dominated much of Eurasia between the 16th and 18th centuries

Standard 4: Economic, political, and cultural interrelations among peoples of Africa, Europe, and the Americas, 1500-1750

Standard 5: How Asian societies responded to the challenges of expanding European power and forces of the world economy

Standard 6: Major global trends from 1450 to 1770

Era 7: An Age of Revolutions, 1750-1914

Standard 1: The causes and consequences of political revolutions in the late 18th and early 19th centuries

Standard 2: The causes and consequences of the agricultural and industrial revolutions, 1700-1850

Standard 3: The transformation of Eurasian societies in an era of global trade and rising European power, 1750-1850

Standard 4: Patterns of nationalism, state-building, and social reform in Europe and the Americas, 1830-1914

Standard 5: Patterns of global change in the era of Western military and economic domination, 1850-1914

Standard 6: Major global trends from 1750 to 1914

Era 8: The 20th Century

Standard 1: Global and economic trends in the high period of Western dominance

Standard 2: The causes and global consequences of World War I

Standard 3: The search for peace and stability in the 1920s and 1930s

Standard 4: The causes and global consequences of World War II

Standard 5: How new international power relations took shape following World War II

Standard 6: Promises and paradoxes of the second half of the 20th century

Egyptian women
British Museum

ERA 1

The Beginnings of Human Society

Giving Shape to World History

So far as we know, humanity's story began in Africa. For millions of years it was mainly a story of biological change. Then some hundreds of thousands of years ago our early ancestors began to form and manipulate useful tools. Eventually they mastered speech. Unlike most other species, early humans gained the capacity to learn from one another and transmit knowledge from one generation to the next. The first great experiments in creating culture were underway. Among early hunter-gatherers cultural change occurred at an imperceptible speed. But as human populations rose and new ideas and techniques appeared, the pace of change accelerated. Moreover, human history became global at a very early date. In the long period from human beginnings to the rise of the earliest civilization two world-circling developments stand in relief:

▶ **The Peopling of the Earth:** The first great global event was the peopling of the earth and the astonishing story of how communities of hunters, foragers, or fishers adapted creatively and continually to a variety of contrasting, changing environments in Africa, Eurasia, Australia, and the Americas.

▶ **The Agricultural Revolution:** Over a period of several thousand years and as a result of countless small decisions, humans learned how to grow crops, domesticate plants, and raise animals. The earliest agricultural settlements probably arose in Southwest Asia, but the agricultural revolution spread round the world. Human population began to soar relative to earlier times. Communities came into regular contact with one another over longer distances, cultural patterns became far more complex, and opportunities for innovation multiplied.

Why Study This Era?

▶ To understand how the human species fully emerged out of biological evolution and cultural development is to understand in some measure what it means to be human.

▶ The common past that all students share begins with the peopling of our planet and the spread of settled societies around the world.

▶ The cultural forms, social institutions, and practical techniques that emerged in the Neolithic age laid the foundations for the emergence of all early civilizations.

▶ Study of human beginnings throws into relief fundamental problems of history that pertain to all eras: the possibilities and limitations of human control over their environment; why human groups accept, modify, or reject innovations; the variety of social and cultural paths that different societies may take; and the acceleration of social change through time.

What Students Should Understand

Standard 1: **The biological and cultural processes that gave rise to the earliest human communities**

    A. **Early hominid development** in Africa [RELATED]

    B. **How** humans **populated** the major regions of **the world** [CORE]

Standard 2: **The processes that led to the emergence of agricultural societies around the world.**

    A. Establishment of **settled communities and** experimentation with **agriculture** [CORE]

    B. The development of **agricultural societies worldwide** [RELATED]

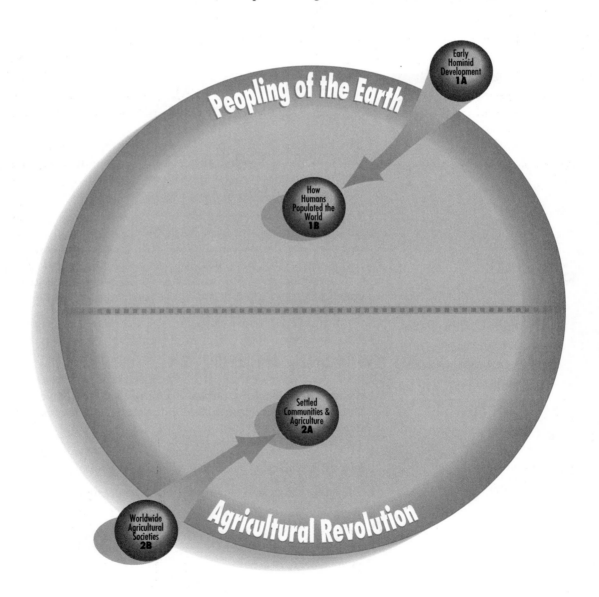

**Relationships Among Major Developments,
Core Standards, and Related Standards for Era 1**

S T A N D A R D   1

Students Should Understand: *The biological and cultural processes that gave rise to the earliest human communities.*

Students Should Be Able to:

1A Demonstrate understanding of early hominid development in Africa by:

[5-12] Inferring from archaeological evidence the characteristics of early African hunter-gatherer communities, including tool kits, shelter, diet, and use of fire. **[Interrogate historical data]**

[7-12] Describing types of evidence and methods of investigation that anthropologists, archaeologists, and other scholars have used to reconstruct early human evolution and cultural development. **[Interrogate historical data]**

[7-12] Tracing the approximate chronology, sequence, and territorial range of early hominid evolution in Africa from the *Australopithecines* to *Homo erectus*. **[Establish temporal order in constructing historical narratives]**

Grades 5-6

Examples of student achievement of Standard 1A include:

▶ Having studied historical evidence, describe a day in the life of an early African woman or man in a hunter-gatherer group. *For which parts of your description was the most, and for which the least, evidence available? How would you account for the differences in the availability of evidence? How does your description differ from a fictional account?*

▶ From historical evidence describe in drawing and writing the ways in which hunter-gatherers lived together in communities. *What do we know about early humans' "lifestyle"? How do we know it? How reliably do we know it?*

▶ Locate the Rift Valley and Ethiopian Highlands on a map of Africa and read about the archaeological discoveries of Louis, Mary, and Richard Leakey and those of Donald Johanson. *How do skeletal remains of Lucy (Australopithecus) compare with the structure of students' own bodies?*

Grades 7-8

Examples of student achievement of Standard 1A include:

▶ Assume the role of a carbon 14, fluorine, or DNA analyst and explain to a class on a field trip to your lab how this dating technique works. *How have these techniques helped us understand early human biological or cultural development?*

▶ Write job descriptions for an archaeologist, geologist, and anthropologist who might be working on a team on hominid evolution in East Africa. *How do these scientists help us to understand earliest human history?*

◗ Draw upon pictorial evidence of human remains to construct a time line showing a possible chronological sequence of human biological and cultural development. Compare your sequence with others that have been proposed by scholars.

Grades 9-12

Examples of student achievement of Standard 1A include:

◗ Draw on scholarly evidence and debate the question: *Were early hominid communities in East Africa hunters, scavengers, or collectors?*

◗ Classify pictures of skeletal remains such as skulls, jaws, and teeth as nonhominid primate, hominid, or *Homo sapiens*. Cite reasons based on evidence, and place them appropriately on a time line. *How may such evidence assist us in understanding human evolution?*

◗ Write a plan to study a newly discovered site of hominid remains, explaining who would join your team and how and why various investigative techniques are to be used. *In what ways do newly-discovered sites affect the ways in which we study and understand our earliest history?*

◗ Compare the inferences that could be made based on examination of a week's worth of household garbage about your own way of life, with those that can be made based on examination of the remains associated with an early human hunter-gatherer community. *What types of inferences can you draw from common refuse?*

◗ Using archaeological evidence, map the distribution and dates of *Australopithecine*, *Homo erectus*, Neanderthal, and the earliest *Homo sapiens sapiens* remains, along with the major features of flora, fauna, and climate associated with them. Based on this information, draw conclusions about the adaptability and success of hominids.

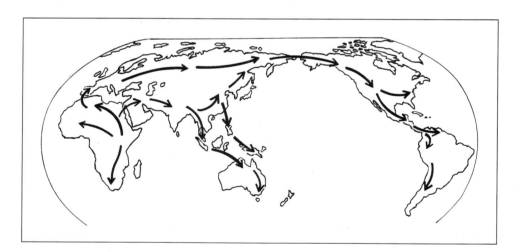

The Peopling of the World

Students Should Be Able to:

1B **Demonstrate understanding of how human communities populated the major regions of the world and adapted to a variety of environments by:**

7-12 Analyzing current and past theories regarding the emergence of *Homo sapiens sapiens* and the processes by which human ancestors migrated from Africa to the other major world regions. [**Evaluate major debates among historians**]

5-12 Comparing the way of life of hunter-gatherer communities in Africa, the Americas, and western Eurasia and explaining how such communities in different parts of the world responded creatively to local environments. [**Compare and contrast differing behaviors and institutions**]

7-12 Assessing theories regarding the development of human language and its relationship to the development of culture. [**Evaluate major debates among historians**]

5-12 Inferring from archaeological evidence the characteristics of Cro-Magnon hunter-gatherer communities of western Eurasia including tool kits, shelter, clothing, ritual life, aesthetic values, relations between men and women, and trade among communities. [**Analyze cause-and-effect relationships and multiple causation**]

7-12 Analyzing possible links between environmental conditions associated with the last Ice Age and changes in the economy, culture, and organization of human communities. [**Analyze cause-and-effect relationships and multiple causation**]

| **Grades 5-6** | **Examples of student achievement of Standard 1B include:** |

▶ Using available resources such as *The Days of the Cave People*, *The Mammoth Hunt*, *Maroo of the Winter Caves*, and material from *Timeframe* (Time-Life series), compare and contrast life in hunter-gatherer communities in Africa, Eurasia, and the Americas. *How were earliest human communities and their life similar in different areas of the world?*

▶ Create a Paleolithic tool kit and explain the possible uses of each implement. *In what ways did humans develop tools to help control their environment?*

▶ Using sources such as *Timeframe* (Time-Life series), describe the Shanidar Cave in present-day Iraq and other such discoveries to understand the Neanderthal culture and community life.

▶ Develop a set of criteria that establishes what factors made a particular geographic location an advantageous place for hunter-gatherers to settle. *How do geography, climate, and other natural factors affect human life?*

| **Grades 7-8** | **Examples of student achievement of Standard 1B include:** |

▶ Examine illustrations of Late Paleolithic cave paintings found in Spain or France and discuss the possible social and cultural meanings of these paintings. *Can we infer the existence of religious beliefs from the evidence of these cave paintings?*

◗ Analyze the story of the Piltdown Man hoax. *Why did people at first believe that the Piltdown Man fossils were genuine? What methods did scholars use to expose Piltdown Man as a hoax?*

◗ Using maps, pictorial evidence of art forms, and other evidence, explain why Cro-Magnon and other early human groups were nomadic.

◗ After reading historical accounts, explain the ways in which hunter-gatherers may have communicated, maintained memory of past events, and expressed religious feelings.

Grades 9-12

Examples of student achievement of Standard 1B include:

◗ Explain what scholars have learned about the Neanderthals and assess theories about the biological and cultural relationships between this hominid and *Homo sapiens sapiens.*

◗ Based on the evidence of Neanderthal burials on the one hand and Cro-Magnon carvings and paintings on the other, infer answers to such questions as: *Were both these groups religious? How reliable is nonverbal evidence for peoples' thoughts and feelings?*

◗ Construct an account based on archaeological evidence of what differences would most strike a girl from a fishing camp who found herself in a mammoth hunters' camp. *What features of everyday life and relations between people were influenced by climate, geographic location, and economic specialization?*

◗ Summarize the evidence in favor of and against the proposition that Mesolithic peoples, such as lake-dwelling Maglemosians, were pioneer innovators taking advantage of opportunities offered by changing climate, rather than its victims.

◗ Hypothesize reasons why language developed as a way for humans to communicate. *How would language be useful to hunters who wished to trap and kill a mammoth? How might naming and classifying tools help in spreading technology from one community to another? How would language have helped communities make complex rules governing social relationships between men and women or adults and children?*

Person gathering honeycomb from a hole in a rock
Late prehistoric cave drawing from Spain
Illustrated by Carole Collier Frick

STANDARD 2

Students Should Understand: *The processes that led to the emergence of agricultural societies around the world.*

Students Should Be Able to:

2A Demonstrate understanding of how and why humans established settled communities and experimented with agriculture by:

5-12 Inferring from archaeological evidence the technology, social organization, and cultural life of settled farming communities in Southwest Asia. [**Draw upon visual sources**]

9-12 Describing types of evidence and methods of investigation by which scholars have reconstructed the early history of domestication and agricultural settlement. [**Evidence historical perspectives**]

9-12 Describing leading theories to explain how and why human groups domesticated wild grains as well as cattle, sheep, goats, and pigs after the last Ice Age. [**Evaluate major debates among historians**]

7-12 Identifying areas in Southwest Asia and the Nile valley where early farming communities probably appeared, and analyzing the environmental and technological factors that made possible experiments with farming in these regions. [**Incorporate multiple causation**]

Grades 5-6

Examples of student achievement of Standard 2A include:

▶ Define wild and domestic plants and animals and draw charts illustrating differences between wild and domestic crops during the early agricultural period.

▶ Draw upon resources such as *Skara Bare* by Oliver Dunrea, the story of a prehistoric village in Scotland, in order to create illustrations or dioramas of early farming villages. Dioramas can include cultivated fields and domesticated animals. *How did the practice of agriculture influence patterns of human settlement?*

▶ Create a "you are there" travel brochure for the early agricultural era. Include information on geographic sites, food production, shelter, specialization, government, and religion.

Grades 7-8

Examples of student achievement of Standard 2A include:

▶ Write an account comparing the daily life of a hunter-gatherer and of an early farmer. *What problems and benefits are associated with each way of life?*

▶ Analyze illustrations of some of the new tools and other objects, such as sickles, grinding stones, pottery, blades, and needles, that appeared in the early era of agriculture. *In what ways are these objects likely to have affected daily life in early farming settlements?*

▶ Use a source such as Richard Leakey's *Dawn of Man* to determine how human communities might have unconsciously domesticated wheat.

♦ Draw upon evidence developed by scholars to describe the role of fishing as a sedentary but nonagricultural way of life.

Grades 9-12

Examples of student achievement of Standard 2A include:

♦ Drawing evidence from scholarly sources, debate the questions: *Did human beings invent or discover agriculture?*

♦ Examine archaeological reconstructions of hunter-gatherer and agricultural sites, including objects found there. Compare and contrast these sites posing questions such as: *Is the presence of permanent structures evidence for an agricultural community? Is the presence of tools such as grinding stones or sickles evidence for an agricultural society? Is a spear an indication of a hunter-gatherer society? What kind of evidence would reliably distinguish a hunter-gatherer from an agricultural site?*

♦ Debate questions such as: *What do historians mean by the "Neolithic revolution" and is the term "revolution" used here in a valid way? What does the term "Neolithic" mean? Is this term adequate to explain the complexities of early farming life?*

♦ Hypothesize ways in which hunter-gatherer societies could try to gain control over food supplies (such as fertility and hunting magic, protection of self-sown seeds, or confinement of a herd). *What part did the ability to store, as well as to control food supplies, play in the "Neolithic revolution"? Were gourds, baskets, and pottery integral or peripheral to the shift toward settled agriculture?*

♦ Construct historical arguments to assess the interconnection between agricultural production and cultural change (such as division of labor, change in concept of time, gender roles).

♦ Based on scholarly accounts, construct a hypothesis to explain the development of wild grain husbandry in Southwest Asia.

Fragment of a vessel with carved relief, Temple of Shamash, Mari

Students Should Be Able to:

2B **Demonstrate understanding of how agricultural societies developed around the world by:**

[5-12] Analyzing differences between hunter-gatherer and agrarian communities in economy, social organization, and quality of living. [**Compare and contrast differing behaviors and institutions**]

[5-12] Describing social, cultural, and economic characteristics of large agricultural settlements such as Çatal Hüyuk or Jericho. [**Obtain historical data**]

[7-12] Analyzing how peoples of West Africa, Europe, Southeast Asia, East Asia, and the Americas domesticated food plants and developed agricultural communities in response to local needs and conditions. [**Compare and contrast behaviors and institutions**]

[7-12] Assessing archaeological evidence from agricultural village sites in Southwest Asia, North Africa, China, or Europe that indicates the emergence of social class divisions, occupational specialization, and differences in roles between men and women. [**Hold interpretations of history as tentative**]

[7-12] Assessing archaeological evidence for long-distance trade in Southwest Asia. [**Draw upon visual sources**]

[9-12] Assessing archaeological evidence for the emergence of complex belief systems, including worship of female deities. [**Interrogate historical data**]

Grades 5-6

Examples of student achievement of Standard 2B include:

▶ Locate on a map the site of the ancient town of Çatal Hüyuk and describe the natural environment surrounding this town. Construct a model or illustration of Çatal Hüyuk and describe daily life in the community. *What problems needed to be solved that resulted from large numbers of people living together on a permanent basis?*

▶ Formulate evidence for the comparative lifestyles of hunter-gatherers, fishermen, and farmers. *What tools would these different groups need to make a living? How would they make these tools and where would they find materials for manufacturing them?*

▶ Explain the development of tropical agriculture in Southeast Asia. *What role did bamboo play as a major tool in this area?*

Grades 7-8

Examples of student achievement of Standard 2B include:

▶ Construct a map demonstrating possible long-distance trade routes in Southwest Asia. *How does archaeological evidence support the routes in this map? What is obsidian, and why was it such an important item of trade?*

▶ Make a time line tracing the emergence of agriculture worldwide up to about 4000 BCE, and identify on a world map both the major areas of agricultural production and the distribution of human settlements. *Why was it in these areas rather than elsewhere that agriculture became a way of life? What connections are there between the practice of agriculture and the pattern of settlement?*

▶ Make a chart comparing the positive and negative effects of agricultural life compared to hunter-gatherer life and debate the following question: *Did the emergence of agriculture represent an advance in human social development? What criteria would you use to evaluate whether or not it was an advance?*

| Grades 9-12 | **Examples of student achievement of Standard 2B include:** |

▶ Analyze pictures of hunter-gatherer sites in places such as Danube fishing villages, the Lascaux caves in France, and hunter sites in northern regions. Contrast these with agricultural sites such as those found in Jericho, Çatal Hüyuk, Banpo village in North China, and the Tehuacán Valley in Mexico. *How do hunter-gatherer sites differ from agricultural sites?*

▶ Chart the probable differences between a hunting/gathering community of a few dozen people, a village of a few hundred, and a town of several thousand in relation to storage needs, sanitation, social hierarchy, division of labor, gender roles, and protection. Find evidence for your hypotheses.

▶ Map the distribution of sites where each of the following kinds of communities was found in the period of about 10,000-4000 BCE: hunter/gatherers; wheat/barley/cattle/sheep farmers; millet farmers; yam farmers; rice farmers; maize/squash farmers. List possible explanations why some groups developed or accepted completely sedentary agriculture, while others partly or fully kept to earlier patterns.

▶ Make inferences based on scholarly evidence to explain the level of social specialization and political organization in such sites as Çatal Hüyuk and Jericho. *How might the development of patterns for layout, fortification, and standardization transform human culture?*

▶ Analyze scholarly evidence to explain the varied methods of crop cultivation. *How were methods of agriculture different in Southwest Asia as compared to West Africa and Southeast Asia?*

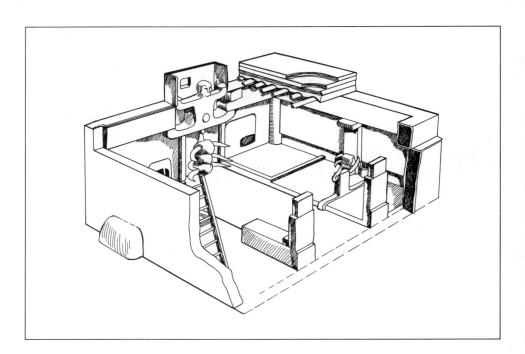

Sketch of a shrine room,
Çatal Hüyuk, Turkey
Illustration by Carole Collier Frick

ERA 2

Early Civilizations and the Emergence of Pastoral Peoples, 4000-1000 BCE

Giving Shape to World History

When farmers began to grow crops on the irrigated floodplain of Mesopotamia in Southwest Asia, they had no consciousness that they were embarking on a radically new experiment in human organization. The nearly rainless but abundantly watered valley of the lower Tigris and Euphrates rivers was an environment capable of supporting far larger concentrations of population and much greater cultural complexity than could the hill country where agriculture first emerged. Shortly after 4000 BCE, a rich culture and economy based on walled cities was appearing along the banks of the two rivers. The rise of civilization in Mesopotamia marked the beginning of 3,000 years of far-reaching transformations that affected peoples across wide areas of Eurasia and Africa.

The three standards in this era present a general chronological progression of developments in world history from 4000 to 1000 BCE Two major patterns of change may be discerned that unite the developments of this period.

‣ **Early Civilizations and the Spread of Agricultural Societies:** Societies exhibiting the major characteristics of civilization spread widely during these millennia. Four great floodplain civilizations appeared, first in Mesopotamia, shortly after in the Nile valley, and from about 2500 BCE in the Indus valley. These three civilizations mutually influenced one another and came to constitute a single region of inter-communication and trade. The fourth civilization arose in the Yellow River valley of northwestern China in the second millennium BCE. As agriculture continued to spread, urban centers also emerged on rain-watered lands, notably in Syria and on the island of Crete. Finally, expanding agriculture and long-distance trade were the foundations of increasingly complex societies in the Aegean Sea basin and western Europe. During this same era, it must be remembered, much of the world's population lived in small farming communities and hunted or foraged. These peoples were no less challenged than city-dwellers to adapt continually and creatively to changing environmental and social conditions.

‣ **Pastoral Peoples and Population Movements:** In this era pastoralism — the practice of herding animals as a society's primary source of food — made it possible for larger communities than ever before to inhabit the semi-arid steppes and deserts of Eurasia and Africa. Consequently, pastoral peoples began to play an important role in world history. In the second millennium BCE migrations of pastoral folk emanating from the steppes of Central Asia contributed to a quickening pace of change across the entire region from Europe and the Mediterranean basin to India. Some societies become more highly militarized, new kingdoms appeared, and languages of the Indo-European family became much more widely spoken.

Why Study This Era?

▶ This is the period when civilizations appeared, shaping all subsequent eras of history. Students must consider the nature of civilization as both a particular way of organizing society and a historical phenomenon subject to transformation and collapse.

▶ In this era many of the world's most fundamental inventions, discoveries, institutions, and techniques appeared. All subsequent civilizations would be built on these achievements.

▶ Early civilizations were not self-contained but developed their distinctive characteristics partly as a result of interactions with other peoples. In this era students will learn about the deep roots of encounter and exchange among societies.

▶ The era introduces students to one of the most enduring themes in history, the dynamic interplay, for good or ill, between the agrarian civilizations and pastoral peoples of the great grasslands.

What Students Should Understand

Standard 1: The major characteristics of civilization and how civilizations emerged in Mesopotamia, Egypt, and the Indus valley.

   A. How **Mesopotamia, Egypt, and the Indus Valley** became centers of dense population, urbanization, and cultural innovation [CORE]

   B. How **commercial and cultural interactions** contributed to change in the Tigris-Euphrates, Indus, and Nile regions [RELATED]

Standard 2: How agrarian societies spread and new states emerged in the third and second millennia BCE

   A. The emergence of **civilization in** northern **China** [CORE]

   B. How **new centers of agrarian society** arose in the third and second millennia BCE [RELATED]

Standard 3: The political, social, and cultural consequences of population movements and militarization in Eurasia in the second millennium BCE

   A. How **population movements** from western and central Asia affected peoples of India, Southwest Asia, and the Mediterranean region [CORE]

   B. The social and cultural effects that **militarization and** the emergence of **new kingdoms** had on peoples of Southwest Asia and Egypt [CORE]

   C. The expansion of urban society in **the Aegean region** in the era of Mycenaean dominance [RELATED]

   D. The development of new cultural patterns in **northern India** [RELATED]

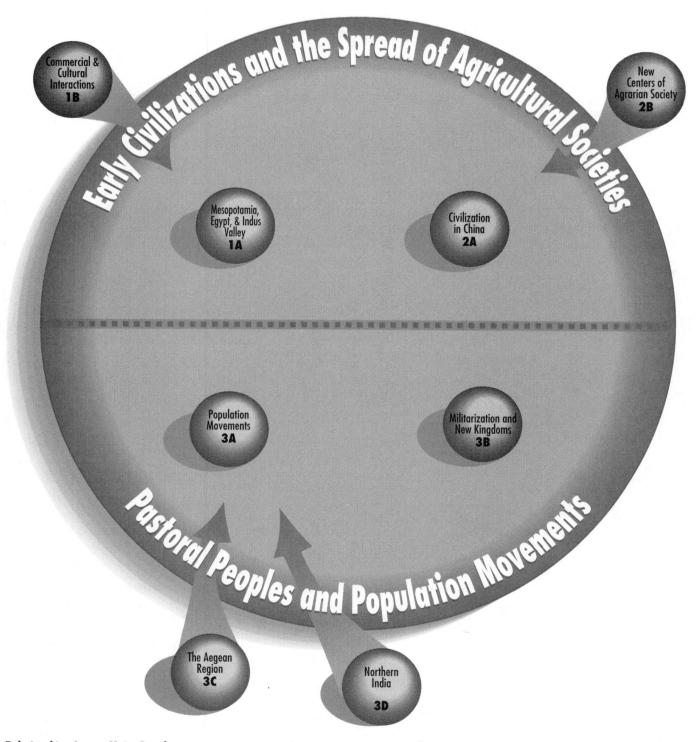

**Relationships Among Major Developments,
Core Standards, and Related Standards for Era 2**

S T A N D A R D   1

Students Should Understand: *The major characteristics of civilization and how civilizations emerged in Mesopotamia, Egypt, and the Indus valley.*

Students Should Be Able to:

1A Demonstrate understanding of how Mesopotamia, Egypt, and the Indus valley became centers of dense population, urbanization, and cultural innovation in the fourth and third millennia BCE by:

5–12 Analyzing the various criteria that have been used to define "civilization" and explaining fundamental differences between civilizations and other forms of social organization such as hunter-gatherer bands and Neolithic agricultural societies. [**Analyze cause-and-effect relationships**]

5–12 Analyzing how the natural environments of the Tigris-Euphrates, Nile, and Indus valleys shaped the early development of civilization. [**Compare and contrast differing sets of ideas**]

5–12 Comparing the character of urban development in Mesopotamia, Egypt, and the Indus valley, including social hierarchy, occupational specialization, and differentiation of the roles of men and women. [**Compare and contrast differing values and institutions**]

5–12 Comparing the forms of writing that developed in the three civilizations and how written records shaped political, legal, religious, and cultural life. [**Compare and contrast differing sets of ideas, values, and institutions**]

7–12 Comparing the development of religious and ethical belief systems in the three civilizations and how they legitimized the political and social order. [**Compare and contrast differing sets of ideas**]

9–12 Analyzing the character of government and military institutions in Egypt and Mesopotamia and ways in which central authorities commanded the labor services and tax payments of peasant farmers. [**Consider multiple perspectives**]

9–12 Describing architectural, artistic, literary, technological, and scientific achievements of these civilizations and relating these achievements to economic and social life. [**Analyze cause-and-effect relationships**]

Grades 5-6

Examples of student achievement of Standard 1A include:

▶ Create a list of the defining characteristics of a "civilization." *At what point in their development could Mesopotamian, Egyptian, and Indus valley societies be called "civilizations" according to these criteria?*

▶ Analyze some of the Indus valley seals. *What can you infer about life in the Indus valley from these seals?*

▶ Locate the Tigris-Euphrates, Indus, and Nile river valleys on a map. Compare the geographic features of these valleys using maps, photographs, and other appropriate pictorial sources. Identify common features that affect agriculture and food supplies. *Why did agriculture develop near rivers that flooded?*

Grades 7-8

Examples of student achievement of Standard 1A include:

▶ Research the technology for flood control and irrigation in the Nile and Tigris-Euphrates valleys. *How did irrigation ensure a reliable food supply? Why did large-scale irrigation projects require more complex political and administrative organization?*

▶ Create a skit entitled "A Day in the Life of Ur," and role-play characters such as ruler, priest, warrior, scribe, artisan, farmer, merchant, slave, mother, and father. Characters must explain why they are important to the overall economic and social welfare of the city.

▶ Read selections from the *Epic of Gilgamesh* and show how this story of a hero-king reflects ancient Mesopotamian religious and cultural values.

▶ Analyze a description of Mohenjo-Daro. *What evidence is there that Mohenjo-Daro was a planned community? Why did the people develop such extensive plumbing? What do you think were the purposes of the buildings of the citadel?*

▶ On a map plot the places where the Indus valley cities have been discovered. Compare the size of the Indus valley civilization with the sizes of Sumerian and Egyptian civilizations. *How do you think the Indus leaders influenced such a large area?*

Grades 9-12

Examples of student achievement of Standard 1A include:

▶ Draw upon selections from the Code of Hammurabi to analyze what it suggests about ethical values, social hierarchy, and attitudes toward and roles of women in Mesopotamia. *How does the Mesopotamian value system compare with modern American ethical and legal standards?*

▶ Using stories such as the Biblical account of creation in Genesis and the *Enuma Elish* from Babylon, compare and contrast the different beliefs these stories reflect.

▶ Draw on historical evidence to role-play a lesson given to a teenager by a Sumerian or Egyptian scribe, explaining the principles of their script and why learning it is important.

▶ Construct a theory to account for why early Egypt united into a kingdom under one ruler, whereas early Mesopotamia was a battleground of competing city-states; and find evidence to support the theory.

▶ Compare and contrast Mesopotamian ziggurats and Egyptian pyramids. *What economic and social preconditions had to exist to make their building possible? What motives impelled their building? What difference did they make to the lives of those who ordered them built and those who actually labored in the building process?*

▶ Examine the way the Indus people laid out and constructed their cities. *What does this evidence suggest about their government and values? What kind of centralized control would be required to build and maintain these cities?*

Students Should Be Able to:

1B **Demonstrate understanding of how commercial and cultural interactions contributed to change in the Tigris-Euphrates, Indus, and Nile regions by:**

5-12 Analyzing the importance of trade in Mesopotamian civilization of the fourth and third millennia and describing the networks of commercial exchange that connected various regions of Southwest Asia. **[Interrogate historical data]**

5-12 Assessing the importance of commercial, cultural, and political connections between Egypt and peoples of Nubia along the upper Nile. **[Identify issues and problems in the past]**

7-12 Tracing the network of trade routes connecting Egypt, Mesopotamia, and the Indus valley in the third millennium and assessing the economic and cultural significance of those commercial connections. **[Analyze cause-and-effect relationships]**

Grades 5-6

Examples of student achievement of Standard 1B include:

▶ Analyze why Mesopotamian civilization was heavily dependent on trade. *What products did Mesopotamians import, from where, and how were they imported? Compare Mesopotamian trade with Egyptian trade.*

▶ Locate on a map of northeastern Africa the cataracts on the Nile River, the regions of Nubia and Kush, and the wind patterns in this part of Africa. From this information show how the geography and climate of the region affected trade in the Nile valley. *What items were traded? What evidence is there for cultural as well as commercial exchanges?*

Grades 7-8

Examples of student achievement of Standard 1B include:

▶ Trace on a map long-distance trade routes by land and sea connecting India, Mesopotamia, and Egypt. List goods traded along these routes and methods of record keeping and ownership. *Why were these goods important to the different societies?*

▶ Role-play a meeting of the king of Kush with an Egyptian official detailing plans for trade. *What goods and tools will they trade? What will the methods of transport be?*

Grades 9-12

Examples of student achievement of Standard 1B include:

▶ Gather evidence for fundamental inventions in Egypt, India, and Mesopotamia and hypothesize: *In what ways might groups borrow aspects of culture from one another? What evidence is there that these three societies borrowed from each other? What effects might cultural innovations have on a receiving society? Why are foreign innovations sometimes rejected? What are some modern examples of both cultural borrowing and rejection?*

◗ Prepare advice from an experienced Mesopotamian trader to his son in the third millennium BCE, including a map of trade routes and information about merchandise known to have been carried by others, transport, dangers, and possible religious or bureaucratic problems in the areas traders visited.

◗ Construct a chart showing the geographical features in Mesopotamia that encouraged trade with others (e.g., their lack of raw materials and their access to the sea) and those features that inhibited trade (e.g., mountain barriers). Find evidence to decide whether the favorable features outweighed the unfavorable.

◗ Construct historical explanations for the shifting political relationship between Egypt and Nubia. *How would you account for Egyptian conquests in Nubia?*

◗ Using Indus seals and other archaeological and geographic evidence, develop an explanation of the type of boats the Indus people used, their navigational techniques, and trade routes.

◗ Gather evidence that people in the Indus valley were in contact with other areas of the world. *What kinds of evidence are available? How wide was the Indus trading network?*

Egyptian laborers in the fields along the Nile. Library of Congress

STANDARD 2

Students Should Understand: *How agrarian societies spread and new states emerged in the third and second millennia BCE.*

Students Should Be Able to:

2A Demonstrate understanding of how civilization emerged in northern China in the second millennium BCE by:

5-12 Explaining the fundamentals of bronze-making technology and assessing the uses and significance of bronze tools, weapons, and luxury goods in the third and second millennia BCE. [**Analyze cause-and-effect relationships**]

5-12 Comparing the climate and geography of the Huang He (Yellow River) valley with the natural environments of Mesopotamia, Egypt, and the Indus valley. [**Clarify information on the geographic setting**]

9-12 Describing royal government under the Shang Dynasty and the development of social hierarchy, religious institutions, and writing. [**Evidence historical perspectives**]

5-12 Inferring from archaeological or written evidence the character of early Chinese urban societies and comparing these centers with cities of Mesopotamia or the Indus valley. [**Formulate historical questions**]

9-12 Assessing the part that Chinese peasants played in sustaining the wealth and power of the Shang political centers. [**Consider multiple perspectives**]

| **Grades 5-6** | **Examples of student achievement of Standard 2A include:** |

▶ Hypothesize how people might have first discovered copper and later created bronze. Write a short story or series of journal entries on your hypothesis. *Why was the making and use of metal work important for humanity?*

▶ Research the writing tools and writing surfaces, and the nature and uses of writing in early Chinese society. Compare with how writing was done and used in early Mesopotamia.

▶ Create a relief map of the Huang He (Yellow River) civilization. Discuss the natural environment of the civilization including its natural resources, and analyze how the environment influenced the civilization that arose there.

▶ Describe Shang ancestor worship. *What attitudes toward the living and dead would ancestor worship encourage? How do Shang practices compare with the Egyptian concept of the afterlife?*

▶ Having looked at pictures of Shang dynasty objects, make a list of all you can tell about people living in that place and time based on this evidence. *What kinds of information about the lives of people who made and used the objects cannot be gained from the evidence of physical objects alone?*

Grades 7-8

Examples of student achievement of Standard 2A include:

▶ Examine illustrations of early Chinese inscriptions on oracle bones. *Why did people write on these animal bones and undershells of tortoises? How has the deciphering of these inscriptions enriched our knowledge of Chinese history during the Shang period? How reliable are these inscriptions as a source of information about Shang China?*

▶ Compare the climate and geography of the Huang He with that of the Tigris-Euphrates valley. *How did environmental factors affect the way early civilization developed differently in these two areas?*

▶ Examine maps illustrating the changes in the course of the Huang He. *What challenges would these changes present to the Chinese people and their government?*

▶ Examine Chinese bronze vessels to determine both their practical and ritual uses.

Grades 9-12

Examples of student achievement of Standard 2A include:

▶ Look at a physical map of Eurasia and consider both geographical barriers and potential routes of communication between China and India or Southwest Asia. *What evidence is there for cultural contacts between China and these other centers of civilization in antiquity?*

▶ Compare the part that prevailing wind, current, and flooding patterns in the Nile, Tigris, and Huang He valleys played in influencing features of the civilizations

▶ Chart the similarities and differences between the military-religious leadership of the Shang kings and the divine kingship of the Egyptian pharaohs.

▶ Taking on the role of a Shang ruler, one of the king's noble vassals, a woman of the upper classes, a bonded peasant, and a slave, describe your rights and responsibilities and your relationship to those above and below you on the social scale.

▶ Gather evidence that the Chinese had developed settlements, sophisticated social cooperation to maintain flood and irrigation systems, and a written language before 1700 BCE. Write an essay presenting your findings.

Students Should Be Able to:

2B Demonstrate understanding of how new centers of agrarian society arose in the third and second millennia BCE by:

5–12 Describing the relationship between the development of plow technology and the emergence of new agrarian societies in Southwest Asia, the Mediterranean basin, and temperate Europe. [**Analyze cause-and-effect relationships**]

7–12 Analyzing how an urban civilization emerged on Crete, and evaluating its cultural achievements. [**Marshal evidence of antecedent circumstances**]

9–12 Explaining the development of commercial communities in such Mediterranean cities as Byblos and Ugarit, and analyzing the cultural significance of expanding commercial exchange among peoples of Southwest Asia, Egypt, and the Aegean Sea. [**Reconstruct patterns of historical succession and duration**]

5–12 Inferring from the evidence of megalithic stone building at Stonehenge and other centers the emergence of complex agrarian societies in temperate Europe. [**Draw upon visual sources**]

9–12 Analyzing evidence for the growth of agricultural societies in tropical West Africa and Southeast Asia in the second millennium BCE. [**Interrogate historical data**]

| Grades 5-6 | Examples of student achievement of Standard 2B include: |

- Using pictorial evidence and historical resources hypothesize how the invention and use of the plow, the bow and arrow, and pottery may have changed the life of humankind.

- Create an illustrated Venn diagram comparing the use of bronze in early civilizations with its use today. *What metals serve as substitutes for bronze today?*

- Assume the role of an archaeologist exploring King Tutankhamen's tomb. Compare the findings to those of other archaeological sites. *What do the treasures from the tomb indicate about Egypt? What conclusions can be drawn about the life of the pharaoh?*

| Grades 7-8 | Examples of student achievement of Standard 2B include: |

- Research the archaeological work of Sir Arthur Evans at Knossos and study a reconstruction of the palace and city. *What do we learn of Minoan culture from Evans's endeavors?*

- Play the role of a craftsman of Syria who is expert in making bronze swords. Explain to a group of apprentices the technological procedures of making these weapons. *In what ways were bronze weapons superior to those made from stone?*

- Defend or refute this statement: *"The plow is the most important invention of early man."* Compare its development and importance to that of pottery, the bow and arrow, and the wheel. *In what ways may the plow and other inventions have led to the creation of different gender roles?*

▶ Prepare a plan for the building of Stonehenge. *How are the stones to be obtained, transported, and erected? How are the laborers to be recruited, provisioned for, and supervised? How will the enterprise be financed? How will the structure be used?*

Grades 9-12

Examples of student achievement of Standard 2B include:

▶ Drawing upon illustrations of Egyptian and Minoan murals and pottery, develop hypotheses on the nature and extent of cultural contact between these two civilizations.

▶ List objects found on Minoan sites that are known to have come from elsewhere, and Minoan wares found outside of Crete. On the basis of this list indicate on a map the places that were in contact with Minoan civilization, and hypothesize the influence of trade on the development of Minoan civilization.

▶ Create a map indicating the most important urban centers of Southwest Asia, Egypt, and the Aegean basin as of about 2000 BCE. *What has archaeology revealed about the development of cities along the eastern Mediterranean coast, notably Byblos and Ugarit? In what ways did these cities form a commercial bridge between the networks of Southwest Asia, Egypt, and the eastern Mediterranean?*

▶ From historical sources create a chart of important technological advances such as the bow and arrow, pottery, the wheel, weaving, the sail, bronze casting, the plow, etc., showing their possible sources, approximate time of introduction, and uses. *What impact did these technologies have on the lives of the people who used them? On the social organization and on the political or economic power of the groups who used them?*

▶ Research pictorial and written evidence on agriculture and agricultural societies in tropical West Africa. *In what ways did agricultural developments stimulate the growth of societies in this part of Africa?* Compare this development with that occurring in Southeast Asia at the same time.

▶ Gather evidence that rice was first domesticated in Southeast Asia, and trace the spread of rice cultivation throughout Asia.

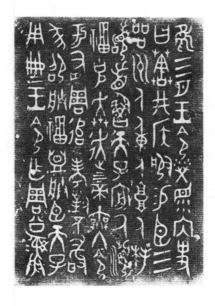

Chinese calligraphy inscribed on a bronze vessel. British Museum

STANDARD 3

Students Should Understand: *The political, social, and cultural consequences of population movements and militarization in Eurasia in the second millennium BCE.*

Students Should Be Able to:

3A Demonstrate understanding of how population movements from western and central Asia affected peoples of India, Southwest Asia, and the Mediterranean region by:

5-12 Defining pastoralism as a specialized way of life and explaining how the climate and geography of Central Asia were linked to the rise of pastoral societies on the steppes. [**Analyze multiple causation**]

7-12 Identifying the probable geographic homeland of speakers of early Indo-European languages and tracing the spread of Indo-European languages from north of the Black and Caspian seas to other parts of Eurasia. [**Reconstruct patterns of historical succession and duration**]

5-12 Explaining the concept of kinship as the basis of social organization among pastoral peoples and comparing the structure of kinship-based societies with that of agrarian states. [**Compare and contrast differing behaviors and institutions**]

9-12 Describing major characteristics of economy, social relations, and political authority among pastoral peoples and analyzing why women tended to enjoy greater social equality with men in pastoral communities than in agrarian societies of Eurasia. [**Identify issues and problems in the past**]

9-12 Analyzing why relations between pastoral peoples and agrarian societies have tended to involve both conflict and mutual dependence. [**Consider multiple perspectives**]

Grades 5-6	Examples of student achievement of Standard 3A include:

▶ Define the term "kinship." *Why was maintaining peace and harmony so important among pastoral people?*

▶ Research the climate and geography of Central Asia. *How would this kind of climate and geography lead to the formation of pastoral societies? What are the characteristics of this kind of society?*

▶ Role-play either a representative of a pastoral or an agrarian society and create a mural showing several kinds of social relationships, marriage ties, and the role of women.

Grades 7-8	Examples of student achievement of Standard 3A include:

▶ Describe the climate and geography of the land mass of Central Asia and hypothesize why animal breeding enabled successful human adaptation to the steppe.

◗ Make charts of some of the major languages of the world today, including languages from Indo-European and Afro-Asiatic families. *How can linguists tell that languages are related to one another? If two languages are related, does that mean that the speakers of those languages will necessarily share other aspects of culture?*

◗ Research, as part of a group, Indo-European languages, and create a language tree with Indo-European as the "trunk" of the tree. *Where are English and Spanish placed on this tree in relation to other languages?* Name some languages spoken in the United States today that would not be on this tree.

Grades 9-12

Examples of student achievement of Standard 3A include:

◗ Construct a map showing the migrations of Indo-European language speakers from their homeland, showing approximate dates for arrivals in new locations, and adding an overlay map showing the distribution of Indo-European language speakers today.

◗ Drawing on historical information, create a conversation between a pastoral nomad woman and a man from a village of agriculturalists about what is expected of women and men in each of their societies.

◗ Draw on scholarly evidence to describe the characteristics of the relations between early herders and farmers. *In what ways could relations between pastoral peoples and agrarian societies involve both conflict and mutual dependence?*

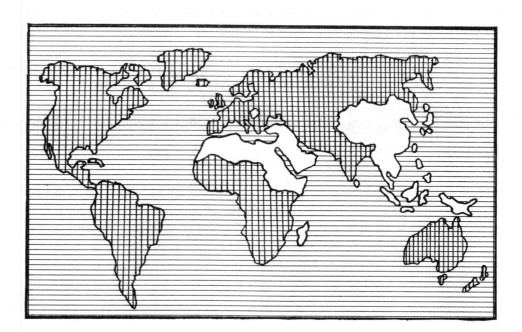

Regions of the World where an Indo-European language is either primary or an official language of state

Students Should Be Able to:

3B Demonstrate understanding of the social and cultural effects that militarization and the emergence of new kingdoms had on peoples of Southwest Asia and Egypt in the second millennium BCE by:

5-12 Analyzing ways in which chariot transport and warfare affected Southwest Asian societies. [**Analyze cause-and-effect relationships**]

7-12 Analyzing the origins of the Hittite people and their empire in Anatolia and assessing Hittite political and cultural achievements. [**Marshal evidence of antecedent circumstances**]

7-12 Describing the spread of Egyptian power into Nubia and Southwest Asia under the New Kingdom and assessing the factors that made Egyptian expansion possible. [**Analyze multiple causation**]

9-12 Explaining the religious ideas of Akhenaton (Amenhotep IV) and assessing the viewpoint that Atonism was an early form of monotheism. [**Interrogate historical data**]

Grades 5-6

Examples of student achievement of Standard 3B include:

▶ Draw on visual data to explain how the invention of chariots affected transportation in Southwest Asian societies.

▶ Investigate the development of chariot warfare. *In what ways were chariots both effective and ineffective weapons of war?*

▶ Use a case study of the Hittites to describe how chariot transport contributed to the spread of new ideas and technology in Southwest Asia.

Grades 7-8

Examples of student achievement of Standard 3B include:

▶ Write entries in the "Who's Who" of Egyptian history describing the political and cultural achievements of Thutmose III, Ramses II, and Queen Hatshepsut. Based on their achievements, debate the question: *Who should get "top billing"?*

▶ As a military commander of the Hittite army, write an argument in favor of spending more of the revenues on chariots. Justify the argument with reasons historically known to be valid.

▶ Write epitaphs for Hatshepsut, outlining her achievements during the New Kingdom. Display epitaphs on a homemade obelisk.

▶ As a member of a group, develop a chart that graphically shows Egyptian expansion during the Old, Middle, and New kingdoms. These graphic representations can take the form of an illustrated time line, transparency overlay, or relief map and should include the factors that made expansion possible.

Grades 9-12

Examples of student achievement of Standard 3B include:

▶ Draw a map of the major states existing in Southwest Asia, Egypt, and the eastern Mediterranean in the later second millennium, and consider why the wars and diplomatic relations among these states probably represent the first era of "internationalism" in world history.

▶ Survey visual and written sources (e.g., *The Iliad*, Egyptian wall paintings, and Assyrian bas reliefs) and describe the effects of introducing chariot warfare onto the battlefield.

▶ Compare the accomplishments of Sargon and Akhenaton (Amenhotep IV), and evaluate which of them had a greater historical impact, giving reasons to justify the assessment.

▶ Create a chart showing the main features of Egyptian religious beliefs during the Old Kingdom; Akhenaton's beliefs; and Hebrew monotheistic beliefs. Then determine to what extent it would be accurate to describe Akhenaton as a "monotheist."

Assyrian chariot

Students Should Be Able to:

3C **Demonstrate understanding of how urban society expanded in the Aegean region in the era of Mycenaean dominance by:**

5-12 Describing the political and social organization of the Mycenaean Greeks as revealed in the archaeological and written record. [Interrogate historical data]

7-12 Assessing the cultural influences of Egypt, Minoan Crete, and Southwest Asian civilizations on the Mycenaeans. [Analyze cause-and-effect relationships]

9-12 Analyzing the impact of Mycenaean expansion and city-building on commerce and political life in the eastern Mediterranean. [Analyze cause-and-effect relationships]

| Grades 5-6 | **Examples of student achievement of Standard 3C include:** |

▶ Assume the role of a Minoan visiting Mycenae. Write an account describing what you find different about Mycenaean society and lifestyle.

▶ Investigate how geography influenced the development of Mycenaean society.

▶ Draw upon selections from the *Iliad*, the *Aeneid*, and pictures of jars and red-clay portraits to retell the story of the siege of Troy.

| Grades 7-8 | **Examples of student achievement of Standard 3C include:** |

▶ Read passages from the *Iliad* about the Mycenaeans and the Trojan War. Locate Mycenaean and Trojan areas on a map. Having investigated archaeological evidence for trade and warfare in these areas, and the successive levels of occupation at the site of Troy, write a critique of Homer's account.

▶ Show the cultural influences of Egypt, Minoan Crete, and Southwest Asian civilizations on the Mycenaeans by using pictures. Explain your reasons for assuming that the direction of the influence was toward Mycenae. *How was the influence accomplished?*

| Grades 9-12 | **Examples of student achievement of Standard 3C include:** |

▶ Drawing on the physical evidence in Mycenaean shaft tombs, write a description of society, government, and trade in the second millennium BCE.

▶ Compare Mycenaean with Egyptian royal tombs. Hypothesize what these tombs suggest about class roles and the nature and role of government.

▶ Using descriptions by archaeologists, ground plans based on excavations, and pictures of remains and of reconstructions, compare Mycenaean fortresses with Minoan palaces. *What conclusions about their respective societies may be drawn from this evidence? How does investigation of other available evidence support, modify, or negate your conclusions?*

Students Should Be Able to:

3D Demonstrate understanding of the development of new cultural patterns in northern India in the second millennium BCE by:

`7-12` Inferring from geographical and archaeological information why Indo-Aryan-speaking groups moved from Central Asia into India beginning in the second millennium. **[Draw upon visual sources]**

`9-12` Analyzing possible causes of the decline and collapse of Indus valley civilization. **[Hypothesizing the influence of the past]**

`9-12` Assessing the early political, social, and cultural impact of Indo-Aryan movements on peoples of North India. **[Analyze cause-and-effect relationships]**

| Grades 5-6 | Examples of student achievement of Standard 3D include: |

▶ Look at slides or photos of the ruins of Mohenjo-Daro and research reasons why this city disappeared. *What are some of the possible causes of the decline or disappearance of cities in history? How could changes in the environment have contributed to the fall of Mohenjo-Daro and other Indus cities?*

| Grades 7-8 | Examples of student achievement of Standard 3D include: |

▶ Hypothesize on the causes of Indo-Aryan and Mycenaean-speaking peoples' movements into India and the eastern Mediterranean. *In what ways may these migrations be seen as a part of the patterns of movement of all Indo-European peoples?*

▶ Drawing upon books such as A.K. Ramanijan's *Folktales from India,* examine the values that governed Indian society. *How is the rigid varna system introduced by the Aryans reflected in these folktales?*

▶ Develop a presentation of possible factors such as climatic, population, technological, or social changes that might have caused Aryan pastoral peoples to leave Central Asia. *What might have pushed them from the steppes? What might have attracted them to the Iranian plateau and into the Indus valley?*

▶ Hypothesize on what caused Aryans and Mycenaean-speaking peoples to move into India and the eastern Mediterranean. *In what ways may these migrations be seen as a part of the pattern of movement of all Indo-European peoples? Should these movements be called a "chariot revolution"?*

▶ Examine photographs and descriptions of excavations of Indus cities such as Mohenjo-Daro to determine what happened to these cities. *What might have caused a decline in trade and overcrowding? Why were people left unburied in the streets?*

▶ Analyze *Rig Veda* 10.90 to determine what the Aryans believed were the ideal divisions of society. *What is the significance of the term "varna"? What privileges and restrictions were placed on the various varna?*

▶ Select odes from the Vedas that praise the major Vedic gods — Indra, Varuna, Soma, and Agni — to determine important Aryan values.

▶ Retell the story of the conflict between the Pandavas and Kauravas in the *Mahabharata. What does it suggest about tensions among Aryan tribes as they began to settle down in the Indo-Gangetic plain? Why did the cousins fight? Who ruled and what was the basis of a ruler's legitimacy?*

Examples of student achievement of Standard 3D include:

▶ Analyze various Vedic hymns. *What do they say about people's beliefs?*

▶ Research the origins of the word "Aryan" and the peoples who came to be called Indo-Aryan. *Based on works such as the* Vedas *and* Mahabharata, *what was Aryan culture in India like? How was the term "Aryan" used by Nazis in the 20th century? Where were the implications of the Nazi definition? How did it differ from the way historians of early India used the term?*

▶ Compare linguistic (shared vocabulary), literary (*Vedas*), and archaeological evidence for the way of life and beliefs of India's Aryan immigrants in the second millennium BCE, and assess what information is most reliably known.

▶ Hypothesize from historical information what factors (disease, famine, environment, invasion, etc.) led to the collapse of the Indus valley civilization. *How does this decline compare with that of other peoples such as the Sumerians?*

▶ Assess how reliable the *Iliad* and *Odyssey* and the *Mahabharata* and *Ramayana* are as sources of historical information about this period. *How do historians determine to what extent these epics reveal information about the time period when they were first written down or the earlier time period during which the stories were set?*

Excavation of a public drain at Lothal, Indus Valley. Archaeological survey, Government of India, New Delhi

ERA 3

Classical Traditions, Major Religions, and Giant Empires, 1000 BCE-300 CE

Giving Shape to World History

By 1000 BCE urban civilizations of the Eastern Hemisphere were no longer confined to a few irrigated river plains. World population was growing, interregional trade networks were expanding, and towns and cities were appearing where only farming villages or nomad camps had existed before. Iron-making technology had increasing impact on economy and society. Contacts among diverse societies of Eurasia and Africa were intensifying, and these had profound consequences in the period from 1000 BCE to 300 CE. The pace of change was quickening in the Americas as well. If we stand back far enough to take in the global scene, three large-scale patterns of change stand out. These developments can be woven through the study of particular regions and societies as presented in Standards 1-4, below.

▶ **Classical Civilizations Defined:** The civilizations of the irrigated river valleys were spreading to adjacent regions, and new centers of urban life and political power were appearing in rain-watered lands. Several civilizations were attaining their classical definitions, that is, they were developing institutions, systems of thought, and cultural styles that would influence neighboring peoples and endure for centuries.

▶ **Major Religions Emerge:** Judaism, Christianity, Buddhism, Brahmanism/Hinduism, Confucianism, and Daoism all emerged in this period as systems of belief capable of stabilizing and enriching human relations across much of the world. Each of these religions also united peoples of diverse political and ethnic identities and offered fertile avenues of cultural interchange between one region of Afro-Eurasia and another.

▶ **Giant Empires Appear:** Multi-ethnic empires became bigger than ever before and royal bureaucracies more effective at organizing and taxing ordinary people in the interests of the state. Empire building in this era also created much larger spheres of economic and cultural interaction. Near the end of the period the Roman and Han empires together embraced a huge portion of the hemisphere, and caravans and ships were relaying goods from one extremity of Eurasia to the other.

Why Study This Era?

▶ The classical civilizations of this age established institutions and defined values and styles that endured for many centuries and that continue to influence our lives today.

▶ Six of the world's major faiths and ethical systems emerged in this period and set forth their fundamental teachings.

◗ Africa and Eurasia together moved in the direction of forming a single world of human interchange in this era as a result of trade, migrations, empire-building, missionary activity, and the diffusion of skills and ideas. These interactions had profound consequences for all the major civilizations and all subsequent periods of world history.

◗ This was a formative era for many fundamental institutions and ideas in world history, such as universalist religion, monotheism, the bureaucratic empire, the city-state, and the relation of technology to social change. Students' explorations in the social sciences, literature, and contemporary affairs will be enriched by understanding such basic concepts as these.

◗ This era presents rich opportunities for students to compare empires, religions, social systems, art styles, and other aspects of the past, thus sharpening their understanding and appreciation of the varieties of human experience.

What Students Should Understand

Standard 1: **Innovation and change from 1000-600 BCE: horses, ships, iron, and monotheistic faith**

    A. How **state-building, trade, and migrations** led to increasingly complex interrelations among peoples of the Mediterranean basin and Southwest Asia [CORE]

    B. The **emergence of Judaism** and the historical significance of the Hebrew kingdoms [CORE]

    C. The development of the **civilization of Kush** in the upper Nile valley and iron technology's contribution to the spread of agricultural societies in Sub-Saharan Africa [RELATED]

    D. How **pastoral nomadic peoples** of Central Asia began to play an important role in world history [RELATED]

Standard 2: **The emergence of Aegean civilization and how interrelations developed among peoples of the eastern Mediterranean and Southwest Asia, 600-200 BCE**

    A. Achievements and limitations of the democratic institutions that developed in Athens and other **Aegean city-states** [CORE]

    B. Major **cultural achievements of Greek civilization** [RELATED]

    C. The development of the **Persian (Achaemenid) Empire** and the consequences of its conflicts with the Greeks [RELATED]

    D. Alexander of Macedon's conquests and the interregional character of **Hellenistic society** and culture [CORE]

Standard 3: How major religions and large-scale empires arose in the Mediterranean basin, China, and India, 500 BCE-300 CE

    A. The unification of the Mediterranean basin under the **Roman empire** [CORE]

    B. The **emergence of Christianity** in the context of the Roman empire [CORE]

    C. The **unification of China** under the early imperial dynasties [CORE]

    D. Religious and cultural developments in India in the era of the Gangetic states and the **Maurya empire** [CORE]

Standard 4: **The development of early agrarian civilizations in Mesoamerica**

    A. The achievements of **Olmec civilization** [CORE]

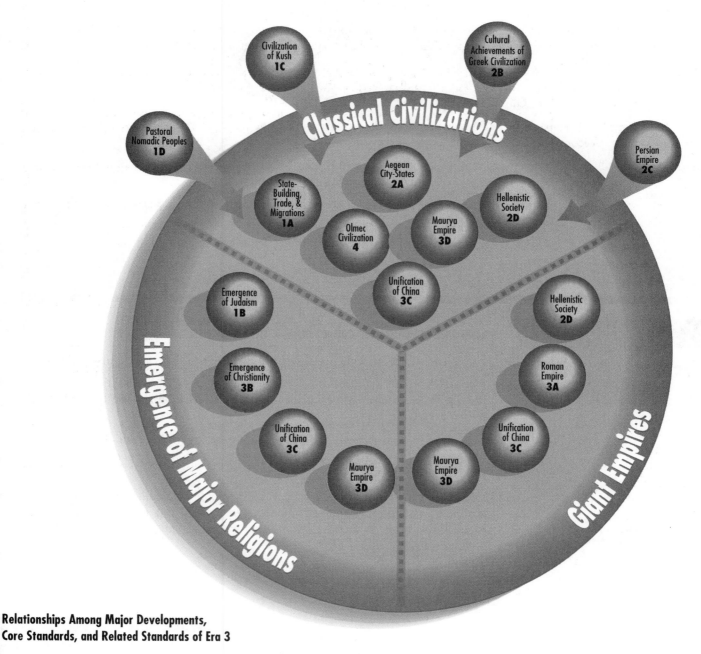

**Relationships Among Major Developments,
Core Standards, and Related Standards of Era 3**

STANDARD 1

Students Should Understand: *Innovation and change from 1000 to 600 BCE: horses, ships, iron, and monotheistic faith.*

Students Should Be Able to:

1A **Demonstrate understanding of state-building, trade, and migrations that led to increasingly complex interrelations among peoples of the Mediterranean basin and Southwest Asia by:**

7-12 Explaining the fundamentals of iron-making technology and analyzing the early significance of iron tools and weapons in Southwest Asia and the Mediterranean region. [**Analyze cause-and-effect relationships**]

7-12 Describing the extent of the Assyrian and New Babylonian empires and assessing the sources of their power and wealth. [**Obtain historical data**]

5-12 Explaining the patterns of Phoenician trade, political organization, and culture in the Mediterranean basin. [**Reconstruct patterns of historical succession and duration**]

5-12 Describing the emergence of Greek city-states in the Aegean region and the political, social, and legal character of the polis. [**Marshal evidence of antecedent circumstances**]

7-12 Analyzing the factors that led Greeks to found colonies in the Mediterranean and Black Sea regions. [**Analyze multiple causation**]

9-12 Analyzing the social and cultural effects of the spread of alphabetic writing in Southwest Asia and the Mediterranean basin. [**Analyze cause-and-effect relationships**]

Grades 5-6

Examples of student achievement of Standard 1A include:

▶ Locate on a map of the Mediterranean Sea the major Phoenician port cities and colonies such as Carthage, and show the trade routes that linked these cities. *Why did the Phoenicians establish cities throughout the Mediterranean? With whom did they trade? What items were traded?*

▶ Make a relief map showing the mountainous Greek peninsula and the major Greek city-states. *How did geography influence the location and development of city-states?*

▶ Construct a model or describe a typical Greek polis, including such features as an acropolis, the temple of the patron deity, gymnasium, and agora. Construct a dialogue with a friend in another city, each of you describing your polis and why it is so important to you.

Grades 7-8

Examples of student achievement of Standard 1A include:

▶ Explain the importance of iron weapons and cavalry in the rise of the Assyrian empire. *What were the consequences of this new technology? How do the consequences compare to the consequences of adopting chariot warfare earlier?*

▶ Prepare a map showing the location of the important Greek city-states and colonies established in the Black Sea, northern Africa, and the western Mediterranean basin. *Why did the Greeks establish colonies in the Mediterranean and Black Sea basins? Did these colonies together constitute a Greek empire? What sort of relations did the Greeks have with the Phoenicians?*

▶ Locate the Assyrian and New Babylonian empires on a map of Southwest Asia. *What are the geographic features of these two empires? Why were the river valleys so important to these empires?*

▶ Analyze Assyrian bas reliefs and answer the questions: *How do these depict hunting, warfare, and the use of weapons? What do these art forms and their subject matter tell us about Assyrian culture and society?*

Grades 9-12

Examples of student achievement of Standard 1A include:

▶ Research the laws of Hammurabi and the role of lawmakers such as Draco and Solon. *How do their perspectives suggest differing views on the role of law in society? How did the differences in the societies they lived in influence their views?*

▶ Examine the early Phoenician, Greek, Hebrew, and Etruscan alphabets. Infer connections between the alphabets. *How would you account for similarities? What evidence can you give to support your argument? Why was it easier for people to learn an alphabetic system of writing than to learn cuneiform or Egyptian hieroglyphics?*

▶ As a 7th- or 6th-century BCE Greek tyrant, compose a proclamation justifying your rule to the inhabitants of the city you rule over.

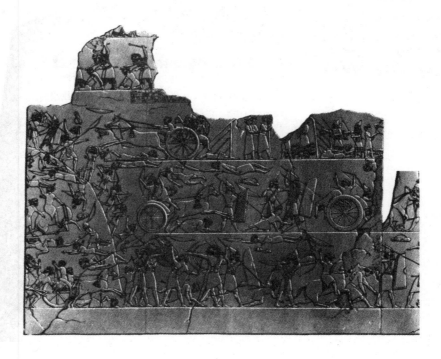

Assyrian warriors in combat
Library of Congress

Students Should Be Able to:

1B **Demonstrate understanding of the emergence of Judaism and the historical significance of the Hebrew kingdoms by:**

5-12 Explaining the fundamental teachings and practices of Judaism and comparing Jewish monotheism with polytheistic religions of Southwest Asia. [**Compare and contrast differing sets of ideas**]

7-12 Explaining the development of the Jewish kingdoms and analyzing how the Jews maintained religious and cultural traditions despite the destruction of these kingdoms. [**Reconstruct patterns of historical succession and duration**]

9-12 Assessing the significance of the Babylonian captivity for the survival of Judaism. [**Evidence historical perspectives**]

9-12 Analyzing the significance of the Jewish diaspora for the transmission of Judaism in the Mediterranean region and Southwest Asia. [**Analyze cause-and-effect relationships**]

Grades 5-6

Examples of student achievement of Standard 1B include:

▶ Construct a time line tracing important periods in ancient Hebrew history from the earliest times through the Babylonian captivity. Illustrate the time line with drawings depicting events in Hebrew history. *In which of the events you show did religion play an important part?*

▶ Construct a model of King Solomon's temple. *What are the central features of the temple complex? What is the role of the temple in Jewish history?* Compare Solomon's temple and a Greek temple of the same period. *What similarities do you see, and how would you explain them?*

▶ Read selections from the Hebrew Scriptures such as stories about the Creation, Noah, the Tower of Babel, Abraham, the Exodus, the Ten Commandments, David, and Daniel and the Lion's Den. Explain the ethical teachings shown in the stories.

Grades 7-8

Examples of student achievement of Standard 1B include:

▶ Write an account describing the political and social structure of Israel during the reigns of Kings Saul, David, and Solomon. *What political role did the judges play? What were the reasons for discontent during the rule of King David? What were the foreign influences in the kingdom during Solomon's reign? Why did the kingdom split into the kingdoms of Israel and Judah?*

▶ Read selections from the Hebrew Scriptures, including the Torah and Psalms, and analyze the basic beliefs of Judaism: its basis in ethical monotheism; its historic belief in the Covenant between God and the Jewish people; the Torah as the source of Judaism's beliefs, rituals, and laws; and the Torah's ethical injunction, "Do justice, love mercy, and walk humbly with thy God."

| Grades 9-12 | **Examples of student achievement of Standard 1B include:** |

- ◗ Read selections from the books of Ezra and Nehemiah and prepare a presentation explaining how the Hebrew people were able to preserve their identity during the Babylonian captivity. *What effect did the captivity have on the subsequent history of the people and their beliefs?*

- ◗ Read selections from the Hebrew Scriptures, the Torah, and Hebrew literature before 300 CE. Based on your reading, write an essay on Hebrew culture focusing on its ethical aspects. *What values are reflected in Hebrew prescriptions for personal behavior? In what ways did religious beliefs in ethical monotheism support ethical prescriptions for human behavior?*

- ◗ Trace the dispersion of Jewish communities on a map. Explain the reasons for and the consequences of the Hebrew diaspora. *What are the modern implications of the diaspora?*

- ◗ Chart the differences between the characteristics of Yahweh and his relationship to the Hebrew people on the one hand, and the characteristics of Southwest Asian nature deities and their relationship to their worshipers on the other. Construct a historical argument to account for the differences.

Shout joyfully to God, all you on earth,

   sing praise to the glory of his name;

   proclaim his glorious praise.

Say to God, "How tremendous are your deeds!

   for your great strength your enemies fawn upon you,

   sing praise to your name!"

THE BOOK OF PSALMS, PSALM 66: 1-4

Students Should Be Able to:

1C Demonstrate understanding of how the civilization of Kush developed in the upper Nile valley and how iron technology contributed to the expansion of agricultural societies in Sub-Saharan Africa by:

9–12 Assessing the importance of political, commercial, and cultural relations between Egypt and Nubia/Kush. [**Analyze multiple causation**]

5–12 Assessing the importance of Nile valley trade as a factor in the rise of the Kushite state in the first millennium BCE. [**Analyze cause-and-effect relationships**]

7–12 Evaluating the linguistic, architectural, and artistic achievements of Kush in the Meroitic period. [**Interrogate historical data**]

7–12 Analyzing how Kushite and Assyrian invasions affected Egyptian society. [**Evidence multiple perspectives**]

9–12 Describing the Nok culture of West Africa and assessing theories of how iron-using societies emerged in Sub-Saharan Africa. [**Evaluate major debates among historians**]

Grades 5-6

Examples of student achievement of Standard 1C include:

▶ Locate Egypt and Kush on a map and draw in the geographic features that either assisted or hampered communication between these two kingdoms.

▶ Analyze pictures of the pyramids in Kush. *What do these pyramids seem to suggest about the relationship between Egypt and Kush? What questions would you need to ask to find out whether the relationship suggested really did exist?*

▶ Assume the role of an iron smelter in Kush and explain the process of making iron to a new king. *What uses of iron were most important in Kushite society?*

▶ Write an account of the Kushite conquest of Egypt from the point of view of both a Kushite and an Egyptian. *In what respects would two such accounts be most likely to differ?*

Grades 7-8

Examples of student achievement of Standard 1C include:

▶ Assume the role of an artist commissioned to commemorate the conquest of Egypt by the Kushites. Draw a series of pictorial representations of the conquest for a public building in Thebes, the city adopted by the victorious Kushites as their capital.

▶ Analyze the social and political consequences of economic contacts between Kush and Egypt.

Grades 9-12

Examples of student achievement of Standard 1C include:

◗ Debate the question: *Was Kush a cultural satellite of Egypt, a distinctive civilization in its own right, or both? What archaeological or other evidence might be used to argue either side of the question?*

◗ Evaluate current theories about the spread of iron technology in Sub-Saharan Africa. *By what routes is the technology likely to have reached West Africa? What evidence might support the theory of independent development of iron technology in Sub-Saharan Africa?*

◗ Analyze illustrations of Nok terra cotta figures and metal implements. *What can be inferred from these physical remains about the culture and society of the West African people who created them?*

◗ Construct assessments, based on historical evidence, of Kushite achievements during the Meroitic period, as they might have been composed by contemporaries from societies known to have been in contact with Kush, such as people from the Nile delta, from Sub-Saharan Africa, and Assyria. *What would observers from each of these different cultures have been likely to single out as noteworthy among Kushite achievements? Why?*

A Nok figurine from the village interior of Nigeria, West Africa. New York Public Library

Students Should Be Able to:

1D Demonstrate understanding of how pastoral nomadic peoples of Central Asia began to play an important role in world history by:

5–12 Explaining the relationship between the mastery of horse riding on the steppes and the development of pastoral nomadism and cavalry warfare. [**Analyze cause-and-effect relationships**]

9–12 Analyzing how the warrior states of the Scythians and the Xiongnu arose among pastoral nomadic peoples of Central Asia. [**Analyze multiple causation**]

7–12 Inferring from archaeological or other evidence basic characteristics of Scythian or Xiongnu society and culture. [**Formulate historical questions**]

5–12 Analyzing why relations between pastoral nomadic peoples of Central Asia and major agrarian states of Eurasia involved both conflict and economic interdependence. [**Analyze cause-and-effect relationships**]

Grades 5-6	**Examples of student achievement of Standard 1D include:**

▶ Construct a map showing the location and range of pastoral nomadic peoples in the first millennium BCE. *How did nomadic groups travel and move their belongings and herds?*

▶ Create a story, a song, or a poem relating the importance of the horse to the pastoral nomadic peoples of Central Asia.

Grades 7-8	**Examples of student achievement of Standard 1D include:**

▶ Write an account, based as much as possible on historical evidence, of a day in the life of a pastoral nomadic person of Central Asia. *For which parts of your account did you have the most, and the least, abundant and accurate evidence? How would you account for the differences in the availability of evidence?*

▶ Label on a map of the Eastern Hemisphere the great chain of arid regions extending from the Sahara Desert to the Gobi Desert of China. *Where did major river valley civilizations exist in relation to this arid belt? How were human communities able to adapt to the environments of these desert and steppe lands? What was the relationship between peoples of the "steppe and the sown"?*

▶ Evaluate the importance of the horse in nomadic life including its use with the chariot, in the cavalry, and as a beast of burden. *How did the horse change life on the steppes?*

Grades 9-12

Examples of student achievement of Standard 1D include:

◗ Analyze drawings or pictures of the remains in the royal Scythian tombs and research archaeological accounts to explain Scythian society and culture.

◗ Use Scythian and Xiongnu nomads as case studies to explain how the horse facilitated territorial expansion and changed leadership roles. *In what ways did leadership among pastoral nomads such as these differ from leadership in settled agricultural communities? What questions would you ask to gain the information you would need should you try to come up with an explanation for the differences?*

◗ Construct a chart showing what pastoral nomadic peoples had to offer that was of value to major agrarian states and vice versa. Hypothesize under what circumstances reciprocal needs and wants would lead to economic interdependence and what other circumstances would lead to conflict. Find information about contacts such as those of the Xiongnu with China and assess how well it supports your hypotheses.

Sculptured relief of an Assyrian king hunting on horseback, from the walls of an Assyrian palace at Nineveh British Museum

STANDARD 2

Students Should Understand: *How Aegean civilization emerged and how interrelations developed among peoples of the eastern Mediterranean and Southwest Asia, 600-200 BCE.*

Students Should Be Able to:

2A **Demonstrate understanding of the achievements and limitations of the democratic institutions that developed in Athens and other Aegean city-states by:**

5-12 Comparing Athenian democracy with the military aristocracy of Sparta. [**Compare and contrast differing sets of ideas, values, and institutions**]

5-12 Explaining the class divisions of Greek society and the social and political roles of major classes, including slaves. [**Evidence historical perspectives**]

7-12 Describing the changing political institutions of Athens in the 6th and 5th centuries BCE and analyzing the influence of political thought on public life. [**Reconstruct patterns of historical succession and duration**]

7-12 Analyzing the place of women in Athenian society. [**Interrogate historical data**]

9-12 Assessing the importance of participatory government in Greek city-states for the development of Western political thought and institutions. [**Hypothesize the influence of the past**]

Grades 5-6

Examples of student achievement of Standard 2A include:

▶ Assume the role of either a citizen, a merchant, a foreign resident, or a slave in both Athens and Sparta. Describe your life in each of these city-states. Compare the rights and responsibilities of a citizen in each city. After the class shares their findings, answer the question: *How did life differ depending on social class?*

▶ Construct a comparative chart that graphically depicts similarities and differences between Athenian democracy and the military aristocracy of Sparta.

▶ *If you were a woman in the 6th or 5th century BCE, would you rather have lived in Sparta or in Athens?* Give reasons based on historical evidence for your decision.

▶ Create a map of the Aegean area and depict each of the major Greek city-states. Delineate each city-state as to its form of government (democracy, oligarchy, tyranny, aristocracy, monarchy) by a symbol or color. *How many other Greek city-states followed the political lead of Athens or Sparta, and how many followed neither?*

Grades 7-8

Examples of student achievement of Standard 2A include:

▶ Prepare a chart listing the major political systems of Greek city-states in the 6th and 5th centuries BCE and explain the evolution of these governmental systems. *What are the advantages and disadvantages of each system?*

▶ Construct a chart showing the major changes in Athenian political organization from the initial monarchy to the forms under Solon and Cleisthenes. *What innovations did Cleisthenes make?*

▶ Describe the roles that women had in Athenian society and their rights under the law. Hypothesize why "democracy" was limited to males only.

▶ Analyze Pericles' *Funeral Oration* to discern Athenian values during the 5th century BCE. *Did daily life in classical Athens reflect these ideals?*

Grades 9-12

Examples of student achievement of Standard 2A include:

▶ Describe the Greek concept of the "barbarian" as set forth in the works of Aristotle and other writers, and explain the position of "barbarians" in Greek city-states. *Could a "barbarian" become a Greek? How could the Greek concept of "barbarian" provide a foundation for greater communication between Greeks and outsiders? What is ethnocentrism? Are all modern societies and nations ethnocentric to some degree?*

▶ Analyze selections from *The Republic*. Prepare a report on how Plato's ideal polis has influenced political thought in the modern world.

▶ Develop a hypothesis to explain why the maturing of democratic institutions in Greece resulted in greater restrictions on the rights and freedoms of women. *What evidence can you give to support your hypothesis?*

▶ Explain the social strata in Athens and Sparta in the 5th century BCE. Choose one of the two, and compare its social structure to that of another Greek city-state such as Corinth or Thebes. *How would you account for similarities and differences?*

▶ Draw evidence from Thucydides' *Melian Dialogue* to examine the concepts of political freedom, national security, and justice. Appraise Pericles' "Funeral Oration" from the perspective of a Melian following the Athenian conquest.

▶ Support or refute the statement: "Athens was the laboratory of democracy and democratic law."

Pericles
Library of Congress

Students Should Be Able to:

2B Demonstrate understanding of the major cultural achievements of Greek civilization by:

5-12 Identifying the major characteristics of Hellenic architecture and sculpture and assessing the ways in which architecture, sculpture, and painting reflected social values and attitudes. **[Draw upon visual sources]**

7-12 Identifying major works of Greek drama and mythology and assessing how they reflected social values and attitudes. **[Formulate historical questions]**

9-12 Explaining the leading ideas of Socrates, Plato, Aristotle, Herodotus, and other philosophers and historians. **[Evidence historical perspective]**

Grades 5-6

Examples of student achievement of Standard 2B include:

♦ Participate in a role-play of the trial of Socrates. *What does the story of Socrates tell us about his values?*

♦ Find local examples of art and architecture that reflect the influence of Classical Greece.

♦ Read and compare several Greek myths using a source such as Charles and Rosalie Baker's *Myths and Legends of Mt. Olympus* or Ingri and Edgar Parin d'Aulaire's *Book of Greek Myths. How are gods and goddesses depicted in Greek mythology? What is anthropomorphism in relation to Greek mythology and how do Greeks and their gods and goddesses relate in these myths?*

♦ Study photographic evidence of Greek pottery and explain how the images on the pottery reflect life in ancient Greece. With this reference construct a replica of a piece of Greek pottery and illustrate this with scenes from life in your community. *How can art reflect culture and values?*

♦ Analyze illustrations of classical Greek sculpture and evaluate them for evidence of social ideals of manhood, womanhood, and athletic prowess.

Grades 7-8

Examples of student achievement of Standard 2B include:

♦ Read selections from Greek dramatists such as Sophocles, Euripides, and Aeschylus and discuss what evidence they offer of ancient moral values and civic culture.

♦ Compare creation myths from Sumer, Egypt, Babylon, and Greece and then compare them to the nationalized myths in China. *What images of the gods are presented in these myths? What human characteristics do they evidence? What similarities and differences in world view do these myths suggest?*

♦ Examine photographic and other evidences of Greek art and architecture and read selections from Greek literature to determine how the arts reflected cultural traditions and values.

Grades 9-12

Examples of student achievement of Standard 2B include:

▶ Present dramatic readings from selections of Greek tragedies and comedies, such as Sophocles' *Antigone* and Aristophanes' *The Clouds*. *What are the lessons transmitted through Greek tragedy and comedy? How does drama reflect values?*

▶ Compare Egyptian and Sumerian deities with the Greek gods and goddesses. Draw upon visual evidence of deities and humans as depicted in bas reliefs, statues, and monuments to discover how each of these societies saw themselves in relation to their gods and goddesses. *What do depictions of goddesses suggest about attitudes toward women? Is there other evidence in Egyptian, Sumerian, and Greek life to support their depiction of goddesses?*

▶ Using contemporary literature such as Dorothy Mills's *Book of the Ancient Greeks*, Mary Renault's *The Mask of Apollo*, and the works of Greek playwrights, reconstruct what daily life was like in ancient Greece between 600 and 200 BCE.

▶ Read excerpts from the introductory sections of Herodotus's and Thucydides' works that reveal their working methods as historians. *What would you praise or criticize about them as historians, and why?*

▶ Compare the ideas of Plato and of Aristotle about the most desirable form of government. *How closely did the government they considered the best resemble the one they themselves lived under?*

Greek pottery, red-figured drinking cup, c. 490 B.C.E.
Illustration by Carole Collier Frick

Students Should Be Able to:

2C Demonstrate understanding of the development of the Persian (Achaemenid) empire and the consequences of its conflicts with the Greeks by:

5-12 Describing the basic teachings of Zoroastrianism. [Interrogate historical data]

5-12 Explaining the founding, expansion, and political organization of the Persian empire. [Reconstruct patterns of historical succession and duration]

7-12 Analyzing the major events of the wars between Persia and the Greek city-states and the reasons why the Persians failed to conquer the Aegean region. [Analyze multiple causation]

Grades 5-6

Examples of student achievement of Standard 2C include:

- Explain the struggle between good and evil as presented in the Persian religion of Zoroastrianism.

- Create a map of the eastern Mediterranean and Aegean, and indicate the location of the major Greek city-states. Using colored pencils or other delineations, show the growth of the Persian state from the time of Cyrus I through the wars with Greece. *What were the geographic advantages of the Persians and the Greeks?*

- Explain why Persia wanted to conquer Greece. *What were the Achaemenid goals?*

- Create maps of the four famous battles in the Persian Wars — Marathon, Thermopylae, Salamis, and Plataea. Use different colors for the Spartans, the Athenians, and the Persians. Include a key to indicate what each color means.

Grades 7-8

Examples of student achievement of Standard 2C include:

- Tell the story of the struggle between the Persians and Greeks from different perspectives. Use conflicts such as the battles of Marathon, Thermopylae, or Salamis. *How were Greeks and Persians likely to have differed in telling this story?*

- Devise a plan for the governing of an ethnically diverse empire such as that of the Persians. *How effectively did the Persians deal with specific problems related to the vast size of their empire?*

- Describe the organization that Darius I (the Great) created, delineating the "chain of command" and explaining the duties of this highly effective construct. *Who did the Achaemenids rule and how?*

- Compare and contrast the basic ideas and teachings of Zoroastrianism with religious beliefs of the Greeks, Hebrews, and Sumerians. *In what ways were these religions inclusive? What was their relationship to the political construct of "their" state?*

- Drawing on Jill Paton Walsh's *Persian Gold* and *Crossing to Salamis* analyze how the Persian Wars affected the daily lives of the people of ancient Greece. *Based on these accounts and others, what are we able to infer about the changes these wars wrought on the lives of the Persian "peoples"?*

Grades 9-12

Examples of student achievement of Standard 2C include:

▶ Read selections from Herodotus's *History* describing key events of the Persian Wars. Debate the accuracy of his reports. *What might indicate a bias in Herodotus's story? What questions would you ask to help decide how reliable his account is?*

▶ Analyze various accounts and histories of Persian rule such as Herodotus and the Book of Esther. *To what extent did the Persians respect the cultural traditions and religious beliefs of peoples living within their empire?*

▶ Analyze the basic tenets of Zoroastrianism, the relationship of religion to political entity, and the place of religion within the various levels of Persian society.

▶ Compare and contrast the Greek city-states' military "establishment" with that of the Persians at the time of the Persian Wars. *In what ways did the political makeup of the two antagonists dictate their military organization? What were the overall strategies of these antagonists, and in what ways is this a reflection of their political and military organizations?*

▶ In an essay respond to the statements: "It was not so much Greek military superiority as Persian weakness and demoralization that caused the Persian defeat in these wars! The end result of the Persian Wars clearly established that a small, highly efficient, and well trained and coordinated force will always defeat a much larger but inefficient force." *How were the Greek city-states able to defeat the monolithic Persian armies and navies?*

▶ Explain how the victories over Persia led to a restructuring of the Greek political balance, and ultimately, the ruinous internecine Peloponnesian Wars. *How do writers such as Thucydides explain the rise and fall of Athens and the Delian League?*

Xerxes's bridge at the Hellespont
Illustration by Carole Collier Frick

Students Should Be Able to:

2D **Demonstrate understanding of Alexander of Macedon's conquests and the interregional character of Hellenistic society and culture by:**

7-12 Analyzing the rise of Macedonia under Philip II and explaining the campaigns and scope and success of Alexander's imperial conquests. **[Reconstruct patterns of historical succession and duration]**

5-12 Assessing Alexander's achievements as a military and political leader and analyzing why the empire broke up into successor kingdoms. **[Analyze cause-and-effect relationships]**

7-12 Evaluating major achievements of Hellenistic art, philosophy, science, and political thought. **[Evidence historical perspectives]**

9-12 Assessing the character of Greek impact on Southwest Asia and Egypt in the 4th and 3rd centuries and the influence of Greek, Egyptian, Persian, and Indian cultural traditions on one another. **[Analyze cause-and-effect relationships]**

9-12 Analyzing the significance of the interaction of Greek and Jewish traditions for the emergence of both Rabbinic Judaism and early Christianity. **[Reconstruct patterns of historical succession and duration]**

Grades 5-6

Examples of student achievement of Standard 2D include:

‣ Tell the story of *The House of Pindar*, the Poet of Thebe*s. How does the story portray Alexander?*

‣ Construct a map tracing the route of Alexander's army through the Persian Empire to India. Indicate major battles that his army fought and cities he founded. *How do Alexander's conquests compare in size to that of the original Persian Empire?*

‣ Assume the role of a soldier in Alexander's army and write a letter to a friend describing the peoples and events you encounter during your conquest of the Persian Empire.

‣ List Hellenistic achievements in astronomy and measurement of the earth. *How accurate were these early scientists?*

‣ Identify illustrations of the "Seven Wonders of the Ancient World." *Which of these "seven wonders" reflect accomplishments of the Hellenistic period? What would you consider to be the "seven wonders" of the modern world?*

Grades 7-8

Examples of student achievement of Standard 2D include:

‣ Explain how Alexander of Macedon came to power and built a vast empire. *How did Alexander's empire differ from that of the earlier Assyrian, Egyptian, and Persian empires? What methods did Alexander use to unite his empire?*

‣ Compare Greek images of gods such as Apollo, with Indian images of the Buddha from Gandhara and Mathura to assess the cultural impact of Hellenism on Indian art.

‣ As one of Alexander's generals, Seleucus, Antigonus, or Ptolemy, develop a dialogue to justify ruling part of Alexander's empire.

▶ Analyze architecture to assess the extent of Greek and Macedonian influence in west Asia after the conquests of Alexander.

▶ Analyze the major achievements of Hellenistic mathematics, science, and philosophy. In an oral report or written essay, explain the significance of these achievements. *What were Indian contributions? What impact have these achievements had on the modern world?*

| Grades 9-12 | Examples of student achievement of Standard 2D include: |

▶ Draw from the teachings of Socrates, Zeno, Epicurus, and other Greek philosophers to debate the question: *What makes for a "good life"?*

▶ Research the status of women during the Hellenistic era. *What new opportunities were open to women during this period? What limitations were placed upon them?*

▶ Construct an explanation of the cultural diffusion of art and architecture through assimilation, conquest, migration, and trade. *How has Hellenistic art and architecture influenced civilizations in central Asia and the western Mediterranean?*

▶ Construct a balance sheet assessing the benefits and costs of Alexander's conquests. *Did his conquests lead to an intermingling of cultures?*

▶ Research Hellenistic religions. Assess the impace of Greek thought on Judaism and the other religions in this period.

Mosaic depicting Alexander's victory over Persian Emperor Darius III. Naples Museum

STANDARD 3

Students Should Understand: *How major religions and large-scale empires arose in the Mediterranean basin, China, and India, 500 BCE-300 CE.*

Students Should Be Able to:

3A Demonstrate understanding of the causes and consequences of the unification of the Mediterranean basin under Roman rule by:

`5-12` Assessing the contributions of the Etruscans and the western Greek colonies to the development of Roman society and culture. **[Analyze multiple causation]**

`5-12` Describing the political and social institutions of the Roman Republic and analyzing why Rome was transformed from republic to empire. **[Analyze cause-and-effect relationships]**

`9-12` Describing the major phases in the expansion of the empire through the 1st century CE. **[Reconstruct patterns of historical succession and duration]**

`9-12` Assessing ways in which imperial rule over a vast area transformed Roman society, economy, and culture. **[Analyze cause-and-effect relationships]**

`7-12` Evaluating the major legal, artistic, architectural, technological, and literary achievements of the Romans and the influence of Hellenistic cultural traditions on Roman Europe. **[Evidence historical perspectives]**

Grades 5-6

Examples of student achievement of Standard 3A include:

▶ Retell the legends of the founding and early history of Rome such as the fable of Romulus and stories from the *Aeneid*. *What do legends tell us about the beliefs and values of the ancient Romans? How do historians use myths and legends in describing ancient civilizations?*

▶ Locate the different ethnic groups and city-states of the Italian peninsula ca. 509 BCE. *Who were the Etruscans and what influence did they have in early Roman history? Where were the Greek settlements located? What influence did they have on the Latins?*

▶ Draw on evidence from David Macaulay's *City* to reconstruct a typical Roman city and explain the function of the public areas and buildings. Include diagrams of Roman residences and sketches of Roman aqueducts. Find examples of public buildings that use Roman architectural styles. Compare a Roman city to a modern U.S. city. *How are these cities different and similar?*

▶ Develop short biographies and sketches of famous Romans such as Cincinnatus, Scipio Africanus, Tiberius Gracchus, Cicero, Julius Caesar, Augustus, Nero, Marcus Aurelius, and Constantine for a class magazine entitled, "Roman Stars." *What do the lives of these famous people tell about Roman values? What changes in values can be determined from the early Republic to the last years of the empire?*

♦ Compare the military leadership of famous generals in ancient history such as Alexander of Macedon, Hannibal, and Julius Caesar.

♦ Draw on stories such as Ellis Dillon's *Rome under the Emperors* and Chelsea Yarbro's *Locadio's Apprentice* to discuss what life was like for common people living in Rome. and Pompeii.

Grades 7-8

Examples of student achievement of Standard 3A include:

♦ Develop an oral account reporting the conclusion of the Punic Wars. Include interviews with important participants, a summary of each war, and an explanation of the importance of these wars to Rome.

♦ Read selections from Plutarch's *Lives of Famous Greeks and Romans* on Tiberius and Gaius Gracchus. *What were the reforms championed by the Gracchi? How did these measures arouse hostility among the great landowners? How did the Senate deal with the Gracchi brothers?*

♦ Construct a comparative study of the status and role of women in Rome and the earlier Greek city-states. Prepare a debate between a Roman woman and one from Periclean Athens in which they discuss their positions in society.

♦ Develop a set of overlay transparencies or charts to describe the major phases of Roman expansion during this era.

♦ Use Rosemary Sutcliff's *Outcast Song for a Dark Queen* to explain the Roman occupation of Britain. *What was the nature of the conflict between the British and the Romans?*

Grades 9-12

Examples of student achievement of Standard 3A include:

♦ Compare innovations in ancient military technology such as the Macedonian phalanx, the Roman legion, the Persian cataphract, the Chinese crossbow, and the Greek trireme, and explain how they affected patterns of warfare and empire building.

♦ Compare Latin and Greek as universal languages of the Roman Empire. *What political, cultural, and commercial purposes did these two languages have?*

♦ Read selections from Polybius's treatment of the Roman Constitution. Identify those elements that he describes that influenced the American political system.

♦ Examine the reign of Augustus and analyze its significance in the transition from Roman Republic to imperial government. Compare the Roman Republic with Imperial Rome. Assess the relative merits of the two types of government. *How did one form of government turn into the other? What were the causes and consequences of the change?*

♦ Explain how Rome governed its provinces during the late Republic and the Empire and compare the Roman system with that of the Persians.

♦ Construct an explanation of the cultural diffusion of Hellenistic arts and architecture upon the Romans. *What major Roman artistic and technological achievements were influenced by Hellenistic traditions?*

Students Should Be Able to:

3B Demonstrate understanding of the emergence of Christianity in the context of the Roman Empire by:

5-12 Describing the lives of Jesus and Paul and explaining the fundamental teachings of Christianity. [**Evidence historical perspectives**]

5-12 Analyzing how Christianity spread widely in the Roman Empire. [**Analyze multiple causation**]

9-12 Tracing the extent and consequences of Christian expansion in Asia, Africa, and Europe to the 4th century. [**Reconstruct patterns of historical succession and duration**]

Grades 5-6

Examples of student achievement of Standard 3B include:

▸ Tell the story of the life of Jesus of Nazareth. *What did he teach?*

▸ Analyze several of Jesus's parables such as "the good shepherd," "the good Samaritan," or "the prodigal son." *What message do these parables illustrate?*

▸ Prepare a short biography of Paul the Apostle and explain how he helped spread Christian beliefs.

▸ Analyze accounts from the New Testament that describe early Christian principles. *What were the morals and values expressed in these teachings?*

Grades 7-8

Examples of student achievement of Standard 3B include:

▸ Analyze the moral code contained in Jesus's teachings of "love thy neighbor." *In what ways did his teachings both confirm the prohibitions of the Ten Commandments in the Hebrew Torah (e.g., you shall not kill, bear false witness, covet your neighbor's possessions) and expand upon them by calling for active commitment to the essential worth and good of others?*

▸ Construct a map locating the centers of the early Christian church in the 1st century CE and the extent of the spread of Christianity by the end of the 4th century CE.

▸ Explain the impact of Christianity on the Roman Empire. *Why did the Romans attempt to destroy Christianity? How did Christians respond to the persecutions? What was the significance of Constantine's conversion to Christianity? of Theodosius's antipagan legislation in the late 4th century?*

▸ Examine illustrations of early Christian religious art and explain the impact of these mosaics and paintings. Compare to religious art of other ancient civilizations. *What are the stories told in these art works? What values do they express?*

| **Grades 9-12** | **Examples of student achievement of Standard 3B include:** |

▸ Compare Jesus's teachings of love of neighbor with Paul's summation, "You shall love your neighbor as yourself." *How are these teachings connected, in Christianity, to belief in God's love of all humanity and in the equality of all people in the sight of God?*

▸ Analyze the similarities and differences between Judaism and Christianity in their respective beliefs concerning the Deity: Judaism's basic belief in ethical monotheism; Christianity's continuity with Judaism and its view of the ongoing story of God's relationship with humankind in the Persons of the Father Creator, the Son Redeemer, and the Holy Spirit, always present, supporting, and sustaining.

▸ Read selections from the lives of early Christian martyrs, such as the *Martyrdom of St. Polycarp*, and construct an account explaining the role of the martyr in the spread and ultimate success of Christianity in the Roman Empire.

▸ Examine the teachings Jesus expressed in the Sermon on the Mount and make a summary of his ethical message.

▸ Compile a listing of the fundamental teachings of Christianity. *Which of these teachings is distinctive to Christianity and no other faiths? In which way has the development of Christianity been affected by Hebrew, Greek, Persian, or other influences?*

▸ Map the areas in which there were recorded Christian communities by the end of the 1st century CE, and the areas that were predominantly Christian by the end of the 4th century CE. *Who were the people, and what were the events and circumstances that helped the spread of the Christian religion from its location of origin to other parts of Asia and to Africa and Europe during this period?*

Love one another with the affection of brothers. . . . Bless your persecutors. . . . Never repay injury with injury. . . . Beloved do not avenge yourselves; leave that to God's wrath, for it is written: "'Vengeance is mine; I will repay,' says the Lord." But if your enemy is hungry feed him; if he is thirsty, give him something to drink . . ." Do not be conquered by evil but conquer evil with good.

ROMANS, CHAPTER 12

Students Should Be Able to:

3C Demonstrate understanding of how China became unified under the early imperial dynasties by:

`7-12` Assessing the significance of the Zhou dynasty for the development of imperial rule and the concept of the Mandate of Heaven. **[Analyze cause-and-effect relationships]**

`5-12` Assessing the policies and achievements of the Qin emperor Shi Huangdi in establishing a unified imperial realm. **[Evaluate the implementation of a decision]**

`9-12` Analyzing the political and ideological contributions of the Han to the development of the imperial bureaucratic state and the expansion of the empire. **[Analyze cause-and effect relationships]**

`7-12` Evaluating the literary, artistic, and technological achievements of the Han dynasty. **[Evidence historical perspectives]**

`7-12` Analyzing the importance of iron technology and family division of labor on the expansion of agriculture and southeastward migration of Chinese farmers. **[Analyze multiple causation]**

`5-12` Analyzing the commercial and cultural significance of the trans-Eurasian "silk roads." **[Interrogate historical data]**

`5-12` Describing the life of Confucius and explaining comparatively the fundamental teachings of Confucianism and Daoism. **[Compare and contrast differing sets of ideas]**

| Grades 5-6 | Examples of student achievement of Standard 3C include: |

▶ Draw upon visual data to evaluate the contents of Shi Huangdi's tomb and the building of the first Great Wall as evidence of the achievements of the Qin period.

▶ Use excerpts from Chinese folktales to explain what life was like for ordinary people in ancient China.

▶ Define the Mandate of Heaven and the idea of virtuous rule.

▶ Use the following three passages expressing the "Golden Rule" and explain how Confucius, Aristotle, and Jesus sought to promote harmony in society. Confucius: *"What you do not want done to yourself, do not do to others."* Aristotle: *"We should behave to our friends as we would wish our friends to behave to us."* Jesus: *"So whatever you wish that men would do to you, do so to them."*

▶ Describe the "silk roads" connecting the Chinese and Roman empires in trade, and assess their impact on these societies and on the peoples of Central Asia through which they passed.

▶ Use excerpts from Marilee Heyer's *The Weaving of a Dream* to describe Chinese values and belief systems.

Grades 7-8

Examples of student achievement of Standard 3C include:

▶ Based on Sima Qian's *Records of the Historian*, assume the role of an adviser to a Chinese ruler in the 3rd century BCE. Suggest ways the ruler should act toward the nomadic people on the borders of his empire. *Should he trade, use military action, forbid any contact, or follow some other policy? Explain your suggestions.*

▶ Use overlays or a series of maps to trace the lands controlled by the Shang, Zhou, Qin, and Han dynasties. Research the methods used by different dynasties to govern the provinces. Compare the Han empire to that of Alexander the Great and the Roman Empire at the time of the emperor Trajan.

▶ Diagram the social hierarchy in China including the scholar-officials, farmers, artisans, merchants, soldiers, women, and slaves. Compare the stratification of Chinese society with that of other ancient societies. *What gave people status in China? How was the composition of Chinese society similar to or different from that of other ancient societies?*

▶ Explain how the Zhou used the concept of the "Mandate of Heaven" to justify the overthrow of the Shang dynasty. *How does this concept compare with ideas about the power of rulers in other ancient civilizations?*

▶ Create a graphic organizer of Chinese achievements in science, technology, the arts, and practical methods of farming and irrigation. *How did these achievements compare with those of the Greeks and Romans?*

▶ Explain the development of iron technology and the family division of labor system. *What were the outcomes of technology and collective responsibility systems?*

Grades 9-12

Examples of student achievement of Standard 3C include:

▶ Read selections from texts such as *John* in the New Testament and the *Analects* of Confucius, and describe their teachings on living a moral life.

▶ Stage a debate among a Confucianist, Daoist, and Legalist over which philosophy would end the era of warring states.

▶ Read selections of Qin laws on penal servitude and debate history's verdict on Shi Huangdi. *Was he a cruel tyrant or a great builder?*

▶ Prepare a museum display using illustrations from Chinese art up to the end of the Han dynasty. *How does the art reflect the history and philosophy of China during this period?*

▶ Research the role and status of women in the Confucian tradition. Compare the Confucian definition of women's roles with those of Ban Zhao (ca. 45-120 CE) as recorded in *Lessons for Women*.

Students Should Be Able to:

3D Demonstrate understanding of religious and cultural developments in India in the era of the Gangetic states and the Mauryan Empire by:

`7-12` Explaining the major beliefs and practices of Brahmanism in India and how they evolved into early Hinduism. [**Evidence historical perspectives**]

`5-12` Describing the life and teachings of the Buddha and explaining ways in which those teachings were a response to the Brahmanic system. [**Analyze cause-and-effect relationships**]

`9-12` Explaining the growth of the Mauryan Empire in the context of rivalries among Indian states. [**Consider multiple perspectives**]

`5-12` Evaluating the achievements of the emperor Ashoka, and assessing his contribution to the expansion of Buddhism in India. [**Evaluate the implementation of a decision**]

`9-12` Analyzing how Brahmanism responded to the social, political, and theological challenges posed by Buddhism and other reform movements. [**Analyze cause-and-effect relationships**]

`7-12` Analyzing how Buddhism spread in India, Ceylon, and Central Asia. [**Analyze multiple causation**]

Grades 5-6 — Examples of student achievement of Standard 3D include:

▶ Analyze excerpts from the *Jataka* tales. *What do the* Jataka *tales reveal about Buddhist teachings?*

▶ Tell the story of the life of Siddhartha Gautama. *Why is he called the Buddha? What are the "four truths" of Buddhism? What values did Buddha teach?*

▶ Assume the role of Ashoka and establish a code of laws to govern your empire. *How would Ashoka advise people to treat one another? What laws might Ashoka recommend? How do you think Buddhism influenced Ashoka's ideas?*

▶ Examine selections from Brian Thompson's *The Story of Prince Rama* and describe how Indian epic stories reflect social values.

Grades 7-8 — Examples of student achievement of Standard 3D include:

▶ Examine the teachings of the Brahmanic religion using excerpts from the *Laws of Manu* to determine the ideal social relationships Manu reveals, especially the emphasis on doing one's dharma (appropriate action). What was the Brahmanic justification for these arrangements? *What did Buddha offer as alternatives to this structure?*

▶ Analyze several animal stories from the Panchatantra. *What advice do they offer people with little power? How could the insights be applied to power struggles between small states? Which of these strategies did Chandragupta Maurya use? How does the advice compare with morals in Aesop's fables?*

⬧ Describe the basic features of social relationships during this period, showing how emphasis was placed on group membership, not the individual. *How did this affect such institutions as marriage and one's choice of occupation? How did the belief in dharma, one's fundamental duty in life, determine social behavior?*

⬧ Read selections from the rock edicts of Ashoka, and analyze what evidence they yield concerning Indian society, religion, and history in the Maurya period. Construct a chart listing the achievements of Ashoka and evaluate his accomplishments. *How do these accomplishments compare to those of other ancient leaders such as Alexander of Macedon and the Han emperors of China?*

⬧ Trace the expansion of Buddhism and Christianity on an outline map of Eurasia and Africa. *What are the similarities and differences between these religions?*

⬧ Read the story of Shvetaketu from the *Chandogya Upanishad* and compare these teachings with the Buddhist idea of *nirvana*. *What does Shvetaketu's father teach his son about Brahman and moksha?*

Grades 9-12

Examples of student achievement of Standard 3D include:

⬧ Draw evidence from literature to compare the roles for women in India, China, and Greece. Use literary works such as the *Ramayana*, the Chinese *Book of Songs*, and the plays of Sophocles. *Do these works accurately reflect the status of women in ancient India, China, and Greece? What other evidence might be available from which women's roles during this period and in these cultures could be inferred?*

⬧ Debate the statement: *"Women were better off as Buddhists than they were in Brahmanic society."*

⬧ Explain how Buddhist teachings challenged the Brahmanic social system, especially caste, dietary practices, language usage, and the role of women. *How did Buddha's reforms contribute to the spread of Buddhism in India and beyond?*

⬧ Examine images of the Buddha from Gandharan and Mathura schools of art in India. *What evidence is there of Persian or Greek influences on these images?*

⬧ Interpret selections from Kautilya's *Arthashastra* as a source of knowledge of Indian political thought and culture in the Maurya period. *What must a ruler do in order to be successful in foreign relations and domestic policy?*

⬧ Research how Ashoka's support for Buddhism affected the spread of that religion in India. Compare with the effects of the Roman emperors' tolerance for and support of Christianity on the spread of that faith in the later empire. *Would religious beliefs have spread as rapidly without the backing of a strong empire?*

⬧ Examine the religious ideas associated with the *Upanishads*. *How did these later books of the* Vedas *reflect Brahmanic teachings? How do Brahmanic teachings compare with Buddhist teachings?*

STANDARD 4

Students Should Understand: *How early agrarian civilizations arose in Mesoamerica.*

Students Should Be Able to:

4 **Demonstrate understanding of the achievements of Olmec civilization by:**

5-12 Analyzing the relationship between maize cultivation and the development of complex societies in Mesoamerica. [**Analyze cause-and-effect relationships**]

7-12 Interpreting archaeological evidence for the development of Olmec civilization in the second millennium BCE. [**Formulate historical questions**]

5-12 Evaluating major Olmec contributions to Mesoamerican civilization, including the calendar, glyphic writing, sculpture, and monumental building. [**Evidence historical perspectives**]

9-12 Assessing Olmec cultural influence on the emergence of civilization in the Oaxaca valley or other regions. [**Analyze multiple causation**]

Grades 5-6

Examples of student achievement of Standard 4 include:

▶ Construct a topographical map of Mesoamerica. *How did various features of geography influence Olmec civilization?*

▶ Create a Venn diagram comparing the religion, social class structure, and monumental architecture of the Olmec and Egyptian civilizations. *As a historian, what questions would you ask to help explain reasons for the similarities and differences?*

▶ Research the land of the Olmec, including the nature of the soil, and plant and animal life. Become "A Farmer for a Day," and describe in words and/or pictures your experiences. *What plants do you cultivate, and how? What animals are part of your daily life? What problems do you have, and what solutions to them do you try? How is it that information about the daily life of an Olmec farmer is known to American students today?*

▶ Compare the way people in the Olmec ritual centers relied on flooding rivers with how people in the Nile civilization relied on the inundations of the Nile. *How did the flooding rivers contribute to centralized power in both areas?*

Grades 7-8

Examples of student achievement of Standard 4 include:

▶ Construct a ground plan or a model of an Olmec city, such as La Venta or San Lorenzo. Explain what the ground plan of the buildings and ball courts might reveal about the Olmec people. *What questions do you have about the Olmec that could not be answered based on the evidence of ground plans alone?*

▶ Explain the importance of maize to the Olmec civilization. *What methods of farming were used? How did farming in Mesoamerica differ from that of other agrarian societies in the ancient world?*

▶ Suppose that archaeologists found a stone sculpture in a new site all by itself. *The presence of what features would lead them to label the sculpture as "Olmec"?*

▶ Make posters of Olmec farming methods. Evaluate their demographical and environmental impact. *What connections can you make between Olmec agriculture and the development of Olmec society? In what ways are agricultural strategies such as the chinampas (floating gardens) sound ecologically? Are they still used? Why or why not?*

▶ Examine pictures of the Olmec monumental stone heads. *What can you infer about the type of political and economic control needed to produce this monumental sculpture? Why did people ritually mutilate these heads?*

Grades 9-12

Examples of student achievement of Standard 4 include:

▶ Having examined archaeological and historical records, explain the political, economic, and social structure of Olmec society. *How can we give an accurate record of the development of the Olmec civilization without having deciphered their written records?*

▶ Research the archaeological or pictorial evidence available to support the hypothesis that the Olmecs had cultural influences on the development of Zapotec and Mayan civilizations. *What role can trade play in the diffusion of culture?*

▶ Plan a museum exhibit of Olmec archaeological finds. Write labels for the various objects you include in the exhibit and explain how they reflect how people lived and worked in Olmec communities. *What can be inferred about Olmec beliefs from the objects in your exhibition? How would you change the exhibition if your aim was to show "the development of Olmec civilization"?*

▶ Debate the validity of the statement that the Olmec were the "mother civilization" of Mesoamerica.

Olmec sculpture

ERA 4

Expanding Zones of Exchange and Encounter 300-1000 CE

Giving Shape to World History

Beginning about 300 CE almost the entire region of Eurasia and northern Africa experienced severe disturbances. By the seventh century, however, peoples of Eurasia and Africa entered a new period of more intensive interchange and cultural creativity. Underlying these developments was the growing sophistication of systems for moving people and goods here and there throughout the hemisphere — China's canals, trans-Saharan camel caravans, high-masted ships plying the Indian Ocean. These networks tied diverse peoples together across great distances. In Eurasia and Africa a single region of intercommunication was taking shape that ran from the Mediterranean to the China seas. A widening zone of interchange also characterized Mesoamerica.

Beyond these developments, a sweeping view of world history reveals three other broad patterns of change that are particularly conspicuous in this era.

▶ **Islamic Civilization:** One of the most dramatic developments of this 700-year period was the rise of Islam as both a new world religion and a civilized tradition encompassing an immense part of the Eastern Hemisphere. Commanding the central region of Afro-Eurasia, the Islamic empire of the Abbasid dynasty became in the 8th-10th-century period the principal intermediary for the exchange of goods, ideas, and technologies across the hemisphere.

▶ **Buddhist, Christian, and Hindu Traditions:** Not only Islam but other major religions also spread widely during this 700-year era. Wherever these faiths were introduced, they carried with them a variety of cultural traditions, aesthetic ideas, and ways of organizing human endeavor. Each of them also embraced peoples of all classes and diverse languages in common worship and moral commitment. Buddhism declined in India but took root in East and Southeast Asia. Christianity became the cultural foundation of a new civilization in western Europe. Hinduism flowered in India under the Gupta Empire and also exerted growing influence in the princely courts of Southeast Asia.

▶ **New Patterns of Society in East Asia, Europe, West Africa, and Mesoamerica:** The third conspicuous pattern, continuing from the previous era, was the process of population growth, urbanization, and flowering of culture in new areas. The fourth to sixth centuries witnessed serious upheavals in Eurasia in connection with the breakup of the Roman and Han empires and the aggressive movements of pastoral peoples to the east, west, and south. By the seventh century, however, China was finding new unity and rising economic prosperity under the Tang. Japan emerged as a distinctive civilization. At the other end of the hemisphere Europe laid new foundations for political and social order. In West Africa towns flourished amid the rise of the Ghana empire and the rise of the trans-Saharan gold trade. Finally, this era saw a remarkable growth of urban life in Mesoamerica in the age of the Maya.

Why Study This Era?

▶ In these seven centuries Buddhism, Christianity, Hinduism, and Islam spread far and wide beyond their lands of origin. These religions became established in regions where today they command the faith of millions.

▶ In this era the configuration of empires and kingdoms in the world changed dramatically. Why giant empires have fallen and others risen rapidly to take their place is an enduring question for all eras.

▶ In the early centuries of this era Christian Europe was marginal to the dense centers of population, production, and urban life of Eurasia and northern Africa. Students should understand this perspective but at the same time investigate the developments that made possible the rise of a new civilization in Europe after 1000 CE.

▶ In this era no sustained contact existed between the Eastern Hemisphere and the Americas. Peoples of the Americas did not share in the exchange and borrowing that stimulated innovations of all kinds in Eurasia and Africa. Therefore, students need to explore the conditions under which weighty urban civilizations arose in Mesoamerica in the first millennium CE.

What Students Should Understand

Standard 1: Imperial crises and their aftermath, 300-700 CE

    A. The **decline** of the **Roman and Han empires** [CORE]

    B. The expansion of **Christianity and Buddhism** beyond the lands of their origin [CORE]

    C. The synthesis of **Hindu civilization** in India in the era of the Gupta Empire [CORE]

    D. **Hindu and Buddhist expansion** in Southeast Asia in the first millennium CE [RELATED]

Standard 2: Causes and consequences of the rise of Islamic civilization in the 7th-10th centuries

    A. The **emergence of Islam** and how Islam spread in Southwest Asia, North Africa, and Europe [CORE]

    B. The significance of **the Abbasid Caliphate** as a center of cultural innovation and hub of interregional trade in the 8th-10th centuries [CORE]

    C. The **consolidation of the Byzantium** in the context of expanding Islamic civilization [RELATED]

Standard 3: Major developments in East Asia in the era of the Tang dynasty, 600-900 CE

    A. Political and cultural expansion in **Tang China** [CORE]

    B. Chinese influence on the peoples of **Inner Asia, Korea, Vietnam, and Japan** [RELATED]

Standard 4: The search for political, social, and cultural redefinition in Europe, 500-1000 CE

    A. The foundations of a new civilization in **Western Christendom** in the 500 years following the breakup of the western Roman empire [CORE]

    B. The **coalescence** of political and social order **in Europe** [RELATED]

Standard 5: State-building in Northeast and West Africa and the southward migrations of Bantu-speaking peoples [CORE]

Standard 6: The rise of centers of civilization in Mesoamerica and Andean South America in the first millennium CE

    A. The origins, expansion, and achievements of **Maya civilization** [CORE]

    B. The rise of the **Teotihuacán, Zapotec**/Mixtec, **and Moche** civilizations [RELATED]

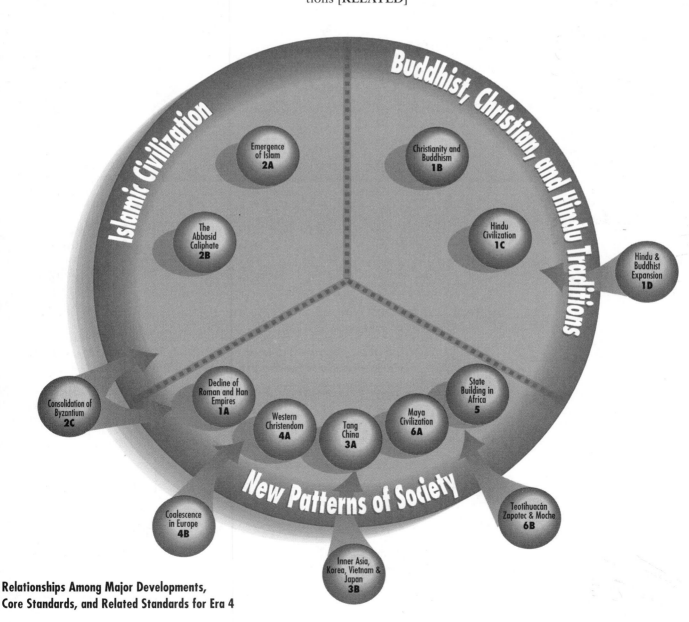

Relationships Among Major Developments, Core Standards, and Related Standards for Era 4

STANDARD 1

Students Should Understand: *Imperial crises and their aftermath, 300-700 CE*

Students Should Be Able to:

1A Demonstrate understanding of the decline of the Roman and Han empires by:

5-12 Analyzing various causes that historians have proposed to account for the decline of the Han and Roman empires. **[Evaluate major debates among historians]**

5-12 Tracing the migrations and military movements of major pastoral nomadic groups into both the Roman Empire and China. **[Reconstruct patterns of historical succession and duration]**

7-12 Comparing the consequences of these movements in China and the western part of the Roman Empire. **[Analyze cause-and-effect relationships]**

9-12 Analyzing comparatively the collapse of the western part of the Roman Empire and the survival of the eastern part. **[Compare and contrast differing sets of ideas]**

9-12 Describing the consolidation of the Byzantine state after the breakup of the Roman Empire, and assessing how Byzantium transmitted ancient traditions and created a new Christian civilization. **[Reconstruct patterns of historical succession and duration]**

| **Grades 5-6** | **Examples of student achievement of Standard 1A include:** |

▶ Construct a time line showing major historical milestones in the period from the late Roman Empire through the rule of Justinian. *What inferences can be made from the information in your time line about possible causes of the decline of the Roman Empire? What other possible causes can you think of that would be hard to show on a time line?*

▶ Compare evidences of typical architectural styles in Rome and Byzantium. *How did the architecture differ? What might these differences tell you about the unity of the two parts of the Roman Empire? What problems might growing East-West differentiation have created for the Roman Empire?*

▶ Construct a map showing the migratory movements of the Xiongnu, Germanic tribes, Huns, and Slavs. *What ecological, economic, or political factors motivated these groups to move in the directions they did?*

▶ In a chart, list the causes for the decline of the Han and Roman empires. From your chart determine similar and differing problems. *Do all empires suffer from the same problems and failures that will lead to decline and fall?*

| Grades 7-8 | **Examples of student achievement of Standard 1A include:** |

◗ Write an account of the nomadic invasions of the Roman Empire in the 5th century CE, including information derived from primary sources such as Orosius, Tacitus, Ammianus Marcellinus, and Priscus, and from secondary sources. *Why did the Romans call these invaders "barbarians"?*

◗ Create a time line labeling major battles, events, and political changes that occurred from the 3rd through 7th centuries in China and Europe. Clearly delineate the division of the Roman Empire, the incursions of invaders into the Han and Roman worlds, and the fall of each.

◗ Draw on historical evidence to write a "state of the empire" speech as it might have been given by one of the late Han or Roman emperors, outlining the strengths and weaknesses of each empire in his time.

◗ Write an essay comparing the strengths and weaknesses of the Roman, Byzantine, and Han empires. Infer from your comparison why each declined and fell and why one lasted longer than the others.

| Grades 9-12 | **Examples of student achievement of Standard 1A include:** |

◗ Identify key trends or events in the weakening and decline of the Han and Roman empires, such as internal corruption and graft, overextension of political capacity to rule, communication, generals setting themselves up as rulers, or the settlement of previously hostile nomads within the borders, and explain the significance of what was identified in the process of imperial decline. *How were political, military, social, and economic causes of imperial decline linked to one another?*

◗ Draw evidence from the writings of the Roman historian Tacitus regarding the Germanic peoples and analyze the way in which he represents Germanic family life. *According to Tacitus, what is the role and status of women? How does the status of Germanic women compare to that of Roman women?*

◗ Construct a chart with Europe, China, and India as headings and list the characteristics under each of these regions that changed after the arrival of the invading and conquering nomadic peoples. Based on the chart, write an essay assessing the relative impact of the barbarian movements on the regions of Europe, China, and India by the close of the 7th century.

◗ Construct a "balance sheet" or chart delineating the differences between the Roman and Byzantine empires in the 4th century CE. Show the strengths and weaknesses of each and from this hypothesize as to why one empire fell and the other continued. *What caused Rome to fall and the Byzantine Empire to continue?*

◗ Investigate the eastern portion of the Roman Empire at the beginning of the 4th century CE and write a position paper for Constantine showing what aspects of Roman rule and society should be continued and what exorcised in favor of truly Eastern institutions. *How will the emperor use such knowledge to fuse the Eastern empire into a "new," independent state that will avoid the failures of the West? How would the Eastern emperors seek to "marry" western and eastern institutions and ideas into a cohesive state?*

Students Should Be Able to:

1B Demonstrate understanding of the expansion of Christianity and Buddhism beyond the lands of their origin by:

5-12 Assessing how Christianity and Buddhism won converts among culturally diverse peoples across wide areas of Afro-Eurasia. [**Demonstrate and explain the influence of ideas**]

7-12 Analyzing causal connections between the breakup of the unified Roman and Han empires and the spread of Christianity and Buddhism. [**Analyze cause-and-effect relationships**]

7-12 Analyzing comparatively the changing image and status of women in early Christian and Buddhist societies. [**Compare and contrast differing values, behaviors, and institutions**]

| Grades 5-6 | **Examples of student achievement of Standard 1B include:** |

▶ Compile a chart showing the basic beliefs of Buddhists and Christians. *Which aspects of each religion might appeal to people of the 3rd-5th centuries CE and why?*

▶ Define the goals of Buddhists and Christians of the first 1,000 years with regard to their intent to spread their faith to new peoples and lands. *What was the importance of the messianic nature of these new faiths?*

▶ Develop a map of Europe, the Mediterranean world, Southwest Asia, India, Southeast Asia, and China. Delineate the extent of the spread of Buddhism, Christianity, Hinduism, and Confucianism. Indicate with alternating colors areas where they overlap.

▶ Investigate the ways in which Buddhism and Christianity spread their "faith" to new areas and new peoples. *What role did monks play in doing so?*

| Grades 7-8 | **Examples of student achievement of Standard 1B include:** |

▶ Locate on a map and illustrate the emerging centers of Christian and Buddhist teachings, and trace the routes used by believers to spread their faith.

▶ Compare and contrast the roles that Ashoka and Constantine played in spreading Buddhism in India and Christianity throughout Europe. *How did these emperors legitimize their religions and spread the teachings of their respective faiths?*

▶ *"Times of trouble lead to an increased interest in religion."* Investigate this statement with regard to the demise of the Han and Roman empires and the commensurate growth of Buddhism and Christianity. *How important was the concept of universal salvation in preaching these two religions in their early history? Did the growth of these religions hasten the fall of the Han and Roman empires or did the decline and fall of these empires stimulate the spread of Buddhism and Christianity?*

▶ Describe the methods and routes used to introduce Christianity to Ethiopia and Ireland. *How was this "new" religion received in these parts of the world?*

♦ Research the role of women in Buddhist and Christian teachings. *How did the status of women differ in Buddhist and Christian teachings?*

Examples of student achievement of Standard 1B include:

♦ Read and analyze selections from the letters of the Apostle Paul on the subject of the moral Christian life, centered in selfless love of one another (e.g., Colossians 3:12-17; Galations 5:13-14; Corinthians 13:1-13). Analyze how these views unified Christian faith and moral life and influenced the spread of Christianity.

♦ Compare and contrast the spread of religious Daoism and Buddhism in China.

♦ Investigate the relationship between the growth of international trade and the spread of Christianity and Buddhism in the 3rd-6th centuries CE. *Did the commercial enterprise follow or precede the extension of these new religions? What was the relationship between teachers and traders?*

♦ Read Buddha's sermon at Benares (Varanasi) and Jesus's *Sermon on the Mount*. Compare and contrast the messages delivered by these teachers to disciples, potential converts, and all peoples.

♦ Discuss the relationship between "patronage" and the advancement of religion in the context of the spread of Buddhism and Christianity during this era. *What was the role of kings and princes in the recognition and promotion of religion? How and why did the concept of "peace" appeal to the rising middle class and their interest in commercial extension?*

♦ *If you were a woman in late imperial Rome, in what ways would you be better off as a Christian than a pagan? In what ways would you be worse off? Would your social class and marital status make any difference in whether you were better or worse off as a Christian?*

A cross, the symbol of Christianity and a wheel with spokes representing the Noble Eight fold Path, the symbol of Buddhism

Students Should Be Able to:

1C **Demonstrate understanding of the synthesis of Hindu civilization in India in the era of the Gupta Empire by:**

`5-12` Describing fundamental features of the Hindu belief system as they emerged in the early first millennium CE. **[Evidence historical perspectives]**

`7-12` Explaining the rise of the Gupta Empire, and analyzing factors that contributed to the empire's stability and economic prosperity. **[Analyze multiple causation]**

`7-12` Analyzing how Hinduism responded to the challenges of Buddhism and prevailed as the dominant faith in India. **[Reconstruct patterns of historical succession and duration]**

`7-12` Analyzing the basis of social relationships in India and the social and legal position of women during the Gupta era. **[Interrogate historical data]**

`5-12` Evaluating Gupta achievements in art, literature, and mathematics. **[Evidence historical perspective]**

`9-12` Analyzing the Gupta decline and the importance of Hun invasions in the empire's disintegration. **[Analyze multiple causation]**

Grades 5-6	Examples of student achievement of Standard 1C include:

‣ Construct a diorama based on an episode from the *Ramayana. How does the story present dharma as the primary social value? What is the dharma of the ideal king, husband and wife, brother, and friend?*

‣ Study pictures of the cave structures at Ajanta and Ellora. *To whom are these sanctuaries dedicated? What does the art and architecture suggest about the relationship among various religions in India during Gupta times?*

‣ Construct a chart with definitions of the fundamental beliefs of Hinduism including Brahma, dharma, the caste system, ritual and sacrifice, reincarnation, and karma.

‣ Compare a long-division problem using Roman numerals with Indian/Arabic numerals. Imagine a world without zero and explain the difficulties this would cause.

Grades 7-8	Examples of student achievement of Standard 1C include:

‣ Construct a physical map of India and label the Gupta Empire. Draw the path from China to India that the Chinese pilgrims Fa Xian and Xuan Zang might have followed. *What gifts might these pilgrims have taken back to China?*

‣ Read selections from *Shakuntala* by Kalidasa and discuss the ways in which this play represents gender relationships in Gupta India. *How reliable a source is drama for the actual beliefs and behaviors of people? What restrictions were placed on women in Gupta India? How did women fit into the caste system?*

- Assume the roles of different castes and role-play an episode in the daily life in an Indian village. *Did affiliation with an unprivileged caste provide any advantages? What were some disadvantages? What were the criteria for ranking castes?*

- Explain in an essay the causes for the Gupta rise in India, the collapse of the Mauryan-Buddhist power, and the reinstatement of the Brahmans under the Guptas. *Was it a political move on the part of the Guptas to ally themselves with the Brahmans?*

- Read the account of Gupta India by the Chinese monk Fa Xian. *What impressed him about life in India? How did Gupta kings promote Hinduism while fostering Buddhist culture at the same time? How did they integrate marginal groups into the political system?*

- Determine the major achievements of scholars in technology, mathematics, astronomy, and medicine during the Gupta period.

Grades 9-12

Examples of student achievement of Standard 1C include:

- Compare the Gupta golden age during the reign of Chandragupta II to that of Athens during the Age of Pericles.

- Trace the route of the Hun invasion of India and explain its consequences to Indian society. *What was the impact of the invasion on India? How similar were its consequences in India to "barbarian" invasions of Europe at the end of the Roman Empire? To what extent did Harsha revive the golden age of the Guptas?*

- Since the Guptas did not write history, assess how contemporary historians use art, literature, archaeology, temple inscriptions, and foreign travelers' accounts as a basis for knowledge of Gupta India.

- Explain how Buddhist monks influenced education, literature, and higher learning in India during the Gupta era. *What were the famed centers of learning in India in the 4th and 5th centuries, and what did they teach? What comparable educational centers existed in the world at this time?*

- Explain how the development of South Indian temple architecture such as the temple at Madurai reveals the resurgence of Hinduism in India and the spread of Hinduism to South India. *What were the various functions carried out in the temple complex? How did temple towns stimulate urban and economic growth?*

Students Should Be Able to:

1D Demonstrate understanding of the expansion of Hindu and Buddhist traditions in Southeast Asia in the first millennium CE by:

5-12 Assessing the relationship between long-distance trade of Indian and Malay peoples and the introduction of Hindu and Buddhist traditions in Southeast Asia. [**Analyze cause-and-effect relationships**]

7-12 Evaluating monumental religious architecture as evidence for the spread of Buddhist and Hindu belief and practice in Southeast Asia. [**Draw upon visual sources**]

9-12 Explaining how aspects of Buddhism and Hinduism were combined in Southeast Asian religious life. [**Interrogate historical data**]

5-12 Explaining how Malayo-Polynesian peoples of East and Southeast Asian origin settled the Pacific islands and New Zealand. [**Evidence historical perspectives**]

Grades 5-6

Examples of student achievement of Standard 1D include:

▶ Draw a map of Southeast Asia and, using different colors, indicate those countries that were influenced by Buddhism and those influenced by Hinduism. *Which countries were influenced by both beliefs? Draw an overlay map of long-distance trade routes. How significant a connection does there seem to be between the spread of religions and trade? What questions would you ask to help establish a connection more reliably?*

▶ Look at pictorial evidence depicting gods and goddesses of India, Malaysia, and Southeast Asia and note similarities. *In what ways may these depictions indicate a relationship with Buddhism and Hinduism?*

▶ Research the monsoons and the ocean currents, and construct a model of a seaworthy boat of this era. Map a trip from Mahabalipuram in India to a destination in Southeast Asia. *How would a knowledge of the monsoons and ocean currents affect ship construction? How did the ocean currents promote cultural diffusion?*

▶ Prepare shadow puppets like those from Southeast Asia and put on a shadow puppet play. *What are the subjects of these puppet plays? What do they reveal about contact between India and Southeast Asia? What other evidence is there of contact between these two areas?*

Grades 7-8

Examples of student achievement of Standard 1D include:

▶ Research sources on the history of Southeast Asia and the Pacific islands of Polynesia and New Zealand. From your reading discern aspects of the cultures of these peoples that indicate that there is a "link" between these areas. Did the islanders have ancestors who came from Southeast Asia? How did they get to these islands?

▶ Research and prepare a map with icons showing plants and animals introduced by Polynesian settlers. *Where did these plants and animals come from? How did these "introductions" affect the existing island flora and fauna or culture?*

♦ Study the history of Southeast Asia and the Malayo-Polynesians and note the presence or absence of Hinduism and Buddhism in these areas by the end of the first millennium. *Did Hindu and Buddhist clerics precede or follow trade between India and these areas?*

♦ On a map of the Southeast Asian and Polynesian areas trace lines of known or potential trade routes. Discuss the geographic problems that a trader would encounter traveling to the Pacific islands.

Grades 9-12

Examples of student achievement of Standard 1D include:

♦ From evidence of art and architecture, such as temple sculpture and adornment and tower-temple structures, explain the spread of Hindu and Buddhist thought in Southeast Asia. Make a drawing of one of the Indian temples such as Borobudur in Java and note in written form the similarities between Indian and Southeast Asian temple architecture. *What do the temple sites tell about the spread of Indian influence? What were the functions of the temples?*

♦ Find a devotional poem or prayer directed to a particular deity, such as Vishnu, Shiva, Krishna, or Devi, and analyze this attitude (bhakti) toward divinity. *Does this same form appear in the adaptations of the Buddhist-Hindu culture of Southeast Asia?*

♦ Examine Hindu-Buddhist architecture, such as stupas, cave structures at Ajanta and Ellora, and temples at Angkor Wat and Borobudur. From your examination hypothesize the influence of Indian religions on Southeast Asia.

♦ Compare and contrast the different types of boats and related navigational skills developed in several regions of the world at this time and decide what advantages each design offered the sailors. *How did sailors/shipbuilders adapt their vessels to the particular areas to be sailed and the needs of trade?*

♦ Write an essay examining the evidences of Hinduism and Buddhism in Southeast Asia. From your examination determine the influence of Indian culture on this area, the acceptance of these religions by the "rulers" and peoples of the area, and the ways in which Southeast Asians adopted and adapted these religions. *Did the peoples of Southeast Asia initiate this contact with India or was it Indian entrepreneurial commerce that opened this area to the Buddhist-Hindu influence?*

♦ Research the history of the Pandyas and Pallavas in South India. Map their trade relationships with West Asia, Greece, Rome, and Southeast Asia. How did the Pallavas help spread Hindu and Buddhist ideas to Southeast Asia?

♦ Research the Indian concept of ideal kingship and trace how this concept was introduced and spread throughout the emerging states of Southeast Asia.

STANDARD 2

Students Should Understand: *Causes and consequences of the development of Islamic civilization between the 7th and 10th centuries.*

Students Should Be Able to:

2A Demonstrate understanding of the emergence of Islam and how Islam spread in Southwest Asia, North Africa, and Europe by:

`9-12` Analyzing the political, social, and religious problems confronting the Byzantine and Sassanid Persian empires in the 7th century and the commercial role of Arabia in the Southwest Asian economy. **[Analyze multiple causation]**

`5-12` Describing the life of Muhammad, the development of the early Muslim community, and the basic teachings and practices of Islam. **[Assess the importance of the individual]**

`7-12` Explaining how Muslim forces overthrew the Byzantines in Syria and Egypt and the Sassanids in Persia and Iraq. **[Interrogate historical data]**

`5-12` Analyzing how Islam spread in Southwest Asia and the Mediterranean region. **[Analyze the influence of ideas]**

`9-12` Analyzing how the Arab Caliphate became transformed into a Southwest Asian and Mediterranean empire under the Umayyad dynasty, and explaining how the Muslim community became divided into Sunni and Shi'ite Muslim groups. **[Reconstruct patterns of historical succession and duration]**

`7-12` Analyzing Arab Muslim success in founding an empire stretching from western Europe to India and China, and describing the diverse religious, cultural, and geographic factors that influenced the ability of the Muslim government to rule. **[Analyze cause-and-effect relationships]**

| Grades 5-6 | Examples of student achievement of Standard 2A include: |

▶ Explain the effects of geography on the lifestyle of nomads and town-dwellers of the Arabian peninsula. Describe the conditions that led to the growth of trade. *Why were the oases important to trade? What goods were traded, and where did they originate?*

▶ Describe the life of Muhammad and his devotion to God. *What basic beliefs and values did Muhammad proclaim?*

▶ Identify and explain the importance of the Qur'an, the Hegira (Hijrah), the Ka'abah, the Sunnah, the Hajj, the daily prayer (Salat), the poor due (Zakat), and Ramadan to Islam.

▶ Draw evidence from art and architecture to illustrate Muslim influence on the Iberian peninsula. *How did Muslims come to exert an influence in this area?*

Grades 7-8

Examples of student achievement of Standard 2A include:

▶ Read accounts of the story of Abraham, Moses, and Jesus in the Old and New Testaments and in the chapter of the Qur'an entitled "The Cow" (2:40-96; 2:124-136); and "Maryam" (19:1-58), and make a chart showing the differences between each version.

▶ Read selections from the short chapters at the end of the Qur'an and describe the morals and values they express. Compare Islamic morals and values to those of other faiths. *What made Islam attractive to new converts and what actions by Muslims aided the process of increasing the number of adherents?*

▶ Describe the campaigns that brought areas from Spain to India under Muslim rule. *Who were the important individuals and groups who participated? What obstacles did they overcome?*

Grades 9-12

Examples of student achievement of Standard 2A include:

▶ Compare the Byzantine and Sassanid empires. *How different were their political institutions? To what extent did their economies depend on trade? How did their social structures differ? What factors weakened these empires in the 7th century?*

▶ Read excerpts from the Qur'an that deal with women. *What can you infer from these excerpts about the position of women in Islamic communities? How did the statements of the Qur'an and the actions and sayings of the Prophet change women's position from what it had been in these communities before Islam?*

▶ Describe a typical mosque (masjid) and explain how its layout reflects the relationship between people, their spiritual leaders, and God in Islam. Compare this to an early Christian church and Jewish synagogue.

▶ Write an historically valid account of the battle of Tours in 733, and explain its significance from the perspectives of a Frankish Christian chronicler and an Arab Muslim scholar of Iberia, both writing in the 9th century. *How do the accounts agree and differ? What conclusions may be drawn from the differing accounts? What are the changing views of this event in modern historiography?*

▶ Discuss the process by which Arabic became a widely spoken language and the main medium of written communication in the early Islamic centuries. *What was the importance of Arabic in the Islamic religion? In what regions of Africa and Eurasia was Arabic an important language in the 8th century as compared with the 6th century? Why did Muslim converts in such regions as Egypt and North Africa learn to speak and write Arabic? Why did many Christians and Jews in Southwest Asia learn Arabic?*

▶ Prepare a chart showing steps taken by early Muslim leaders and scholars to record and transmit the Qur'an and Hadith. Show what branches of scholarship developed from study and compilation of these documents, and compare the importance of oral and written transmission.

Students Should Be Able to:

2B **Demonstrate understanding of the significance of the Abbasid Caliphate as a center of cultural innovation and hub of interregional trade in the 8th-10th centuries by:**

9-12 Comparing Abbasid government and military institutions with those of Sassanid Persia and Byzantium. **[Compare and contrast differing values and institutions]**

7-12 Analyzing why the Abbasid state became a center of Afro-Eurasian commercial and cultural exchange. **[Analyze cause-and-effect relationships]**

5-12 Analyzing the sources and development of Islamic law and the influence of Islamic law and Muslim practice on such areas as family life, moral behavior, marriage, women's status, inheritance, justice, and slavery. **[Examine the influence of ideas]**

7-12 Describing the emergence of a center of Islamic civilization in Iberia and evaluating its economic and cultural achievements. **[Evidence historical perspectives]**

9-12 Describing the cultural and social contributions of various ethnic and religious communities, particularly the Christian and Jewish, in the Abbasid lands and Iberia. **[Evidence historical perspectives]**

7-12 Evaluating Abbasid contributions to such fields as mathematics, science, medicine, and literature, and the preservation of Greek learning. **[Interrogate historical data]**

5-12 Assessing how Islam won converts among culturally diverse peoples across wide areas of Afro-Eurasia. **[Analyze cause-and-effect relationships]**

| Grades 5-6 | **Examples of student achievement of Standard 2B include:** |

▶ Chart the trade routes that converged on Baghdad. *Why was Baghdad a center of trade and commerce? What items were traded? How did trade promote cultural exchanges?*

▶ Trace the route whereby knowledge of the way to manufacture paper reached Europe through Muslim lands. *Why was paper such an important invention, and what role did it play in Chinese, Muslim, and later European culture?*

▶ Role-play a conversation between a Muslim and a non-Muslim in the Abbasid era, with the former pointing out the benefits of conversion to the latter.

| Grades 7-8 | **Examples of student achievement of Standard 2B include:** |

▶ Compose a letter from a scholar in Muslim Spain to a colleague in Baghdad, describing economic and cultural conditions in his city. *How did the use of Arabic language promote cultural exchange among Muslims in various regions?*

▶ Read excerpts such as *Sura IV* from the Qur'an to discover what kind of family life and gender relations were prescribed in Islamic society. *How do these compare to prescriptions concerning these topics in the Old and New Testaments?*

▶ Examine how the Abbasids promoted learning and advanced science, mathematics, and medicine. Research individuals such as Ibn Sina (Avicenna), Abu Hanifa, Hunayn, or al Biruni, and explain how they advanced scientific knowledge.

Grades 9-12

Examples of student achievement of Standard 2B include:

▶ Research the lives of prominent women such as scholars, philanthropists, poets, and artists during the Abbasid period. *What factors in Muslim society enabled them to reach prominence?* (Resources: N. Abbot, *Two Queens of Baghdad*, Univ. of Chicago Press, 1946; E. W. Fernea and B. Q. Bezirgan, *Middle Eastern Muslim Women Speak*, Univ. of Texas Press, 1977)

▶ Explain the social roles and relative status of government bureaucrats, landowning notables, scholars, peasants, urban artisans, and slaves within the Abbasid empire. *What influence did religion have on social roles and social standing? What advantages did conversion to Islam confer?*

▶ Research the treatment of non-Muslims in the Abbasid empire. *What was the legal status of Christians and Jews living in the empire? In what ways did they contribute to the achievements of Abbasid society?*

▶ Role-play the part of an adviser to an Abbasid ruler, and review Sassanid Persian and Byzantine government and military institutions in comparison with Abbasid ones. *What are the strengths and weaknesses of each?*

▶ Make a list of the effects that the Muslim practice of veiling and seclusion of women on the one hand, and the Muslim law giving women control over their own property, income, and inheritance even after marriage on the other, are likely to have had on women's lives. *In the 9th and 10th centuries CE, was there seclusion of women among Christians? Jews? Did women control their own property, inheritance, and income among Christian and Jewish communities, which in the Islamic empire had their own laws of personal status?*

▶ Assuming the role of an Arab merchant, write a letter to a fellow merchant in Baghdad describing your voyage from the Persian Gulf to the city of Guangzhou (Canton) on the South China coast. *What was the voyage like? What sort of relations do you have with the Chinese government? What goods are you trading in? Why did you travel such a long distance to trade?*

Calligraphy has been one of the high arts in Muslim civilization
Ross Dunn, slide collection

Students Should Be Able to:

2C **Demonstrate understanding of the consolidation of the Byzantine state in the context of expanding Islamic civilization by:**

`5-12` Explaining how the Byzantine state withstood Arab Muslim attacks between the 8th and 10th centuries. [**Analyze cause-and-effect relationships**]

`9-12` Comparing Byzantium's imperial political system with that of the Abbasid state. [**Compare and contrast differing values and institutions**]

`7-12` Evaluating the Byzantine role in preserving and transmitting ancient Greek learning. [**Reconstruct patterns of historical succession and duration**]

`9-12` Analyzing the expansion of Greek Orthodox Christianity into the Balkans and Kievan Russia between the 9th and 11th centuries. [**Analyze multiple causation**]

Grades 5-6	**Examples of student achievement of Standard 2C include:**

▸ Construct a map showing the expansion of Orthodox Christianity in Eastern Europe.

▸ Draw and label typical weapons of this period such as the compound bow and arrow, lance, body and horse armor, and Greek fire. *How valuable were these weapons in the defense of the Byzantine Empire? Why was Greek fire a closely guarded secret? Is the fact that they had these weapons sufficient to explain the success of Byzantium in resisting Arab Muslim attacks?*

Grades 7-8	**Examples of student achievement of Standard 2C include:**

▸ Research and make models of various military and merchant ship designs of the 9th century such as the Mediterranean galley, the dhow, and Viking ships. *What accounts for the differences in these designs? To what uses were each of these kinds of ships put? What was the relative importance of the army and the navy in Byzantine defense against Arab Muslim attacks?*

▸ Describe the weapons, fortifications, and military preparedness of the Byzantine Empire and explain how it was able to withstand Bulgar and Arab attacks.

Grades 9-12	**Examples of student achievement of Standard 2C include:**

▸ Describe the spread of Greek Orthodox Christianity into the Balkans, Ukraine, and Russia between the 9th and 11th centuries. *What explains the acceptance of Greek over Latin Christianity in the Slavic world?*

▸ Construct an appeal to the Byzantine emperor on the importance of preserving the works of the ancient Greek and Hellenistic scholars. *What arguments would you use to convince the emperor of the necessity of maintaining Greek learning?*

◗ Compare and contrast Constantinople and Baghdad as centers of manufacturing and long-distance trade. *How did economic power translate into military and political power in each?*

◗ Draw evidence from the legends in the Russian Chronicle regarding Vladimir of Kiev and his conversion to Eastern Orthodox Christianity. *Why was Vladimir inclined to accept the Greek Orthodox Church rather than Judaism, Islam, or Latin Christianity? What do the stories reveal regarding the relationship of church and state in Kievan Russia?*

◗ Assume the role of a foreign traveler and describe your impressions of Constantinople and the imperial government of the Byzantine emperor. *How would your impressions differ if you were a traveler to Baghdad describing that city and the Abbasid imperial government?*

Detail of Constantinople for a 15th-century woodcut
Library of Congress

STANDARD 3

Students Should Understand: *Major developments in East Asia in the era of the Tang dynasty, 600-900 CE*

Students Should Be Able to:

3A Demonstrate understanding of China's sustained political and cultural expansion in the Tang period by:

`9-12` Describing political centralization and economic reforms that marked China's reunification under the Sui and Tang dynasties. [**Analyze cause-and-effect relationships**]

`5-12` Describing the territorial expansion of the empire to Southeast and Central Asia. [**Reconstruct patterns of historical succession and duration**]

`5-12` Describing the cosmopolitan diversity of peoples and religions in Chinese cities of the early- and mid-Tang period. [**Evaluate historical perspectives**]

`7-12` Assessing explanations for the spread and power of Buddhism in Tang China, Korea, and Japan. [**Analyze cause-and-effect relationships**]

`7-12` Evaluating creative achievements in painting and poetry in relation to the values of Tang society. [**Evidence historical perspectives**]

| Grades 5-6 | **Examples of student achievement of Standard 3A include:** |

▶ On a map of China, show the physical features of the land, locate the network of canals, and indicate the greatest extent of the Tang dynasty. *How did China's geography affect farming techniques? How did the Grand Canal change life in China?*

▶ Assume the role of a diplomat or traveler from Constantinople or Baghdad to one of the cities of Tang China, and write accounts to government officials back home of what you have observed. *What could your empire learn from Tang China?*

▶ Describe the development of cities in Tang China. *Where did major cities develop? Who went to live there? What caused people to migrate to cities?*

| Grades 7-8 | **Examples of student achievement of Standard 3A include:** |

▶ Assume the role of an adviser to a Tang emperor and argue for the development of a network of roads and canals in the empire. *How would you justify the cost of these public works? How might you raise the money needed? How would you organize the building project? How would they benefit the state and the public?*

▶ Explain how Buddhism was introduced from China to Korea and Japan. Tell the story of how the Korean emperor encouraged Japan to adopt Buddhism. *Why did the Soga clan advise the Japanese emperor to accept Buddhism?*

- Map the extent of the Tang empire and mark the major trade routes used. *What products were exchanged? How might the introduction of the crystallization process for sugar have affected Chinese life?*

- Analyze Tang landscape painting and examples of Tang pottery. *What ideas and values about everyday life are expressed?*

- Summarize the technologies developed during the Tang dynasty and how they were used. *What impact did these technologies have in China? By what routes might knowledge of these technologies have spread?*

Grades 9-12

Examples of student achievement of Standard 3A include:

- Research living conditions in China and compare urban with rural society during the Tang dynasty. *How did life differ in rural areas from urban communities? How did urban centers influence growth in the arts?*

- Reading retrospectives such as *Journey to the West*, discuss the story of the journey of the Tang monk Xuan Zang to India in quest of Buddhist scriptures and discuss the role of the "Monkey King," who accompanied him. *What was the legendary significance of this story in Chinese popular culture from the Tang dynasty onward?*

- Read poems by Tang poets such as Bo Juyi, Wang Wei, Du Fu, and Li Bo, and create an exhibit of painting and calligraphy done during this period. Discuss the place of poetry and painting in the lives of the scholar-officials in China. *What do we know about the values of the Chinese elite at this time? What is the attitude of the poets toward common people?*

- Read Li Gongzuo's *Governor of the Southern Tributary State* and analyze the role of women, the family, and government. Write a summary of one of the passages to depict a main idea in the story.

Japanese painting of the Nara period using a style similar to Chinese painting Kokusai Bunka Shinkokai

Students Should Be Able to:

3B Demonstrate understanding of Chinese influence on the peoples of Inner Asia, Korea, Southeast Asia, and Japan by:

7-12 Explaining how relations between China and pastoral peoples of Inner Asia in the Tang period reflect long-term patterns of interaction along China's grassland frontier. **[Reconstruct patterns of historical succession and duration]**

9-12 Analyzing changes in Inner Asia, Korea, and Vietnam under the impact of Tang state and culture. **[Marshal evidence of antecedent circumstances]**

5-12 Describing the indigenous development of Japanese society up to the 7th century CE **[Reconstruct patterns of historical succession and duration]**

7-12 Assessing the patterns of borrowing and adaptation of Chinese culture in Japanese society from the 7th to the 11th century. **[Analyze the influence of ideas]**

5-12 Describing the establishment of the imperial state in Japan, and assessing the role of the emperor in government. **[Reconstruct patterns of historical succession and duration]**

5-12 Assessing the political, social, and cultural contributions of women in the Japanese imperial court. **[Evidence historical perspectives]**

Grades 5-6

Examples of student achievement of Standard 3B include:

▶ Construct a map of the Japanese islands showing elevation and the proximity of the islands to Korea and the Chinese mainland. *What role did geography play in the development of Japan? How did it influence Japan's relations with China and Korea?*

▶ Draw upon evidence from diaries to describe the lives of women in the court of the emperor. *What was the position of women in Heian Japan?*

▶ Investigate the importance of rice in Japan. *How is the importance of rice reflected in family life? In popular celebrations?*

▶ Research how wet rice is cultivated and outline the agricultural cycle associated with it. *What role did the family play in rice cultivation in Japan? How did the family accommodate the rice cycle? How are popular festivals in Japan related to the agricultural cycle?*

Grades 7-8

Examples of student achievement of Standard 3B include:

▶ Reading selections from the *Kojiki* in *Sources of Japanese Tradition*, explain the legends of the creation of Japan. Explain the differences between history and legend. *What do these stories tell you about Japanese history?*

▶ On a time line, trace the development of the early cultures of Japan from the Jomon, ca. 10,000 BCE, through the "tomb culture," ca. 200 CE. *What did each of these cultures introduce to the islands of Japan?*

- Explain the basic beliefs of Shinto. Using works of art and literature, describe the impact of Shinto on Japan.

- Assume the role of a Buddhist monk making two voyages to Japan; the first to the capital of Nara (710-784) and second to the new capital of Heian (Kyoto) (794-857), some seventy years later. Record your impression of the influence of Buddhism in Japan and explain changes that occurred over time. *How would you regard the changes? Why did the emperor in Heian restrict the Buddhist clergy?*

- Investigate how the Chinese language was used as a written "lingua franca" for government throughout East Asia at this time. *How does this compare with the use of Latin in the West?*

- Describe courtly life and the search for beauty in Heian Japan. *Why was calligraphy so important in pottery?*

Grades 9-12

Examples of student achievement of Standard 3B include:

- Examine how the Tang dynasty extended its influence in East Asia. *To what extent did Korea and Vietnam adopt Chinese traditions? To what extent did Korea and Vietnam resist Chinese political domination? What was the relationship between Tang China and Japan? Why do you think a historian who has studied the influence of Confucianism and Chinese government on Vietnam referred to the latter as a "smaller dragon"?*

- Analyze Prince Shotoku's "Constitution" for evidence of borrowing and adapting Chinese ideas in ancient Japan. *If the Taika reforms had endured, how might Japan's imperial government have changed?*

- Read selections from the *Diary of Murasaki Shikibu* and *The Pillow Book* by Sei Shonagon. Discuss the importance of women as authors at the Japanese court of the Heian period. *Who were these women? How did their writings reflect social roles and values of the imperial court?*

- Examine the difference between spoken language and writing systems. *How many writing systems are there in the world? What is unique about the Chinese writing system?* Explain how the Japanese adapted the Chinese writing system to fit the spoken language of Japan.

- Select poems from the *Kokinshu*. *What is distinctive about the* waka *(or* tanka) *form that developed in Japan at this time?*

- Research the history of the commercial state of Srivijaya in Southeast Asia. Studying a map of the region, explain why the Strait of Malacca was such a strategic waterway for interregional trade. *How did the pattern of the monsoon winds make Srivijaya a "hinge" of trade between China and India? Why do you think Srivijaya became a rich and powerful kingdom?*

STANDARD 4

Students Should Understand: *The search for political, social, and cultural redefinition in Europe, 500-1000 CE*

Students Should Be Able to:

4A Demonstrate understanding of the foundations of a new civilization in Western Christendom in the 500 years following the breakup of the western Roman Empire by:

5-12 Assessing the importance of monasteries, the Latin Church, and missionaries from Britain and Ireland in the Christianizing of western and central Europe. [**Analyze cause-and-effect relationships**]

5-12 Explaining the development of the Merovingian and Carolingian states, and assessing their success at maintaining public order and local defense in western Europe. [**Reconstruct patterns of historical succession and duration**]

7-12 Analyzing how the preservation of Greco-Roman and early Christian learning in monasteries and Charlemagne's royal court contributed to the emergence of European civilization. [**Reconstruct patterns of historical succession and duration**]

7-12 Analyzing the changing political relations between the popes and the secular rulers of Europe. [**Identify issues and problems of the past**]

9-12 Comparing the successes of the Latin and Orthodox churches in introducing Christianity and Christian culture to eastern Europe. [**Compare and contrast differing sets of ideas**]

Grades 5-6	Examples of student achievement of Standard 4A include:

▶ Explain the function of monasteries in western Europe during the early medieval period and sketch a plan for a monastery that reflects those functions. *What services did monasteries perform? How did monasteries preserve ancient learning? Why did monks become missionaries? Did monks and nuns fulfill the same functions?*

▶ Read the description of Charlemagne given by his friend and biographer Einhard, and an account of Charlemagne's government, laws, and conquests in a secondary source. *What can you infer from this information about his values and aims? About the difficulties he had to overcome?*

Grades 7-8	Examples of student achievement of Standard 4A include:

▶ Map the Carolingian world, including the tributary peoples. *How did the Carolingian influence expand, what were its greatest extensions, and why did it contract?*

▶ Write a biography of Clovis including his conversion and its results, and map the lands he conquered. *What part did his wife Clothilde, and other royal women of the time, play in the Christianization of Frankish and Saxon peoples? What part did conquest play?*

▶ From illustrations and written accounts (Einhard), describe the coronation of Charlemagne. *At his coronation what did Charlemagne expect of his people and himself? What were his expectations and perhaps his goals? How were they fulfilled?*

▶ Research and compare the lives of Charlemagne, Harun al-Rashid, and the Empress Irene. *How did each of these secular leaders influence the political order within Europe?*

▶ Discuss the usefulness of the term "Dark Ages" to characterize medieval Europe, and consider the factors that might make for a "dark age" in any society.

▶ Examine the Rules of St. Benedict. *Why did St. Benedict prescribe times for prayer and meditation? How harsh were these rules? Why were men and women willing to live by these rules? What importance did these rules have for monks, nuns, and missionaries?*

Grades 9-12

Examples of student achievement of Standard 4A include:

▶ Compare Charlemagne's empire with Byzantium, the Abbasid empire, and the Islamic caliphate of Iberia in regard to their size, wealth, and political organization.

▶ Construct a chart showing several significant similarities and differences in the governance and worship in the Latin Catholic and Byzantine churches. *How did the "governors" of these churches seek to promote conversion in eastern and western Europe?*

▶ Map the extent of the Frankish conquests under Clovis and mark the four areas he divided among his sons. Predict the consequences of this division and then compare them with the actual results.

▶ Relate the life of the Anglo-Saxon missionary, Boniface. *How did he represent "the romanization of Europe"? In what ways did he serve as an exemplar for other monks/missionaries?*

▶ Read excerpts from *The Song of Roland*. Evaluate it as a factual account of Charlemagne's campaign in 778. *What other purposes might the document have had? How did the campaign change the relationship between the Roman Church and western Europe? How does it express the growing relationship between the secular and religious leaders of Western civilization?*

Students Should Be Able to:

4B Demonstrate understanding of the coalescence of political and social order in Europe by:

5–12 Assessing the impact of Norse (Viking) and Magyar migrations and invasions, as well as internal conflicts, on the emergence of independent lords and the knightly class. **[Analyze cause-and-effect relationships]**

7–12 Assessing changes in the legal, social, and economic status of peasants in the 9th and 10th centuries. **[Interrogate historical data]**

7–12 Analyzing how Christian values changed the social and economic status of women in early medieval Europe. **[Examine the influence of ideas]**

9–12 Explaining how royal officials such as counts and dukes transformed delegated powers into hereditary, autonomous power over land and people in the 9th and 10th centuries. **[Reconstruct patterns of historical succession and duration]**

Grades 5-6

Examples of student achievement of Standard 4B include:

▶ Sketch a Viking ship and, on a map, locate major Norse settlements. Trace Viking ships' travel routes to the North Atlantic, Russia, western Europe, and the Black Sea. *Where did the Vikings come from? Why did peoples of England or northern France fear them so much? Why do you think the Viking settlement in North America (Newfoundland) did not endure?*

▶ Write a biographical report on King Alfred of England. *Why was he called Alfred the Great? How did he defend his lands against the Vikings?*

Grades 7-8

Examples of student achievement of Standard 4B include:

▶ Keep two journals, one for a day in the life of an early medieval noble woman and one for a peasant woman. Include subjects such as marriage, family, food, work, household organization, and religion. *How were the roles of women in differing social classes similar and varying? What additional burdens and disabilities affected a peasant woman who was a serf? What legal rights and protections did women have in the feudal order?*

▶ Construct a map of major Norse settlements and routes of communication in the region extending from North America to Russia and the Black Sea. *What contributions did Vikings make to long-distance trade? Should they be credited with the European "discovery" of America? Why did Norse settlements in Newfoundland and Greenland fail to survive?*

▶ Research the status of peasants in 9th- and 10th-century Europe. *Were peasants better or worse off in these centuries than they had been under Roman rule? How did the political fragmentation of Europe after Charlemagne affect the lives of peasants?*

Grades 9-12

Examples of student achievement of Standard 4B include:

◆ Research reasons why the Carolingian empire did not endure after the death of Charlemagne. *What would a political map of western and central Europe have looked like in the 10th century? Why were European nobles able to assert independent power? What connection may have existed between Viking and Magyar invasions and the political fragmenting of large areas of Europe?*

◆ Construct a chart comparing how the Magyar cavalry and the Viking longboat gave an advantage to invaders. *How did Norse invasions of Britain affect Christian culture and learning? What happened to the Magyar invaders after the 10th century?*

A Viking ship
Norwegian Information Service

STANDARD 5

Students Should Understand: *State-building in Northeast and West Africa and the southward migrations of Bantu-speaking peoples.*

Students Should Be Able to:

5 Demonstrate understanding of state-building in Northeast and West Africa and the southward migrations of Bantu-speaking peoples by:

9–12 Analyzing how maritime trade contributed to the growth of the kingdom of Aksum in Northeast Africa. [**Analyze cause-and-effect relationships**]

9–12 Analyzing how the contrasting natural environments of West Africa defined agricultural production, settlement patterns, and trade. [**Analyze cause-and-effect relationships**]

7–12 Explaining how Ghana became West Africa's first large-scale empire and the role of divine kingship in its development. [**Interrogate historical data**]

7–12 Assessing the importance of gold and salt production, trans-Saharan camel trade, and Islam in the growth of the Ghana empire and urbanization in West Africa. [**Analyze multiple causation**]

9–12 Inferring from archaeological evidence the importance of Jenné-jeno or Kumbi-Saleh as early West African commercial cities. [**Interrogate historical data**]

9–12 Analyzing causes and consequences of the settling of east, central, and southern Africa by Bantu-speaking farmers and cattle herders up to 1000 CE. [**Analyze cause-and-effect relationships**]

Grades 5-6

Examples of student achievement of Standard 5 include:

▶ Create a diorama of West Africa illustrating the topography of the region. Use symbols to locate agricultural products, settlements, and trade items. Include a legend and brief explanation interpreting the display.

▶ Compare Jenné-jeno with earlier river valley civilizations such as Mesopotamia. *What influence did the natural environment have on agriculture, settlement patterns, and trade in each case?*

▶ Read Ethiopian legends of the introduction of Christianity to that region. *By what routes do you think Christianity might have reached Ethiopia in the 4th century? What part did exchange with other countries play in the growth of Aksum? What else besides religious ideas was passed along these routes?*

Grades 7-8

Examples of student achievement of Standard 5 include:

▸ Identify a person in your family who is the family historian, the "keeper of tales." Interview this person for a family story and share it with the class. *What functions did the griot "keeper of tales" have in West African society? Besides oral tradition, what other sources are there for West African history during this era? In what different ways do oral traditions and other kinds of evidence, verbal and physical, give historians access to the past?*

▸ Write a traveler's guide to the routes taken by the salt-gold trade. Include a description of Jenné-jeno. *How did the salt-gold trade promote urbanization in West Africa?*

▸ View slides or pictures that portray the physical and cultural diversity of West Africa and write a few words describing each. Compile the descriptions in a paragraph beginning with "West Africa is. . . ."

▸ Drawing on archaeological evidence for the growth of Jenné-jeno, interpret the commercial importance of this city in West African history. *How did the commercial importance of Jenné-jeno in this era compare with that of contemporary western European commercial centers such as early Venice?*

▸ Describe the royal court in Ghana and how it ruled Ghana. *How did belief in the king's divinity contribute to Ghana's imperial success?*

Grades 9-12

Examples of student achievement of Standard 5 include:

▸ Construct an abstract analytical model of an empire using comparative information from the Ghana and Carolingian states. *What characteristics must a state have to be considered an empire? What were some major differences between the Ghana and Carolingian empires? What similarities and differences do you find in these two empires in agriculture, trade, standard of living, expansionary tendencies, and the role of religious ideas?*

▸ Discuss the unique characteristics and strengths of the oral tradition, and the role of the griot in West African society. Compare this to the role of the monk in medieval Europe in keeping knowledge alive. Assess the strengths of each method of recording history.

▸ Design a room for an exhibit in an archaeological museum for West African artifacts. Choose the items you would display and label them in a way that would contribute to the understanding of reasons for the development of Ghana into a large-scale empire.

▸ Read selections from the *Periplus of the Erythraean Sea*, the Greek shipping manual of the 1st century CE, for evidence of the importance of trade in the African state of Aksum. *What are some of the goods that passed through Adulis, the Aksumite Red Sea port? How was Aksum well situated to play a large role in long-distance trade? What reasons do historians give for the decline of Aksum in the 8th century?*

▸ Map the spread and pattern of settlement of Bantu-speaking farmers and herders in eastern, central, and southern Africa by the 4th to 7th centuries CE. *In what ways did knowledge of ironworking, the introduction of bananas and the Asian yam from Southeast Asia, and the presence of the tsetse fly influence settlement patterns?*

STANDARD 6

Students Should Understand: *The rise of centers of civilization in Mesoamerica and Andean South America in the first millennium CE.*

Students Should Be Able to:

6A Demonstrate understanding of the origins, expansion, and achievements of Maya civilization by:

5-12   Describing the natural environment of southern Mesoamerica and its relationship to the development of Maya urban society. [**Analyze cause-and-effect relationships**]

7-12   Analyzing the Mayan system of agricultural production and trade and its relationship to the rise of city-states. [**Analyze cause-and-effect relationships**]

9-12   Interpreting the Mayan cosmic world view as evidenced in art and architecture, and evaluating Mayan achievements in astronomy, mathematics, and the development of a calendar. [**Evaluate historical perspectives**]

5-12   Analyzing the role and status of elite women in Mayan society as evidenced in monumental architecture or other sources. [**Draw upon visual sources**]

7-12   Assessing interpretations of how and why Mayan civilization declined. [**Evaluate major debates among historians**]

Grades 5-6

Examples of student achievement of Standard 6A include:

▶ Locate Mayan city-states on a map of Mesoamerica using symbols to indicate road systems and sea routes. Hypothesize reasons for the development of urban societies in these locations.

▶ Select a Mayan deity and construct a clay figure or a mask depicting its attributes. Explain the importance of religion and religious beliefs in Mayan society.

▶ Compare the Mayan pok a tok (a ceremonial ball game) with our modern sports. *Which modern sport is pok a tok most like?* Illustrate the similarities on a double drawing. *Were the reasons for playing the games also similar?*

▶ Compare Mesopotamian ziggurats with the Mayan pyramids. *In what ways are they similar? In what ways are they different? Were the purposes they served similar or different?*

▶ Study portrayals of women in Mayan monumental architecture. *What can be inferred from these about the roles elite women played in Mayan society?*

Grades 7-8

Examples of student achievement of Standard 6A include:

▶ Draw a map illustrating the exchange of trade items, commodities, and luxury goods such as cacao, salt, feathers, jade, and obsidian. *What conclusions may be drawn from the extent of Mayan trade? How important was trade to the Mayan economy?*

▶ Use visual data, such as graphs and charts, to illustrate how the Maya altered their methods of farming depending on the topography and climate. *How important was agricultural production to the Maya?*

▶ Construct a model or visual representation of a Mayan city-state such as Palenque. Estimate the number of people who are likely to have lived in such an urban settlement. *What conditions had to be met to allow such numbers to live together?*

▶ List the major achievements of Mayan civilization and explain their relationship to everyday life. *How did achievements in astronomy impact Mayan society? How valuable were mathematical innovations and the calendar to farmers?*

▶ Research interpretations of why classical Mayan society declined and prepare an oral presentation analyzing and evaluating these factors.

▶ Read excerpts from Douglas Gifford's *Warriors, Gods and Spirits from Central and South American Mythology* to examine the ways in which Mayan myths reflect social values and daily survival skills.

Grades 9-12

Examples of student achievement of Standard 6A include:

▶ Select two contrasting Mayan deities and, as a comparative model, select two comparable Hindu deities and through a drawing show comparisons. Write a paper discussing their commonalities.

▶ Using methods of an archaeologist and historian, explain how we have knowledge of Mayan civilization from deciphered hieroglyphics. *How has the Mayan "Long Count" calendar served as a tool for learning about Mayan civilization? To what extent did the destruction of Mayan books by the Spanish hamper our understanding of Mayan culture? How have recent historical interpretations altered our knowledge of Mayan political organization and warfare?*

▶ Create a schematic design including a temple/pyramid, cave, cenote, ball court, and planetarium, and explain their relationship to each other and to Mayan religious belief.

▶ Create a mural in the Bonampak style using glyphs integrated into the design, illustrating social organization, ritual practices such as blood letting, and warfare. Explain the mural, relating it to historical evidence of Mayan society and religious beliefs.

▶ Read excerpts from the *Popul Vuh*. Compare it with Christian views of creation. *Is the* Popul Vuh *a reliable account of the Mayan world view? Why or why not?*

Students Should Be Able to:

6B Demonstrate understanding of the rise of the Teotihuacán, Zapotec/Mixtec, and Moche civilizations by:

7–12 Analyzing the character of the Zapotec state in the valley of Oaxaca as reflected in the art and architecture of Monte Albán. [**Draw upon visual sources**]

9–12 Explaining the growth of the urban society centered on Teotihuacán and the importance of this city as a transmitter of Mesoamerican cultural traditions to later societies. [**Examine the influence of ideas**]

5–12 Analyzing how the diverse natural environment of the Andes region shaped systems of agriculture and animal herding. [**Analyze cause-and-effect relationships**]

7–12 Describing how archaeological discoveries have led to greater understanding of the character of Moche society. [**Hold interpretations of history as tentative**]

Grades 5-6

Examples of student achievement of Standard 6B include:

▶ On a map of the Western Hemisphere, locate the Zapotec, Teotihuacán, and Moche civilizations. *In what modern countries would you find archaeological sites of each of these civilizations?*

▶ Explain how the peoples of Teotihuacán and Moche adapted to the environment. *How did these civilizations make use of available water resources? What methods did the Moche use to farm desert lands? How did these differ from the methods used at Teotihuacán?*

▶ Construct a model of Monte Albán based on pictorial representations and site plans. *What does the model tell about the Zapotec civilization?*

▶ Locate Monte Albán and Teotihuacán on a topographical map. Write a short description of each environment and discuss the ways that they might be similar or different.

▶ Analyze examples of Moche pottery. *How can pottery help us learn about societies such as the Moche who left no written records? What can we learn from the Moche pottery and clay figures?*

Grades 7-8

Examples of student achievement of Standard 6B include:

▶ Examine Mayan and Teotihuacán murals, and speculate on reasons for their differences. *What inferences may be drawn from these murals about the societies that produced them? Why do the Teotihuacán murals lack battle scenes?*

▶ Research *ayllus* (kinship groups) and explain how they regulated family and community life in Andean societies.

▶ Examine Moche art and artifacts to determine patterns of daily life among the people. *What do these artifacts tell about the interests, occupations, and religious concerns of the people?*

◆ Make a map showing the different types of agriculture practiced in the Moche/Andean area.

Grades 9-12

Examples of student achievement of Standard 6B include:

◆ Compare religion and ritual practices of Teotihuacán and Mayan civilizations. *Based on the 1988 discovery of the tomb of a Moche warrior priest, what is known about religion and ritual practices in Moche society? How does this compare to what is known about the Maya or Teotihuacán?*

◆ Construct a two-layer calendar using a 360-day year, 30-day month, and overlay with a different Mesoamerican calendar. *What accounts for the differences in these calendars?*

◆ Research the cultures of the Moche, Tihuanaco, Chimu, or other Andean societies, exploring such aspects as textile production, gold metallurgy, burial practices, and social relations between men and women.

◆ Develop a hypothesis to assess possible methods of contact between Mesoamerica and the Andean world. Use examples of agriculture, societal structure, and artisan crafts to consider cultural diffusion.

Ritual ball court at Monte Albán.
Ross Dunn, slide collection

ERA 5

Intensified Hemispheric Interactions 1000-1500 CE

Giving Shape to World History

In this era the various regions of Eurasia and Africa became more firmly interconnected than at any earlier time in history. The sailing ships that crossed the wide sea basins of the Eastern Hemisphere carried a greater volume and variety of goods than ever before. In fact, the chain of seas extending across the hemisphere — China seas, Indian Ocean, Persian Gulf, Red Sea, Black Sea, Mediterranean, and Baltic — came to form a single interlocking network of maritime trade. In the same centuries caravan traffic crossed the Inner Asian steppes and the Sahara Desert more frequently. As trade and travel intensified so did cultural exchanges and encounters, presenting local societies with a profusion of new opportunities and dangers. By the time of the transoceanic voyages of the Portuguese and Spanish, the Eastern Hemisphere already constituted a single zone of intercommunication possessing a unified history of its own.

A global view reveals four other "big stories" that give shape to the entire era.

▶ **China and Europe — Two Centers of Growth:** In two regions of the Eastern Hemisphere, China and Europe, the era witnessed remarkable growth. China experienced a burst of technological innovation, commercialization, and urbanization, emerging as the largest economy in the world. As China exported its silks and porcelains to other lands and imported quantities of spices from India and Southeast Asia, patterns of production and commerce all across the hemisphere were affected. At the opposite end of the hemisphere western and central Europe emerged as a new center of Christian civilization, expanding in agricultural production, population, commerce, and military might. Powerful European states presented a new challenge to Muslim dominance in the Mediterranean world. At the same time Europe was drawn more tightly into the commercial economy and cultural interchange of the hemisphere.

▶ **The Long Reach of Islam:** In this era Islamic faith and civilization encompassed extensive new areas of Eurasia and Africa. The continuing spread of Islam was closely connected to the migrations of Turkic conquerors and herding folk and to the growth of Muslim commercial enterprise all across the hemisphere. By about 1400 CE Muslim societies spanned the central two-thirds of Afro-Eurasia. New Muslim states and towns were appearing in West Africa, the East African coast, Central Asia, India, and Southeast Asia. Consequently, Muslim merchants, scholars, and a host of long-distance travelers were the principal mediators in the interregional exchange of goods, ideas, and technical innovations.

▶ **The Age of Mongol Dominance:** the second half of the era saw extraordinary developments in interregional history. The Mongols under Chinggis Khan created the largest land empire the world had ever seen. Operating from Poland to Korea and Siberia to Indonesia, the Mongol warlords intruded in one way or another on the lives of almost all peoples of Eurasia. The conquests were terrifying, but the stabilizing of Mongol rule led to a century of fertile commercial and cultural interchange across the continent. Eurasian unification, however, had a disastrous consequence in the 14th century — the Black Death and its attendant social impact on Europe, the Islamic world, and probably China.

▶ **Empires of the Americas:** In the Western Hemisphere empire building reached an unprecedented scale. The political styles of the Aztec and Inca states were profoundly different. Even so, both enterprises demonstrated that human labor and creative endeavor could be organized on a colossal scale despite the absence of iron technology or wheeled transport.

Why Study This Era?

▶ The civilizations that flourished in this era — Chinese, Japanese, Indian, Islamic, European, West African, Mesoamerican, and others — created a legacy of cultural and social achievements of continuing significance today. To understand how cultural traditions affect social change or international relations in the contemporary world requires study of the specific historical contexts in which those traditions took form.

▶ The modern world with all its unique complexities did not emerge suddenly in the past 500 years but had its roots in the developments of the 1000-1500 era, notably the maturing of long-distance trade and the economic and social institutions connected with it.

▶ To understand both the history of modern Europe and the United States requires a grasp of the variety of institutions, ideas, and styles that took shape in western Christendom during this era of expansion and innovation.

What Students Should Understand

Standard 1: The maturing of an interregional system of communication, trade, and cultural exchange in an era of Chinese economic power and Islamic expansion

    A. **China's** extensive urbanization and commercial **expansion** between the 10th and 13th centuries [CORE]

    B. The development of **Japanese civilization** between the 11th and 15th centuries [RELATED]

    C. How pastoral migrations and religious reform movements between the 11th and 13th centuries contributed to the rise of new states and the **expansion of Islam** [CORE]

    D. How interregional communication and trade led to **intensified cultural exchanges** among diverse peoples of Eurasia and Africa [RELATED]

Standard 2: The redefining of European society and culture, 1000-1300 CE

    A. The growth of **centralized monarchies** and city-states in Europe **[CORE]**

    B. The **expansion of** Christian **Europe** after 1000 **[CORE]**

    C. Patterns of **social change** and cultural achievement **in Europe** **[RELATED]**

Standard 3: The rise of the Mongol empire and its consequences for Eurasian peoples, 1200-1350

    A. The world-historical significance of the **Mongol empire [CORE]**

    B. The **significance of Mongol rule** in China, Korea, Russia, and Southwest Asia **[RELATED]**

Standard 4: The growth of states, towns, and trade in Sub-Saharan Africa between the 11th and 15th centuries

    A. The growth of **imperial states in Africa [CORE]**

    B. Indian Ocean **trade and Bantu settlement** in East, Central, and South Africa **[RELATED]**

Standard 5: Patterns of crisis and recovery in Afro-Eurasia, 1300-1450

    A. The **Black Death** and recurring plague pandemic in the 14th century **[CORE]**

    B. Transformations in **Europe following** the **14-century** economic and demographic **crises [CORE]**

    C. Major political **developments in Asia** in the aftermath of the collapse of Mongol rule and the plague pandemic **[RELATED]**

Standard 6: The expansion of states and civilizations in the Americas, 1000-1500

    A. The development of complex **societies and states in North America and Mesoamerica [CORE]**

    B. The development of the **Inca empire** in Andean South America **[CORE]**

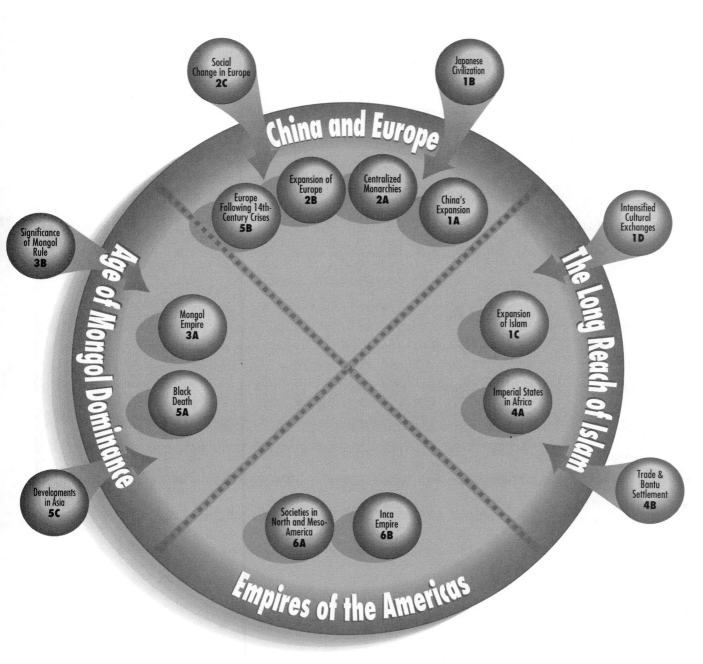

**Relationships Among Major Developments,
Core Standards, and Related Standards for Era 5**

S T A N D A R D   1

Students Should Understand: *The maturing of an interregional system of communication, trade, and cultural exchange in an era of Chinese economic power and Islamic expansion.*

Students Should Be Able to:

1A   Demonstrate understanding of China's extensive urbanization and commercial expansion between the 10th and 13th centuries by:

7-12   Explaining the major dynastic transitions China experienced and the changes in Confucianism between the 10th and 13th centuries. **[Analyze cause-and-effect relationships]**

7-12   Analyzing how improved agricultural production, population growth, urbanization, and commercialization were historically interconnected. **[Analyze multiple causation]**

5-12   Identifying major technological and scientific innovations, and analyzing their effects on Chinese life. **[Examine the influence of ideas]**

5-12   Analyzing the expansion of China's external trade with peoples of Southeast Asia and the lands rimming the Indian Ocean. **[Analyze cause-and-effect relationships]**

7-12   Analyzing the growth of an economically powerful merchant class in China. **[Formulate historical questions]**

7-12   Assessing the importance of women of gentry families in preserving and transmitting Chinese cultural values. **[Interrogate historical data]**

Grades 5-6

Examples of student achievement of Standard 1A include:

▶ Investigate the development of paper currency in China during the Song dynasty. *How did the introduction of paper money stimulate the economy?*

▶ Assume the role of an ambassador to Song China and write an account of Chinese innovations in warfare. Describe the use of gunpowder in crossbow arrows, bombs, and guns. *What were the consequences of these weapons?*

▶ Map the expansion of China's external trade with Southeast Asia and the lands rimming the Indian Ocean. *What effect did this trade expansion have on China? What effect did this trade expansion have on Southeast Asia?*

▶ Investigate the use and spread of wood-block book printing. *What kinds of purposes were prints first used for in China? Once printing spread, how did it change gentry life?*

Grades 7-8

Examples of student achievement of Standard 1A include:

‣ Explain the factors that led to the development of a merchant class in Song China. *How did the expansion of trade and commerce influence the growth of cities? What were the traditional social attitudes in China toward merchants and commercial activity?*

‣ List the significant achievements during the Song dynasty. *How did these achievements change China?*

‣ Write an essay comparing the city of Hangzhou with London or other cities of this era.

‣ Write a personal journal entry of a young Chinese man who has just taken the state civil service examination. *What social class was this man a member of? What did he have to do to prepare for the exams? What was a typical exam day like?*

‣ Make a three-section chart on the basic beliefs of Confucianism, Daoism, and Buddhism. *How did Zhu Xi blend these into a new synthesis called neo-Confucianism?*

Grades 9-12

Examples of student achievement of Standard 1A include:

‣ Research how economic changes in China affected society. *How mobile was the gentry class?*

‣ Study reproductions of Song art. *How do Song paintings reflect Confucian, Daoist, and Buddhist ideas?*

‣ Research Chinese achievements in alchemy, astronomy, and medicine during the Song dynasty. *How did Chinese advances in science and medicine compare with those in Europe and Southwest Asia?*

‣ Read the instructions Zhu Xi gave on rites for honoring ancestors in his *Family Rituals,* and discuss the relationship between popular rites and Zhu Xi's Neo-Confucian philosophy.

‣ Investigate the arguments and political conflicts during the Song dynasty over how the government should deal with rapid social change and a growing economy. *What were the main positions? Which position won out for the long term in China?*

‣ Describe footbinding of women as a social practice in Song China and analyze ways in which this practice might reflect changes in the social and moral status of women.

‣ Investigate the life of a typical Chinese gentlemen. *What were his attitudes toward (a) family, (b) women, (c) servants, tenants, and social inferiors?*

‣ Read selections from the philosopher Zhu Xi's conversations with his followers and from the *Schedule for Learning,* and discuss the basic ideas of Neo-Confucianism. Analyze how these ideas affected Chinese society, government, and education.

Students Should Be Able to:

1B Demonstrate understanding of the development of Japanese and Southeast Asian civilization between the 11th and 15th centuries by:

`5-12` Describing Japanese government in the Kamakura and early Ashikaga periods, and assessing the applicability of the concept of feudalism to Japan. **[Interrogate historical data]**

`5-12` Analyzing the rise of the warrior class and the changes in the economic and social status of peasants and women in the context of feudal society. **[Reconstruct patterns of historical succession and duration]**

`7-12` Explaining the development of distinctive forms of Japanese Buddhism. **[Examine the influence of ideas]**

`5-12` Evaluating the arts and aesthetic values in warrior culture. **[Evidence historical perspectives]**

`7-12` Explaining the sources of wealth of the Southeast Asian states of Vietnam (Dai Viet), Champa, and Angkor (Cambodia), and comparing the influence of Confucianism, Hinduism, and Buddhism in these states. **[Compare and contrast differing institutions]**

Grades 5-6	**Examples of student achievement of Standard 1B include:**

▶ Write an account of the daily life of a boy in training as a warrior. *How would your training change as you grew older?*

▶ Tell the story of the Mongol invasions of Japan in 1274 and 1281 and how the Japanese defeated the invaders. *What part did the "divine wind" (kamikaze) play in the defeat of the Mongols and how was this depicted by the Japanese?*

▶ Research the art of Japanese screens and describe the values they represent. Make a Japanese screen painting based on designs of the period.

Grades 7-8	**Examples of student achievement of Standard 1B include:**

▶ Study a physical geography map of mainland Southeast Asia. Locate the Red River and the states of Champa, Dai Viet, and Angkor. *Why do you think Dai Viet and Angkor were both strong agricultural societies? Why did Champa's prosperity depend heavily on maritime trade?*

▶ Describe the system of feudalism that developed in Japan. *What led to the development of feudalism? How powerful were the daimyo? What are the similarities and differences between the institutions of feudalism in Japan and medieval Europe?*

▶ Construct a time line showing the important political events of the Kamakura period of Japanese history.

▶ Read excerpts from *The Tale of Heike. Why were military tales of particular importance at this time?* Discuss how the political and military developments affected the lives of common people. Analyze how the development of the sects of Buddhism took place in this context.

♦ Read excerpts from *An Account of My Hut* by Kamo no Chomei and discuss the life of the author. Analyze how his decision to become a monk reflected the political, social, and religious developments of the time.

Grades 9-12

Examples of student achievement of Standard 1B include:

♦ Construct a table to analyze the degree to which women's experiences in feudal Japanese society were determined by social class, area, time, and stage of life.

♦ Research Noh drama and compare Noh to Greek tragedy. *How does each demonstrate philosophical values and traditions?*

♦ Examine the development of Buddhist sects in Japan and explain the appeal of each of these communities. *How was Japanese society affected by Zen Buddhism? Why did Zen Buddhism have wide appeal among the samurai? What accounted for the popularity of Jodo ("Pure Land") Buddhism and Nichiren Buddhism?*

♦ Research different art forms of the Kamakura and Ashikaga periods such as painting, pottery, literature, dance, flower arranging, and rock gardens. *How do the arts reflect Buddhist and Shinto philosophy?*

♦ Draw evidence from art and literature to examine the lives of common people in Japan.

♦ Write a speech defending the samurai revolt against the Kamakura shogunate following the defeat of the Mongols. *What were the economic problems caused by the wars with the Mongols?*

♦ Study pictures of the temple of Angkor Wat that was built in Cambodia beginning in the 12th century. *Why was this enormous temple built? How does it combine Indian and Southeast Asian art and architecture? Why has this temple been called one of the most impressive structures ever built?*

The 12th century Cambodian city of Angkor Thom reflecting Indian influence. Library of Congress

Students Should Be Able to:

1C Demonstrate understanding of how pastoral migrations and religious reform movements between the 11th and 13th centuries contributed to the rise of new states and the expansion of Islam by:

> **7-12** Analyzing how the migrations of Turkic peoples from Turkestan into Southwest Asia and India in the 11th and 12th centuries contributed to Islamic expansion and the retreat of Byzantium and Greek Christian civilization. [**Analyze cause-and-effect relationships**]

> **9-12** Assessing the growth of North African Islamic reform movements and the success of the Almoravids and Almohads in creating empires spanning Iberia and North Africa. [**Examine the influence of ideas**]

> **5-12** Evaluating scientific, artistic, and literary achievements of Islamic civilization between the 11th and 13th centuries. [**Evidence historical perspectives**]

> **9-12** Assessing Sufism as an important dimension of Islamic faith and practice and how it enriched Muslim life and contributed to Islamic expansion. [**Examine the influence of ideas**]

Grades 5-6

Examples of student achievement of Standard 1C include:

> ◗ Create a chart listing the scientific achievements of Islamic civilization between the 11th and 13th centuries. *How did new discoveries encourage communication among the different peoples of the Islamic state?*

> ◗ Read excerpts from *A Thousand and One Nights*. *How do the tales reflect the multiethnic character of the Islamic state? What do the tales teach us about life in this era?*

Grades 7-8

Examples of student achievement of Standard 1C include:

> ◗ Research the kind of life that students led in an Islamic college in Cairo, and compare it with the lives of European university students in this period.

> ◗ Write a tourist's guide to Cairo in the age of the Fatimids. *Under what circumstances did Cairo become an international center of trade and Islamic culture in that age? What are the* geniza *documents, and what have historians learned from them about the life of Jewish and Muslim communities in Egypt and the Mediterranean in the Fatimid period?*

> ◗ Develop overlay maps showing Turkic migrations, Islamic expansion, and the retreat of Byzantium and Greek Christian civilization.

> ◗ Read excerpts from Ibn Jubayr's account of his travels between Spain and Mecca (1183-1185). *What was the purpose of his journey? What characteristics of Muslim society does he find worth writing about?*

Grades 9-12

Examples of student achievement of Standard 1C include:

▶ Compare the way of life of Turkic peoples such as the Seljuks with that of earlier peoples of the steppes such as the Huns, or the early Germanic tribes.

▶ Discuss basic ideas of Sufism and the meaning of mysticism as an aspect of religious belief and practice. *How did Sufi organizations contribute to the spread of Islam?*

▶ Compare the origins and growth of the Seljuk and Ghaznavid empires as Turkic military states.

▶ Interpret selections from Muslim chronicles and literary works regarding Muslim military, political, and cultural responses to the Christian crusades in Syria-Palestine.

▶ Read excerpts from Ibn Jubayr's account of Cairo, Damascus, and Sicily during the Crusades. *What interactions does he describe among Muslims and Christians in these places, and how is society affected by the Christian campaigns?*

▶ Read selections from the *Rubaiyat* of Omar Khayyam and the writings of al-Ghazali, and discuss ways in which these writings exemplify Sufi ideas. *What aspects of Islamic society do these writings reflect?*

▶ Assess the role played by Sufi orders in rural and urban areas of Muslim lands. *What was their relationship to organizations of artisans in the cities? What was their relationship to landowners and peasants?*

▶ Research the origins of the North African Islamic reform movements. *How did the reform message of the Almoravids transform rival clans into a unified force? How did the Almoravid and Almohad states boost the trans-Saharan gold trade?*

The Hassan Mosque, Rabat, Morocco, built in the 12th century under the Almohad dynasty

A Berber girl of the Middle Atlas Mountains, Morocco

Students Should Be Able to:

1D Demonstrate understanding of how interregional communication and trade led to intensified cultural exchanges among diverse peoples of Eurasia and Africa by:

`5-12` Identifying the maritime routes extending from East Asia to northern Europe, and assessing the importance of trade across the Indian Ocean for societies of Asia, East Africa, and Europe. [**Draw upon data in historical maps**]

`5-12` Explaining how camel caravan transport facilitated long-distance trade across Central Asia and the Sahara Desert. [**Interrogate historical data**]

`7-12` Explaining connections between trade and the spread of Islam in Central Asia, East Africa, West Africa, the coasts of India, and Southeast Asia. [**Analyze cause-and-effect relationships**]

Grades 5-6

Examples of student achievement of Standard 1D include:

▶ Using an outline map of the Eastern Hemisphere, identify the chain of seas that stretches from East Asia to Scandinavia; then draw routes sea travelers might take to sail across the major regions extending from the South China Sea to the Baltic Sea.

▶ Identify the major commercial cities involved in Indian Ocean trade and use icons to indicate their trade goods.

▶ Research why a camel is the best mode of transportation across the desert. *Are camel caravans still used in long-distance trade across Central Asia and the Sahara Desert?*

Grades 7-8

Examples of student achievement of Standard 1D include:

▶ Construct a chart showing the pattern of the seasonal monsoon winds in the Indian Ocean basin. *What climatic factors account for this pattern? How did the monsoon winds affect the possibilities and limitations of seaborne navigation and trade in the Indian Ocean? What importance did products such as gold, silks, woolens, pepper, ivory, cowry shells, and slaves have for the economies of Asian, African, or European societies?*

▶ Research the architecture and position in the city of caravansaries and khans in Central Asia and the Middle East. Describe their functions and the sort of people you might meet there. *Why did they become gathering places for local people as well as travelers?*

▶ Make a model or drawing of a typical lateen-rigged sailing craft of the Indian Ocean. *How did this type of vessel take advantage of the monsoon winds?* Describe positive and negative aspects of making a long voyage on a lateen-rigged ship. *How did the large Chinese junks that plied the China seas and Indian Ocean differ in construction and technology from lateen-rigged vessels? What technology enabled Chinese ships to be so large?*

Grades 9-12

Examples of student achievement of Standard 1D include:

◗ Debate the proposition: The economic and commercial expansion of Song China was the single most important factor in the intensification of interregional communication and trade across Eurasia.

◗ Analyze the relationship between Indian Ocean trade and the rise of city-states along the East African coast. *In what ways did the spread of Islam expand trade routes?*

◗ Write a reaction paper to the following statement: Ideas are carried along trade routes together with goods and products. Therefore, the direction of trade routes can affect the course of history in very important ways. Suppose trade caravans had been unable or traders unwilling to cross the Sahara. *How might African society be different today? What effect might such isolation have had on the spread of Islam?*

Ruins of Sijilmasa, caravan center of the northern Sahara
Ross Dunn, slide collection

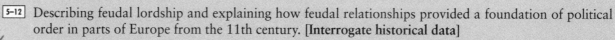

STANDARD 2

Students Should Understand: *The redefining of European society and culture, 1000-1300 CE.*

Students Should Be Able to:

2A Demonstrate understanding of feudalism and the growth of centralized monarchies and city-states in Europe by:

`5-12` Describing feudal lordship and explaining how feudal relationships provided a foundation of political order in parts of Europe from the 11th century. **[Interrogate historical data]**

`5-12` Describing manorialism as an economic system in 11th- and 12th-century Europe and analyzing the legal, social, and economic position of serfs. **[Evidence historical perspective]**

`7-12` Analyzing how European monarchies expanded their power at the expense of feudal lords and assessing the growth and limitations of representative institutions in these monarchies. **[Analyze cause-and-effect relationships]**

`7-12` Explaining the changing political relationship between the Roman Catholic Church and secular states. **[Analyze cause-and-effect relationships]**

`7-12` Describing roles that upper-class women played in dynastic and aristocratic medieval politics. **[Formulate historical questions]**

`9-12` Analyzing how prosperous city-states arose in Italy and northern Europe and comparing the political institutions of city-states with those of centralizing monarchies. **[Compare and contrast differing institutions]**

Grades 5-6

Examples of student achievement of Standard 2A include:

▶ Construct a map of medieval Europe showing the extent of kingdoms and location of city-states. *How does such a map show that Europe was still dominated by feudal rulers? Where was their power most limited?*

▶ Prepare a report on William the Conqueror and explain how he was able to win control of England after the Battle of Hastings. *Why did William invade England? What sort of changes did William make in governing England?*

Grades 7-8

Examples of student achievement of Standard 2A include:

▶ Using the Bayeux Tapestry write an account of the conflict between William of Normandy and Harold of England. *Why did the Normans invade England? What factors contributed to William's success at the Battle of Hastings? Which kind of political changes did William initiate? How did England change culturally and socially in the two centuries following the Norman Conquest?*

◗ Investigate events leading to Runnymede (1215). Analyze the Magna Carta from the perspective of a serf, free man, noble, and monarch. *Was it important to establish the principle that the king had to live by the same law that he demanded be followed by the nobles?*

◗ In an essay discuss the changing position and power of the papacy from the Early Middle Ages to the High Middle Ages. *What stimulated this change? How did the relationship between popes and feudal rulers change?*

Grades 9-12

Examples of student achievement of Standard 2A include:

◗ Analyze the historical significance of the Magna Carta in establishing the principle of the rule of law and the foundation of the English legal system and constitutional liberties. *How were these principles reinforced with the establishment of the English Parliament in the 13th century?*

◗ Discuss those common features or activities that allowed city-states such as Genoa, Venice, and Bruges to become commercial, financial, and economic leaders of Europe. *How did they maintain their independence? In what ways did their political structure differ from that of the centralizing monarchies?*

◗ Prepare an oral report evaluating the relative importance of mercenary armies, bureaucracies, and earlier feudal options such as marriage alliances and the building of fiefs in the growth of centralized royal power. *In what ways did these institutions assist monarchs in assuming greater powers?*

◗ Make a diagram showing the structure of the English and French governments, and compare and contrast the workings of the English Parliament and the French Estates-General. *To what extent did these institutions involve popular participation in government? How much real power did these representative bodies have in how their nations were run?*

◗ Based on reading Christine de Pisan's advice to princesses and other elite women in *Treasure of the City of Ladies* and the Parisian manual *The Good Wife*, infer the part played by women in 14th-century political and family life. *To what extent do secondary sources support or challenge your inferences?*

◗ Assume the role of a serf on the manor and describe your daily activities, your rights, obligations, legal and economic position, and relationship to freemen, slaves, and lords. *In what ways was manorialism an economic system? How did it promote economic growth, the accumulation of wealth, and eventually entrepreneurialism?*

◗ Compare the European feudal system with the Byzantine or Abbasid political systems. *How did the systems differ? Which system offered the greatest security? What is political legitimacy? How did kings in western Europe exercise legitimacy in comparison with the Byzantine emperor or Abbasid caliph?*

◗ Research and create a historical narrative or dramatization of a prominent woman of this period who exercised intellectual, religious or political influence over the developments of her day such as Catherine of Siena or Hildegard of Bingen. *What do their lives tell us about the opportunities open to them and the obstacles they faced?*

Students Should Be Able to:

2B Demonstrate understanding of the expansion of Christian Europe after 1000 by:

7-12 Analyzing how population growth occurred and its relationship to increased agricultural production and technological innovation. [**Analyze cause-and-effect relationships**]

9-12 Explaining urban growth in the Mediterranean region and northern Europe, and analyzing causes for the expansion of manufacturing, interregional trade, and a money economy in Europe. [**Analyze cause-and-effect relationships**]

5-12 Analyzing the success of Christian states in overthrowing Muslim powers of central and southern Iberia between the 11th and 13th centuries. [**Interrogate historical data**]

5-12 Analyzing the causes and consequences of the European Crusades against Syria and Palestine. [**Analyze cause-and-effect relationships**]

7-12 Assessing the consequences of German expansion into Poland and the Baltic region. [**Analyze cause-and-effect relationships**]

| Grades 5-6 | Examples of student achievement of Standard 2B include: |

▶ Construct a map tracing the route of the First Crusade and write a letter from a crusader describing where he traveled and what he did along the way. Compare his experiences to those of later crusaders. *What caused the Crusades? What were the goals of the popes and those of the kings?*

▶ Draw and label a plan of a typical medieval manor. *What effect did being isolated have on the people of the manor? What was the position of the peasant in the manor's life? In what ways did a free peasant's and a serf's life differ?*

▶ Construct a model of a European castle of the 12th or 13th century and explain daily activities in and around the castle. *What were the purposes of castles? In what ways did the life of the castle depend on the work of serfs? In what ways did serfs depend on the castle and its inhabitants?*

| Grades 7-8 | Examples of student achievement of Standard 2B include: |

▶ Explain how the development of agricultural technologies such as the iron plow-share and the wheeled plow stimulated greater agricultural production. *How did increased agricultural production lead to increased economic development and the growth of population in medieval Europe?*

▶ Using bar graphs, compare the increase in population and agricultural production ca. 1000-1300. Infer from these graphs the relationship between population and agricultural production.

▶ Assume the role of a young adult from a noble family in training for knighthood and give an account of the training you would receive. *What responsibilities and rights did this squire learn? How did he approach his relationship to his lord, his church, noblewomen, and serfs?*

▶ Drawing on sources such as Scott O'Dell's *The Road to Damietta,* discuss the role that saints played in the spread of Christianity.

▶ Draw a recruiting poster for the Crusades for either the Christian or Muslim armies. *How did the Christian and Muslim leaders entice common soldiers and knights to commit so much of their lives to the Crusades? What benefits might be derived from such service? How does the concept of Muslim* jihad *compare to the concept of "crusade"?*

▶ Investigate the legend of El Cid and explain why he is a legendary Spanish hero. *What does the legend tell about the conditions in Spain during the Reconquest? How much of the legend is based on historical evidence? How would you regard El Cid if you were a Muslim? a Castilian? What was the Almoravid empire and why was El Cid opposing it?*

Grades 9-12

Examples of student achievement of Standard 2B include:

▶ Drawing on literature such as Rudyard Kipling's *Puck of Pook's Hill,* describe what daily life was like as feudalism was developing in the last century of the first millennium CE. *How were the lives of serfs, knights, and lords interrelated? What difference does it make to learn about daily life under feudalism from a novelist like Kipling, from a history textbook, or from looking at the actual tools used by people living in feudal times, the plans of their homes, and legal documents of the time listing their possessions?*

▶ Compare and contrast the population growth, economic growth, and urbanization in Europe, Abbasid Southwest Asia, and Song China after 1000 CE. *What similarities and differences may be found in the causes for this development?*

▶ Describe the developing financial institutions of North Italian cities, and analyze the relationship between banking, trade, and the power of feudal aristocrats.

▶ Research the anti-Semitism of the Crusades. *Why did the call for Crusades arouse anti-Semitic sentiments? How and why did crusaders ravage Jewish communities in western Europe on their way to fight the Muslims?*

▶ Analyze why Latin Christian states and maritime cities achieved commercial and naval dominance over Muslim power in the Mediterranean and Black Sea basins between the 11th and 13th centuries. *What caused these European states to develop a naval power? What is the relationship between commercial and naval development and political strength?*

▶ Define the term "guild" and describe the rise of guilds as economic and social institutions. *What was a guild? How did a guild work? How effective were guilds in promoting economic growth, product quality, and the rights of workers?*

The Bayeux Tapestry recording Duke William of Normandy's conquest of Britain in 1066

Students Should Be Able to:

2C Demonstrate understanding of patterns of social change and cultural achievement in Europe's emerging civilization by:

5-12 Analyzing the changing status of women in medieval European life and ways in which ideals of chivalry and courtly love changed feudal society. [**Analyze cause-and-effect relationships**]

5-12 Describing the life of Jewish communities and their contributions to Europe's cultural and economic development. [**Examine the influence of ideas**]

5-12 Analyzing how the rise of schools and universities in Italy, France, and England contributed to literacy, learning, and scientific advancement. [**Analyze cause-and-effect relationships**]

7-12 Evaluating major works of art, architecture, and literature, and analyzing how they shed light on values and attitudes in Christian society. [**Draw upon visual sources**]

9-12 Assessing the importance of the Islamic states of Iberia and Sicily as well as the Byzantine empire in transmitting scientific and philosophical knowledge to and influencing literature and the arts of western and central Europe. [**Analyze the importance of ideas**]

9-12 Assessing the importance of both Orthodox and Latin Christianity in the cultural and social life of eastern Europe and Russia. [**Examine the importance of ideas**]

| Grades 5-6 | Examples of student achievement of Standard 2C include: |

▶ Collect pictures that demonstrate the architectural differences between houses of worship of this period, for example a Romanesque church, a Gothic cathedral, and a mosque of the Fatimid or Mamluk period in Egypt. Look at your community and locate buildings illustrating architectural elements from this period. Prepare an album of pictures or drawings and explain how these designs relate to the medieval period, and speculate on why modern builders chose to use them.

▶ Define the term "university" and on a map of Europe locate the cities that were home to the major universities of later medieval times. *What was the purpose of the university in medieval Europe? Whom did it educate and why? How did people of that time view the university? Why were universities founded in certain cities? Which country had the most universities?*

▶ Describe a Jewish community in Europe. *What jobs or professions did Jews engage in? How did their work contribute to the development of medieval Europe?*

| Grades 7-8 | Examples of student achievement of Standard 2C include: |

▶ Examine photographic evidence of interior decorations of Gothic churches and Spanish mosques. *How do these designs reflect cultural and religious beliefs and values?*

▶ Read excerpts from literature on courtly love such as Ibn Hazm's essay "The Dove's Necklace" and examples of Andalusian poetry. Compare these works with troubadour poetry and medieval European works on chivalry. *What do they tell about women's lives and their position in society? How did the civilization of Muslim Spain encourage these works and attitudes? What musical influences accompanied this literature?*

▶ Research the origins of Christian universities of Europe and describe their organization and studies. *How did Muslim scholarship and universities influence their development?* Locate important universities in both societies. *By what means did Muslim scholarship become available to Europeans?*

▶ Use evidence from David MacCaulay's video, *Cathedral: The Story of Its Construction,* to explain the cultural importance of Gothic cathedrals. *What role did the craft guilds play in the building of cathedrals? What did these structures indicate about the place of religion in society?*

| Grades 9-12 | **Examples of student achievement of Standard 2C include:** |

▶ Construct a grid to analyze the degree to which women's experiences in feudal European society were determined by social class, area, time, and stage of life. *What life choices were available to women of various classes and marital status in medieval Europe? What was the basis for women's "education"?*

▶ Compare the political and societal influences of Orthodox and Latin Christianity in eastern and western Europe. *How did the religious authority of the papacy differ from that of the patriarch? How did the political influence of the patriarch in the Russian and Greek Orthodox churches differ from that of the pope?*

▶ Trace the ways in which classical works such as those of Aristotle and Plato became a part of medieval philosophy in western Europe. *Was philosophy a part of the offerings of the university? What was the Church's attitude to this non-Christian philosophy?*

▶ Describe the kinds of contact that took place between Spanish and other European Christians and the Muslims of Spain. *How did Muslim Spain absorb information from eastern Muslim culture, India, and China? How did these contacts allow the diffusion of ideas and culture from Muslim Spain into other parts of Europe?*

▶ Compare medieval women's lives as they appear from a reading of excerpts from the 12th-century *Art of Courtly Love* (edited by F. Wilocke, 1957), verses of *Women Troubadours* (M. Byron, 1974), and the late 14th/early 15th-century Pisan's *Treasure of City of Ladies* and Dati's diary (in *Two Memoirs,* edited by G. Buckley, 1972). *In what ways were women subordinate? How did the ideals of courtly love affect them? How did social class influence their experience?*

Women working with wool
Bettmann Archive

STANDARD 3

Students Should Understand: *The rise of the Mongol empire and its consequences for Eurasian peoples, 1200-1350.*

Students Should Be Able to:

3A Demonstrate understanding of the world-historical significance of the Mongol empire by:

5-12 Assessing the career of Chinggis Khan as a conqueror and military innovator in the context of Mongol society. [**Assess the importance of the individual**]

7-12 Describing the destructive Mongol conquests of 1206-1279 and assessing their effects on peoples of China, Southeast Asia, Russia, and Southwest Asia. [**Analyze cause-and-effect relationships**]

9-12 Describing the founding and political character of Mongol rule in China, Central Asia, Southwest Asia, and Russia, and explaining why the unified empire divided into four major successor kingdoms. [**Reconstruct patterns of historical succession and duration**]

9-12 Assessing the usefulness and limitations of the concept of the "Pax Mongolica," and analyzing how long-distance communication and trade led to cultural and technological diffusion across Eurasia. [**Interrogate historical data**]

| **Grades 5-6** | **Examples of student achievement of Standard 3A include:** |

▶ Dramatize major events from the life of Chinggis Khan after reading accounts of his life. *On what basis did you decide what was a "major" event?*

▶ Construct a map showing the extent of Chinggis Khan's conquests. *How far can his success as a conqueror be explained by his use of horses, of bows and arrows, and of military tactics such as feigned retreats?*

▶ Create or illustrate costumes representative of what would have been worn by Mongol warriors and construct models of the weapons used in the conquest of China, Southwest Asia, and Russia. *Does this equipment explain Mongol success?*

| **Grades 7-8** | **Examples of student achievement of Standard 3A include:** |

▶ Write a short story as told by someone your age about the siege of their home city in Persia by a Mongol army. *How would the story differ if it were told by a Mongol warrior?*

▶ Explain the differences in social, political, and economic organization between Mongol steppe nomads and sedentary populations such as those of China and Russia. *What were the relative strengths and weaknesses of each? Why did the Mongols prevail?*

◗ Use the reported remarks of Chinggis Khan — "Man's highest joy is in victory: to conquer one's enemies, to pursue them, to deprive them of their possessions, to make their beloved weep . . ." — to examine the record of Mongol conquests. *Is this an accurate appraisal of Mongol warriors?*

Grades 9-12

Examples of student achievement of Standard 3A include:

◗ Examine the Mongol conquests between 1206 and 1279, and construct a historical argument explaining the relationship between military success and Mongol army organization, weapons, tactics, and policies of terror.

◗ Read the report of John of Plano Carpini, the 13th-century papal emissary, on the Mongol threat and analyze his social and cultural biases about the Mongols.

◗ Prepare a schematic diagram explaining the system of succession followed by Mongol rulers after the death of Chinggis Khan. *How important were the disputes over succession, the absence of a bureaucracy, and increasing divisions between those favoring traditional steppe ways and those adopting the ideas of conquered urban cultures, in the division of the Mongol empire and its eventual decline?*

◗ Analyze the pattern of trade routes that emerged under Mongol domination; explain the location of these routes and list the commodities exchanged. *How do we know about the existence and location of these trade routes?*

◗ Compare selections from the travels in Asia of Marco Polo and Ibn Battuta. Using the descriptions of their travels, account for the flourishing city life in the areas of Mongol domination.

◗ Debate the concept of the "Pax Mongolica," comparing it to the Pax Romana. *Is it worth the cost of terror to have an enforced peace?*

Chinggis Khan
National Palace Museum, Taiwan

Students Should Be Able to:

3B Demonstrate understanding of the significance of Mongol rule in China, Korea, Russia, and Southwest Asia by:

`5-12` Analyzing how Mongol rule affected economy, society, and culture in China and Korea. [**Analyze cause-and-effect relationships**]

`7-12` Explaining the growth of the kingdom of the Golden Horde (Khanate of Kipchak) and its impact on peoples of Russia, Ukraine, Poland, and Hungary. [**Interrogate historical data**]

`9-12` Explaining how the Golden Horde and the Khanate of Persia-Iraq became Islamicized in the 13th and 14th centuries. [**Formulate a position or course of action on an issue**]

`9-12` Describing major characteristics of the Mamluk and Delhi sultanates, and assessing the Mongol failure to conquer Egypt and India. [**Identify issues and problems in the past**]

| Grades 5-6 | **Examples of student achievement of Standard 3B include:** |

▶ Conduct a conversation between two Chinese people under Mongol rule in China, one praising and the other complaining about Mongol rule. *What might each one have to say?*

▶ Find information to debate the proposition that for the Chinese and Koreans, Mongol rule was a disaster.

| Grades 7-8 | **Examples of student achievement of Standard 3B include:** |

▶ Research the accomplishments of Batu and explain what is meant by the "Golden Horde." *How did the Mongols gain control in Russia? Describe their rule.*

▶ As a member of the Golden Horde, write a letter to Khubilai Khan describing your rule in eastern Europe. *How would the description of Mongol rule there differ if written by a Christian Hungarian to the pope?*

| Grades 9-12 | **Examples of student achievement of Standard 3B include:** |

▶ Use historical information to debate the accuracy of the statement by Chinggis Khan's adviser that "the empire was won on horseback but it will not be governed on horseback" when applied to Mongol rule in China.

▶ Construct a museum exhibit using illustrations of selected works of art from the Yuan dynasty and explain the relationship of Chinese artists to the Mongol court. *To what extent did the Yuan dynasty support the arts? What can be discerned about Chinese history from the art of the period?*

▶ Compare the consequences of the Great Khan Ogodei's death for the Mongol enterprise in eastern Europe with the consequences of the Great Khan Mongke's death for Mongol invasion plans of Egypt. *What Mamluk strengths helped to bring about their defeat of the Mongols?*

▶ Construct a graphic organizer to show characteristics of Mongol society and culture, of Muslim society and culture, and of contacts between Mongols and Muslim peoples that would help explain the Islamization of the Golden Horde and the Khanate of Persia-Iraq.

▶ Debate from the points of view of the Chinese, the Russians, and the Southwest Asians the advantages of living under Mongol rule; and evaluate the impact of technological advances, political and fiscal policy, foreign trade, warfare, and military domination.

▶ Trace the extent of the Mongol control in Europe and Southwest Asia on a map. Research reasons for the success of the Mamluks in halting their advance in Egypt.

Architecture of Cairo in the age of the Mamluk dynasty, 13th and 14th centuries
Ross Dunn, slide collection

S T A N D A R D   4

Students Should Understand: *The growth of states, towns, and trade in Sub-Saharan Africa between the 11th and 15th centuries.*

Students Should Be Able to:

4A Demonstrate understanding of the growth of imperial states in West Africa and Ethiopia by:

5-12 Analyzing the importance of agriculture, gold production, and the trans-Saharan caravan trade in the growth of the Mali and Songhay empires. [**Analyze cause-and-effect relationships**]

7-12 Explaining how Islam expanded in West Africa, and assessing its importance in the political and cultural life of Mali and Songhay. [**Examine the influence of ideas**]

5-12 Inferring from bronze sculpture or other evidence the characteristics of the West African forest states of Ile-Ife and Benin. [**Draw upon visual sources**]

5-12 Explaining how a Christian kingdom thrived in the Ethiopian highlands. [**Interrogate historical data**]

Grades 5-6

Examples of student achievement of Standard 4A include:

◗ Draw visual portrayals of desert, semi-arid steppe, savanna, and rain forest climatic zones, and hypothesize how life in each area may be similar and different. *Why is there no permanent settlement in extreme climatic zones?*

◗ Read the story of Solomon and Sheba in the Old Testament and Ethiopian legends of Solomon's role in founding the first dynasty there. *What evidence is there to show that the queen of Sheba was an African monarch?*

◗ Research military technology and tactics of Mali, Bornu, and Songhay as a factor in their success. *Why were horses important in the development of these empires? Why did horses have to be continually imported from North Africa.?*

◗ Draw a map of Africa showing the outline of major kingdoms such as Ghana, Mali, Songhay, Kanem Bornu, and Ethiopia and identify major centers such as Timbuktu, Kilwa, Meroe, and Axum and infer how trade may have moved in Sub-Saharan Africa. *Was trade important to these peoples of Africa? How did it move?*

◗ Look at photography of the bronze works of Benin and Ile-Ife and explain how these may have been created. *What do these art works tell us about the life of these peoples? What do they tell us about the power of monarchs such as Ewuane the Great?*

Grades 7-8

Examples of student achievement of Standard 4A include:

- Diagram one of the churches of Lalaibela. Compare it to the rock temple of Kalash at Ellora in India. *How did such architecture show the influence of other states of Africa and the retreat of African isolation?*

- Compare the political, economic, and social structure of Mali and Songhay. *How important was trade to the two empires? How did the rule of Mansa Musa differ from that of Askia Muhammad? How did the wealth and power of these monarchs compare with that of Christian and Islamic rulers? What roles did Muslim scholars play in governing the cities?*

- Read Ibn Battuta's and Leo Africanus's accounts of travels in Mali and Songhay and evaluate their reports. *What did they admire about these empires? What did they criticize? Why did Ibn Battuta disapprove of the social relations between men and women in Mali?*

- Create a summary evaluation of the Zagwe dynasty of Ethiopia from the view of an Egyptian Coptic Christian. *How would a Muslim from Adal have evaluated the Zagwe history?*

- Investigate the Mali Kingdom of Mansa Musa and accounts of his pilgrimage to Mecca in 1324. *What can you discover about the wealth, power, and capability of this monarch and his kingdom? Given later history, was this pilgrimage a mistake on Mansa Musa's part?*

Grades 9-12

Examples of student achievement of Standard 4A include:

- Compare and contrast the West African Sudan and the East African coast in terms of political, social, economic, and religious developments between the 8th and 13th centuries. *How were these areas of Africa affected by outside influences? What role did commerce play in their development?*

- Draw upon architectural evidence to infer the power of the government in different African states.

- Evaluate the achievements of the Zagwe dynasty of Ethiopia as patrons of Christian art and architecture and explain Ethiopian decorative art. *How did Ethiopians construct rock-hewn churches? What are some of the characteristics of painting in Ethiopian art?*

- Draw evidence from bronze sculpture and other art forms from Ile-Ife and Benin, to infer the role of the ruler, class and gender differences, contact with other peoples, and technology. *How does reading of secondary sources confirm, modify, amplify, or challenge your inferences?*

- Compare Coptic Christianity as to sources, institutions, practices, and art to Latin and Orthodox Christianity. *In what ways did Coptics adapt African traditions to Christian practice?*

- Construct a map of Africa and indicate different religions including the extent of the expansion of Islam. *Why did Islam have such success in Africa? Why did indigenous states give up their tribal religions in favor of Islam or Christianity? How much did commerce and missionaries have to do with the extension of these non-African religions?*

Students Should Be Able to:

4B **Demonstrate understanding of Bantu settlement and Indian Ocean trade in East, Central, and South Africa by:**

`7-12` Explaining the role of Bantu-speaking peoples in the rise of commercial towns on the East African coast and the significance of Swahili as a language of trade. [**Interrogate historical data**]

`5-12` Assessing the importance of Islam, Arab settlement, and maritime trade in the economic and cultural life of Kilwa and other East African coastal cities. [**Analyze cause-and-effect relationships**]

`5-12` Analyzing the importance of Great Zimbabwe as a Bantu state and commercial center with links to the Indian Ocean trade. [**Interrogate historical data**]

| Grades 5-6 | Examples of student achievement of Standard 4B include: |

▸ As an Indian merchant trading in Kilwa, write a letter home about a visit to Great Zimbabwe. Include your reasons for going there, what you saw, and the advantages you will derive from the visit.

▸ Construct a vocabulary chart of Swahili words.

| Grades 7-8 | Examples of student achievement of Standard 4B include: |

▸ Construct a model of the "Great Enclosure" at Great Zimbabwe and develop hypotheses about the purpose of this building. *What questions would need to be answered to help check the validity of your hypotheses? What types of evidence have historians used to reconstruct the history of Bantu-speaking peoples?*

▸ After watching a film on the Khoisan hunter-gatherer peoples of southwest Africa, discuss what sort of encounters are likely to have occurred between the Khoisan and southward-moving Bantu farmers in the early centuries of the second millennium CE. *Why is the territory of Khoisan peoples so restricted today?*

| Grades 9-12 | Examples of student achievement of Standard 4B include: |

▸ Make a simplified chart of the family of Bantu languages. Make a list of basic words in Swahili, Zulu, or other Bantu languages and compare these words for similarities and differences. *What can the relationships among the Bantu languages tell us about the migrations of Bantu-speaking peoples? What major cultural or social differences were found among Bantu-speaking groups? What part did Swahili play as a lingua franca of trade?*

▸ Explain the role of gold in the trade patterns of East Africa during this period. *Where did the traded gold come from and who controlled its source? What else was traded besides gold?* Map the network of trade stretching to Southeast Asia and the Persian Gulf in which the east African KiSwahili-speaking city states such as Kilwe were involved.

◗ Read excerpts from Ibn Battuta about his visit to East Africa and secondary sources on the Swahili-speaking commercial towns there. From them, construct an account of the class structure and Arab-Swahili-Persian influences in these towns. *Who were the ruling elites? How did religion interact with wealth, language, and country of origin in influencing social status?*

Curved steps in one of the structures at Great Zimbabwe, Southern Africa

STANDARD 5

Students Should Understand: *Patterns of crisis and recovery in Afro-Eurasia, 1300-1450.*

Students Should Be Able to:

5A Demonstrate understanding of the Black Death and recurring plague pandemic in the 14th century by:

5-12 Explaining the origins and characteristics of the plague pandemic of the mid-14th century, and describing its spread across Eurasia and North Africa. [**Reconstruct patterns of historical succession and duration**]

7-12 Analyzing the demographic, economic, social, and political effects of the plague pandemic in Eurasia and North Africa in the second half of the 14th century. [**Evidence historical perspectives**]

9-12 Assessing ways in which long-term climatic change contributed to Europe's economic and social crisis in the 14th century. [**Interrogate historical data**]

Grades 5-6 | Examples of student achievement of Standard 5A include:

▶ Describe what might happen to the daily life of a Southwest Asian or European town suddenly afflicted with plague.

▶ Write a short story or script a play about families in Christian Europe and Islamic Europe and Southwest Asia during the height of the Black Death. Include information on topics such as: *Did people know the causes of the plague? How did they respond to the plague? Was the response different in Christian and Islamic areas? How did the plague change the lives of those who survived?*

Grades 7-8 | Examples of student achievement of Standard 5A include:

▶ Map the origin and spread of the plague on a physical relief map. Hypothesize about the connection of the spread of the disease with the flow of goods along the Silk Route due to Mongol control of the region. Connect the spread of the disease in Europe to heavy rains and poor crops that had already weakened the population. *What areas were spared the ravages of the plague?*

▶ Draw evidence from primary source documents and visual materials to infer how villagers in western Europe and Southwest Asia responded to the Black Death. Write an account describing how you would have reacted if you were a villager and a deadly mysterious disease was threatening your village. Record whether or not your reactions would have been the same as those shown in the sources, explaining why or why not.

▶ Chart the population before the plague and after the plague in areas affected by the disease. *How consistent were mortality rates in different areas? What other causes for high mortality besides the plague were present in Europe in the 14th and 15th centuries? What results followed from the high mortality?*

▶ Drawing information from books such as Ann Turner's *The Way Home*, and Ann Cheetham's *The Pit*, discuss the impact of the plague on young people. *What options were available to them? What evidence would the authors have had to draw on to construct their accounts?*

Grades 9-12

Examples of student achievement of Standard 5A include:

▶ Read and discuss accounts of the effects of the Black Death by Europeans writing at the time, such as Boccaccio. Read Ibn Battuta's accounts of its effects on Syria and Egypt. Compare these accounts. *What aspects of the disease and of its effects did contemporaries focus on?*

▶ Examine primary sources, such as Jacob von Konigshofen's chronicle of the cremation of Strasbourg Jews, and secondary accounts of scapegoating during the Great Plague. *How did the pogroms affect Jewish communities in the Holy Roman Empire? Why did Jews flee to Poland and Russia in the mid-14th century? What do the accounts of scapegoating tell you about attitudes and values in Europe during the Middle Ages?*

▶ Describe the medical, administrative, and psychological measures taken in attempts to cope with the plague in the 14th century. *What other measures could have been taken under 14th-century conditions had the transmission of plague through fleas and rats, as well as by direct human-to-human contagion, been known?*

▶ Make a list of what you consider to be the likely consequences of the high mortality, prolonged fear, loss of close human ties, and breakdown in public services that went with the recurrent pandemics of the 14th and 15th centuries, and check your hypotheses against historical evidence. *What impact did the Black Death have on economic, social, political, and religious life?*

Illustration of the Black Death, Art Resources

Students Should Be Able to:

5B Demonstrate understanding of transformations in Europe following the economic and demographic crises of the 14th century by:

`5-12` Analyzing major changes in the agrarian and commercial economies of Europe in the context of drastic population decline. [**Evidence historical perspective**]

`7-12` Assessing the effects of crises in the Catholic Church on its organization and prestige. [**Analyze cause-and-effect relationships**]

`5-12` Analyzing causes and consequences of the Hundred Years War and repeated popular uprisings in Europe in the 14th century. [**Analyze cause-and-effect relationships**]

`9-12` Analyzing the resurgence of centralized monarchies and economically powerful city-states in western Europe in the 15th century. [**Reconstruct patterns of historical succession and duration**]

`7-12` Defining humanism as it emerged in Italy in the 14th and 15th centuries, and analyzing how study of Greco-Roman antiquity and critical analysis of texts gave rise to new forms of literature, philosophy, and education. [**Examine the influence of ideas**]

`5-12` Evaluating the aesthetic and cultural significance of major changes in the techniques of painting, sculpture, and architecture. [**Evidence historical perspectives**]

Grades 5-6

Examples of student achievement of Standard 5B include:

▶ Look at examples of Greek and Roman and then of Renaissance art and architecture. *How did the former influence the latter?*

▶ Study peasant uprisings such as that of Wat Tyler, 1381 to understand what led the peasants to rebel. Plot on a map and create a time line for the major rebellions in Europe between 1300 and 1500. *Were these rebellions due to the same causes?*

▶ Write short biographies of persons involved in the Hundred Years War such as the English kings Edward III and Henry V, French king Charles VII, and Joan of Arc, focusing on their part in the war.

Grades 7-8

Examples of student achievement of Standard 5B include:

▶ Use examples from European history, following the Great Plague, to explain how a substantive decrease in population raised the price of labor. *How did governments seek to maintain previous wage levels? What were the results of these attempts?*

▶ In dyads, assume the roles of an English and a French chronicler and debate the causes of the Hundred Years War.

▶ Develop a role-play activity or write a skit of the conflict between King Philip IV of France and Pope Boniface VIII. *How do you think Holy Roman Emperor Henry IV or King John of England would have responded to the conflict if they were alive at this time? How would Pope Gregory VII or Innocent III have responded? What does the conflict between Philip and Boniface indicate about the power of the papacy in the early 14th century?*

Grades 9-12

Examples of student achievement of Standard 5B include:

▶ Assess the impact of climatic change in an agricultural system that already reached the upper limit of productivity, and the social and political consequences (famine, disorder).

▶ Explain how decreasing revenues led to competition between nobles for other sources of income, raising the incidence of civil war (e.g., German robber barons).

▶ Compare the power and prestige of the papacy at the time of the Babylonian captivity and Great Western Schism to the papacy of Innocent III, a century and a half earlier. *How might the conflict between the popes at Avignon and Rome have stimulated reform movements within the Catholic Church? To what extent did the problems within the Catholic Church stimulate kings and princes to challenge papal authority? Did the Great Western Schism pave the way for the Protestant Reformation?*

▶ Read the accounts of the trial of Joan of Arc from the official report of the proceeding. *Why was Joan tried in a church court? What was the charge brought against her? What accounts for the Catholic Church's review of her trial a quarter of a century later? Why is Joan revered as a patron saint of France?*

▶ Develop a list of the characteristics of Italian 15th-century humanism. *What reasons can you give for its emergence in this time and place? Which segments of the population were most significantly influenced by Italian humanism?*

▶ Create a Venn diagram showing the relationship between economic changes and population decline.

▶ Research the European role of gunpowder in weaponry, compared to traditional weaponry (mounted knights with lances, longbow, etc.). *What social and political effects did the use of gunpowder have? How did it strengthen royal power?*

▶ Write a set of educational recommendations in accordance with humanist ideals. *Who should be educated, how, and what should they learn?*

Erasmus dictating to his secretary. Wood cut from Erasmus' On the Duties of Secretaries. 1531

Students Should Be Able to:

5C Demonstrate understanding of major political developments in Asia in the aftermath of the collapse of Mongol rule and the plague pandemic by:

9-12 Analyzing reasons for the collapse of the Mongol rule in China and the reconstituting of the empire under the Chinese Ming dynasty. [Reconstruct patterns of historical succession and duration]

7-12 Assessing the impact of the conquests of Timur (Tamerlane) on Central Asia, Southwest Asia, and India and evaluating Timurid contributions to arts and sciences. [Assess the importance of the individual]

5-12 Analyzing the origins and early expansion of the Ottoman state up to the capture of Constantinople. [Reconstruct patterns of historical succession and duration]

Grades 5-6 | Examples of student achievement of Standard 5C include:

▶ Write a biography of Osman. *How did his achievements lay the foundations of the Ottoman empire?*

▶ Using overlays, map the expansion of the Ottoman State during the 1st century-and-a-half of its existence. *How would you account for the Ottomans' success?*

Grades 7-8 | Examples of student achievement of Standard 5C include:

▶ Research the empire of Timur the Lame (Tamerlane) and assess the impact of his conquests on Southwest Asia and India. *What part was played in Timur's successes by mobility, opponents' weakness, and a strategy of terror? How would you compare and contrast Timur and Chinggis Khan as conquerors, destroyers, and empire builders?*

▶ Compare Samarkand under Timur with Baghdad under the Abbasids. *How did their rulers contribute to the flourishing cultural life in each? How important was governmental support of the arts and sciences?*

▶ Compare the Ottoman *ghazi* warriors to European knights.

Grades 9-12 | Examples of student achievement of Standard 5C include:

▶ Make a list of the weaknesses of Mongol rule in China (such as problems of succession, corruption, and laxity) and reasons for Chinese discontent (such as favoring of Mongols for high government positions and inability to maintain order). *What part did these factors play in the collapse of Mongol rule in China?*

▶ Write a biography of the Hongwu emperor, focusing on his economic and political reforms. *To what extent was he restoring continuity with pre-Yuan conditions?*

▶ Compare the conquests of Timur with those of Chinggis Khan. *How did their treatment of resisting and submitting peoples contribute to their successes? What were the benefits and disadvantages of their rule for their Mongol followers, and for their subject peoples? To what extent was each influenced by values or ideas from the cultures they came in contact with?*

▶ Compare and contrast Timur's patronage of scholars, artists, and scientists at Samarkand with the patronage taking place in Italian city-states at the same time. *To what extent was the "Republic of Letters" a widespread phenomenon in the civilized world during this period? What evidence is there for communication among scholars and artists across cultural and religious lines?*

▶ Trace the rise of the Ottoman Empire from its beginning in Asia Minor under Osman to the conquest of Constantinople by Sultan Mohammed II. *What accounts for the success of the Ottoman Empire?*

Tamerlane's forces attacking a Moslem fort, British Library

STANDARD 6

Students Should Understand: *The expansion of states and civilizations in the Americas, 1000-1500.*

Students Should Be Able to:

6A **Demonstrate understanding of the development of complex societies and states in North America and Mesoamerica by:**

7-12 Explaining major characteristics of Toltecs, Anasazi, Pueblo, and North American mound-building peoples. [**Compare and contrast differing values and institutions**]

5-12 Analyzing how the Aztec empire arose in the 14th century. [**Interrogate historical data**]

7-12 Analyzing patterns of long-distance trade centered in Mesoamerica. [**Formulate historical questions**]

| Grades 5-6 | **Examples of student achievement of Standard 6A include:** |

▶ Research the different types of sources (archaeological, artistic, written, etc.) that can be used to illustrate life in the Americas before the coming of the Europeans.

▶ Construct a model of Tenochtitlán and label the most important buildings in the city. *Why did the Aztecs call this city the "Foundation of Heaven"?*

| Grades 7-8 | **Examples of student achievement of Standard 6A include:** |

▶ Compare and contrast the ways in which the natural environments of the North American plains, the southwestern deserts, and the tropical forests of Yucatan affected the organizations of societies in these regions.

▶ Demonstrate a knowledge of the Aztecs by constructing an example of an artifact such as a royal robe or the Aztec calendar or a floating garden (chinampa) and describing its use and relationship to Aztec culture.

▶ Read excerpts from Bernal Diaz's *True History of the Conquest of New Spain* comparing Tenochtitlán to European cities. *What were the unique qualities of Tenochtitlán as described by Bernal Diaz?*

▶ Read excerpts of Bernardino de Sahagún's *The General History of the Things of New Spain* that pertain to the proper behavior for different roles of both men and women in Aztec society. *What does this account by a Spanish missionary reveal about the characteristics of Aztec culture?*

Grades 9-12

Examples of student achievement of Standard 6A include:

▸ Locate on a map the territory occupied by the Aztecs in their early nomadic warrior period (to 1325), the settlement at Tenochtitlán about 1325, and its emergence to a dominant position over the other city-states of Mexico by the late 15th century.

▸ Interpret evidence from codices or archaeological remains for the social role and status of women in Aztec society. *Among the Maya, Inca, and Aztec societies, which seemed the most positive and which seemed the most negative for women?*

▸ Write an account from the point of view of residents of Tenochtitlán or Spanish soldiers or priests, including descriptions of the complex organization of markets providing food and luxury goods to the population (partly from tribute of subject peoples); the use of efficient, intensive agriculture in chinampas in the lake; fishing in the lake; well-engineered causeways; canals; dikes to separate salt water from fresh water; and the central temple and palace complex.

▸ Draw upon slides or pictures of the mound center located at Cahokia in Illinois. Consider the evidence for this center being a city comparable to cities of the same period in Eurasia or Africa. Develop arguments for and against the proposition that a major civilization developed in the Mississippi valley after about 1000 AD.

▸ Investigate evidence to establish the development of the Mississippi valley center. *How do legends of various Indian nations reflect the introduction of the bow and arrow (ca. 400 CE) and a new dependency upon eastern flint corn around the time that Mississippian center began to develop? How do 18th-century French accounts of the Natchez help to illuminate the Mississippian ceremonial associated with mound-building centers in this era?*

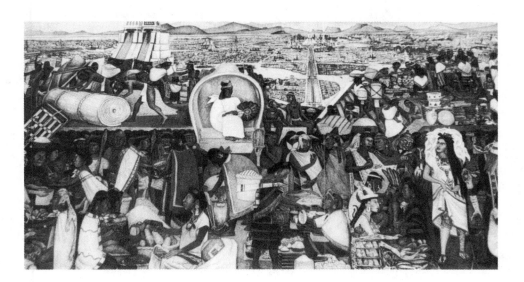

Great Tenochtitlán from a mural by Diego Rivera National Palace, Mexico City

Students Should Be Able to:

6B Demonstrate understanding of the development of the Inca empire in Andean South America by:

`5-12` Analyzing Inca expansion and methods of imperial unification. [**Evidence historical perspectives**]

`7-12` Analyzing the Inca social, political, religious, and economic institutions and their development. [**Interrogate historical data**]

`7-12` Comparing Aztec and Inca in government, economy, religion, and social organization. [**Compare and contrast differing values and institutions**]

Grades 5-6

Examples of student achievement of Standard 6B include:

▶ Draw graphic diagrams comparing the structure of Inca and Aztec societies indicating the roles of groups such as family, class, priests, warriors, and governors.

▶ Make a list of the different food plants that were the basis of Inca and Aztec agriculture.

▶ Construct a mural showing various aspects of Incan society, and explain what the illustrations reveal about the structure of society. *What was everyday life like for the common people living in the empire?*

Grades 7-8

Examples of student achievement of Standard 6B include:

▶ Construct a three-dimensional map of the Inca empire, and use different colors to show the expansion of the empire over time (ca. 1230 to 1525). *What problems did the geography of the empire present? What were the variations in climate within the empire? How did altitude and terrain affect Inca agriculture?*

▶ Describe the Inca communication system and consider how it contributed to both effective central government and long-distance trade.

▶ Compare Inca and Aztec temples. *What do Inca and Aztec artistic styles in metalwork, textiles, and pottery reveal about their cultural achievements?*

▶ Describe the discovery of Machu Picchu, and explain what the site can tell us about the Inca civilization.

Grades 9-12

Examples of student achievement of Standard 6B include:

▶ Analyze gender roles in the Caribbean, Mesoamerican, and Andean societies using visual source material such as religious images and myths. *Which of the qualities of the gods seem to fit descriptions of roles expected and admired in men and women?*

‣ Compare the Inca capital of Cuzco and Inca engineering of roads and bridges and irrigation systems with the Aztec capital of Tenochtitlán and its attendant technology, as well as with technology and urbanism of the Mound-builders in North America.

‣ Evaluate the argument by some historians that the Inca empire was an early "welfare state." *How does Inca government compare with that of the Aztecs?*

‣ Explain how the Inca rulers overcame the problems of governing an enormous, geographically and climatically diverse group of territories. *What impelled the Inca conquests and expansion?*

A Chimu god forming the handle of a ceremonial knife
Museo Ora del Peru, Monterrico, Lima

ERA 6

The Emergence of the First Global Age 1450-1770

Giving Shape to World History

The Iberian voyages of the late 15th and early 16th centuries linked not only Europe with the Americas but laid down a communications net that ultimately joined every region of the world with every other region. As the era progressed ships became safer, bigger, and faster, and the volume of world commerce soared. The web of overland roads and trails expanded as well to carry goods and people in and out of the interior regions of Eurasia, Africa, and the American continents. The demographic, social, and cultural consequences of this great global link-up were immense.

The deep transformations that occurred in the world during this era may be set in the context of three overarching patterns of change.

▶ **The Acceleration of Change:** The most conspicuous characteristic of this era was the great acceleration of change in the way people lived, worked, and thought. In these 300 years human society became profoundly different from the way it had been in the entire 5,000 years since the emergence of civilizations. Five aspects of change were especially prominent. Though American Indian populations declined catastrophically in the aftermath of the first European intrusions, world numbers on the whole started their steep upward curve that continues to the present. The globalizing of communications produced intensified economic and cultural encounters and exchanges among diverse peoples of Eurasia, Africa, and the Americas. Capitalism emerged as the dominant system for organizing production, labor, and trade in the world. Innovations in technology and science multiplied and continuously built on one another. European thinkers, drawing on a worldwide fund of ideas, formulated revolutionary new views of nature and the cosmos, ideas that challenged older religious and philosophical perspectives.

▶ **Europe and the World; the World and Europe:** Europeans came to exert greater power and influence in the world at large than any people of a single region had ever done before. In the Americas Europeans erected colonial regimes and frontiers of European settlement that drew upon various European traditions of law, religion, government, and culture. Europeans seized relatively little territory in Africa and Asia in this era, but their naval and commercial enterprises profoundly affected patterns of production and interregional trade. The trade in human beings between Africa and the Americas to provide a labor force for European commercial agriculture was a particularly catastrophic aspect of the expanding global economy. Closely linked to Europe's far-reaching global involvement was its own internal transformation — political, social, economic, and intellectual. In this era peoples almost everywhere had at some time to come to terms with European arms and economic clout, but as of 1750 Europe by no means dominated the world scene.

▶ **Empires of Eurasia:** Indeed, the greater share of the world's peoples, cities, agrarian wealth, and land-based military power were in this era and still concentrated in the region stretching from the eastern Mediterranean to China. Between the late 14th and early 16th centuries four huge empires arose to dominate the greater part of Eurasia and northern Africa. Effectively employing artillery and other firearms to expand territorially and maintain law and order among diverse populations, the Ming, Ottoman, Mughal, and Safavid states have sometimes been called "gunpowder empires." They unified such large areas of Afro-Eurasia — politically, economically, and culturally — that they contributed much to processes of globalization.

Why Study This Era?

▶ All the forces that have made the world of the past 500 years "modern" were activated during this era. A grasp of the complexities of global interdependence today requires a knowledge of how the world economy arose and the ways in which it produced both enormous material advances and wider social and political inequalities.

▶ The founding of the British colonies in North America in the 17th century took place within a much wider context of events: the catastrophic decline of American Indian populations, the rise of the Spanish empire, the African slave trade, and the trans-Atlantic trade and migration of Europeans. The history of colonial America makes sense only in relation to this larger scene.

▶ Any useful understanding of American political institutions and cultural values depends on a critical grasp of the European heritage of this era.

▶ The great empires of Eurasia — Ottoman, Persian, Mughal, and Ming/Qing — all experienced cultural flowerings that paralleled the Renaissance in Europe. These achievements are an important part of our contemporary global heritage.

What Students Should Understand

Standard 1: How the transoceanic interlinking of all major regions of the world from 1450 to 1600 led to global transformations

    A. **European overseas expansion** in the 15th and 16th centuries [CORE]

    B. **Encounters** between Europeans and peoples of Sub-Saharan Africa, Asia, and the Americas in the late 15th and early 16th centuries [CORE]

    C. The consequences of the worldwide exchange of **flora, fauna, and pathogens** [RELATED]

Standard 2: How European society experienced political, economic, and cultural transformations in an age of global intercommunication, 1450-1750

    A. Demographic, economic, and social **trends in Europe** [CORE]

    B. **Renaissance,** Reformation, **and** Catholic **Reformation** [CORE]

    C. The rising military and bureaucratic **power of European states** between the 16th and 18th centuries [CORE]

    D. The **scientific revolution and** the **Enlightenment** [CORE]

Standard 3: How large territorial empires dominated much of Eurasia between the 16th and 18th centuries

    A. The extent and limits of **Chinese regional power** under the Ming dynasty [CORE]

    B. How Southeast Europe and Southwest Asia became unified under the **Ottoman Empire** [CORE]

    C. The rise of the **Safavid and Mughal empires** [RELATED]

Standard 4: Economic, political, and cultural interrelations among peoples of Africa, Europe, and the Americas, 1500-1750

    A. How **European** powers asserted **dominance in the Americas** between the 16th and 18th centuries [CORE]

    B. The origins and consequences of trans-Atlantic **African slave trade** [CORE]

    C. Patterns of **change in Africa** in the era of the slave trade [RELATED]

Standard 5: How Asian societies responded to the challenges of expanding European power and forces of the world economy

    A. The development of **European** maritime **power in Asia** [CORE]

    B. **Transformations in India, China, and Japan** in an era of expanding European commercial power [CORE]

    C. Major **cultural trends in Asia** between the 16th and 18th centuries [RELATED]

Standard 6: Major global trends from 1450 to 1770 [RELATED]

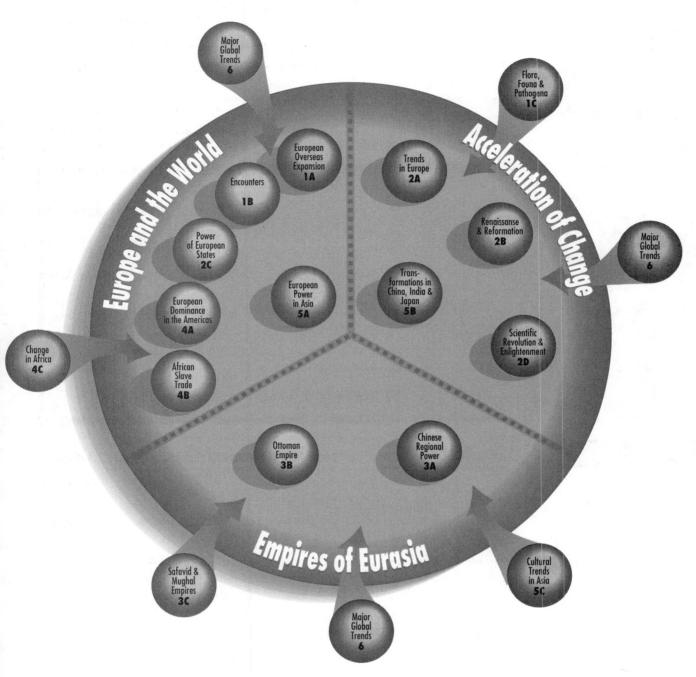

**Relationships Among Major Developments,
Core Standards, and Related Standards for Era 6**

STANDARD 1

Students Should Understand: *How the transoceanic interlinking of all major regions of the world from 1450 to 1600 led to global transformations.*

Students Should Be Able to:

1A Demonstrate understanding of the origins and consequences of European overseas expansion in the 15th and 16th centuries by:

5–12 Explaining major characteristics of the interregional trading system that linked peoples of Africa, Asia, and Europe on the eve of the European overseas voyages. [**Consider multiple perspectives**]

9–12 Analyzing the major social, economic, political, and cultural features of European society, and in particular of Spain and Portugal, that stimulated exploration and conquest overseas. [**Identify issues and problems in the past**]

5–12 Identifying major technological innovations that the Portuguese and Spanish made in shipbuilding, navigation, and naval warfare. [**Analyze cause-and-effect relationships**]

7–12 Analyzing the motives, nature, and short-term significance of the major Iberian military and commercial expeditions to Sub-Saharan Africa, Asia, and the Americas in the late 15th and early 16th centuries. [**Identify issues and problems in the past**]

Grades 5-6

Examples of student achievement of Standard 1A include:

▶ Trace the routes of Zheng He, Díaz, Vasco da Gama, Columbus, and the Polynesians on a world map and explain how they used prevailing wind currents to reach their destinations. Select two locations to travel between by a sail boat and use information from maps and wind currents to chart the best route.

▶ Research an invention for navigation such as the compass, astrolabe, or quadrant. Find out where it originated and how it was used. Demonstrate, using visuals, its impact on exploration and trade. *How did mariners navigate before these inventions? What is used today for the same purpose?*

▶ Compare diagrams of a Portuguese caravel, Indian Ocean dhow, and Chinese junk of the 15th or 16th centuries to assess their sailing abilities. *What advantages for long-distance travel did each type of vessel have? What advantages did innovations such as the stern-post rudder offer?*

▶ Construct a picture story of the life of Columbus. Use a map to locate his voyages while in service of the Portuguese off Africa and during his voyages to America. *How would you have viewed Columbus if you were one of the sailors during the first voyage to America? What would you think about Columbus if you had been one of the Taino "Indians" on the island of Guanahaní (San Salvador) in 1492?*

| Grades 7-8 | **Examples of student achievement of Standard 1A include:** |

◆ Create a poster, diorama, or a three-dimensional model of a rudder, smooth and clinker-built hull, compass, astrolabe or types of sails as used in navigation and shipbuilding in the latter part of the 15th century. *Where did these technologies originate? How did they affect trade?*

◆ Construct a historical argument or debate on such questions as: *Were the voyages of Columbus a "discovery"? To what extent were the contacts between Amerindians and Europeans "conquest" and/or "exchange"?*

◆ Examine images of the Portuguese that Benin craftsmen created to ascertain the relationship between the people of Benin and the Portuguese during their first years of contact. *How was a person's relative status shown in Benin art? What types of Benin art objects were in demand in Europe?*

◆ In dyads, role-play interviews with Jewish and Muslim scholars and artisans to determine their contributions to Iberian culture. Theorize and draw conclusions about the effects on Iberia of the loss of the talents of Jews and Muslims after they were expelled. *Where did Jews settle? Where did Muslims go? What did these groups contribute to their new home states?*

| Grades 9-12 | **Examples of student achievement of Standard 1A include:** |

◆ Analyze Chinese naval and commercial activities in the Indian Ocean in the early 15th century. *What do Chinese fleets reveal about Chinese technology and wealth at this time? How did the Chinese use a tribute system as a means of trade?*

◆ Taking the point of view of a Spanish general and a Muslim court official of Granada, debate the likely consequences of the Spanish conquest of Granada in 1492. Taking the point of view of a Spanish bishop, explain the forced conversion or exile of Jews and Muslims from Spain in the early 16th century.

◆ Assume the role of an adviser to King João II of Portugal and develop a position paper outlining Portugal's trade goals and potential routes to attain these goals. *Why did the Portuguese monarch reject Columbus's scheme to reach the Indies by sailing west?*

◆ Write an illustrated essay on how the lateen sail, the sternpost rudder, or the magnetic compass contributed to the technology of shipbuilding and navigation in 15th-century Portugal. *Where are these three inventions likely to have been first used? How did the magnetic compass, which was in use in earlier centuries in China, give mariners of the Mediterranean or Atlantic greater confidence in sailing out of sight of land during the winter months? How is the lateen sail idea likely to have diffused from the Indian Ocean to the western Mediterranean? What are the advantages and disadvantages of a "fore-and-aft" sail like the lateen in comparison with a square sail?*

◆ Analyze the Iberian states' organization for overseas trade and colonization. Assess the influence of the Reconquista campaigns. *What measures were taken to exclude Mudejar Muslims, converts, and Jews from settling in the Americas? How effective were these measures?*

Students Should Be Able to:

1B Demonstrate understanding of the encounters between Europeans and peoples of Sub-Saharan Africa, Asia, and the Americas in the late 15th and early 16th centuries by:

5-12 Analyzing the character of Portuguese maritime expansion to Africa, India, and Southeast Asia and assessing the impact of Portuguese intervention on society and commerce in these regions. [**Formulate historical questions**]

7-12 Analyzing the success of the Ottoman, Indian, Chinese, and Japanese powers in restricting European commercial, military, and political penetration in the 16th century. [**Analyze cause-and-effect relationships**]

5-12 Describing the political and military collision between the Spanish and the Aztec and Inca empires and analyzing why these empires collapsed. [**Identify issues and problems in the past**]

7-12 Explaining the founding and organization of Spanish and Portuguese colonial empires in the Americas and assessing the role of the Church in colonial administration and policies regarding American Indian populations. [**Interrogate historical data**]

Grades 5-6

Examples of student achievement of Standard 1B include:

▶ Research and write an account of King Affonso II of the Kongo and his relations to the Portuguese.

▶ Investigate stories of the lives of Montezuma, Malinche, Cortés, Atahualpa, and Pizarro. Sketch pictures of the encounters of Aztecs, Incas, and the Spanish.

▶ Research the life of Bartholomew de las Casas and explain why las Casas has been called the defender of the Indians. *Does he deserve that title?*

▶ Map Cortés's journey into Mexico and examine both indigenous and European depictions of the conquest of Tenochtitlán. Evaluate the point of view of the sources.

▶ Using books such as Scott O'Dell's *The King's Fifth*, discuss the motivations behind Spanish conquests of the New World, and particularly, of the Aztec and Inca empires.

Grades 7-8

Examples of student achievement of Standard 1B include:

▶ Research the possible reasons the strong Inca empire fell to Pizarro. *What caused the Inca to delay in defending themselves against the Spanish? What strategies did the Spaniards use to capture Atahualpa?*

▶ Construct a map identifying the major ports and enclaves held by the Portuguese in Africa and Asia in the 16th century. Explain how the Portuguese succeeded in dominating seaborne trade in the Indian Ocean basin for several decades. *How much military or political influence did the Portuguese have over the states and empires of Africa and Asia? How did the leaders in these areas view the Portuguese?*

◆ Conduct a debate among las Casas, Sepúlveda, the Quakers in North America, and the Jesuits in Paraguay over the treatment of Amerindians. Evaluate the role of religious sects in the treatment of the Amerindians.

◆ Drawing on books such as Scott O'Dell's *The Amethyst Ring*, *The Captive*, and *The Feathered Serpent* and Gloria Duran's *Malinche: Slave Princess of Cortez*, discuss the impact of Spanish conquest on the day-to-day lives of Aztec, Maya, and Inca peoples.

Grades 9-12	**Examples of student achievement of Standard 1B include:**

◆ Examine the tradition of free trade on the Indian Ocean's northern rim. *How did that tradition influence the response of local rulers to European penetration?*

◆ Examine the causes and explain the consequences of the conflict between Portuguese and Ottoman Turkish military power in the Red Sea, Arabian Sea, and Ethiopia in the early 16th century.

◆ Compare the Portuguese impact on West African and East African peoples in the late 15th and the 16th centuries. *Did the presence of Portuguese naval vessels and merchants have any impact on the kingdom of Benin? What consequences did the coming of the Portuguese have for the maritime trade of the East African city-states? Why did the Portuguese settle in the Zambezi River valley and how did they affect African trade and politics?*

◆ Investigate the impact Christian missionaries had on Sub-Saharan Africa and Asia during the 16th century.

◆ Construct a comparative balance sheet of early Iberian colonialism in the Americas and Asia. *How did the European military impact on these two regions differ?*

◆ Research the role of the Catholic Church in the colonial administration of Spanish America. *How did the Church become both the defender and the oppressor of Indians?*

◆ Compare the strategies, tactics, and assumptions of Turks, Indians, Japanese, and Chinese in dealing with foreign merchants in the 16th century. *In what ways did they underestimate the threat posed by European naval power?*

◆ Research the Japanese reactions to activities of the Portuguese and Spanish. *In what ways were Hideyoshi's invasions of Korea a response to Spanish takeover of the Philippines?*

◆ Assess the means by which Spain and Portugal ruled their colonial empires in the Americas. *What effect did the encomienda system have on the local people? How was military and civil authority exercised? What role did the Church play?*

◆ Compare the Spanish organization of labor in the Americas with the system of labor in a European manor.

Students Should Be Able to:

1C Demonstrate understanding of the consequences of the worldwide exchange of flora, fauna, and pathogens by:

5-12 Assessing ways in which the exchange of plants and animals between the Americas and Afro-Eurasia in the late 15th and the 16th centuries affected European, Asian, African, and American Indian societies and commerce. [**Analyze cause-and-effect relationships**]

5-12 Analyzing why the introduction of new disease microorganisms in the Americas after 1492 had such devastating demographic and social effects on American Indian populations. [**Analyze cause-and-effect relationships**]

9-12 Assessing the effects that knowledge of the peoples, geography, and natural environment of the Americas had on European religious and intellectual life. [**Clarify information on the geographic setting**]

| **Grades 5-6** | **Examples of student achievement of Standard 1C include:** |

- Explain the origins of "cowboy" culture in the Americas. *Where did the equipment and methods of livestock farming originate?*

- Research a different plant or domestic animal that was transported by exploration and, on a large outline map of the world, graphically represent its route. On the same map, indicate the direction and route of diseases that spread during the age of exploration and colonization.

- Keep a journal of foods you eat for a day. Cross out those items that would not be available had the worldwide exchange not taken place. Diagram on a map where the various foods you are eating were first grown.

- Research the characteristics of so-called weeds brought to the Americas during the 15th and 16th centuries. *How do they attempt to stabilize the soil and prevent erosion? How do they affect other plants?*

- Research the effects of the horse, sheep, and pig on life in the Americas. *How did they change land use and agricultural patterns?*

| **Grades 7-8** | **Examples of student achievement of Standard 1C include:** |

- Construct graphs of estimated population trends in the Americas, Europe, and East Asia in the 16th and 17th centuries. *Why did populations drastically decline in parts of the Americas but rise in Europe and East Asia?*

- Draw a map and place the items of flora and fauna exchange at their points of origin. Illustrate on the map the global dispersions of these items. Select a place in Africa, Asia, Europe, or the Americas and plan a menu for two banquets, one before "the exchange" and the other after.

- Distinguish between commercial and domestic crops. Assume the role of a plantation owner in colonial Spanish or Portuguese America and list the requirements for crop growth, including a labor force.

▶ Draw evidence from primary and secondary source materials to describe the effects of disease on the Amerindian population. Examine the effects of disease on the psyche of the Amerindians in terms of their belief in their leaders and their long-held traditions. *Why was it possible for so few Europeans to dominate the indigenous peoples? To what extent may the spread of disease have made it easier to make converts to Christianity?*

Grades 9-12

Examples of student achievement of Standard 1C include:

▶ Trace the "travels" of one item from the flora (sugar, coffee, cassava, corn, potato) and one from fauna (horse, cattle, chicken, pig) from the first transfer forward through the 16th through 18th centuries. Explain the impact of these on the world economy.

▶ Develop a chart that catalogs the diseases that were transferred as a result of the explorations and colonizations of the 16th and 17th centuries. Include the areas they would affect, the means by which they were spread, the immunities of native populations to these diseases, and the impact that the spread of disease had upon individual societies, globalization, world trade, and political expansion and control.

▶ Select a specific native population such as Aztec, Inca, Zuni, Tuscarora, Powhatan, or Iroquois and, using primary and secondary sources, explain the demographic changes that transpired. Hypothesize as to the effects disease-driven demographics might have on the psyche of the selected Indian nation.

▶ Examine the fundamental plantation systems introduced to the New World as a result of the explorations, and investigate the ways in which disease and the plantation were interrelated.

▶ Draw on sources such as *Seeds of Change: A Quincentennial Commemoration*, edited by Herman J. Viola and Carol Margolis, to analyze the impact of worldwide exchange of people, flora, fauna, and pathogens on contemporary ecology, economy, and culture.

▶ Assess how the encounter with Amerindian civilizations contributed to European ideas such as romanticized images of the "noble savage," systems of classifications of peoples, natural history, and cartography.

Ancient Incas harvesting corn. From Guamán Poma de Ayala, Nueva Cronica, courtesy of Det Kongelige Bibliotek, Copenhagen.

STANDARD 2

Students Should Understand: *How European society experienced political, economic, and cultural transformations in an age of global intercommunication, 1450-1750.*

Students Should Be Able to:

2A Demonstrate understanding of demographic, economic, and social trends in Europe by:

5-12 Describing characteristics of the family and peasant society in early modern Europe, and assessing changes in social relations, including serfdom and the status of women, in eastern and western Europe. **[Analyze cause-and-effect relationships]**

7-12 Analyzing the social and economic consequences of population growth and urbanization in Europe from the 15th to the 18th centuries. **[Utilize visual and mathematical data]**

9-12 Describing major institutions of capitalism, and analyzing how the emerging capitalist economy transformed agricultural production, manufacturing, and the uses of labor. **[Analyze cause-and-effect relationships]**

Grades 5-6

Examples of student achievement of Standard 2A include:

▶ Compare selections from Leon Battista Alberti's *Book of the Family* with ideas about current families. *Under what circumstances do our ideas of family change?*

▶ Research one of the social classes of early modern Europe and construct a project that illustrates occupations, a typical home, and the roles of men, women, and children.

▶ Research what factors reveal a woman's status in the period 1450-1750. Determine the relative changes in status among women in different social classes from earlier periods and during these centuries. Role-play a conversation among women representing various classes, discussing how their positions in society have changed and why.

▶ Consult manuals from this period explaining the responsibilities of husbands and wives. *How do the expectations of wives compare with earlier attitudes? How did Protestants and Catholics differ in their attitudes toward marriage?*

Grades 7-8

Examples of student achievement of Standard 2A include:

▶ Research the Spanish silver trade from America and its effect on world trade.

▶ Locate on a map the major cities of Europe at the beginning of the 17th century. On an overlay indicate the major urban areas toward the end of the 18th century. *How do the maps differ? What accounts for the development of large urban centers?*

◆ Explain the "agrarian revolution." *What factors caused the "revolution"? How did the agricultural revolution change society? Were the effects of the agricultural revolution felt throughout western and eastern Europe?*

Grades 9-12

Examples of student achievement of Standard 2A include:

◆ Investigate the "price revolution" in 16th-century Europe. *What is the evidence that it happened? What caused it?*

◆ Using data from the period 1550-1700, graph the increase of agricultural production, the increase in productivity, and population increase in Europe. Hypothesize why production increased while productivity showed little increase. Relate this to population and technology changes during the period.

◆ Assume the role of a merchant and prepare a rationale for trading in the world economy of the 16th century. *What products would you select to trade? What are the existing markets and what markets need to be created? How would you finance, transport, and market goods? What problems are peculiar to each market item? What role would you expect the state to take in trade and commerce?*

◆ Research how Dutch and English merchants amassed enough capital to explore and make significant investments in overseas areas. Create a brochure aimed at attracting investors.

◆ Using historical evidence, draw a chart showing changes in men's and women's work options resulting from developments such as the increased division between capital and labor, and the increasing emphasis on wages as a defining characteristic of "work." *What effect did family roles, class, and geographical location have on women's work in this period? In what ways did their work situation remain unchanged?*

A banker and his wife by Flemish painter Quentin Matsys
Alinari, Art Resources Bureau

Students Should Be Able to:

2B Demonstrate understanding of the Renaissance, Reformation, and Catholic Reformation by:

5-12 Analyzing the social and intellectual significance of the technological innovation of printing with movable type. [**Demonstrate and explain the influence of ideas**]

7-12 Explaining connections between the Italian Renaissance and the development of humanist ideas in Europe north of the Alps. [**Compare and contrast differing sets of ideas and values**]

5-12 Evaluating major achievements in literature, music, painting, sculpture, and architecture in 16th-century Europe. [**Draw upon visual data and literary sources**]

5-12 Explaining discontent among Europeans with the late medieval Church, and analyzing the beliefs and ideas of the leading Protestant reformers. [**Marshal evidence of antecedent circumstances**]

5-12 Explaining the aims and policies of the Catholic Reformation, and assessing the impact of religious reforms and divisions on European cultural values, family life, and relations between men and women. [**Analyze cause-and-effect relationships**]

9-12 Analyzing causes of religious wars in 16th and 17th century Europe, and their effects on the establishment of religious pluralism. [**Marshal evidence of antecedent circumstances**]

Grades 5-6

Examples of student achievement of Standard 2B include:

▶ Research the development of linear perspective in art in 15th-16th-century Europe and make a camera obscura.

▶ Keep a record of the time it takes to copy a page of a textbook by hand. Multiply this by the number of pages in the book to determine how many hours it might take to reproduce one book by hand. Discuss how the printing press increased the spread of knowledge.

▶ Select a leading person during the Renaissance and Reformation and research the life of the individual. Assemble information about the person using illustrations to help explain his or her contributions to society.

Grades 7-8

Examples of student achievement of Standard 2B include:

▶ Compare the Gutenberg printing press with that used by Benjamin Franklin and with a modern printing press. *How has the technology changed? How has the new technology influenced learning and communication?*

▶ Research the changing gender roles during the Renaissance and Reformation. Using a television panel show format, interview a cross section of women about their lives and interests. *Did the status of women improve during this period of time? Who were the leading women of the period?*

▶ Construct a map showing the geographical patterns of religious affiliation in Europe in the early 17th century. *What factors might have contributed to the conversion of specific populations to Protestant faiths?*

▸ Study examples of Renaissance architecture and examine local buildings, churches, and homes to determine the influence of Renaissance architecture. Collect photographs of public buildings in the United States and display them with pictures of the Renaissance buildings that inspired them.

▸ Select illustrations to display in a classroom "museum" that show the changes in art and architecture from the Middle Ages through the High Renaissance. Describe the changes and draw conclusions about how the points of view of artists changed.

Grades 9-12

Examples of student achievement of Standard 2B include:

▸ Read excerpts from Machiavelli's *The Prince* and compare his understanding of "realpolitik" with earlier writers like Kautilya (*Arthashastra*) and the Qin Legalists such as Han Fei. *Could Machiavelli have been influenced by these earlier philosophies?*

▸ Examine excerpts from Renaissance writers such as Petrarch, Boccaccio, Cervantes, Erasmus, More, and Shakespeare. *How did authors reflect the spirit of Renaissance humanism in their works?* Compare and contrast northern humanism with that of the Italian Renaissance.

▸ Assess the impact of the rediscovery of Greco-Roman antiquity in the 15th century and its role in the development of new forms of art and scholarship. *Who were the leading figures in the revival of Classical architecture and sculpture? What factors stimulated the rediscovery?*

▸ Analyze the theological views of leading reformers of the Reformation such as Luther, Calvin, and the Anabaptists. *How did their central beliefs challenge the practices and authority of Roman Catholicism of their day? What were the consequences?*

▸ Assume the role of a Protestant woman writer, such as Katherine Zell, and respond to Luther's assertion, *"The rule remains with the husband, and the wife is compelled to obey him by God's command. . . . The woman . . . should stay at home and look after the affairs of the household."*

▸ Examine the major political, social, and economic consequences of the religious wars in Europe in the 16th and 17th centuries. *What were the political repercussions of these conflicts? To what extent does modern Europe reflect the consequences of these struggles?*

▸ Use books such as Irving Stone's *The Agony and the Ecstasy*, Claudia Van Canon's *The Inheritance*, and Barbara Willard's *A Cold Wind Blowing* to discuss social oppression and conflict in Europe during the Renaissance. *How did such conditions conflict with prevailing humanist principles?*

Martin Luther,
an engraving by Cranach

Students Should Be Able to:

2C Demonstrate understanding of the rising military and bureaucratic power of European states between the 16th and 18th centuries by:

`7-12` Analyzing the nature and development of strong bureaucratic monarchies in the 16th century. [**Analyze cause-and-effect relationships**]

`9-12` Explaining how the Dutch Republic emerged as a powerful European state. [**Formulate historical questions**]

`5-12` Explaining how the English civil war and the Revolution of 1688 affected government, religion, economy, and society in that country. [**Analyze cause-and-effect relationships**]

`5-12` Comparing characteristics of absolutist monarchy in France, Prussia, and the Habsburg empire. [**Compare and contrast differing sets of ideas**]

`5-12` Analyzing the nature and growth of the Russian monarchy and the success of Russian expansion in the Caucasus, Central Asia, and Siberia. [**Reconstruct patterns of historical succession and duration**]

Grades 5-6

Examples of student achievement of Standard 2C include:

- Explain the impact gunpowder had on European warfare and collect pictures to show how fortifications changed after the introduction of gunpowder.

- Working within small groups, examine the lives of leading political figures such as Henry VIII, Elizabeth I, Philip II, James I, Oliver Cromwell, Louis XIV, or Peter the Great. Incorporate pictures and sketches with information regarding the life and accomplishments of the selected leader.

- Develop a list of newly won freedoms that an English person would have after the Revolution of 1688.

Grades 7-8

Examples of student achievement of Standard 2C include:

- Research Elizabeth I's reign and explain her accomplishments as queen of England. *How effective was Elizabeth's leadership? To what extent did her actions contribute to the development of a strong national state?*

- Trace the spread of gunpowder from China to Europe, and assess the role of gunpowder in establishing and maintaining the power of leaders of the European states during this period.

- Assume the role of Catherine the Great or one of her chief ministers and prepare a manual for leadership to advise future Russian rulers on how to govern.

- Research the founding of St. Petersburg. *Why was St. Petersburg called the "window on the West"?*

- Drawing on books such as E. M. Almedingen's *The Crimson Oak* and Erik Christian Haugaard's *Cromwell's Boy*, describe what life was like for people living in European monarchies. *How were conditions in various states different?*

♦ Identify three characteristics of an "absolute" monarch and debate the extent to which James I of England, Louis XIV of France, and Peter I of Russia were absolute monarchs. *Which other rulers would you characterize as absolute? How does their authority compare with that of the emperors of China or the Ottoman sultans?*

♦ Identify the long-range and immediate causes of the English Revolution of 1688. Debate the extent to which this revolution was "Glorious." *What were the effects of English ideas of popular resistance and liberty upon the development of self-government in the American colonies?*

♦ Trace the spread of gunpowder from China to Europe, and assess the role of gunpowder in establishing and maintaining the power of leaders of the European states during this period.

Grades 9-12

Examples of student achievement of Standard 2C include:

♦ Compare the pressures for building and maintaining a large army today with those of states in the 17th and early 18th centuries. *What was Machiavelli's advice regarding the use of mercenaries? Was this advice followed in early modern Europe?*

♦ Write a defense of your position during the English Civil War from the perspective of a Cavalier or Roundhead.

♦ Write a biographical sketch of the Louis XIV, emphasizing ways in which royal pomp and ceremony were used to represent absolutist power.

♦ Construct a map of Russia with overlays showing the expansion of territory from the close of the 16th century through the end of the 18th century. *What appear to be Russia's goals in territorial expansion? What lands did Russia acquire during the reigns of Peter the Great and Catherine the Great?*

♦ Research the reign of Frederick the Great, Catherine the Great, and Joseph II. *Which of these monarchs best deserves the title "Enlightened Despot"?*

♦ Compare the characteristics of government and the growth of power of the Dutch Republic with the characteristics of other states during this period. *What role did commerce play in determining who exercised political power? What were the results of the Dutch attitude toward various religious groups?*

♦ Write an essay explaining how Amsterdam gained commercial supremacy from the northern Italian city-states in the latter part of the 16th century. Compare Amsterdam's ascendancy with the decline of Venice.

♦ Use books such as Barbara Willard's *A Flight of Swans* and *Harrow and Harvest* to analyze some of the divisions and conflicts within European monarchies.

♦ Contrast English political development which established Parliament's supremacy over the crown with the development of absolutism in France under Louis XIV. *What were the long-term effects of these separate developments?*

Students Should Be Able to:

2D Demonstrate understanding of the Scientific Revolution and the Enlightenment by:

`5-12` Analyzing the cultural, religious, and scientific impact of astronomical discoveries and innovations from Copernicus to Newton. [**Assess the importance of the individual in history**]

`5-12` Analyzing the importance of discoveries in mathematics, physics, biology, and chemistry on 17th- and 18th-century European society. [**Examine the influence of ideas**]

`7-12` Accounting for the coexistence of the new scientific rationalism in 17th- and 18th-century Europe with traditional learning and practices such as astrology, magic, and witchcraft. [**Examine the influence of ideas**]

`9-12` Explaining the principal ideas of the Enlightenment and how these ideas contributed to the reform of church and state. [**Demonstrate and explain the influence of ideas**]

`7-12` Analyzing ways in which scientific and philosophic knowledge was communicated throughout Europe. [**Examine the influence of ideas**]

Grades 5-6

Examples of student achievement of Standard 2D include:

▶ Define the word "revolution" and explain what is meant by the Scientific Revolution.

▶ Research one of the great thinkers and scientists of the Scientific Revolution such as Copernicus, Vesalius, Galileo, Bacon, or Newton. Use information gathered through research to construct a short essay, poem, or play emphasizing what was new about his ideas.

▶ Research the life of Denis Diderot. *How did he exemplify Enlightenment ideas? What similar works like the encyclopedia, dictionary, and thesaurus existed in other cultures?*

Grades 7-8

Examples of student achievement of Standard 2D include:

▶ Using the scientific method, chart the major constellations and note the position of the sun as it rises and sets over a period of two to three weeks. *Does such a chart indicate that the stars and planets revolve around the earth or that the earth revolves around the sun?* Debate the statement: *Superstitions prevented people from accepting the scientific method.*

▶ Investigate the concepts of scientific method advanced by Francis Bacon and René Descartes. *What other scientists influenced these thinkers?*

▶ Research the trial of Galileo. Assuming the roles of defense and prosecution, conduct a simulated trial presenting evidence of Galileo's innocence and guilt. Evaluate the arguments presented in the context of the 17th century.

▶ Analyze one of Shakespeare's plays such as Macbeth or Hamlet and cite examples of references to ghosts, witches, or spirits. *What do such references tell us about 16th- or 17th-century belief in the supernatural? What consequences resulted from those beliefs? Were such beliefs considered scientifically sound at the time?*

◆ Construct a chart or a time line showing the important events that marked the Scientific Revolution and the person or persons associated with each. Write a biography of one person for a science "hall of fame." Select from major fields of endeavor such as astronomy, mathematics, biology, earth science, physics, chemistry, botany, and medicine.

Grades 9-12

Examples of student achievement of Standard 2D include:

◆ Draw evidence from Galileo's letter to the Grand Duchess Christina (1615) to explain Galileo's ideas about the solar system. Discuss Galileo's points in light of religious conservatism and the Scientific Revolution. *Why does Galileo feel it is dangerous to apply scriptural passages to science-related problems?*

◆ Draw from excerpts of René Descartes's *Discourse on Method* to explain his approach to discovering truth. In dyads, assume the role of a scientist and a churchman and debate the apparent conflict between religion and science in the context of the 17th century.

◆ Analyze the proposition that the Newtonian vision of a universe of order, predictability, and harmony influenced Enlightenment thought and generated optimism that progress and perfectability were possible in human affairs.

◆ Research the Parisian salons and their influence in spreading Enlightenment thought. *What were the roles of aristocratic and bourgeois women in promoting the Enlightenment? What influence did the salons have on French political affairs? Why did some men criticize the salons as superficial and organize exclusively male salons?*

◆ Write an appraisal of Immanuel Kant's "motto" of the Enlightenment, "Dare to Know! Have the courage to use your own intelligence!" *To what extent was the Enlightenment dependent on the Scientific Revolution?*

◆ Assume the role of an Enlightened philosopher and appraise the laws and governmental system of an early 18th-century monarchy. Devise a plan to re-structure that system having it conform with the Enlightenment.

◆ Research and cite specific examples of how Chinese humanist philosophy influenced the ideas of Voltaire, Leibniz, and Quesnay. *How did these European thinkers learn about Chinese philosophy? What rationale did Chinese philosophy offer these Enlightenment thinkers as a basis for human morality and ethics?*

◆ Research the titles of some important books translated from non-European languages like Arabic and Chinese that were found in the libraries of European universities and scientists during this period. *Who undertook these translations?*

A Parisian salon,
an engraving by Moreau le Jeune

STANDARD 3

Students Should Understand: *How large territorial empires dominated much of Eurasia between the 16th and 18th centuries.*

Students Should Be Able to:

3A Demonstrate understanding of the extent and limits of Chinese regional power under the Ming dynasty by:

5-12 Analyzing the power and limits of imperial absolutism under the Ming dynasty. [**Analyze cause-and-effect relationships**]

9-12 Analyzing the effects of commercialization on social relations among gentry elites, urban merchants, and peasants. [**Analyze cause-and-effect relationships**]

5-12 Analyzing China's changing attitudes toward external political and commercial relations following the Zheng He voyages (1405-33). [**Formulate historical questions**]

7-12 Assessing the effects of the introduction of American food crops and importation of American silver on demographic, economic, and social change in China. [**Analyze cause-and-effect relationships**]

9-12 Comparing the role of Neo-Confucianism, Buddhism, and Daoism in Chinese government and society. [**Compare and contrast differing sets of ideas**]

Grades 5-6

Examples of student achievement of Standard 3A include:

▶ Research the reign of Emperor Taizu (reign title: Hongwu), founder of the Ming dynasty, and compare his policies and actions with those of Suleiman. Analyze the extent to which they were reformers or despots.

▶ Research the voyages of Zheng He in order to assess Chinese naval and commercial activities in the Indian Ocean in the early 15th century and assess explanations for cessation of government-sponsored activities in this region. *What do the fleets of Zheng He reveal about Chinese maritime technology at this time? What might have been a Ming ruler's cost-benefit analysis of overseas trade? Where was the major military threat to China?*

▶ Playing the role of a Chinese scholar-bureaucrat, explain why China is the "Middle Kingdom" in the world and why other countries have a tributary relationship to the celestial empire. *In what way are this gentleman's views an expression of ethnocentrism? Have other peoples seen themselves as the "central" place in the world?*

Grades 7-8

Examples of student achievement of Standard 3A include:

▶ Assess the power of the Ming emperors at various stages of Ming rule. *Should Ming government be called despotic? To what extent was the ruler's control absolute? What aspects of Chinese society did the emperor control? What high offices did the Ming eliminate? What officials were responsible to the emperor?*

▶ Compare the services the state expected from the various groups in society. *What services were expected from the gentry? What were the roles of the military, merchant, and commoner classes? In what ways was a separation among the gentry, merchants, and peasants established and maintained in Ming society? What use did Ming leaders make of such things as jobs, clothes, taxation, and corvée?*

▶ Assess the military strategy of the Ming. *Where was the political threat to their empire? To what extent was defense their main concern?*

▶ Research rice production and reforestation projects under the Ming. *What was the importance of new crops and/or new technology? Why and how were people relocated?*

Grades 9-12

Examples of student achievement of Standard 3A include:

▶ Explain the methods that the Ming used to bring cultural unity to China, particularly in eliminating Mongol influences and re-establishing Confucian and Daoist values. *How does this compare with efforts at tolerance and cultural pluralism in other empires at the time such as the Mughal and Ottoman?*

▶ Write an essay demonstrating that under the Ming, neo-Confucianism overshadowed Buddhism and Daoism. *How did neo-Confucian philosophers like Wang Yangming absorb Buddhist teachings into official Confucianism?*

▶ Drawing on selections from the satirical novel *The Scholars* or from *China's Examination Hell* by Conrad, assess the role of the imperial examination system. *Why did the Ming reestablish it? What types of questions were included? How did the examination system foster neo-Confucian values and assure the appointment of bureaucrats of merit? How does the examination system compare with our civil service exams and SATs?*

▶ Evaluate the evidence that more than one-third of the silver mined in the Americas between 1527 and 1821 ended up in China. *Why did China receive so much silver? What were the implications for Chinese society in moving from payment in kind to payments in silver? In what ways was the Ming court in Beijing isolated from the commercial activity of the south?*

▶ List the various ways the central government in China controlled people's lives; mention, for example, job allocation, service to the government including taxation and *corvée*, and where one lived. *What were the symbols of central authority that surrounded the ruler? What power did eunuchs in the service of the court have?*

Students Should Be Able to:

3B Demonstrate understanding of how Southeast Europe and Southwest Asia became unified under the Ottoman Empire by:

`5-12` Analyzing how the capture of Constantinople and the destruction of Byzantium contributed to the expansion of Ottoman power. [**Hypothesize the influence of the past**]

`5-12` Analyzing reasons for Ottoman military successes against Persia, Egypt, the North African states, and Christian European kingdoms. [**Analyze cause-and-effect relationships**]

`7-12` Analyzing the political, institutional, and economic development of the empire in the context of its religious and ethnic diversity. [**Analyze multiple causation**]

`5-12` Evaluating the artistic, architectural, and literary achievements of the empire in the 15th and 16th centuries. [**Draw upon visual, literary, and musical sources**]

`9-12` Analyzing how Muslim, Greek Orthodox, and Roman Catholic peoples interacted in southeastern Europe under Ottoman rule. [**Examine the influence of ideas, human interests, and beliefs**]

Grades 5-6

Examples of student achievement of Standard 3B include:

▶ Research the life of Suleiman the Magnificent. *Why is he given the title "the Magnificent"? What leader living today would you call "the magnificent"? Why?*

▶ Make overlay maps of the extent of the Byzantine and Ottoman empires at various periods, particularly focusing on the 14th and 15th centuries, to determine their relative strength. *How can you account for the changes in territory each empire controlled?*

▶ Research the events in Constantinople in 1453 and write a report of the events from the perspectives of different people, such as a Christian resident of Constantinople, or an Ottoman soldier, or someone living in Spain or the Vatican.

▶ Research and describe the various aspects of the Ottoman military and explain the importance of firearms in Ottoman expansion. *What motivated the troops? How did they combine cavalry and infantry? What made their enemies consider the janissaries such a formidable foe?*

▶ Make a model of one of the buildings designed by Sinan Pasha such as the Suleimaniye mosque in Constantinople. Compare the use of space with buildings such as St. Peter's in Rome.

Grades 7-8

Examples of student achievement of Standard 3B include:

▶ Compare the *ghazi* warrior with the European feudal knight or the Japanese samurai as social types.

▶ Describe and compare the military, political, and cultural achievements of Mehmet the Conqueror and Suleiman the Magnificent. *What contributed to their successes?*

♦ Construct a map of the main trade routes passing through the Ottoman Empire. *How important was international trade in the empire's economy? How did the development of the sea route around Africa affect trade in the empire?*

♦ Assume the role of a journalist and report on the Ottoman seizure of Constantinople in 1453. *Why did Christian Europeans regard the fall of the city as such a catastrophic event?*

Grades 9-12	**Examples of student achievement of Standard 3B include:**

♦ Compare the emergence of the Ottomans as a world power between 1450 and 1650 with that of the Spanish during the same period. *How did both Ottoman Turks and Castilians come to dominate richer neighbors and ultimately rule vast territories? How did they enlist the support of their subject peoples?*

♦ Analyze in what ways the Ottoman Empire was similar to the Byzantine Empire. *What administrative and legal practices were retained? What influences from Islamic and Turkic models of administration and law are evident? What role did the Sultan's household play in ruling the state?*

♦ After reading excerpts from Ghislain de Busbecq's book describing the life of the Ottomans, write a letter from de Busbecq to the Austrian and Russian monarchs recommending changes they need to make in order to meet the threat from the Ottomans.

♦ On a map or map overlays, show the lands of the Ottoman Empire at different periods: the fall of Constantinople (1453); the defeat of the Safavids (1514); the second siege of Vienna (1683); and the rapid contraction of the empire at the end of the 17th century. Assess the difficulties in holding such a vast empire, especially noting the many different religious communities under Ottoman control.

♦ Research the role of women and the family in the Ottoman Empire. *What was the legal position of women in the empire? How did the legal status of women compare to that of other Islamic states? What political and social roles did women of the imperial harem play in the Ottoman state? What rules applied to non-Moslem women within the Ottoman Empire?*

♦ Assess the state revenues of the Ottoman court under Suleiman. *What were the sources of revenue? How were they collected? On what did the Ottoman court spend its revenues? How important were building projects such as state-supported mosques, schools, and public baths? What role did pious charitable foundations play in establishing hospitals, schools, soup kitchens, and other public projects?*

♦ Assess the ethnic and religious diversity of peoples within the Ottoman Empire. Evaluate the effects of Ottoman governance on the various social, religious, and ethnic groups. *Why did many Jews expelled from Spain in 1492 settle under the Ottomans? How were Orthodox Christian populations such as those in Serbia and Bosnia treated by the Ottoman Turks?*

Students Should Be Able to:

3C Demonstrate understanding of the rise of the Safavid and Mughal empires by:

5–12 Explaining the unification of Persia under the Turkic Safavids, and evaluating Safavid political and cultural achievements under Shah Abbas. [**Analyze cause-and-effect relationships**]

5–12 Explaining the Mughal conquest of India and the success of the Turkic warrior class in uniting the diverse peoples of the Indian subcontinent. [**Formulate a position or course of action on an issue**]

7–12 Analyzing the relationship between Muslims and Hindus in the empire, and comparing Akbar's governing methods and religious ideas with those of other Mughal emperors, such as Aurangzeb. [**Examine the influence of ideas, human interests, and beliefs**]

9–12 Evaluating the interplay of indigenous Indian, Persian, and European influences in Mughal artistic, architectural, literary, and scientific achievements. [**Draw upon the visual and literary sources**]

5–12 Assessing the importance of Indian textiles, spices, and other products in the network of Afro-Eurasian trade in the 16th and 17th centuries. [**Formulate historical questions**]

| **Grades 5-6** | **Examples of student achievement of Standard 3C include:** |

▶ Research and report on the achievements of the Safavid ruler Shah Abbas. *In what ways did he support trade and commerce? How did he encourage trade with European merchants?*

▶ Write a letter to a European court describing the grandeur of the Safavid golden age during the reign of Shah Abbas I. Assemble illustrations of Safavid art and architecture to illustrate architectural style, paintings, ceramics, and carpets.

▶ Imagine you were a member of Babur's army as it conquered the armies of the Sultanate of Delhi. Report your impressions of the military campaign and of North India.

▶ What spices did Vasco da Gama buy from the local Indian merchants in 1498? What was included in the Indian mixture of spices that the early European traders called "curry"? How did the sale of the spices da Gama brought back to Europe set off a rush to India to deal in the spice trade?

| **Grades 7-8** | **Examples of student achievement of Standard 3C include:** |

▶ On a map of southwestern Asia show the extent of the Safavid Empire and create a time line to show its expansion. *How did Shi'a Islam become dominant in Persia during the Safavid period? What other factors contributed to the success of the Safavid rule?*

▶ Construct a map showing the locations from which the Safavid state began and indicate the movement of people into Iran and Afghanistan. Show the extension of the empire and the key cities of Tabriz and Isfahan.

▶ What Indian textiles were popular among Europeans during the 16th and 17th centuries? *How did the large market for Indian cloth in Europe undermine the East India Company's goal of selling more British goods in India than it imported?*

◗ Describe Isfahan during the reign of Shah Abbas I, including such buildings as the Isfahan mosque. Compare Isfahan with Ottoman Istanbul, or with Agra or Delhi under the Mughals. *How does it compare with cities in Europe at this time?*

Examples of student achievement of Standard 3C include:

◗ Assess the reasons Ismail was able to create the Safavid empire. *How did he win the support of the Qizilbash nomadic tribesmen? What was the basis of his legitimacy? What was his attitude toward Sufi, Shi'i, and Sunni forms of Islam?*

◗ Draft a statement to be sent throughout the Mughal empire listing Akbar's methods for creating harmony among the various groups he ruled. *How do his strategies compare with the way the Ottoman Empire treated minorities or the way Elizabeth I of England handled Protestant-Catholic tensions?*

◗ How do the Agra Red Fort, the Taj Mahal, and the Audience Hall at Fatehpur Sikri suggest a synthesis of Muslim and Hindu architecture and artistic motifs? How do these buildings combine Hindu and Islamic motifs?

◗ Create a series of maps, charts, and time lines comparing the Ottoman, Safavid, and Moghul empires. Include geographic extension; penetration of other states; dates of their beginning, height, and demise; art and architecture; scholarship; degree of tolerance; and economic endeavors.

◗ Research Akbar's religious attitudes and his attempts to unite his culturally diverse empire. *How did he encourage religious tolerance? How do the policies he established for his religiously pluralistic empire compare with those of Elizabeth I?*

◗ Drawing upon visual and written sources, describe either the monumental architecture or the miniature art of the Mughal empire. *In what ways do these art forms reflect a blending of Persian, Islamic, and Hindu traditions?*

◗ Research the attitude of the six major Mughal emperors from Babur to Aurangzeb on an issue such as how to treat minorities, religious beliefs, military expansion, or architectural and literary accomplishments. Write an essay comparing their ideas. *How can you account for the differences among these rulers?*

◗ Drawing evidence from primary and secondary sources, trace the evolution of the Safavid social and political system from its nomadic-warrior beginnings under Ismail to the golden age of Shah Abbas I.

The Taj Mahal, built by Shah Jahan in the 17th century as a tomb for his wife, Mumtaz

STANDARD 4

Students Should Understand: *Economic, political, and cultural interrelations among peoples of Africa, Europe, and the Americas, 1500-1750.*

Students Should Be Able to:

4A Demonstrate understanding of how European powers asserted dominance in the Americas between the 16th and 18th centuries by:

[5-12] Defining and comparing four major types of European activity and control in the Americas: large territorial empires, trading-post empires, plantation colonies, and settler colonies. [**Compare and contrast differing sets of ideas**]

[9-12] Describing the administrative system of the Spanish viceroyalties of Peru and Mexico, and analyzing the importance of silver production and Indian agriculture in the Spanish colonial economy. [**Interrogate historical data**]

[5-12] Analyzing how Holland, England, and France became naval, commercial, and political powers in the Atlantic basin in the 16th and 17th centuries. [**Marshal evidence of antecedent circumstances**]

[7-12] Assessing the moral, political, and cultural role of Catholic and Protestant Christianity in the European colonies in the Americas. [**Examine the influence of ideas, human interests, and beliefs**]

[7-12] Explaining why historians have called the Seven Years War the first "global war," and assessing its consequences for Britain, France, Spain, and the indigenous peoples of the American colonial territories. [**Analyze cause-and-effect relationships**]

| Grades 5-6 | Examples of student achievement of Standard 4A include: |

- On a map of the Americas and India, locate areas of British and French influence. Explain why the British and French wanted to trade in these regions.

- Research daily life in the Spanish colonies in the Americas. In an illustration, draw yourself and your friends doing what you would be doing if you lived in one of the Spanish colonies during the colonial period.

- Assume the role of an adviser to a European government and argue for or against the establishment of a policy of mercantilism. *How would this policy help the mother country? What advantages would it have for the colonists?*

| Grades 7-8 | Examples of student achievement of Standard 4A include: |

- Working with three other students, create lists of the duties of colonial administrators in the Spanish empire in Peru, a French trading-post empire in the Great Lakes region, a plantation colony of Barbados, and a British settler colony in Massachusetts. *What duties are the same? What duties are different?* Discuss the advantages and disadvantages to serving in the various areas.

- Locate on a world map military campaigns during the Seven Years War. *Why is this war considered a "world" war?*

- Analyze the ways the power of Holland, England, and France were enhanced by their relationships with various American Indian nations.

- Explain how the Dutch East India Company was chartered by the state to conduct diplomatic, economic, and military functions. *How did the Dutch East India Company get monopoly control over the world's supply of nutmeg and mace? What difference did that make?*

- Role-play a 16th-century Catholic missionary sent to the Americas to convert people. Write a letter home describing Amerindian beliefs and explaining how you might go about the conversion.

Grades 9-12

Examples of student achievement of Standard 4A include:

- Define mercantilism and explain why colonial powers adopted this system. *In what ways was mercantilist theory and practice different in Holland, France, and England? Would it be possible for this economic policy to be successful today?*

- Drawing on information contained in Alfred Crosby's books *The Columbian Exchange* and *Ecological Imperialism*, explain why Europeans founded large land empires and settler colonies in the Americas in the 16th and 17th centuries, but asserted these forms of control almost nowhere in Africa or Asia.

- Write an essay hypothesizing why Catholics were generally more successful than Protestants in converting non-Europeans between the 16th and 18th centuries.

- Create a chart showing the diversity of the government, the economy, the military, and the organization of societies in different European colonies around the world. Analyze why colonization differed in trading-post colonies and settled colonies.

- Compare and contrast examples of types of European activity and control: the Spanish empire of Peru, the French trading-post empire in the Great Lakes region, the slave plantation colony of Barbados, and the British settler colony of Massachusetts.

- Research the emergence of Native American prophets such as Neolin (the Delaware Prophet) in the aftermath of the Seven Years War. *In what way was the emergence of the Seneca prophet Handsome Lake related to the aftermath of the American Revolution?*

- Research daily life in the Spanish colonies in the Americas. Explain what you and your friends would be if you lived there during the colonial period. *What part would Indian agricultural and silver production have played in your lives?*

Students Should Be Able to:

4B Demonstrate understanding of the origins and consequences of the trans-Atlantic Af slave trade by:

7–12 Analyzing the ways in which Europeans exploited American Indian labor and why commercial ture came to rely overwhelmingly on African slave labor. [**Evidence historical perspectives**]

7–12 Comparing ways in which slavery or other forms of social bondage were practiced in the Isla Christian Europe, and West Africa. [**Compare and contrast differing sets of ideas**]

5–12 Explaining how commercial sugar production spread from the Mediterranean to the Ame analyzing why sugar, tobacco, and other crops grown in the Americas became so import world economy. [**Analyze cause-and-effect relationships**]

7–12 Explaining the organization of long-distance trade in West and Central Africa, and analyzi cumstances under which African governments, elites, merchants, or other groups participa sale of slaves to Europeans. [**Identify issues and problems in the past**]

5–12 Explaining how European governments and firms organized and financed the trans-Atlantic s and describing the conditions under which slaves made the "middle passage" from Af Americas. [**Evidence historical perspectives**]

9–12 Analyzing the emergence of social hierarchies based on race in both the Iberian empire and colonies in the Americas. [**Interrogate historical data**]

5–12 Describing conditions of slave life on plantations in the Caribbean, Brazil, and British Nor and analyzing ways in which slaves perpetuated aspects of African cults and carried on r plantation servitude. [**Evidence historical perspectives**]

| Grades 5-6 | Examples of student achievement of Standard 4B ind |

▶ Draw a diagram of a slave ship to show how slaves were tr

▶ Read several primary sources recounting the capture and ....aves to the New World. Write an account of the slave trade from ....ves of a West African leader and a European social reformer. *Do thes..... .....differ? Why or why not?*

▶ Study pictures of plantation life in the Americas and write captions for the illustrations from the point of view of a slave and plantation owner.

▶ From the perspective of an Amerindian, write journal entries describing daily life as a pearl diver, silver miner, or plantation worker.

▶ Research the rising popularity of new consumer products such as coffee, tea, sugar, tobacco, and opium all around the world in the 17th and 18th centuries. *Why did these products gain mass acceptance? What is the per capita consumption of these products in various nations today?*

▶ Graphically represent the origins and destinations for slaves taken from Africa to the Americas on a large world map.

Grades 7-8

Examples of student achievement of Standard 4B include:

▶ Examine the working conditions on sugar plantations in the Caribbean. *Why did African slaves come to supply most of the labor needs for commercial plantations? Why not American Indian labor, European indentured servitude, or free wage labor?*

▶ Recount the efforts of the kingdoms of Kongo and Benin to resist the trans-Atlantic slave trade? *Why did some African governments oppose the trade and others participate in it?*

▶ Conduct a read-around using excerpts from the 18th-century autobiography, *The Interesting Narrative of the Life of Olaudah Equiano or Gustavus Vasa. Written by Himself. How authentic is Equiano's account of the "middle passage"? What does it reveal about the treatment of enslaved peoples? What forms of resistance to enslavement were used during the middle passage?*

Grades 9-12

Examples of student achievement of Standard 4B include:

▶ Trace the evolution of systems of labor in 16th-17th-century Spanish America: from encomienda to hacienda.

▶ Explain the encomienda system and assess its effects on Indians. *What was the intent of the encomienda when it was established? How was the encomienda used by Spanish colonists? Is the encomienda comparable to slavery?*

▶ Explain the *Leyenda Negra. How did other countries use the "Black Legend" to build opposition to Spain? To what extent did the dealings of other European states with native populations differ from those of Spain?*

▶ Analyze primary and secondary source material, including illustrations of laborers in silver mines and on plantations, to assess the variety of ways in which Europeans exploited American Indian labor.

▶ Explain the political, social, and economic circumstances under which African merchants, political elites, and other groups participated in the capture of slaves and their sale to European slave traders. *How did the African concept of slavery differ from that adopted by European settlers in the Americas?*

▶ Construct a comparative chart illustrating the ways in which ancient, medieval, and early modern societies instituted social bondage and slavery prior to the Atlantic slave trade. Compare and contrast ways in which bondage was practiced in the Islamic lands, Christian Europe, and West Africa. *How did the Atlantic slave trade differ from previous historical examples of slavery?*

Students Should Be Able to:

4C Demonstrate understanding of patterns of change in Africa in the era of the slave trade by:

7-12 Explaining the emergence of African states such as Ashanti, Dahomey, and Oyo in the context of the slave trade and the expanding world economy. [**Formulate historical questions**]

5-12 Assessing how the slave trade affected population, economic systems, family life, and relations between men and women in West and Central Africa. [**Analyze cause-and-effect relationships**]

7-12 Describing government, trade, cultural traditions, and urban life in the Songhay Empire in the 16th century and analyzing reasons for the empire's collapse at the end of the century. [**Interrogate historical data**]

9-12 Analyzing regional and international circumstances under which large new states such as Lunda and Buganda emerged in East and Central Africa. [**Analyze multiple causation**]

7-12 Analyzing causes and consequences of encounters among Khoisan groups, Bantu-speaking peoples, and European settlers in South Africa in the 17th and 18th centuries. [**Identify the gaps in the available records**]

| Grades 5-6 | **Examples of student achievement of Standard 4C include:** |

▶ Use books such as Scott O'Dell's *My Name Is Not Angelica* and Paula Fox's *Slave Dancer* to describe the experience of Africans sold into slavery.

▶ Explain how the colonial system would have been different had there been no African slave market. *How would this have changed the history of the European colonies? How would this have changed the history of West Africa?*

▶ Listen to a reading of the capture scene at the beginning of *Roots* and describe the visual imagery and express personal reactions.

| Grades 7-8 | **Examples of student achievement of Standard 4C include:** |

▶ Discuss and compare different forms of slave resistance and protest, including cultural defiance, sabotage, rebellion, and the founding of Maroon societies.

▶ Recount the history of the African kingdom of Palmares in Brazil.

▶ Examine the influence of trade on such African states as Ashanti, Dahomey, and Oyo. *With whom did the West African states trade? What commodities were traded? How important was trade to West African kingdoms?*

▶ Explain the meaning of the Ashanti belief that the king was "first among equals." *How does this belief compare with European concepts of the "divine right of kings?"*

▶ Map the terrain of West Africa. On an overlay, indicate the extent of the states of Ashanti, Oyo, Dahomey, and Songhay. *What role did geography play in the development of these states? What items were traded and with whom?*

♦ Research statistical studies related to the numbers of slaves involved in the Atlantic slave trade. Design a bar graph to illustrate the different statistics. *Why are there wide discrepancies in the numbers? How are the different statistics determined? Can we determine the correct number of people taken forcibly from Africa? Why or why not?*

Grades 9-12

Examples of student achievement of Standard 4C include:

♦ Research how the slave trade affected family life and gender roles in West and Central Africa.

♦ Research the institutions, practices, and beliefs of slaves working on plantations in the Western Hemisphere. List the ways in which they preserved their African heritage.

♦ Assume the role of a slave on a plantation in the Caribbean, Brazil, or British North America and explain ways in which you resist the institution of slavery. Examine historical records to determine if slaves organized similar resistance movements. *What were the dangers involved in open rebellion against slavery? What other means of resistance were used?*

♦ Recount the history of the African kingdom of Palmares in Brazil.

♦ Use the song "The Dirge of St. Malo," to examine the way in which the Spanish in New Orleans put down slave revolts. *How extensive were slave revolts in the Spanish and English colonies?*

♦ Assume the perspective of a person sold into bondage in the Caribbean and describe conditions you endured in the middle passage and daily life on a Caribbean sugar plantation. *How was the life of a slave similar and different on a Brazilian plantation? On a plantation in British North America?*

The king of Tombuto hath many plates and scepters of gold, some whereof weigh 1300 poundes . . . and he keeps a manificent and well furnished court. . . . Whosoever will speake unto this king must first fall downe before his feete and then taking up earth must sprinkle it upon his owne head and shoulders . . .

LEO AFRICANUS

STANDARD 5

Students Should Understand: *Transformations in Asian societies in the era of European expansion.*

Students Should Be Able to:

5A Demonstrate understanding of the development of European maritime power in Asia by:

5-12 Explaining how Holland, England, and France became naval and commercial powers in the Indian Ocean basin in the 17th and 18th centuries. [**Evaluate the implementation of a decision**]

5-12 Assessing the impact of British and French commercial and military penetration on politics, economy, and society in India. [**Marshal evidence of antecedent circumstances**]

5-12 Analyzing motives for Dutch commercial and military penetration of Indonesia and the effects of Dutch imperialism on the region's economy and society. [**Analyze cause-and-effect relationships**]

9-12 Assessing the extent of European commercial penetration of China and the ability of Chinese governments to control European trade. [**Analyze cause-and-effect relationships**]

9-12 Analyzing the character and significance of Christian missionary activity in India, the East Indies, and the Philippines. [**Examine the influence of ideas, human interests, and beliefs**]

9-12 Assessing the impact of the Seven Years War on the relative power of Britain and France in Asia. [**Analyze cause-and-effect relationships**]

Grades 5-6

Examples of student achievement of Standard 5A include:

◗ On a map of East Asia, locate Portuguese, Dutch, English, and French trading centers and identify the products that were traded.

◗ Assume the role of a British merchant and prepare a presentation to the Cabinet regarding the importance of the Asia trade. *What arguments would you present? What policies would you propose?*

◗ Compare the life of an average Bengali peasant before and after the East India Company began to collect taxes and administer the area after 1757.

◗ Make a map of Southeast Asia showing the locations of the various spices that the Europeans wanted for trade. Then identify how many of these sites of this spice trade were controlled by the Dutch as of 1770.

Grades 7-8

Examples of student achievement of Standard 5A include:

◗ Make a political map of China showing the major port cities and trade routes used by the European merchants. *Why do you think Guangzhou (Canton) was a good choice by the Chinese government for the center of trade with Europe? How did Chinese authorities control European merchants' activities there?*

◗ Research the growth of British, Dutch, and French naval power in the Indian Ocean from 1600-1700. Assume the role of an English, Dutch, or French admiral and develop a set of arguments on what the other two nations are doing to create a strong navy and what your own country should do to compete with your two rivals.

◗ Research how the Dutch developed a system of forced labor as a basis for their prosperity in Indonesia. Compare this system with the slave economy of sugar production in the Caribbean.

◗ Read the correspondence between the Chinese emperors and the British requests for trading privileges during the period 1700-1770. Write a short dramatic presentation involving one Chinese and one British diplomat debating the issue of increased trading privileges for the British merchants.

Grades 9-12

Examples of student achievement of Standard 5A include:

◗ Research how Joseph François Dupleix developed the French policy of "divide and rule" in South India. *What impact did Dupleix's concept have on Robert Clive and the British East India Company's policy and on life for Indian peasants?*

◗ Research how the Mughal emperors such as Akbar, Jahangir, and Aurangzeb tried to limit and control the expansion and influence of European trading centers in India. Assess their relative success in this effort and compare it to the Chinese and Japanese attempts to regulate foreign trade and outside influences.

◗ Research the historical reasons that the Chinese emperors wanted to limit the amount of foreign trade and the Chinese view of "foreign barbarians." Assume that you are an envoy of the British government sent to Guangzhou in 1770 to find out the reasons for the Chinese limitation on trade and how your government might persuade the Chinese to open their country to more foreign trade. Write a memorandum to parliament summarizing your findings and suggestions.

◗ Research and compare various attempts by the Dutch, British, and French to redress the unfavorable trade balances that each suffered in Asia from 1500 to 1800.

◗ Research the spread of Christianity into predominantly Hindu, Buddhist, and Muslim areas after 1500. Write a dialogue between a Muslim and a Hindu on what they see as the reasons for the spread of Christian missions, what the impact will be on their faiths, and how best to resist the appeals of Christian missionaries.

◗ Assume that you are chief military adviser to the emperor Aurangzeb in 1700. Develop a list of arguments on the best way to defend his empire against the rising maritime power of France and England. *Would you stress the building of a larger army? What would you advise about building a strong navy?*

Students Should Be Able to:

5B Demonstrate understanding of transformations in India, China, and Japan in an era of expanding European commercial power by:

5-12 Analyzing causes of the decline of the Mughal Empire and the rise of regional powers such as the Marathas and Sikhs. [**Analyze multiple causation**]

5-12 Explaining how the Manchus overthrew the Ming dynasty, established the multiethnic Qing, and doubled the size of the Chinese empire. [**Identify issues and problems in the past**]

7-12 Evaluating China's cultural and economic achievements during the reigns of the Kangxi and Qianlong emperors. [**Examine the influence of ideas, human interests, and beliefs**]

5-12 Assessing the extent of European commercial penetration of China and the ability of the Chinese government to control European trade. [**Analyze cause-and-effect relationships**]

5-12 Explaining the origins and character of centralized feudalism in Japan under the Tokugawa shogunate and how the country achieved political stability, economic growth, and cultural dynamism. [**Analyze cause-and-effect relationships**]

5-12 Analyzing Japan's relations with Europeans between the 16th and 18th centuries and the consequences of the policy of limiting contacts with foreigners. [**Reconstruct patterns of historical succession and duration**]

Grades 5-6

Examples of student achievement of Standard 5B include:

- Construct a map of the islands of Japan and the opposite coast of mainland East Asia. Locate on the map the peninsula of Korea, the Ming boundaries, the major warrior states within the island of Honshu, and the major cities predating the Tokugawa shogunate.

- Read sections of *Chushingura* (The Tale of the Forty-seven Ronin) and discuss the samurai ideals.

- Drawing on books such as Erik Haugaard's *The Samurai's Tale* and Robert D. San Souci's *The Samurai Daughter*, describe Japanese society between the 16th and 18th centuries. *Who is left out of the stories about samurai?*

Grades 7-8

Examples of student achievement of Standard 5B include:

- Assume the role of a Jesuit missionary in China during the reign of the Kangxi emperor and prepare an appeal to the pope for recognizing traditional Confucian values in your efforts to spread Christianity in China.

- As a Manchu emperor, decide how to handle the problems stemming from increasing population growth, agricultural output, commerce, and the incursion of European trading networks.

- Use an evaluation form to rate the treatment and opportunities open to women in 17th- and 18th-century China. Rate such items as footbinding, female subordination, patriarchy, a flourishing women's culture, and literature. Develop an oral or written report on one of the topics.

- Assume the role of a Korean before 1800 and explain why Korea was called the "Hermit Kingdom." Write a newspaper or magazine article defending or rejecting that title.

- Read the "Great Learning for Women" and assess the role and status of women in Tokugawa Japan.

- Read excerpts from Saikaku's *The Eternal Storehouse of Japan*, from Chikamatsu's view on the art of the puppet stage (*bunraku*) and his *Love Suicides at Sonezaki*, and from the haiku of Basho. Discuss the life of townsmen in 17th-century Japan and the social, economic, and political context in which these art forms evolved.

Grades 9-12

Examples of student achievement of Standard 5B include:

- Research how the demise of centralized control by the imperial Mughals contributed to the rise of Maratha and Sikh power in India. Write an essay comparing the reasons for the end of Mughal rule with reasons for the end of Ming rule.

- Analyze how importation of American silver affected the economies of China and Japan between the 16th and 18th centuries.

- Prepare a list of Chinese goods desired by Europeans. From the perspective of a European country, devise a commercial treaty with China. *How did trading policies under the Manchus differ from those of the Ming dynasty? What factors contributed to the change?*

- Discuss the life of the elite in China, drawing on selections from the satirical novel *The Scholars*, from an autobiography of a scholar-official out of office, or from *China's Examination Hell.*

- Discuss the family and its role in Chinese society, including family business, property rights vested in the family, not the individual, individual vs. group identity, popular religion and life-cycle events. Draw on reading from *The Dream of the Red Chamber* (*The Story of the Stone*) and from family genealogies.

- Evaluate the different positions of a neo-Confucian scholar, a nativist thinker, and a student of Dutch learning in 18th-century Japan.

- Compare and contrast the unification of Tokugawa Japan with the rise of nation states in early modern Europe. *How did the Tokugawa rulers centralize feudalism in Japan?*

- Compare Japanese attitudes regarding trade with foreign states with those of the Chinese. *What role did the Portuguese and the Dutch have in Japanese trade? Why did the Japanese decide to limit contacts? How successful was Japan in isolating itself from Europe? Why was Japan closed to the West but not to Asia?*

Students Should Be Able to:

5C Demonstrate understanding of major cultural trends in Asia between the 16th and 18th centuries by:

`7-12` Assessing the influence of both new currents in Confucianism and Chinese art, architecture, and literary styles on cultural life in Korea, Vietnam, and Japan. [**Draw upon visual and literary sources**]

`7-12` Describing the varieties of Buddhist and Hindu teaching and practice in Asia, and comparing their influence on social and cultural life. [**Demonstrate and explain the influence of ideas, human interests, and beliefs**]

`7-12` Analyzing how and why Islam continued to expand in India, Southeast Asia, and China. [**Demonstrate and explain the influence of ideas, human interests, and beliefs**]

| Grades 5-6 | **Examples of student achievement of Standard 5C include:** |

▶ Compare Japanese and Chinese brush paintings. *What is their relationship to nature?*

▶ On a current map of East Asia indicate the dominant religion or religions of each nation. Research how these religions spread into these societies.

▶ Research what groups of people in India were most likely to have converted to Islam. *What was the appeal of Islam to these groups and what was the major vehicle for conversion?*

| Grades 7-8 | **Examples of student achievement of Standard 5C include:** |

▶ Read excerpts from *Monkey* translated by Arthur Waley. Act out a scene such as when "Monkey" steals the nectar of immortality from the celestial court. *In what ways is this novel a playful critique of Confucianism, Daoism, and Buddhism in China? In what ways does it affirm the synthesis of these three faiths in China?*

▶ Read the Tulasidas version of the *Ramayana*. *How does the author change the identity of Rama offered in earlier versions of the epic?*

▶ Assess the changing roles of women in Korea and Japan as Confucianism gained in strength among the ruling elites in those countries.

▶ Compare Nikko and Katsuru rikyu, the screens of Sotabu, the brush painting of literati, and the paintings of Shiba Kokan. *To what extent did the Japanese adapt techniques and designs from other parts of the world? What were the recurring themes used in Japanese art? How did art reflect Japanese society?*

▶ Compare the role played by Confucianism in China, Korea, Japan, and Vietnam. *How did differences in government and society affect the practice of Confucianism?*

▶ Research how the new religion of Sikhism represented a synthesis between Hinduism and Islam. *Which major features of the religion are more Hindu and which more Islamic?*

Grades 9-12

Examples of student achievement of Standard 5C include:

◆ Examine the art, architecture, and literature of Korea and Vietnam in the 17th and 18th centuries. *How do they reflect Chinese influence, and how do they express separate identities?*

◆ Compare the major world religions as of the mid-18th century in terms of numbers of adherents worldwide and relative degree of success at winning new converts.

◆ Compare Buddhism as it developed in China and Japan.

◆ Research the life and writings of Mirabai (ca. 1500-1550). *What does her life say about the role of women in Bhakti movements of the period? What metaphors of love infuse her poetry?*

◆ Read selections from the poet Kabir (ca. 1440-1518) in Embree's *Sources of the Hindu Tradition* (pp. 263-265). Debate if his poetry is more Islamic or Hindu.

Painting by an Italian Jesuit missionary, Joseph Castiglione, of a woman in the Chinese emperor's court William McNeill, slide collection

STANDARD 6

Students Should Understand: *Major global trends from 1450 to 1770.*

Students Should Be Able to:

6   **Demonstrate understanding of major global trends from 1450 to 1770 by:**

5-12 Describing major shifts in world demography and urbanization in this era and analyzing reasons for these changes. [**Utilize visual and mathematical data**]

7-12 Analyzing ways in which expanding capitalistic enterprise and commercialization affected relations among states and contributed to changing class relations. [**Analyze cause-and-effect relationships**]

7-12 Assessing the impact of gunpowder weaponry and other innovations in military technology on empire-building and the world balance of naval power. [**Analyze cause-and-effect relationships**]

5-12 Explaining major changes in world political boundaries between 1450 and 1770 and assessing the extent and limitations of European political and military power in Africa, Asia, and the Americas as of the mid-18th century. [**Clarify information on the geographic setting**]

5-12 Assessing how the acceleration of scientific and technological innovations in this era affected social, economic, and cultural life in various parts of the world. [**Analyze cause-and-effect relationships**]

7-12 Identifying regions where Buddhism, Christianity, and Islam were growing in this era and analyzing why these religious and cultural traditions gained new adherents in various parts of the world. [**Examine the influence of ideas**]

7-12 Identifying patterns of social and cultural continuity in various societies and analyzing ways in which peoples maintained traditions and resisted external challenges in the context of a rapidly changing world. [**Explain historical continuity and change**]

Grades 5-6

Examples of student achievement of Standard 6 include:

‣ Compare a map of the Western Hemisphere at the time of first European contacts around 1500 with a map of the area in 1750. *Why did the boundaries change in such a drastic way during this period?*

‣ Research the origins of the major aids for navigation used by the European powers during the age of western European expansion. Develop a chart showing the first use of such essential tools and knowledge as: the mariner's compass, the astrolabe, knowledge of ocean currents, lateen sails, use of place numbers in mathematics, and mounting of cannons on ships.

Grades 7-8

Examples of student achievement of Standard 6 include:

▶ Using *300 Years of Urban Growth* by Tertius Chandler, make a list rank-ordering the twenty major cities of the world in 1450 and compare it with a second list as of 1750. Locate the cities on a world map. *What might account for the changes in the ranking of the cities during this period?*

▶ Prepare a chart showing the number of adherents the three religions — Islam, Buddhism, and Christianity — had in 1450 and make a similar chart for 1750. On two maps, show the areas where followers of these religions lived in these two periods. Compare the charts and maps and account for the changes in both numbers and area over the two-century period.

▶ Make a list of the ten most important technical discoveries and inventions during the period 1500-1770. *Which of these do we regularly use in your own time? How would your life be different now if these things had not been created?*

▶ Research how the Ming and early Qing rulers viewed the European merchants, Christian missionaries, and military personnel who sought trading privileges in China. *Was their view realistic and practical given the circumstances of the time?*

▶ Make a chart of the major breakthroughs in military technology and tactics during the period 1500-1770. *What countries benefited the most from the new military innovations? Which countries suffered most as a result of them?* Write an essay describing how the life of an average soldier changed during this period as a result of the new technology.

Grades 9-12

Examples of student achievement of Standard 6 include:

▶ Research the major reasons for the move of the center of economic power from the Mediterranean Basin to northern Europe during the 16th century. *What factors help explain this dramatic shift in world power?*

▶ How did the expanding capitalist system affect the textile industry in India after 1700? *What groups of people in India joined the new expanding middle class and what occupations did they take up?*

▶ What factors were present in England, Holland, and France that might help explain the rapid development of capitalism in these states? *Why didn't Spain, Portugal, and Italy similarly develop modern capitalism?*

▶ Research the core and periphery thesis of Immanuel Wallerstein. *How does he explain the rise of Western European capitalism? What were its effects on the rest of the world? What, according to Wallerstein, is a "world-system"?*

▶ Research how the Ming and early Qing rulers viewed the European merchants, Christian missionaries, and military personnel who sought trading privileges in China. Was their view realistic and practical given the circumstances of the time?

▶ Research the Confucian and Puritan attitudes toward investing in order to make a profit. Write an essay comparing the attitudes of the Chinese and the first generations of Puritans in Massachusetts toward the practice of buying and selling goods in order to get rich. *To what extent were the policies of the two groups successful?*

▶ Create a series of overlay transparencies showing the political boundaries of Europe, Africa, Asia, and the Western Hemisphere. Make a map for every fifty years beginning in 1500 and ending in 1800. *How would you account for these changing boundaries? What generalizations could you justifiably make about the changing balance of power during this period?*

ERA 7

An Age of Revolutions, 1750-1914

Giving Shape to World History

The invention of the railway locomotive, the steamship, and, later, the telegraph and telephone transformed global communications in this era. The time it took and the money it cost to move goods, messages, or armies across oceans and continents were drastically cut. People moved, or were forced to move, from one part of the world to another in record numbers. In the early part of the era African slaves continued to be transported across the Atlantic in large numbers; European migrants created new frontiers of colonial settlement in both the Northern and Southern Hemispheres; and Chinese, Indian, and other Asians migrated to Southeast Asia and the Americas. International commerce mushroomed, and virtually no society anywhere in the world stayed clear of the global market. Underlying these surges in communication, migration, and trade was the growth of the world population, that moved upward even faster than in the previous era, forcing peoples almost everywhere to experiment with new ways of organizing collective life.

This was an era of bewildering change in a thousand different arenas. One way to make sense of the whole is to focus on three world-encompassing and interrelated developments: the democratic revolution, the industrial revolution, and the establishment of European dominance over most of the world.

▶ **Political Revolutions and New Ideologies:** The American and French revolutions offered to the world the potent ideas of popular sovereignty, inalienable rights, and nationalism. The translating of these ideas into political movements had the effect of mobilizing unprecedented numbers of ordinary people to participate in public life and to believe in a better future for all. Liberal, constitutional, and nationalist ideals inspired independence movements in Haiti and Latin America in the early 19th century, and they continued to animate reform and revolution in Europe throughout the era. At the same time political and social counterforces acted to limit or undermine the effectiveness of democratic governments. Democracy and nationalism contributed immensely to the social power of European states and therefore to Europe's rising dominance in world affairs in the 19th century. Under growing pressures from both European military power and the changing world economy, ruling or elite groups in Asian and African states organized reform movements that embraced at least some of the ideas and programs of democratic revolution.

▶ **The Industrial Revolution:** The industrial revolution applied mechanical power to the production and distribution of goods on a massive scale. It also involved mobilizing unprecedented numbers of laborers and moving them from village to city and from one country to another. Industrialization was a consequence of centuries of expanding economic activity around the world. England played a crucial role in the onset of this revolution, but the process involved complex economic and financial linkages among societies. Together, the industrial and democratic revolutions thoroughly transformed European society. Asian, African, and Latin American peoples dealt with the new demands of the world market and Europe's economic might in a variety of ways. Some groups argued for reform through technical and industrial modernization. Others called for reassertion of established policies and values that had always served them well in times of crisis. Japan and the United States both subscribed to the industrial revolution with rapid success and became important players on the world scene.

▶ **The Age of European Dominance:** In 1800 Europeans controlled about 35 percent of the world's land surface. By 1914 they dominated over 84 percent. In the long span of human history European world hegemony lasted a short time, but its consequences were profound and continue to be played out today. Western expansion took three principal forms: (1) Peoples of European descent, including Russians and North Americans, created colonial settlements, or "neo-Europes," in various temperate regions of the world, displacing or assimilating indigenous peoples; (2) European states and commercial firms established considerable economic domination in certain places, notably Latin America and China; while Japan and the United States also participated in this economic expansionism; (3) in the later 19th century European states embarked on the "new imperialism," the competitive race to establish political as well as economic control over previously uncolonized regions of Africa and Asia. Mass production of new weaponry, coupled with the revolution of transport and communication, permitted this "new imperialism." The active responses of the peoples of Africa, Asia, and Latin America to the crisis of European hegemony are an important part of the developments of this era: armed resistance against invaders, collaboration or alliance with colonizers, economic reform or entrepreneurship, and movements for cultural reform. As World War I approached, accelerating social change and new efforts at resistance and renewal characterized colonial societies far more than consolidation and stability.

Why Study This Era?

▶ The global forces unleashed in the second half of the 18th century continue to play themselves out at the end of the 20th century. Students will understand the "isms" that have absorbed contemporary society — industrialism, capitalism, nationalism, liberalism, socialism, communism, imperialism, colonialism and so on — by investigating them within the historical context of the 18th and 19th centuries.

▶ At the beginning of the 20th century, Western nations enjoyed a dominance in world affairs that they no longer possess. By studying this era students may address some of the fundamental questions of the modern age: How did a relatively few states achieve such hegemony over most of the world? In what ways was Western domination limited or inconsequential? Why was it not to endure?

▶ The history of the United States, in this era, was not self-contained but fully embedded in the context of global change. To understand the role of the United States on the global scene, students must be able to relate it to world history.

What Students Should Understand

Standard 1: The causes and consequences of political revolutions in the late 18th and early 19th centuries

    A. The contributions of the **French Revolution** to transformations in Europe and the world [CORE]

    B. How **Latin American** countries achieved **independence** in the early 19th century [CORE]

Standard 2: **The causes and consequences of the agricultural and industrial revolutions, 1700-1850**

    A. **Early industrialization** and the importance of developments in England [CORE]

    B. The expansion of **industrial economies and the transformations** of societies in Europe and the Atlantic basin [CORE]

    C. The **abolition** of the trans-Atlantic **slave trade** and slavery in the Americas [RELATED]

Standard 3: **The transformation of Eurasian societies in an era of global trade and rising European power, 1750-1850**

    A. The **Ottoman Empire and** the challenge of **Western** military, political, and economic **power** [CORE]

    B. **Russian** imperial **expansion** in the late 18th and the 19th centuries [RELATED]

    C. Political and military encounters between **Europeans and** peoples of **South and Southeast Asia** [CORE]

    D. **China's responses to** economic and political **crises** in the late 18th and 19th centuries [CORE]

    E. The **transformation of Japan** from feudal shogunate to modern nation-state in the 19th century [CORE]

Standard 4: **Patterns of nationalism, state-building, and social reform in Europe and the Americas, 1830-1914**

    A. The effect of **modern nationalism** on European politics and society [CORE]

    B. The impact of new **social movements and ideologies** on 19th-century Europe [CORE]

    C. The contributions of **technological, scientific, and intellectual achievements** to social and cultural change in 19th-century Europe [RELATED]

    D. The political, economic, and social **transformations in the Americas** in the 19th century [RELATED]

Standard 5: **Patterns of global change in the era of Western military and economic domination, 1850-1914**

    A. **European** overseas **settlement** in the 19th century [RELATED]

    B. European, American, and Japanese **imperial expansion,** 1850-1914 [CORE]

    C. The transformations in South, Southeast, and East **Asia in the era of** the "new **imperialism**" [CORE]

    D. **African responses to** world economic developments and European imperialism [CORE]

Standard 6: **Major global trends from 1750 to 1914 [RELATED]**

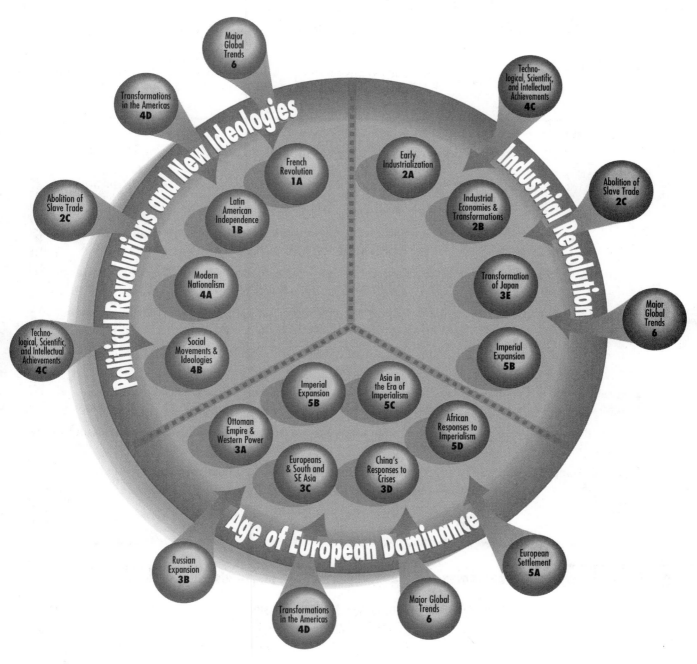

**Relationships Among Major Developments,
Core Standards, and Related Standards for Era 7**

S T A N D A R D   1

Students Should Understand: *The causes and consequences of political revolutions in the late 18th and early 19th centuries.*

Students Should Be Able to:

1A   Demonstrate understanding of how the French Revolution contributed to transformations in Europe and the world by:

[7-12] Analyzing how the Seven Years War, Enlightenment thought, and growing internal economic crisis affected social and political conditions in Old Regime France. [**Analyze multiple causation**]

[5-12] Assessing the character of the American Revolution and evaluating its impact on France. [**Analyze cause-and effect relationships**]

[7-12] Explaining how the French Revolution developed from constitutional monarchy to democratic despotism to the Napoleonic empire. [**Reconstruct patterns of historical succession and duration**]

[5-12] Evaluating leading ideas of the revolution concerning social equality, democracy, human rights, constitutionalism, and nationalism. [**Interrogate historical data**]

[7-12] Analyzing how the revolution changed French society, including political and religious institutions, social relations, education, family life, and the status of women. [**Analyze cause-and-effect relationships**]

[5-12] Analyzing how the wars of the revolutionary and Napoleonic period changed Europe, and assessing Napoleon's effects on the aims and outcomes of the revolution. [**Analyze multiple causation**]

[9-12] Analyzing connections between the French and Haitian revolutions, and assessing the impact of the Haitian movement on race relations and slavery in the Americas and the French empire. [**Analyze cause-and effect relationships**]

Grades 5-6

Examples of student achievement of Standard 1A include:

▶ Design a banner for the beginning of the French Revolution touting "Liberty, Equality and Fraternity." *Which people in France would have been most likely to carry or follow your banner? Which would not? Why?*

▶ Create a time line using pictures or headline statements to label the main political events in the Americas and France from 1770 to 1815. *Which events were the most important? Why? How were events between the continents related?*

▶ Draw evidence from a biography of Napoleon to gather information on both his military and political policies. *Were Napoleon's domestic achievements greater than his military accomplishments? Was France better off under Napoleon than under Louis XVI?*

Grades 7-8

Examples of student achievement of Standard 1A include:

- Construct a series of maps or map overlays showing France during the revolution, Napoleon's Consulate, the empire, and the settlement of the Congress of Vienna. Assume the role of an individual living in 19th-century Europe and write a letter to a friend describing the territorial changes that took place in Europe between 1789 and 1815.

- Construct a time line listing the major events of the French Revolution. Assume the role of a noble, cleric, bourgeois, peasant, or sans-culotte and, from your perspective, record short entries in a journal about each of these major events.

- Recreate the meeting of the Estates-General by assigning representatives of the First, Second, and Third Estates. Write a position paper for each estate, stating which classes they represent, the rights and privileges of each, and what they expect to do at the meeting. Assess the merits of the organization of the Estates-General and its limitations. *What changes did the Third Estate demand? What resulted?*

- Read sections of the "Declaration of the Rights of Man and Citizen" and create "publication committees" to design illustrations and to write short tracts defending the central principles contained in the declaration. *What sections show the influence of Enlightenment ideas and the American Declaration of Independence?*

- After studying a sequence of paintings and drawings of events in the French Revolution, including such works as "The Fall of the Bastille," and David's "Oath of the Tennis Court," and "The March of the Women of Paris on Versailles," write accounts of each event as if you were there.

- Construct a classroom newspaper covering the Congress of Vienna from differing perspectives. Include character sketches of leading figures, editorials, and cartoons dealing with issues discussed at the conference.

Grades 9-12

Examples of student achievement of Standard 1A include:

- Create a chart illustrating the political spectrum showing radical, liberal, moderate, conservative, and reactionary during the French Revolution. Give an example of the actions of an individual or an event that is characteristic of each.

- Compare Olympe de Gouges's "Declaration of the Rights of Women and the Female Citizen" to the French Revolution's "Declaration of the Rights of Man and the Citizen."

- Examine the "Code Napoleon" from the point of view of an early 19th-century reformer. *How would property owners, workers, women, and Catholic and Protestant clerics critique the Civil Code?*

- Using books such as *The Scarlet Pimpernel* and *A Tale of Two Cities*, assess the accuracy of such literary accounts in describing the French Revolution.

- From the perspective of different groups in Haiti such as plantation owners, free blacks and mulattos, and slaves, construct an account of the fears, demands, and actions in the Haitian Revolution.

Students Should Be Able to:

1B Demonstrate understanding of how Latin American countries achieved independence in the early 19th century by:

5-12 Analyzing the influence of the American, French, and Haitian revolutions, as well as late 18th-century South American rebellions, on the development of independence movements in Latin America. [**Analyze multiple causation**]

7-12 Analyzing the effects of Napoleon's invasion of Iberia and the growth of British power in the Atlantic basin on the struggles for independence. [**Evaluate the implementation of a decision**]

5-12 Analyzing the political and ideological objectives of the independence movements between 1808 and 1830, and explaining why these movements succeeded. [**Interrogate historical data**]

9-12 Analyzing the political roles of Creole elites, the Roman Catholic Church, and mestizo, mulatto, and Indian populations in the independence movements. [**Marshal evidence of antecedent circumstances**]

Grades 5-6

Examples of student achievement of Standard 1B include:

▶ Compare maps of Latin America in 1790 with maps in 1828. Identify the key colonial powers of 1790 and the new independent countries,.

▶ Map the territories liberated by Simón Bolívar and those liberated by José de San Martín. *What role did geography play in Latin American independence?*

Grades 7-8

Examples of student achievement of Standard 1B include:

▶ Research the role of Father Miguel Hidalgo in the Mexican Revolution of 1810 and the role of Agustín de Iturbide in the revolt of 1821. *How was the 1810 movement led by Hidalgo different from the independence movements in South America? Which forces supported Hidalgo? What prompted the creole-dominated revolt of 1821 come about?*

▶ Write a short chronological narrative based on the arrival of Napoleonic forces in Portugal and the departure of the Portuguese royal court to Brazil. Contrast the form of independent government set up in Brazil with those of the other Latin American countries.

▶ Assume the role of a Latin American and explain how you would react to news that Napoleon had taken control of Spain, *Would you be willing to support Joseph Bonaparte as your king? Why or why not?*

▶ Write a journalistic account of the Haitian revolution and the role played by Toussaint L'Ouverture. Include background information on the social and economic conditions under French rule. *How important was sugar? slave labor? How did events in France and the rise of Napoleon affect the Haitian revolution?*

▶ Create a time line of events in France, Spain, and Portugal for the period 1770-1825. Construct a parallel time line for the Caribbean, Latin American, and Mexican independence movements. *How did events in France and on the Iberian Peninsula affect the Haitian and Latin American revolutions?*

Grades 9-12

Examples of student achievement of Standard 1B include:

▶ Role-play a meeting of liberal leaders in New Granada and propose a plan for the establishment of an independent government. *What role should the Creole elite play in the new government? What should be the position of the Roman Catholic Church? To what extent should all persons be given the right to vote in the new nation?*

▶ Prepare a chart to compare and contrast a Spanish American independence movement with the American, French, and Haitian revolutions. *How were pre-independence social and political conditions the same? different? What regimes and policies did the movements oppose? How did revolutionaries justify their independence claims? What class forces did they represent? How widespread were the revolutions?*

▶ Compare the status of women in Latin America before and after the independence movements. *How did independence change the status of women? Did this vary by region? by class?*

▶ Debate the provisions of the Monroe Doctrine from the Latin American point of view.

▶ Construct a broadside or political cartoon using the American and French revolutions as models for an independence movement in Latin America.

▶ Write a declaration of independence for a Latin American state in the early 19th century. *What is the ideological basis for your declaration of independence? What are your political objectives in declaring independence? How did Brazilian independence differ from that of the other Latin American countries?*

▶ Create a graphic to illustrate the racial and social divisions, including the position of the creoles, mestizos, mulattoes, Indians, and blacks throughout most of Latin America following the independence movements. *What had changed? What was the attitude toward the Catholic Church?*

▶ Recreate a tertulia, or social gathering, held by woman leaders such as María Josefa Ortiz in Mexico, Manuela Sanz de Santamaria in Colombia, or Manuela Canizares of Quito in the periods before the wars of independence. *How did they serve as arenas for discussion of revolt? How were ideas and discussions of events in Spain and France transmitted through them?*

Mexican patriot, Father Miguel Hidalgo
Courtesy, Organization of
American States

S T A N D A R D   2

Students Should Understand: *The causes and consequences of the agricultural and industrial revolutions, 1700-1850.*

Students Should Be Able to:

2A Demonstrate understanding of early industrialization and the importance of developments in England by:

5-12 Analyzing the characteristics of the "agricultural revolution" that occurred in England and western Europe, and assessing its importance for the growth of industrialization. [**Analyze cause-and effect relationships**]

5-12 Identifying the major characteristics of the industrial revolution, and comparing industrial economies with other forms of economic organization. [**Compare and contrast differing institutions**]

9-12 Analyzing relationships between the expanding world market economy of the 16th through 18th centuries and the development of industrialization. [**Analyze cause-and-effect relationships**]

7-12 Analyzing connections between early industrialization and Britain's commercial relations with continental Europe, the Mediterranean, India, the Caribbean, and other world regions. [**Analyze cause-and-effect relationships**]

7-12 Assessing the relative importance of geographical, economic, technological, and political factors that permitted or encouraged the rise of mechanized industry in England. [**Analyze multiple causation**]

Grades 5-6	Examples of student achievement of Standard 2A include:

▶ Research the inventions of Jethro Tull and Charles Townsend. Graphically show agricultural methods "Before" their inventions and "After." *How did changes in agriculture influence the industrial revolution?*

▶ From visual sources of the period, describe daily life in an English cottage industry before the industrial revolution. Using other visual sources depicting spinning in a factory setting, compare daily life within the two workplaces. *What major changes had taken place?*

▶ On a map of Britain, illustrate the shifts in population caused by the industrial revolution. Write a diary account of what it would have been like to migrate from a rural area to an industrial center.

▶ Write an illustrated biography of an inventor such as John Kay, James Hargreaves, James Watt, Edmund Cartwright, and Richard Arkwright.

Grades 7-8	Examples of student achievement of Standard 2A include:

▶ Brainstorm the reasons why the industrial revolution began in Great Britain. Create a class chart to be displayed on the wall for easy reference.

▶ Using a chart of inventions relating to agriculture such as the seed drill, crop rotation, stock breeding, three-piece iron plow, mechanical reaper, steel plow, barbed wire, and chemical fertilizers, assess the consequences and relative importance of each to the agricultural revolution.

▶ Construct a physical map of Great Britain that identifies the geographic features that were favorable for industrialization. Explain how physical geography and natural resources aided industrialization.

▶ On a world map label Britain's commercial connections during the period of early industrialization. *How did these connections contribute to the industrial revolution?*

▶ Assume the role of an inventor such as John Kay, Richard Arkwright, or Edmund Cartwright and prepare a presentation to persuade business leaders that your invention will revolutionize the textile industry. Include a sketch or drawing of your invention. *What was the effect of new technologies on the textile industry? To what extent was the textile industry the "mother of the industrial revolution?"*

▶ Debate the benefits of interchangeable parts and mass production from the point of view of a craftsman and a factory worker.

Grades 9-12

Examples of student achievement of Standard 2A include:

▶ Explain the distinctions between mercantilist and free-market economies, and assess the influence of new economic theories on industrial policies and practices.

▶ Analyze the paintings of Constable and Turner for what they say about the beauties of the English countryside and villages. *How do they romanticize the pre-industrial world? To what extent is their view real? Why?*

▶ Using primary sources such as Edward Baines's *The History of the Cotton Manufacture in Great Britain* and statistical data, explain the factors that contributed to England's leadership in the Industrial revolution. *Which was the most important factor in the development of England's industrialization? Why? How did England's location in Europe and the world affect its industrial development? What characteristics of English society and government contributed to the rise of the industrial revolution?*

▶ Research the life of an English "factor" or trade agent for a textile company in Aleppo, Syria, in the late 18th century using Ralph Davis's *Aleppo and Devonshire Square*. Write a letter home that describes the goods he handles, his worries and concerns, the people he does business with, and his leisure-time activities.

▶ Construct a flow chart representing the relationships between improvements in agriculture, population increase, the rise of the textile industry, the enclosure movement, urbanization, and industrialization in 18th-century England.

Students Should Be Able to:

2B Demonstrate understanding of how industrial economies expanded and societies experienced transformations in Europe and the Atlantic basin by:

`5-12` Explaining connections among population growth, industrialization and urbanization, and evaluating the quality of life in early 19th-century cities. **[Evidence historical perspectives]**

`5-12` Analyzing the effects of industrialization and urbanization on development of class distinctions, family life, and the political and economic status of women. **[Analyze cause-and effect relationships]**

`5-12` Analyzing connections between industrialization and movements for political and social reform in England, Western Europe, and the United States. **[Analyze cause-and-effect relationships]**

`7-12` Analyzing connections between industrialization and the rise of new types of labor organizations and mobilization. **[Analyze cause-and-effect relationships]**

Grades 5-6

Examples of student achievement of Standard 2B include:

▶ Read selections from *A Christmas Carol* and *Oliver Twist* and write a journal entry about the daily life of a working-class person in Britain during the industrial revolution.

▶ Create an illustrated time line of technological advances in communication and transportation during the industrial revolution. *What special effects did the railroad have on everyday life?*

▶ Study the beginning of labor unions. Working in groups, prepare posters identifying a conflict that might have occurred in 1900 between representatives of workers and big business. As a class, brainstorm possible solutions to the conflict.

▶ Design and label a bar graph showing the growth of population in Europe during the industrial revolution from 1750 to 1900. Show statistics in 50-year increments.

Grades 7-8

Examples of student achievement of Standard 2B include:

▶ Study a bar graph of railway mileage in Great Britain from the 1840s to 1900. Research similar data for the same period in the United States and create a comparative graph. *What conclusions can you make about the pace and extent of the industrialization in both countries?*

▶ Research Robert Owen's New Lanark System. Assume the role of Robert Owen and prepare a speech to European industrialists explaining the benefits of your approach. *How did Robert Owen propose to deal with societal problems caused by the industrial revolution?*

▶ Read excerpts from 19th-century literature describing living and working conditions in an industrialized nation. *What do they say about population, work life, and city life?*

▶ Simulate a parliamentary debate of the Reform Bill of 1832. *How great was the "Great Reform" legislation? What problems connected with the industrial revolution did it address? Which did it leave untouched?*

♦ Create a statistical table showing "Percentage Distribution of the World's Manufacturing Production" for the following countries: Great Britain, United States, Germany, France, Russia, and Italy in the periods 1800, 1850, and 1900. *What new patterns in world manufacturing production can you detect?*

Grades 9-12

Examples of student achievement of Standard 2B include:

♦ Using selections from *The Wealth of Nations* by Adam Smith, identify the characteristics of capitalism and analyze Smith's view of its strengths. *How are free enterprise, the profit motive, and competition the building blocks of capitalism? How does Smith use the "pin" story? Why? How does the Invisible Hand work? What are the strengths and weaknesses of Smith's argument?*

♦ Using descriptions and pictures of "The Great Exhibition of the Works of Industry of All Nations" in London's "Crystal Palace," compare the development of industrialization on the continent with that of England. Explain why there are differences in development.

♦ Read excerpts from 19th-century literature such as Charles Dickens's *Hard Times* or Émile Zola's *Germinal*, describing working and living conditions in an industrialized nation. *What do they say about the new classes that emerged with industrialization, the new human relationships, and the quality of industrial work life?*

♦ Research the condition of children employed in the factories, in trades and manufactures, and in the mines in England in the early 19th century. From primary documents, summarize the debates over child labor and factory legislation. *What changes were brought about by the Factory Act of 1833? the legislation of 1842? the Ten Hours Act of 1847? What general changes were wrought in the lives of women and children, as well as the structure of the family, by the industrial revolution?*

♦ Develop a typology for the types of organizational responses and activities devised by working people in England, western Europe, and the United States in response to the conditions of industrial labor.

♦ Stage a debate on the benefits of the industrial revolution. Write a summary position paper assessing the positive and/or negative aspects of industrialization.

♦ Examine reproductions of advertisements from 19th-century magazines and newspapers. *How do these reflect the rise of industrial economies? the changes in family life? the role of women?*

Gustave Dore's 1872 engraving Over London by Rail. New York Public Library

Students Should Be Able to:

2C **Demonstrate understanding of the causes and consequences of the abolition of the trans-Atlantic slave trade and slavery in the Americas by:**

`9-12` Assessing the relative importance of Enlightenment thought, Christian piety, democratic revolutions, slave resistance, and changes in the world economy in bringing about the abolition of the slave trade and the emancipation of slaves in the Americas. [**Analyze multiple causation**]

`5-12` Describing the organization of movements in Europe and the Americas to end slavery, and explaining how the trans-Atlantic trade was suppressed. [**Reconstruct patterns of historical succession and duration**]

`7-12` Comparing contract labor migration and other forms of coerced labor with slavery as methods of organizing commercial agriculture in the Americas in the later 19th century. [**Compare and contrast differing values, behaviors, and institutions**]

`7-12` Assessing the degree to which emancipated slaves and their descendants achieved social equality and economic advancement in various countries of the Western Hemisphere. [**Interrogate historical data**]

| Grades 5-6 | **Examples of student achievement of Standard 2C include:** |

▶ Assume the role of an abolitionist and write a small pamphlet describing the evils of slavery.

▶ Hypothesize reasons why the slave trade continued even after it was outlawed.

▶ Research the life of Frederick Douglass and his role as a leader in the American abolitionist movement. Explain his statement that slavery "brands your Christianity as a lie."

| Grades 7-8 | **Examples of student achievement of Standard 2C include:** |

▶ Draw on a map the places where slavery was permitted in 1800, 1830, and 1880. *How might this be tied to revolution ideology and economics?*

▶ After reviewing short primary source readings, re-enact the debate on the abolition of slavery in the colonies as it took place in the National Assembly during the French Revolution. *Why would the National Convention have been the body most likely to pass such a declaration?*

▶ Write a series of cameo biographies on the women of the abolitionist movement in America. Include such women as Harriet Tubman, Sojourner Truth, the Grimké sisters, Lucretia Mott, Elizabeth Cady Stanton, and Harriet Beecher Stowe.

▶ Make a chart listing the many strategies employed by different peoples in the Americas resisting slavery. Include some examples from the Caribbean and Brazil. In as many cases as possible, name the people associated with each one and evaluate its success or failure.

▶ Prepare a chart listing the ways in which different peoples in the Americas resisted slavery and evaluate their successes.

♦ Research the life and work of Olaudah Equiano (Gustavus Vasa). *What were Equiano's experiences during the "middle passage"? What were the measures he undertook to help bring an end to the slave trade?*

Grades 9-12

Examples of student achievement of Standard 2C include:

♦ Compare the African slave trade with the migration of Chinese workers to North and South America and Indian workers to the Caribbean or other parts of the world in the 19th century.

♦ Using selections from the writings of Wilbert Wilberforce, analyze the evangelical reasons for the antislavery movement. *To what extent is Britain's abolition of slavery the result of the Evangelical movement? the Enlightenment? economic failures?*

♦ Using trading maps and primary sources, analyze the reason why Brazil was the last nation to abolish slavery and the slave trade.

♦ Analyze the causes and consequences of the Haitian Revolution and its effects on slavery and the slave trade.

♦ Create a chart listing the estimated slave imports to Brazil, Spanish America, the British West Indies, the French West Indies and British North America, and the United States for the years 1701-1810 and 1811-1870. *When was the largest influx of slaves to the Americas? Where? What might account for this?*

♦ Review photocopies of the front pages of William Lloyd Garrison's antislavery newspaper, *The Liberator. How was slavery depicted?* Research the influence of the Second Great Awakening on Garrison's life and how it related to his antislavery position.

♦ Read selections from the writings of the *philosophes,* such as Louis de Jaucourt's "The Slave" (1755) and "Blacks" (1765) from the *Encyclopedia,* Voltaire's "Essay on Morals and Custom" (1756), Rousseau's "The New Heloise" (1761), and Diderot's "Natural Liberty" from the *Encyclopedia* (1765). *On what grounds did they argue against slavery and the slave trade in the French colonies? On what grounds had slavery been justified in the past? How did the views of the* philosophes *influence the speeches on slavery given in the Estates-General (1789) and the National Assembly (1789)?*

♦ Research the organization, participants, and proceedings of the World Antislavery Convention held in London in 1840. *Who were the main participants? Where did they come from? What were the main issues discussed?*

♦ Read excerpts from *The Interesting Narrative of the Life of Olaudah Equiano or Gustavus Vasa, Written by Himself* to examine aspects of the slave trade from the perspective of a captive. *How widely read was Equiano's narrative in Britain and the United States? What are the visual images presented in his narrative? What were the circumstances under which he was enslaved? What actions did he undertake in England to promote the abolition of the slave trade?*

STANDARD 3

Students Should Understand: *How Eurasian societies were transformed in an era of global trade and rising European power, 1750-1850.*

Students Should Be Able to:

3A Demonstrate understanding of how the Ottoman Empire attempted to meet the challenge of Western military, political, and economic power by:

`9-12` Assessing the effects of population growth and European commercial penetration on Ottoman society and government in the 18th and 19th centuries. [**Analyze cause-and-effect relationships**]

`5-12` Analyzing why the empire was forced to retreat from the Balkans and the Black Sea region. [**Analyze multiple causation**]

`7-12` Explaining the defensive reform programs of Selim III and Mahmud II and analyzing the challenges these rulers faced in resolving the empire's political and economic crisis. [**Interrogate historical data**]

`5-12` Explaining the impact of the French invasion of Egypt in 1798 and analyzing the subsequent efforts of Muhammad Ali to found a modern state and economy. [**Analyze cause-and-effect relationships**]

Grades 5-6

Examples of student achievement of Standard 3A include:

▶ Write an historically accurate story about one aspect of Ottoman life such as a day in the life of a janissary, life in the Palace School, or the roles of women.

▶ Create a project illustrating the Western-style reforms made to the Ottoman Empire during the reign of Selim III.

▶ Write a eulogy for Muhammad Ali telling of his life, how he came to power, and what he attempted to do as ruler of Egypt. *How successful was he? Why was he called the "father of modern Egypt"?*

Grades 7-8

Examples of student achievement of Standard 3A include:

▶ Find evidence to support the statement: By the late 19th century the Ottoman Empire was called "the sick man of Europe." Draw a political cartoon to illustrate this evidence and statement.

▶ Compare the training and equipment of the Janissary Corps with that of Japanese samurai, Mongol soldiers, European knights, and modern infantry.

▶ Create an annotated time line listing the major territorial changes in the Ottoman Empire during the first half of the 19th century. *Which new nations were created? Which were made autonomous within the Empire? Which were controlled by other foreign powers?*

◆ Write a script for and present a "You Are There" program covering the main events of the Crimean War. Include dialogue on the background causes of the war, the major nations involved, and the form of fighting and technology used in the war.

Grades 9-12

Examples of student achievement of Standard 3A include:

◆ Describe the changing roles of the janissaries and of Jewish and Christian merchants and landowners by the mid-19th century. *What accounts for their relative prominence?*

◆ Design a chart of the many religious communities and nationalities within the Ottoman Empire in 1800. Include Sunni and Shi'ite Muslims, Druses, Wahabis, Jews, and Christians, as well as the many different nationalities. List the regions or major areas where each group resided. *What was the general picture of the makeup of the Ottoman Empire? What was the prevailing policy toward religions under Ottoman rule? What was the relationship between religion and political authority?*

◆ Create an illustrated biography of Selim III. Describe his education. Give some examples of his poetry, with illustrations, and discuss his accomplishments as a composer of Ottoman music. *What was the rule of Selim like? What were his greatest successes? failures?*

◆ Conduct an interview with English, French, and Ottoman diplomats questioning the motives and strategies for the Crimean War. *What interests did each represent? What military technology, including naval capacity, did each possess? How were each country's interests actually met after the war?*

◆ Prepare a public announcement proclaiming the 1856 reforms in the Hatt-I Humayun issued by Abdul-Mejid. *How did religious leaders react? merchants and artisans? non-Turkish groups such as Armenians, Bulgarians, Macedonians, or Serbs? How successful were the reforms?*

◆ Create a grid listing the political, military, and economic problems of Selim III's rule, the reforms he instituted to deal with those problems, the actual consequences of the reform attempts, and whether they can be said to have succeeded or failed. Summarize the state of affairs in the Ottoman Empire at the death of Selim III. *What other reforms might he have tried to save the empire?*

◆ Read excerpts from the Egyptian historian al-Jabarti's chronicle of the French invasion of Egypt in 1798. *How does he view the impact of the French upon Egyptian culture? What positive and negative aspects of French culture does he note?*

Students Should Be Able to:

3B Demonstrate understanding of Russian imperial expansion in the late 18th and 19th centuries by:

7-12 Analyzing why Russia was successful in wars of expansion with the Ottoman Empire and Muslim Turkic peoples of Central Asia. [**Analyze cause-and effect relationships**]

7-12 Explaining the characteristics of Russian absolutism and reasons for the emergence of movements to reform or oppose the czarist regime. [**Interrogate historical data**]

5-12 Analyzing motives and means of Russian expansion into Manchuria, Siberia, and North America. [**Evidence historical perspectives**]

Grades 5-6

Examples of student achievement of Standard 3B include:

▶ Create a map showing the Russian expansion across Asia and into Alaska and along the California coast. *What did California have to offer that Russia wanted or needed?*

▶ Create an archaeologist's log of cultural and physical artifacts that could describe life in the Russian settlements at Sitka and Bodega Bay.

Grades 7-8

Examples of student achievement of Standard 3B include:

▶ On a map of eastern Europe and central Asia, show the territories conquered during the reign of Catherine the Great, including the territories gained from the Ottoman Empire. Mark the three partitions of Poland with the years 1772, 1793, and 1795. *What port did Russia have on the White Sea? on the Baltic? on the Black Sea? Why was the Black Sea so important to Russia?*

▶ Read an appropriate biography of Catherine the Great and conduct a mock interview of her. *How did she come to rule Russia? What were her literary and intellectual interests? What was palace life like in the Russian court? What problems did she encounter in trying to be an "enlightened" ruler?*

▶ Make a chart describing the general political, social, and economic structure of Russia in 1800s. *What is autocratic rule? What was the relationship between landowners and peasants? How much of Russia was agricultural?*

▶ From the point of view of a Western European journalist, review the events of the Pugachev Rebellion of 1773 and write a story summarizing Catherine the Great's subsequent policies toward the peasantry, serfdom, and the nobility. *What does this reveal about the character of absolutism in Russia?*

Grades 9-12

Examples of student achievement of Standard 3B include:

▶ Construct leaflets, one for distribution to an uneducated peasant audience, the other to army officers, advocating reforms to the czarist regime in the 1820s.

- Examine the causes of the Crimean War. *What consequences did it have for Russia, the Ottoman Empire, Britain, and France?*

- Issue a series of policy statements from Czar Nicholas I on such issues as a constitution, freedom of the press, the Decembrist uprising, the Polish rebellion, and Russification.

- Map Russian expansion eastward across Siberia and southward beyond the Caspian Sea. *Why did Russia invade Ottoman territories in the early 1850s? What was the significance of the Crimean War? What did it show about Russian strength? How did it lead to political and social reforms?*

- Create a poster, banner, or flag depicting Pan-Slavism and how it affected Russian foreign policy in the late 19th century. *Which groups, both within and outside Russia, supported this? on what grounds?*

- Refer to a map of Russian territory and expansion, including diagrams of the Trans-Siberian Railroad and other railroad routes for the period 1801-1914. *Which cities had the most rail service? the least? What would you predict about Russian development from a railway map?*

Painting of the Egyptian ruler Mohammed Ali (1805-1849) conferring with French engineers Courtesy William McNeill

Students Should Be Able to:

3C Demonstrate understanding of the consequences of political and military encounters between Europeans and peoples of South and Southeast Asia by:

7-12 Analyzing causes of the decline of the Mughal empire and the rise of the British East India Company as a political and military power in India. [**Reconstruct patterns of historical succession and duration**]

5-12 Describing the advance of British power in India up to 1850, and assessing both its social and economic impact and the efforts of Indians to resist European conquest and achieve cultural renewal. [**Consider multiple perspectives**]

5-12 Describing patterns of British trade linking India with both China and Europe, and assessing the impact of world trade on Indian agriculture and industry. [**Analyze cause-and-effect relationships**]

9-12 Comparing the British conquest of India with the Dutch penetration of Indonesia, and assessing the role of indigenous elites under these colonial regimes. [**Compare and contrast differing values, behaviors, and institutions**]

| Grades 5-6 | **Examples of student achievement of Standard 3C include:** |

▶ On a world map, draw the main trade route linking India with China and Europe in 1800. *What goods were traded at each port? With which groups of people would trade be carried on? What was the impact of world trade on Indian agriculture and industry?*

▶ Give an oral report on either the history of the British or French East India Company. *How did they receive charters? What did the charters enable them to do? What was the attitude of the home country to the role these companies were to play in India?*

▶ Construct an exchange of letters between a representative of the East India Company and an Indian ruler in the 18th century on the subject of trade.

| Grades 7-8 | **Examples of student achievement of Standard 3C include:** |

▶ Construct a series of map overlays to illustrate the religious and linguistic diversity of India in the early 18th century; compare it with a similar construct illustrating the late 19th century.

▶ Debate the competitive policies of the British and the French in India. *How was the British East India Company able to prevail?*

▶ Compare a map of Dutch territories in South Asia in 1815 with Dutch-ruled territories in 1850. *What factors led to this change?*

▶ View a series of political maps of India from 1798 to 1850. Write a report of your observations about changes in political boundaries, region by region. *What different political forces were present in 1798? How was India organized politically in 1850?*

▶ Show on a world map of the period the trade routes linking India with both China and Europe. Include the Suez Canal in the route. *What products were traded at each station? What goods were imported to India? exported from India?* Speculate on the impact of world trade on Indian agriculture and industry. *How would hand-manufactured goods compete with machine-produced products? How would production and use of Indian resources be different for world market needs than for local needs?*

▶ Construct a time line of the stages of British advancement into India from 1750 to 1858. Include the grant of *diwani* to the East India Company, the battle of Plassey with the French, the defeat of Tipu Sultan of Mysore, the taking of Delhi, the defeat of the Marathas, the First Afghan War, the annexation of the Sind and the conquest of the Punjab, the uprising of 1857, and finally the official transfer of power from the East India Company to the British Crown. *How was India ruled by British Parliament even before 1858? What place did Indians have in the Indian Civil Service that was created by the British to govern India?*

▶ Write a travel diary of a Dutch merchant traveling through the East Indies. *Which Dutch colonies would he visit? What products would he find? How did the Dutch rule their colonies? What language would people speak?*

Grades 9-12

Examples of student achievement of Standard 3C include:

▶ Write a diary entry for a member of the Indian elite and for an average peasant describing your relationship to Europeans and its effect on your life. *In what ways did Western culture influence the lives of elite groups in India or Indonesia? How were Europeans living in those colonies influenced by local cultural styles and practices?*

▶ Role-play a discussion between an upper-class Hindu and a Muslim about their reaction to British presence in India in the late 19th century.

▶ Read original speeches and writings on the life of Ram Mohan Roy. *What was his attitude toward Western science, technology, and culture? toward the use of English in India? What did he hope to achieve for India in the mid-19th century? How did these attitudes change?*

▶ Research the "modernizing" administration of Lord Dalhousie (1848-1856) and British policies in India. Using visual sources of the construction and running of the railroad, evaluate the social and political impact of the railroad on Indian life. *Which people might have benefited most? least? How did the railroad help or hinder the "unity" of India?*

▶ Debate the question: *Did the British "unify" India?*

▶ Create a chart comparing and contrasting the colonial policies of the British in India with Dutch colonial policies in the East Indies. *Where were the areas of greatest similarity? of greatest difference?*

Students Should Be Able to:

3D **Demonstrate understanding of how China's Qing dynasty responded to economic and political crises in the late 18th and the 19th centuries by:**

7-12 Analyzing the economic and social consequences of rapid population growth in China between the 17th and 19th centuries. [**Analyze cause-and-effect relationships**]

7-12 Analyzing causes of governmental breakdown and social disintegration in China in the late 18th century. [**Analyze multiple causation**]

5-12 Analyzing why China resisted political contact and trade with Europeans and how the opium trade contributed to European penetration of Chinese markets. [**Evidence historical perspectives**]

7-12 Assessing causes and consequences of the mid-19th century Taiping rebellion. [**Analyze cause-and-effect relationships**]

9-12 Explaining the reasons for the Chinese diaspora in Southeast Asia and the Americas, and assessing the role of overseas Chinese in attempts to reform the Qing. [**Formulate historical questions**]

| Grades 5-6 | Examples of student achievement of Standard 3D include: |

▸ Write a letter to the editor assuming either the role of a Chinese or a Westerner, and state your reasons for supporting your trade policy. *Why did the Chinese want to keep foreigners out?*

▸ Based on historical evidence, role-play a meeting between a Chinese immigrant to the U.S., one to Southeast Asia, and a Chinese who remained at home, discussing their reasons for leaving and staying.

| Grades 7-8 | Examples of student achievement of Standard 3D include: |

▸ Draw on books such as *Rebels of the Heavenly Kingdom* by Katherine Paterson and *The Serpent's Children* by Lawrence Yep to assess the political and social conflict in China during the late 18th and 19th centuries.

▸ Write an article that might have appeared in a Chinese newspaper of the time about the events of the Opium War or the Boxer Rebellion. Graphically illustrate the main points of your article.

| Grades 9-12 | Examples of student achievement of Standard 3D include: |

▸ Draw evidence from the Qianlong emperor's correspondence (1793) with King George III of England to determine how the Chinese emperor viewed the world. *What are the reasons the emperor gives for denying English trading rights in China? In the emperor's view, how does his Celestial Dynasty compare with other monarchies?*

- Read excerpts from the documents of the Taiping rebels, such as the "Land Regulations of the Taiping Heavenly Kingdom" and discuss the influence of Christianity, rural class relations, problems of rural poverty, and the impending century of revolution.

- Read Lin Zexu's letter to Queen Victoria (1839). Analyze Lin's argument and debate his position on the British sale of opium in China.

- Read Wei Yuan's statement on maritime defense (1842) and selections from Lord Palmerston in parliament on the necessity to go to war with China. *What was Wei Yuan's perception of the West and of imperialism in China?*

- Discuss the terms of the Treaty of Nanjing (1842) following the Opium War and those of the Treaty of Shimonoseki (1895) following the Sino-Japanese War, and analyze the evolution of imperialism in China in the latter half of the 19th century.

- Read Zhang Zhidong's *Exhortation to Study* (1898) and Kang Youwei's memorial to the emperor and discuss the different arguments of these two men. *How do they analyze China's situation? How do they recommend China should respond to the challenge of the West? What does Zhang mean by "Chinese learning for substance (ti), Western learning for function (yong)"?*

- Based on historical information, construct interviews concerning their stand on the opium trade with an English merchant, a Chinese merchant, a Confucian scholar, a Catholic missionary, a Chinese official such as Commissioner Lin Zexu, and a British member of Parliament.

". . . I have heard that the smoking of opium is very strictly forbidden in your country; that is because the harm caused by opium is clearly understood. Since it is not permitted to do harm to your own country, then even less should you let it be passed on to the harm of other countries — how much less to China!"

EXCERPT OF A LETTER FROM LIN TSE-HSU TO QUEEN VICTORIA

Students Should Be Able to:

3E Demonstrate understanding of how Japan was transformed from feudal shogunate to modern nation-state in the 19th century by:

[7-12] Analyzing the internal and external causes of the Meiji Restoration. [Formulate historical questions]

[5-12] Analyzing the goals and policies of the Meiji state and their impact on Japan's modernization. [Obtain historical data]

[5-12] Assessing the impact of Western ideas and the role of Confucianism and Shinto traditional values on Japan in the Meiji period. [Evidence historical perspectives]

[9-12] Explaining the transformation of Japan from a hereditary social system to a middle-class society. [Examine the influence of ideas]

[7-12] Explaining changes in Japan's relations with China and the Western powers from the 1850s to the 1890s. [Reconstruct patterns of historical succession and duration]

| Grades 5-6 | Examples of student achievement of Standard 3E include: |

▶ Make a drawing, using woodblock prints, of the "black ships" and assess their meaning for Japan in the 1850s and 1860s.

▶ Read *Commodore Perry in the Land of the Shogun* by Rhoda Blumberg. Write a biographical sketch or poem on Commodore Perry.

▶ Rewrite the Charter Oath in your own words. Defend this statement: The Charter Oath marked a momentous change in Japan's attitude toward itself and the outside world.

| Grades 7-8 | Examples of student achievement of Standard 3E include: |

▶ Debate the proposition "modernization equals Westernization" in terms of the Japanese experience. *What knowledge did the Japanese have about the West before the arrival of Commodore Perry? What advantages did Japan gain from their "window on the West"?*

▶ Read Sakamoto Ryoma's letters and assume the role of a "samurai man of spirit" (*shishi*) in the events leading up to the Meiji Restoration.

| Grades 9-12 | Examples of student achievement of Standard 3E include: |

▶ Read the Charter Oath and analyze the goals of the new imperial government in 1868. *Which of the goals was achieved and when?*

▶ Read songs and diaries from Tsurumi's *Factory Girls*, and write an autobiography of a factory girl in Meiji Japan.

▶ Read the beginning of Fukuzawa Yukichi's *Encouragement of Learning* and discuss education and social change in Meiji Japan. *What were the changes in social relations from the Tokugawa period?*

♦ Compare the Meiji Restoration to the French and American revolutions.

♦ Analyze the reasons for Japan's rapid industrialization, and compare Japan and China in their response to Western commerce and power in the 19th century.

♦ Read excerpts from writings about visits of 19th-century Japanese travelers to the West, such as Masao Miyoshi's *As We Saw Them*, and hypothesize those features of Western culture and society the Japanese were most likely to take over for themselves; and find evidence to support or modify the hypotheses.

♦ Discuss the meaning of three Meiji slogans: "Civilization and Enlightenment"; "Rich Nation, Strong Army"; and "Increase Production and Promote Industry."

♦ Using stories in Hane's *Peasants, Rebels, and Outcasts*, make a social map showing the people who benefited and those who suffered in the first decades of industrialization and nation-building.

Print of Japanese women of the Meiji era using a telescope National Museum of Modern Art, Tokyo

STANDARD 4

Students Should Understand: *Patterns of nationalism, state-building, and social reform in Europe and the Americas, 1830-1914.*

Students Should Be Able to:

4A Demonstrate understanding of how modern nationalism affected European politics and society by:

[7-12] Identifying major characteristics of 19th-century European nationalism, and analyzing connections between nationalist ideology and the French Revolution, Romanticism, and liberal reform movements. **[Evidence historical perspectives]**

[7-12] Analyzing causes of the revolutions of 1848, and why these revolutions failed to achieve nationalist and democratic objectives. **[Analyze cause-and-effect relationships]**

[5-12] Describing the unification of Germany and Italy, and analyzing why these movements succeeded. **[Analyze multiple causation]**

[9-12] Assessing the importance of nationalism as a source of tension and conflict in the Austro-Hungarian and Ottoman empires. **[Analyze cause-and-effect relationships]**

| Grades 5-6 | Examples of student achievement of Standard 4A include: |

▶ Role-play a young Italian who has joined Garibaldi's redshirts and write a letter home explaining why you became a redshirt.

▶ Research the major leaders of Italian and German unification and write a nationalist speech for each.

| Grades 7-8 | Examples of student achievement of Standard 4A include: |

▶ Review cartoons and drawings of German and Italian unification and create captions or titles for each.

▶ Construct a time line listing the Revolutions of 1848 and, on a map of Europe, locate the areas where the revolts occurred. *To what extent were the Revolutions of 1848 a chain reaction? What was the moving spirit behind each revolution? What were the goals of the revolutions?*

▶ Use a television interview format to conduct a panel discussion of leading figures in the revolutionary era such as: Louis Philippe, Louis Napoleon, Madame de Stael, Louis Kossuth, Pope Pius IX, George Sand, Giuseppe Mazzini, and Klemens von Metternich.

▶ Construct a time line showing each of the events you consider to have been important in the unification of Italy and Germany, and give your reasons for including each event.

▶ Write a speech supporting liberal political reforms from the point of view of a Pole, Hungarian, Austrian, German, Italian, or Spaniard. *What liberal reforms are you supporting? What appeals would you make to arouse nationalist feelings?*

▶ Construct a visual display to accompany a dramatic reading of Bismarck's "Blood and Iron" speech. *What were the previous attempts at unification to which Bismarck referred?*

▶ Construct a poster, patriotic speech, poem, or song to help recruit for the "Red Shirts." *To what extent did Garibaldi reflect 19th-century Romanticism?*

Grades 9-12

Examples of student achievement of Standard 4A include:

▶ Give an account of the Franco-Prussian war as it might have appeared in a French, Bavarian, and a British newspaper.

▶ Define *realpolitik*. Write comparative biographical sketches of Cavour and Bismarck. *To what extent did Cavour and Bismarck exemplify the* realpolitik? *Who would you rank as a master of* realpolitik *today?*

▶ Draw evidence from the original and edited Ems Telegram and role-play Bismarck's editing of the dispatch. *How did Bismarck's understanding of history enter into this editing of the document? What effect did the edited version of the dispatch have on the French?*

▶ Compile a sketchbook of caricatures and cartoons of nationalist movements in Italy and Germany. Explain the meaning of the illustrations.

▶ Research poster art, political cartoons, and news articles from 19th-century Europe and the Mediterranean region to assess the importance of Greek nationalists' and Europeans' roles in the struggle for independence from the Ottomans. Write an editorial for a newspaper taking sides on the topic.

Italian patriot, Giuseppe Mazzini
Library of Congress

227

Students Should Be Able to:

4B **Demonstrate understanding of the impact of new social movements and ideologies on 19th-century Europe by:**

5-12 Analyzing causes of large-scale population movements from rural areas to cities in continental Europe. [**Analyze multiple causation**]

5-12 Analyzing leading ideas of Marxism, other forms of socialism, and labor movements and assessing how they contributed to political and social change in Europe. [**Consider multiple perspectives**]

9-12 Analyzing the influence of industrialization, democratization, and nationalism on these reforms. [**Analyze multiple causation**]

5-12 Analyzing the origins of women's suffrage and other movements in Europe and North America, and assessing their successes up to World War I. [**Marshal evidence of antecedent circumstances**]

9-12 Assessing the extent to which Britain, France, and Italy became more broadly liberal and democratic societies in the 19th century. [**Formulate historical questions**]

7-12 Analyzing changing roles and status of European Jews and the rise of new forms of anti-Semitism. [**Reconstruct patterns of historical succession and duration**]

Grades 5-6

Examples of student achievement of Standard 4B include:

▶ Create and analyze a rural and urban population graph for France and Germany at different points in the 19th century.

▶ Identify a person from the women's suffrage movement and cite important contributions made to women's rights.

▶ Write a slogan for the woman's suffrage movement and create a poster expressing the changes women wanted. Display on a bulletin board. Participate in a class discussion of the posters.

Grades 7-8

Examples of student achievement of Standard 4B include:

▶ On a map of Europe show the rural-to-urban migration in the 19th century. Investigate the causes for each of the major demographic changes.

▶ Trace the development of the women's suffrage movement in Britain. *Who were the leaders in the movement? What was accomplished by the end of the 19th century?*

▶ Construct maps or charts to illustrate and explain the large-scale population movements within Europe and out of Europe in the 19th century.

▶ Write a slogan for the European factory workers who wanted to set up trade unions. Create posters using this slogan and listing their demands.

Grades 9-12

Examples of student achievement of Standard 4B include:

◆ As a member of the English Workingmen's Association, prepare a speech explaining the need for political reform. *How radical were the six major demands of the Chartist movement? How did the ruling classes react to the Chartists? What effect did the continental revolutions of 1848 have on the Chartist movement?*

◆ Construct a late 19th-century newspaper editorial, reflecting both the nature of the agitation for women's suffrage at the time and of the resistance to it.

◆ In the context of the political, economic, and social conditions of the mid-19th century, debate the "10 point program" Marx outlined in the *Communist Manifesto*. *To what extent were these points radical in the context of the late 19th century?*

◆ Draw evidence from Mary Wollstonecraft's *Vindication of the Rights of Women* to list the goals of the women's movement in the 19th century. Debate the various ways to achieve these goals.

◆ Using diverse visual, literary, political, and scientific documents as evidence, debate the benefits and problems of the industrial revolution in at least one European country.

◆ Reading such sources as Émile Zola's indictment of the handling of the Dreyfus Affair, *J'Accuse*, analyze why the French political and military establishment was so resistant to any idea of pardoning Dreyfus in spite of overwhelming proof of his innocence. *To what extent was the Dreyfus Affair a political conflict between conservatives and progressives?*

Émile Zola's letter J'Accuse printed on the front page of L'Aurore, January 1898

Students Should Be Able to:

4C **Demonstrate understanding of how major technological, scientific, and intellectual achievements contributed to social and cultural change in 19th-century Europe by:**

5-12 Assessing the social, economic, and cultural impact of new inventions such as the railroad, telegraph, telephone, internal combustion engine, and photography. [**Analyze cause-and-effect relationships**]

5-12 Assessing the social significance of the work of 19th-century scientists such as Maxwell, Darwin, Pasteur, and Curie. [**Examine the influence of ideas**]

9-12 Analyzing ways in which trends in philosophy and the new social sciences challenged and shaped dominant social values. [**Analyze cause-and-effect relationships**]

9-12 Analyzing how expanded educational opportunities and literacy contributed to changes in European society and cultural life. [**Analyze cause-and-effect relationships**]

5-12 Evaluating major movements in literature, music, and the visual arts and ways in which they shaped or reflected social and cultural values. [**Formulate historical questions**]

7-12 Analyzing elements of the distinctive working and middle-class culture that emerged in industrial Europe. [**Compare and contrast differing values, behaviors, and institutions**]

Grades 5-6

Examples of student achievement of Standard 4C include:

▶ Marshal evidence from primary, literary, and pictorial sources to devise a schedule for an average school day schedule for a male and female student during this period.

▶ Write "A Day in the Life of . . . ." a child from an upper, a middle, or a working class family. Be sure to describe all aspects of your life.

▶ Assume the role of a child of twelve who has never gone to school and will probably never attend school. In pairs, list all of the things you will never be able to do because of your lack of education. Compare your list with other pairs. *How did the lives of people in 19th-century Europe change when they were able to attend school?*

▶ Create, as part of a class, a mural-sized, illustrated, annotated time line of inventors and inventions of 19th-century Europe and America.

Grades 7-8

Examples of student achievement of Standard 4C include:

▶ Construct a comparison chart illustrating the changes in the standard of living from the beginning to the end of the 19th century. *What factors account for the changes? Did everyone benefit from the changes?*

▶ Develop a classroom newspaper profiling the leading scientists of the 19th century and explain how advances in science affected society. *What were the obstacles scientists faced? How did new scientific discoveries improve the health of children and adults?*

◗ Compose a sports and entertainment section for a metropolitan newspaper (ca. 1890) tracing the changes in leisure activity and popular culture through the century. *What factors contributed to the changes? What were the activities most associated with "high culture"? What types of entertainment were open to the middle and working classes?*

◗ Assemble a collection of illustrations to graphically demonstrate the major movements in the arts during the 19th century. Select a literary, musical, art, and architectural work to exemplify one of the major movements. *How did these works reflect changing attitudes in society?*

◗ Analyze various scientific and artistic depictions of the railroad. *What do they say about the source's attitude toward the changes it brought?*

◗ Role-play a discussion between parents of peasant, middle-class, craft, and urban factory worker backgrounds, about the advantages and drawbacks of their children's attending school.

Grades 9-12

Examples of student achievement of Standard 4C include:

◗ Research the new scientific thinkers of the 19th century. *How did they build on or reject each other's theories?*

◗ On a map, identify the countries of the world that had compulsory education and graphically portray the numbers of people who attended school before and during the industrial age.

◗ Examine the effects of Darwin's publication of *The Origin of Species* on traditional patterns of thought with particular regard to religion and social organization.

◗ Bring to class books showing illustrations of the most characteristic examples you can find of Romantic, Realist, and Impressionist art, explaining what features of your examples make them characteristic of the style they illustrate.

◗ Construct a series of diary entries and illustrate the life experiences of 19th-century middle- and working-class women and men. The diaries may be patterned on models such as are available in John Burnett, ed. *The Annals of Labor: Autobiographies of British Working Class People, 1820-1920*; and E. O. Hellerstein et al., eds., *Victorian Women* (a documentary account of 19th-century England, France, and the U.S.).

◗ Read travel accounts, missionary reports, etc., to see how "other" was defined by Europeans. *How did this express or shape Europeans' images of themselves?*

Students Should Be Able to:

4D **Demonstrate understanding of political, economic, and social transformations in the Americas in the 19th century by:**

`5-12` Assessing the successes and failures of democracy in Latin American countries in the decades following independence. [**Formulate historical questions**]

`9-12` Explaining Latin America's growing dependence on the global market economy and assessing the effects of international trade and investment on the power of landowners and the urban middle class. [**Analyze cause-and-effect relationships**]

`9-12` Assessing the consequences of economic development, elite domination and the abolition of slavery for peasants, Indian populations, and immigrant laborers in Latin America. [**Interrogate historical data**]

`5-12` Assessing major events in the United States and their impact on the hemisphere. [**Analyze cause-and-effect relationships**]

`7-12` Assessing the effects of foreign intervention and Liberal government policies on social and economic change in Mexico. [**Analyze cause-and-effect relationships**]

`7-12` Explaining the factors that contributed to nation-building and self-government in Canada. [**Marshal evidence of antecedent circumstances**]

`5-12` Assessing progress in race relations and the status of women during the 19th century. [**Reconstruct patterns of historical succession and duration**]

Grades 5-6

Examples of student achievement of Standard 4D include:

▶ Using a physical map of Latin America, list the ways geography might have influenced nation-building in Latin America.

▶ Construct a diagram of the class system in Latin America. *How was this based on race? How did Creoles take over the Spanish positions of privilege?*

Grades 7-8

Examples of student achievement of Standard 4D include:

▶ Create a visual depiction of caudillo rulers such as Portales and Rosas in Latin America. *What was a caudillo? Which forces backed his rule? How did he maintain himself in power?*

▶ Map the territorial expansion of the United States in the 19th century labeling how each region was acquired and from whom.

▶ Using a provincial map of Canada, draw the routes of the Canadian Pacific Railway to show how the new Dominion of Canada was linked together.

Grades 9-12

Examples of student achievement of Standard 4D include:

▶ Assume the role of a caudillo, a military official, a landowner, a member of the urban bourgeoisie, or a church official, and defend your actions in postindependence Latin America.

▶ Examine the leadership of Benito Juárez within the framework of the Liberal/Conservative civil wars and the French intervention.

▶ Using the economic policies and consequences of the rule of General Porfirio Díaz as an example, write a position paper on the benefits and problems of 19th-century foreign investments.

▶ Using excerpts from *Ariel* (1900) by Juan Enrique Rodó, Domingo Sarmiento's *Facundo* (1845), and the writings of José Martí of Cuba (1870s) or Rubén Darío of Nicaragua, evaluate Latin American attitudes toward nationalism and cultural identity.

▶ Create a graphic showing the governmental structure of the new Dominion of Canada created in 1867. *What was "dominion status," or the Canadian idea?*

Zachary Taylor at the battle of Buena Vista, Library of Congress

STANDARD 5

Students Should Understand: *Patterns of global change in the era of Western military and economic domination, 1850-1914.*

Students Should Be Able to:

5A Demonstrate understanding of the causes and consequences of European settler colonization in the 19th century by:

5-12 Explaining why migrants left Europe in large numbers in the 19th century, and identifying temperate regions of the world where frontiers of European settlement were established or expanded. [**Draw upon data in historical maps**]

5-12 Comparing the consequences of encounters between intrusive European migrants and indigenous peoples in such regions as the United States, Canada, South Africa, Australia, and Siberia. [**Compare and contrast differing values and institutions**]

7-12 Analyzing geographical, political, economic, and epidemiological factors contributing to the success of European colonial settlement of such regions as Argentina, South Africa, Australia, New Zealand, Algeria, Siberia, or Canada. [**Analyze multiple causation**]

| Grades 5-6 | Examples of student achievement of Standard 5A include: |

▶ Make a line graph of the population of Europe from 1650 to 1950. Use increments of 50 years. *Which years mark the highest rate of growth?*

▶ Make a horizontal bar graph of the migration of Europeans from 1840 to 1940. Label the columns "millions of people," and assign intervals of 5 million, from 0 to 60 million. Rows should be labeled "Emigrants to:" the United States, Asiatic Russia, Argentina, Canada, Brazil, Australia, Cuba, South Africa, Uruguay, and New Zealand. Put in the correct information and summarize the information expressed in the graph. *What other visual means could you create to convey this data?*

▶ Write a series of letters back and forth between a European who is considering emigration and an established European in Canada. *What was Canada like around 1870? Which cities were being settled? Who were the other settlers? What things might entice the new settler to Canada?*

| Grades 7-8 | Examples of student achievement of Standard 5A include: |

▶ Recount the rise of the Zulu empire in South Africa. *Did this event have a historical connection to European settlement in the Cape region of South Africa? What were the characteristics of relations between migrating European and African peoples in South Africa in the 19th century? In what ways did these relations lay the foundations of the apartheid system of the 20th century?*

♦ Make a double chart of (a) migrations from European countries, 1846-1932, and (b) immigration into other countries from Europe, citing numbers of people involved. *What inferences about new European settlements can you make?*

♦ Make a line graph of the population of Europe from 1650-1950. Use increments of 50 years. *What is the general trend or pattern of population growth in Europe? Using factors such as birth, death, and infant mortality rates, what accounts for the highest rise in European population? What accounts for the leveling off or stabilizing of the population?*

♦ Design a poster glorifying all the ways that new technologies, such as the steamship or the railroad, can make your emigrant voyage more safe and secure.

♦ Develop a typology of why people left Europe. Use such reasons as overpopulation, political persecution, religious persecution, and improvement of living standards. *Which European countries or peoples would fit some of these categories?*

Grades 9-12

Examples of student achievement of Standard 5A include:

♦ Drawing on historical evidence, explain the settlement of the western part of North America by peoples of European descent. *Was this "westward movement" a unique and exceptional event in world history? Or was it part of a larger pattern of European overseas settlement that included such regions as Argentina, South Africa, and Siberia? Were the consequences of this settlement for indigenous peoples similar in these different regions?*

♦ Select one area of new European settlement and research the foods and raw materials produced by the settlers. *How did settlement and increasing economic ties with Europe change the region?*

♦ Research and develop a case study of one emigrant European group, for example, Italians who went to Argentina. Find out the main factors that led them to leave Italy and the main reasons they chose Argentina. *What backgrounds did they come from? How similar were their new surroundings to the ones they left? What was different?*

♦ Using the case of Australia, research the environmental impact of the new immigrant populations on the land. *What of the indigenous people? Where else might we find a similar case?*

♦ Choose four major cities in the United States where many European immigrants of the 19th century settled. *Where did they settle and why? What were the economic consequences? political consequences? How were they treated by previous settler groups?*

♦ Map the overall settlement of "European communities" throughout the world. *How would this affect the political and economic lives of the local regions in which they settled? What new ways might resources, labor, the flow of goods, and markets change?*

Students Should Be Able to:

5B Demonstrate understanding of the causes of European, American, and Japanese imperial expansion, 1850-1914 by:

7-12 Explaining leading ideas of Social Darwinism and pseudoscientific racism in 19th-century Europe, and assessing the importance of these ideas in activating European imperial expansion in Africa and Asia. [Identify issues and problems in the past]

5-12 Describing advances in transportation, medicine, and weapons technology in Europe in the later 19th century, and assessing the importance of these factors in the success of imperial expansion. [Analyze multiple causation]

7-12 Analyzing the motives that impelled several European powers to undertake imperial expansion against peoples of Africa, Southeast Asia, and China between the 1850s and 1914. [Interrogate historical data]

7-12 Relating the Spanish-American War to United States participation in Western imperial expansion in the late 19th century. [Analyze cause-and effect relationships]

9-12 Assessing the effects of the Sino-Japanese and Russo-Japanese wars and colonization of Korea on the world-power status of Japan. [Analyze cause-and-effect relationships]

7-12 Analyzing the reasons for Japan's imperial expansion in Korea and Manchuria and the rise of Japan as a world power. [Analyze cause-and-effect relationships]

| Grades 5-6 | Examples of student achievement of Standard 5B include: |

▶ On a map or bulletin board graphically depict the motives for European expansion in Africa, Southeast Asia, and China. *What were the motives for imperial expansion? How did they differ depending on the region where expansion was taking place?*

| Grades 7-8 | Examples of student achievement of Standard 5B include: |

▶ Read and report on a biography of Cecil Rhodes. *What were his motives and goals in the "scramble for Africa"? How did the railroad contribute to imperial expansion?*

▶ Read the provisions of the Treaty of Nanking (1842) following the Opium War and discuss what interests the Western powers had in China and what imperialism meant to the Chinese.

▶ Playing the part of a western European journalist reporting on the Russo-Japanese War, draw on historical evidence to explain to your readers why that war was fought and how and why the Japanese won it.

Grades 9-12

Examples of student achievement of Standard 5B include:

◆ Write an essay on the chain of developments in both Europe and Africa that precipitated the so-called "scramble" for African territory. *Is it possible to identify a single precipitating event? In what ways did particular African governments or peoples play a part in shaping the way the European partition of Africa took place?*

◆ Construct a balance sheet listing the positive and negative features of imperialism. *What were the chief benefits of the introduction of new political institutions and advances in communication, technology, and medicine? What were the costs of the introduction of European institutions and new technology?*

◆ Using multiple sources like Kipling's *White Man's Burden*, summarize the intellectual justifications for British imperialism, French *mission civilisatrice*, and German *Kultur* as part of European imperialism.

◆ Read Chinua Achebe's *Things Fall Apart* or Markandaya's *Nectar in a Sieve* to assess the impact of European expansion on village life, including legal, familial, and gender relations in Africa and India.

◆ Develop case studies from Daniel Headrick's *Tools of Empire* to illustrate the role of medical advances, steam power, and military technology in European imperialism.

◆ Prepare a map of Africa and Eurasia showing major national and international railroad lines constructed during the late 19th- and early 20th-century. Gather information about the history of their construction and funding. Write a report assessing the importance of these routes and analyzing the potential benefits to imperial powers and indigenous economies.

◆ Argue Japan's case for its imperial expansion in East Asia, taking either of the following two positions: (1) Japan should "Escape from Asia," treating Asia as the West does, or (2) Japan should be "Leader of Asia," protecting Asia from Western imperialism.

Cartoon image of Cecil Rhodes showing British influence from "Cape to Cairo." Punch, *1892*

Students Should Be Able to:

5C **Demonstrate understanding of transformations in South, Southeast, and East Asia in the era of the "new imperialism" by:**

`7-12` Analyzing the economic and political impact of British rule on India in the 19th century [**Interrogate historical data**]

`7-12` Explaining the social, economic, and intellectual sources of Indian nationalism and analyzing reactions of the British government to it. [**Analyze cause-and-effect relationships**]

`9-12` Comparing French and British colonial expansion in mainland Southeast Asia, and analyzing Thailand's success in avoiding colonization. [**Compare and contrast differing values, behaviors, and institutions**]

`7-12` Analyzing how Chinese began to reform government and society after 1895 and why revolution broke out in 1911. [**Analyze multiple causation**]

`5-12` Analyzing Japan's rapid industrialization, technological advancement, and national integration in the late 19th and early 20th centuries. [**Formulate historical questions**]

| Grades 5-6 | **Examples of student achievement of Standard 5C include:** |

▶ Write an article that might have appeared in a Chinese newspaper of the time about the events of the Boxer Rebellion. Illustrate the main points of your article.

▶ Write an article that might have appeared in a Japanese newspaper after the death of the Meiji emperor in 1912. *What were the main achievements of Meiji Japan?*

| Grades 7-8 | **Examples of student achievement of Standard 5C include:** |

▶ Map the new European presence in South, Southeast, and East Asia in the late 19th century.

▶ Construct a graphic display of the Uprising of 1857 in India and British reaction to the uprising drawing from original works and your interpretations through cartoons or caricatures.

▶ Draw from historical evidence to construct a speech encouraging a sepoy to rebel against British authority.

▶ Hold a dialogue, based on historical information, between Empress Dowager Cixi and a leader of the Righteous Harmonious Fists (Boxers) secret society about the presence and activities of foreigners in China in the late 1890s.

▶ Trace the importance of silk in Japan's trade and economic development.

Grades 9-12

Examples of student achievement of Standard 5C include:

▶ Write a series of newspaper accounts of the Indian uprising of 1857. *Why did the army revolt? What religious policies were they rebelling against?* Describe the march on Delhi and the other forces that joined the soldiers there. *Why did the rebellion spread so quickly? What demands did Muslim rebels make? How did Hindu factions react? Sikhs? What was the reaction of the princes and maharajahs who had made alliances with the East India Company?*

▶ Prepare arguments for why the empress dowager originally supported the Boxer Rebellion.

▶ Trace the life of Sun Yatsen and look at the role of overseas Chinese in the 1911 revolution.

▶ Construct a time line showing the chronology of the introduction of major social, economic, political, and technological changes derived from the West in 19th-century Japan.

▶ Map the French and British expansion in mainland Southeast Asia. *How did their colonial policies differ? Why was Thailand successful in avoiding colonization?*

▶ Analyze the role of the emperor in Meiji Japan. Compare his political and symbolic roles with those of the British or other Western monarchs of the time.

Sepoys charging the Kashmir Gate at Delhi during the Rebellion of 1857. An engraving of M. S. Morgan's painting. National Army Museum, London

Students Should Be Able to:

5D Demonstrate understanding of the varying responses of African peoples to world economic developments and European imperialism by:

[7-12] Analyzing the changing economies of West African societies following the termination of the trans-Atlantic slave trade. [**Reconstruct patterns of historical succession and duration**]

[7-12] Explaining the rise of Zanzibar and other commercial empires in East Africa in the context of international trade in ivory, cloves, and slaves. [**Evidence historical perspectives**]

[9-12] Analyzing the sources and effectiveness of military, political, and religious resistance movements against European conquest in such regions as Algeria, Morocco, West Africa, the Sudan, Ethiopia, and South Africa. [**Analyze cause-and-effect relationships**]

[5-12] Assessing the effects of the discovery of diamonds and gold in South Africa on political and race relations among British colonial authorities, Afrikaners, and Africans. [**Analyze cause-and-effect relationships**]

[5-12] Explaining major changes in the political geography of both northern and Sub-Saharan Africa between 1880 and 1914. [**Draw upon the data in historical maps**]

Grades 5-6

Examples of student achievement of Standard 5D include:

▶ After viewing video clips of the discovery of diamonds and gold in South Africa in Basil Davidson's series *Africa*, predict the events that followed. *How did the British population and British investors react?*

▶ List the products exchanged between Europe and West Africa in the period after the slave trade. *What was the relationship between European and African merchants?*

Grades 7-8

Examples of student achievement of Standard 5D include:

▶ Write, as a part of a group, a description of one of the following resistance leaders or movements: Abd al-Qadir in Algeria, Samori Ture in West Africa, the Mahdist state in the Sudan, Memelik II in Ethiopia, the Zulus in South Africa. Share your findings with the class and attach your description to a map of Africa.

▶ Construct a map of the Eastern Hemisphere. Label the Suez Canal. *How did the Suez Canal affect world trade? World political alliances? What part did the Egyptian government have in its building?*

▶ Recount the career of the East African empire-builder Tippu Tip. *How did 19th-century trade in clover, ivory, and slaves stimulate empire-building in East Africa? Was Tippu Tip a leader of resistance against European imperialism?*

Grades 9-12

Examples of student achievement of Standard 5D include:

◗ Research evidence that slavery and slave trade became more widespread in both West and East Africa in the 19th century, even as the trans-Atlantic slave trade came to an end. *How did world demand for West African products contribute to increased enslavement of people in that region? How was slave labor used in 19th-century West Africa? How did the development of clove plantations on the East African coast, as well as international ivory trade, contribute to an increase in long-distance slave trading in that region? What connections were there between slave and ivory trading in East Africa and the emergence of new empires in the interior?*

◗ Drawing on historical evidence, chart the reasons for both the successes and the failures of resistance movements in Africa such as those led by Abd al-Qadir in Algeria, Samori Ture in West Africa, Menelik II in Ethiopia, the Zulus in South Africa. *What conditions or events favored success? Failure?*

◗ Assess the relative strength of Islam and Christianity in Africa at the beginning of the 20th century. *What attracted people to either of these faiths? What forms did rivalries take among Christian denominations in proselytizing Africans? In what ways were both Islam and Christianity linked to the interests of governments?*

◗ Research the role of Mahdi Muhammad Ahmed in opposing the British in the Sudan. *How effective was the Mahdi uprising? What did it illustrate regarding popular opposition to British imperialism in the Anglo-Egyptian Sudan?*

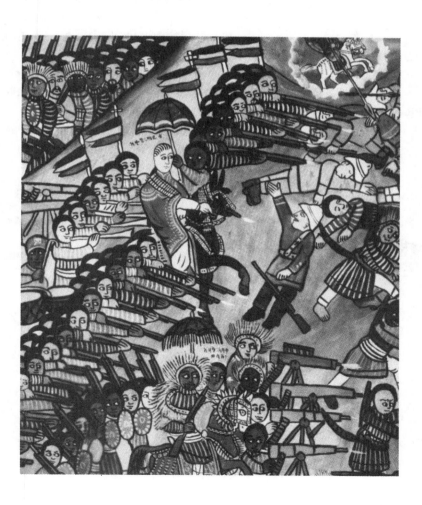

Ethiopian defeat of Italian forces at the Battle of Adowa, 1896
American Museum of Natural History

STANDARD 6

Students Should Understand: *Major global trends from 1750 to 1914.*

Students Should Be Able to:

6 **Demonstrate understanding of major global trends from 1750 to 1914 by:**

5-12 Describing major shifts in world population and urbanization in this era and analyzing how such factors as industrialization, migration, changing diets, and scientific and medical advances affected worldwide demographic trends. **[Interrogate historical data]**

5-12 Describing major patterns of long-distance migration of Europeans, Africans, and Asians and analyzing causes and consequences of these movements. **[Analyze cause-and-effect relationships]**

5-12 Comparing processes by which industrialization occurred in Great Britain, France, Germany, the United States, Russia, Japan, or other countries and analyzing how industrialization in these countries affected class relations and the social position of women. **[Compare and contrast differing values, behaviors, and institutions]**

5-12 Explaining major changes in world political boundaries between 1750 and 1914 and analyzing why a relatively few European states achieved such extensive military, political, and economic power in the world during this era. **[Analyze cause-and-effect relationships]**

5-12 Assessing the importance of ideas associated with republicanism, liberalism, and constitutionalism on 19th-century political life in such states as Great Britain, Germany, Russia, Mexico, Argentina, the Ottoman Empire, China, or Japan. **[Identify issues and problems in the past]**

5-12 Identifying regions where Christianity and Islam were growing in this era, and analyzing causes of 19th-century movements of reform or renewal in Buddhism, Christianity, Hinduism, Islam, or Judaism. **[Interrogate historical data]**

5-12 Identifying patterns of social and cultural continuity in various societies and analyzing ways in which peoples maintained traditions and resisted external challenges in this era of expanding Western hegemony. **[Reconstruct patterns of historical succession and duration]**

Grades 5-6

Examples of student achievement of Standard 6 include:

▶ Create a graphic illustrating immigration and emigration.

▶ View visual sources on North and South American immigrants in the 19th century. Choose one photograph and do a "quickwrite" about what she or he felt, saw, heard, and what they hoped for.

▶ Map Asian or African migrations from 1750-1900. *Where did people go? Why?*

▶ Report on the history, layout, and size of any one of the following cities during this era: Guangzhou, Cairo, Sydney, Tokyo, Buenos Aires, Bombay, Moscow, San Francisco, or London. *How did these cities change?*

| Grades 7-8 | **Examples of student achievement of Standard 6 include:** |

- Using information from a computer data source, create a graph of world population figures by century from 1500-1900. *When did the greatest increases occur? Where? What factors might account for this?*

- Construct a bar graph of major world religion statistics in 1750 and in 1900. Research the regions where both Christianity and Islam expanded.

- Using various visual, literary, and documentary resources from one country, list the ways a rural family unit might have been affected by the industrial revolution. Create a visual representation of the findings. *How were women's roles affected? How did the role of children change?*

- Write a pamphlet or series of newspaper articles describing the daily life of an industrial working man. Write a second series on the daily life of a woman. *How are they similar? Different?*

| Grades 9-12 | **Examples of student achievement of Standard 6 include:** |

- Make two maps showing the location of major cities of the world, one dated about 1750, the other about 1900. *Where did new large cities appear? Why did more large cities appear in Europe? In Latin America? In what regions was migration likely to have contributed to the growth of cities? Where would trade or industrialization most likely have been important? In what regions was urbanization linked to European colonialism?*

- Research and report on two major religious reform movements in Buddhism, Christianity, Hinduism, Islam, or Judaism in the 19th century. *What reforms were undertaken? What problems did they address? How successful were they?*

- Create a series of political slogans or cartoons for the liberal and/or socialist interests of a 19th-century nation-state. *How were these connected to new- or old-class interests? What specific demands were being made?*

- Using excerpts from novels such as Chinua Achebe's *Things Fall Apart*, Buchi Emecheta's *The Joys of Motherhood*, Kamala Markandaya's *Nectar in a Sieve*, and *Child of the Dark: The Diary of Carolina Maria de Jesus*, describe the struggle of traditional forces to maintain themselves in the face of rapid industrial and urban change.

- Research the lives and explore writings of Jamal al-Din al-Afghani, Rashid Rida, and Muhammad Abdul. *What was their vision of progress, and how did they differ in blending Western ideas and values with indigenous values?*

- Research educational reform in various Muslim regions during the 19th century. Make a chart describing and arranging these efforts on a continuum of traditionalist rejection of Western ideas, wholesale embrace of Western forms and ideas, and synthesis of Western and indigenous ideas. *What new institutions were established, and how did older ones change? How did educational reform affect women?*

ERA 8

The 20th Century

Giving Shape to World History

The closer we get to the present the more difficult it becomes to distinguish between the large forces of change and the small. Surveying the long sweep of history from early hominid times to World War I, we might reach at least partial consensus about what is important to the development of the whole human community and what is not. The multifarious trends of the past century, however, are for the most part still working themselves out. Therefore, we cannot know what history students one or two hundred years from now will think was worth remembering about the 20th century. Clearly, the era has been one of tensions, paradoxes, and contradictory trends. Some of these countercurrents provide students with a framework for investigation and analysis.

▶ **Democracy and Tyranny:** Human aspirations toward democratic government, national independence, and social and economic justice were first expressed on a large scale in human affairs in the 1750-1914 era. These aspirations have continued to inspire numerous popular protests and revolutions in the 20th century. Early in the century revolutions in such countries as Mexico, China, and Russia brought drastic political changes but also a variety of new social and economic dilemmas. Before World War II movements of protest and dissent, some largely peaceful, forced a broadening of the democratic base, including voting rights for women, in a number of countries. Under the weight of the two great wars and the resolute pressure of nationalist movements, the empires of the European nations and Japan were dismantled. In the three decades following World War II a multitude of new sovereign states appeared. The breakup of the Soviet Union that began in 1990 introduced fifteen more. Triumphant nationalism, in short, has radically transformed the globe's political landscape. Even so, peoples around the world have had to struggle persistently for democracy and justice against the powerful counterforces of authoritarianism, totalitarianism, neo-colonialism, and stolid bureaucracy. Many of the newer independent states have also faced daunting challenges in raising their peoples' standard of living while at the same time participating in a global economic system where industrialized countries have had a distinct advantage. The political, and in some places economic, reform movements that bloomed in Africa, Eurasia, and Latin America in the 1980s are evidence of the vitality of civic aspirations that originated more than two centuries ago.

▶ **War and Peace:** The powers of destruction that centuries of accumulated technical and scientific skill gave to human beings became horrifyingly apparent in World War I. Because this first global conflict sowed copious seeds of the second one, the entire period from 1914 to 1945 may be characterized as the 20th century's "thirty years war." However, as soon as World War II ended, the Cold War began: forty more years of international crises and the doubtful consolations of mutually assured destruction. When the Soviet empire collapsed, the threat of nuclear war receded. On the other hand, local "hot spots" multiplied as ancient enemies settled old scores and ethnic or nationalist feelings rose to the surface. Amid the fierce confrontations of the century, people around the world have continued to seek peace. The achievements and limitations of the League of Nations, the post-World War II settlements, the U.N., the European Economic Community, Middle East negotiations, and numerous other forms of international cooperation are all worthy of serious study for the lessons they may offer the coming generation.

▶ **Global Links and Communal Identity:** The transformations that the world experienced in the previous two eras appear modest in comparison with the bewildering pace and complexity of change in the 20th century. The revolution of global communication has potentially put everyone in touch with everyone else. Business travelers, scientists, labor migrants, and refugees move incessantly from country to country. Currency transfers ricochet from bank to bank. The youth of Bangkok, Moscow, and Wichita Falls watch the same movies and sport the same brand of jeans. In economy, politics, and culture the human community is in a continuous process of restructuring itself. Global interdependence, however, has a flip side. As the gales of change blow, people seek communal bonds and identities more urgently than ever. Communalism has frequently led to fear and suspicion of the "other." Yet the institutions and values that communities share also protect them in some measure from the shocks of the new and unforeseen. The social and cultural bonds of family, village, ethnic community, religion, and nation provide a framework for estimating how others will think and behave and for calculating with some confidence the pattern of affairs from day to day.

▶ **Countercurrents in the Quality of Life:** The first decade of the 20th century promised, at least in the industrialized countries, a new age of progress through science, technology, and rational policy-making. Fifty years and two world wars later, humanity was far less optimistic about its future. Art and literature starkly reported the era's skepticism and angst. Science, medicine, and techniques of human organization continued to benefit society in wondrous ways. On the other hand, the world population explosion, wretched poverty, environmental degradation, and epidemic disease have defied the best efforts of statesmanship, civic action, and scientific imagination. Amid the distresses and dangers of the era, people have sought not only communal ties but also moral and metaphysical certainties. The major religions have continued to grow and change dynamically. Spiritual quests and ethical questionings have been a vital part of the cultural history of the past century.

Why Study This Era?

▶ If the great forces moving in our contemporary world are difficult to understand, they make no sense at all except in relation to the events of the past century. Historical perspectives on the world wars, the Great Depression, the breakup of empires, the Cold War, the population explosion, and the other sweeping developments of the era are indispensable for unraveling the causes and perhaps even discerning the likely consequences of events now unfolding. Students in school today are going to be responsible for addressing the promises and paradoxes of the age. They will not be able to do this by reading headlines or picking bits of "background" from the past. They must gain some sense of the whole flow of developments and comprehend the contemporary world in all its roundness.

What Students Should Understand

Standard 1: **Global and economic trends in the high period of Western dominance**

    A. Emergence of **industrialized states** in the Northern Hemisphere [CORE]

    B. Causes and consequences of early 20th-century **revolutionary movements** [RELATED]

Standard 2: **The causes and global consequences of World War I**

    A. Multiple causes of **World War I** [CORE]

    B. The global scope and human **costs of World War I** [CORE]

    C. The causes and consequences of the **Russian Revolution** [CORE]

Standard 3: **The search for peace and stability in the 1920s and 1930s**

    A. Postwar efforts to achieve lasting **peace and** social and economic **recovery** [CORE]

    B. Economic, social, and political **transformations** in Africa, Asia, and Latin America [CORE]

    C. How new departures in **science and the arts** altered human views of nature, the cosmos, and the psyche between 1900 and 1940 [RELATED]

    D. Causes and global consequences of the **Great Depression** [RELATED]

Standard 4: **The causes and global consequences of World War II**

    A. Multiple causes of **World War II** [CORE]

    B. The global scope and human **costs of World War II** [CORE]

Standard 5: **How new international power relations took shape following World War II**

    A. **Global power shifts** after World War II [CORE]

    B. How African, Asian, and Caribbean peoples achieved **independence** from European colonial rule [CORE]

Standard 6: **Promises and paradoxes of the second half of the 20th century**

    A. How **population** explosion **and changes in the earth's environment** altered conditions of life [CORE]

    B. The increasing **economic interdependence** of human society [CORE]

    C. How ideologies of **democracy, private enterprise, and human rights** have reshaped political and social life [CORE]

    D. Sources of **tension and conflict** in the contemporary world [RELATED]

    E. Worldwide **social and cultural trends** of the late 20th century [RELATED]

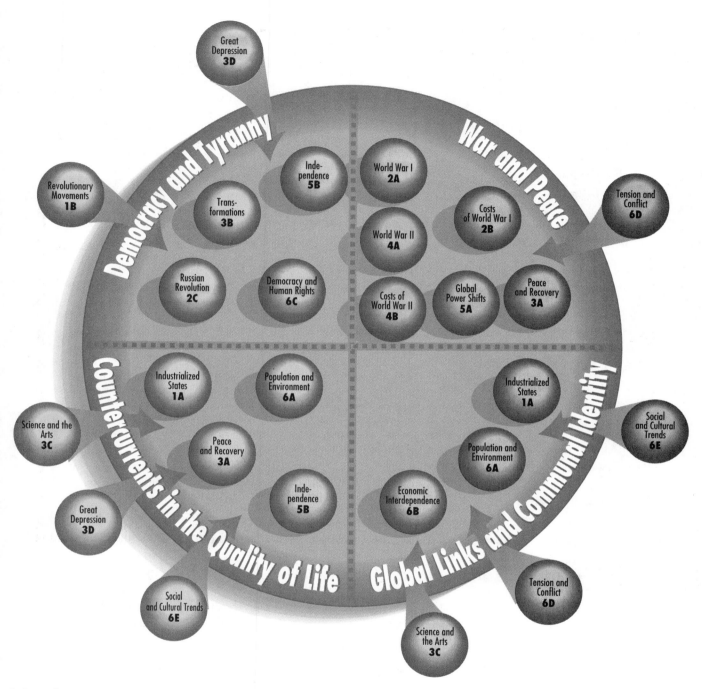

Relationships Among Major Developments, Core Standards, and Related Standards for Era 8

STANDARD 1

Students Should Understand: *Global and economic trends in the high period of Western dominance.*

Students Should Be Able to:

1A Demonstrate understanding of how a belt of industrialized states was emerging in the Northern Hemisphere in the early 20th century by:

7-12 | Comparing the industrial power of Great Britain, France, Germany, and the United States in the early 20th century. [**Utilize visual and mathematical data**]

5-12 | Analyzing the impact of industrial development on the standard of living and lifestyles of middle- and working-class people in Europe and the United States. [**Analyze cause-and-effect relationships**]

5-12 | Describing major scientific, medical, and technological advances in Europe and the United States at the turn of the century, and evaluating popular attitudes regarding material progress and the West's global leadership. [**Interrogate historical data**]

7-12 | Explaining leading ideas of liberalism, social reformism, conservatism, and socialism as competing ideologies in early 20th-century Europe. [**Examine the influence of ideas**]

7-12 | Comparing Japan's economic development and political ideologies in the early 20th century with those of Europe and the United States. [**Compare and contrast differing sets of ideas**]

9-12 | Analyzing why European colonial territories and Latin American countries continued to maintain largely agricultural economies in the early 20th century. [**Identify issues and problems in the past**]

Grades 5-6

Examples of student achievement of Standard 1A include:

▶ Identify the new technologies of the early 20th century and explain how they altered lifestyles. *To what extent did technology bring people closer together? What impact did the automobile have?*

▶ List the major industrial nations of the world at the turn of the century. Draw evidence from art works, photographs, and documentary films to examine the lifestyles of people in these industrialized countries.

▶ Construct a chart listing the major scientific advances at the turn of the century. *How did these innovations in science and medicine affect peoples' lives? What would our life be like today without these innovations?*

Grades 7-8

Examples of student achievement of Standard 1A include:

- Identify the industrial output in Britain, France, Germany, the United States, and Japan in the early 20th century and examine the importance of industrialization in these northern hemisphere nations. Compare and contrast the industrial potential of these states. Write an essay examining the importance of industrial development in the modern world.

- Research the life of a leading European conservative, liberal, or socialist at the beginning of the century such as Stanley Baldwin, Ramsay MacDonald, Emmeline Pankhurst, Jean Jaurès, Raymond Poincaré, Peter Stolypin, Alfred Krupp, or Rosa Luxemburg. *How did the selected individual influence political or social policy in prewar Europe?*

- Examine the impact of Japanese territorial expansion as a result of the Sino-Japanese and Russo-Japanese wars on industrialization and economic development of Japan. *How did the annexation of Taiwan and a sphere of influence in Korea impact Japan's economy?*

- Define the "welfare state" in terms of liberal ideals of the early 20th century. *What were the programs promoted by early 20th-century liberals?*

Grades 9-12

Examples of student achievement of Standard 1A include:

- Examine the role of government in the industrial nations of the Northern Hemisphere in promoting social legislation. Debate the efficacy of Social Security, minimum wage laws, compulsory free public education, and state-financed public works from the point of view of a liberal and a conservative in the early 20th century.

- Research the impact of new technological developments on labor, capital investment, and industrial production. *What social changes resulted from technological developments in manufacturing? How did these changes impact the standard of living?*

- Examine how changes regarding land ownership and government promotion of new technology in Japan in the late 19th century encouraged industrial development. *What impact did government subsidies have in promoting Japanese industry? How did Japan's industrial leaders influence government policy? In what ways was the industrial development of Japan similar to mid- and late-19th century industrialization in western Europe and the United States?*

- Examine the policy of a European country toward industrial development in one of their colonial possessions. Prepare a position paper that assesses policies that promoted or retarded industrial development from the perspective of a member of the colonial office or a prominent citizen in the colonized nation. *Did the policy promote or retard the development of an industrial economy? To what extent was the colonial policy similar to or different from those of the British during the period prior to the American Revolution?*

- Prepare a chart illustrating the agricultural products and raw materials of Latin American states. *On what were the economies of Latin American states based? What countries had large investments in Latin America? Why did Latin American nations fail to develop industrial economies at the turn of the century?*

Students Should Be Able to:

1B Demonstrate understanding of the causes and consequences of important resistance and revolutionary movements of the early 20th century by:

[7–12] Assessing the South African (Anglo-Boer) War as the first "total war" of the 20th century. [Interrogate historical data]

[5–12] Explaining the causes of the Russian rebellion of 1905 and assessing its impact on reform in the succeeding decade. [Analyze cause-and-effect relationships]

[7–12] Analyzing the efforts of the revolutionary government of the Young Turks to reform Ottoman government and society. [Interrogate historical data]

[5–12] Analyzing the significance of the Mexican Revolution as the first 20th-century movement in which peasants played a prominent role. [Evidence historical perspectives]

[7–12] Assessing the promise and failure of China's 1911 republican revolution to address the country's political, economic, and social problems. [Compare and contrast differing values and institutions]

| **Grades 5-6** | **Examples of student achievement of Standard 1B include:** |

♦ Assume the role of a Russian worker in 1905 and describe the events of that year. *Would you have supported the Revolution of 1905?*

♦ Research the lives of Francisco Madero, Emiliano Zapata, and Francisco Villa and write accounts of the role each played in the Mexican Revolution.

♦ Write a biography of Dr. Sun Yatsen. *Why is he called the "Father of Modern China"?*

♦ Study the murals of Diego Rivera and José Clemente Orozco that glorified the Mexican Revolution and the Mexican nation. *How did such works of art create support for the revolution among the peasants?*

| **Grades 7-8** | **Examples of student achievement of Standard 1B include:** |

♦ Construct posters and banners representing the issues raised by Russian workers in 1905 and describe the events of "Bloody Sunday." *As a Russian worker, how would you have reacted to the events of "Bloody Sunday"? What were the consequences of the "Revolution of 1905"?*

♦ Compare the motivations of the peasants and the middle class in the Mexican Revolution. *How did the peasants play a prominent role?*

♦ Investigate the New Culture movement in China. *Who were the leaders of the movement? What were its goals? Why did it fail to win support in rural areas?*

♦ Assume the role of a peasant supporting the Mexican or Chinese revolutions and create a protest poster or banner that reflects the reforms you are demanding. *Does there seem to be a common theme among the peasants' demands?*

▶ Research the rise of the Young Turk movement and its attempts to restore constitutional government in Turkey. *To what segments of the population did the Young Turks appeal? Who were the leaders of the movement? How effective were the Young Turks in using nationalism as a means of promoting their cause?*

▶ Assume the role of a member of the British Foreign Office and debate the measures British troops should take in responding to the guerrilla tactics employed by the Boers in South Africa. *What were the major causes of the war? Why was the Anglo-Boer War considered to be a "total war"? What role did Africans play in the war?*

Grades 9-12

Examples of student achievement of Standard 1B include:

▶ Draw evidence from a variety of primary sources, and visual images from movies such as *Nicholas and Alexandra* and *Dr. Zhivago* to examine the Revolution of 1905. *What impact did the Russo-Japanese War have on heightening discontent in Russia? What were the issues that led to "Bloody Sunday"? What groups of people supported political reform? What groups called for radical structural changes in Russia? How effective was the October Manifesto?*

▶ Examine illustrations of the murals depicting the Mexican Revolution by José Clemente Orozco, David Siqueros, and Diego Rivera, and explain how they were an expression of nationalism. *How did such works of art create support for the revolution among the peasants? How do the muralists portray the revolution? Was the revolution a class struggle?*

▶ Use excerpts from Mariano Azuela's novel *The Underdogs* or Carlos Fuentes's *The Death of Artemoi Cruz* to explain the impact of the Mexican Revolution on peasants.

▶ Write an essay analyzing the social and cultural ferment in China that culminated in the New Culture or May Fourth movement. *What were the consequences of the movement?*

▶ Use a variety of primary sources and excerpts from films such as *Breaker Morant* to examine British attitudes toward non-British people and the use of colonial troops in the Anglo-Boer War. *What were the consequences of the war on the Boers, British and African populations?*

▶ Trace the roots of the Young Turk movement to the Constitution of 1876. *What accounts for the success of the movement? What were the reforms advocated by the Young Turks? How effective were these reforms?*

▶ Draw evidence from Sun Yatsen's *Manifesto* for the Tong Meng Hui (Revolutionary Alliance) to examine the issues raised by the Chinese Revolution of 1911. *What were the four points presented in the* Manifesto*? To whom did the revolutionary goals appeal? What were the "Three People's Principles"?*

STANDARD 2

Students Should Understand: *The causes and global consequences of World War I.*

Students Should Be Able to:

2A **Demonstrate understanding of the multiple causes of World War I by:**

7–12 Analyzing the relative importance of economic and political rivalries, ethnic and ideological conflicts, militarism, and imperialism as underlying causes of the war. **[Analyze multiple causation]**

9–12 Analyzing the degree to which class and other social conflicts in Europe contributed to the outbreak of war. **[Analyze multiple causation]**

7–12 Evaluating ways in which popular faith in science, technology, and material progress affected attitudes toward the possibility of war among European states. **[Formulate historical questions]**

5–12 Analyzing the precipitating causes of the war and the factors that produced military stalemate. **[Analyze cause-and-effect relationships]**

Grades 5-6

Examples of student achievement of Standard 2A include:

▶ Role-play situations when members of an alliance must come to the aid of one of its members. Discuss how the alliances worked or did not work. *What are the advantages and disadvantages of an alliance? What geographic advantage did each alliance have? What countries made up the Allied Powers? The Central Powers?*

▶ Use a pyramid model with the assassination of Archduke Ferdinand of Austria at the apex to show how this event led to the involvement of the countries of the two European alliances eventually leading to World War I.

▶ On a map of Europe and Southwest Asia, locate the major areas of combat. *Why was there a stalemate? What plans would you propose to break the stalemate?*

Grades 7-8

Examples of student achievement of Standard 2A include:

▶ Write a nationalist song expressing loyalty to your country. *How did nationalism threaten the balance of power among the Great Powers? Why was it considered one of the causes of World War I?*

▶ Construct a graphic organizer examining the long-range causes of World War I. Assuming the role of a nationalist leader of one of the major powers, write a speech defending your country's position on the eve of war.

▶ Examine the system of alliances through which nations in Europe sought to protect their interests and explain the role of nationalism and militarism, that contributed to the outbreak of war. *What measure might have been taken to avert war? How did the war expand beyond European boundaries to become a world war?*

- ► Write a position paper from the perspective of one of the Allied or Central Powers in August 1914 explaining the immediate causes for your nation's entry into war.

- ► Analyze photographs and paintings of battle scenes in order to explain the nature of the war in Europe. Investigate how technological developments employed in the "Great War" contributed to the brutality of modern war.

Grades 9-12

Examples of student achievement of Standard 2A include:

- ► Interrogate historical data presented in both primary and secondary sources, including the telegrams between William II and Nicholas II, to determine the arguments presented by political leaders on the eve of the Great War.

- ► Assume the role of a political leader in either France, Germany, Britain, Austria-Hungary, or Russia and debate the recommendation that your government should press an active foreign policy in order to "smother internal problems." *How did ethnic conflicts in European states, particularly Austria-Hungary and Russia, contribute to the outbreak of war? How valid is the argument that the desire to suppress internal disorder encouraged some European political leaders to advocate war?*

- ► Debate the position that France should take regarding the war from the perspective of socialist leader Jean Jaurès, French President Raymond Poincaré or members of the rightist Action Française.

- ► Write an essay from the perspective of an idealist in early 1914 examining how the quality of life and the advances in science and technology would preclude Europe from engaging in a major war. *To what extent did Europeans persuade themselves that a massive war was inconceivable?*

- ► Examine the Schlieffen Plan. *Did the Schlieffen Plan contribute to the stalemate?* Explain.

- ► Draw upon historical narratives and poster art to analyze the relative successes of propaganda campaigns waged by major world powers to influence their colonial possessions and neutral nations to support the war effort. *How successful were the Allied propaganda campaigns in mobilizing support for the war against the Central Powers? How successful was German propaganda?*

- ► Debate the proposition that World War I was inevitable considering the nationalism, militarism, and imperialism of the day. *Did decision-makers in various European countries believe war was unavoidable? What were the miscalculations that ultimately led to the "Great War"?*

U.S. Army recruitment poster during World War I, National Archives

British recruiting poster from World War I picturing Lord Kitchener Library of Congress

Students Should Be Able to:

2B   Demonstrate understanding of the global scope and human costs of the war by:

5-12   Describing the major turning points of the war, and describing the principal theaters of conflict in Europe, the Middle East, Sub-Saharan Africa, East Asia, and the South Pacific. [**Interrogate historical data**]

5-12   Analyzing the role of nationalism and propaganda in mobilizing civilian populations in support of "total war." [**Examine the influence of ideas**]

5-12   Explaining how massive industrial production and innovations in military technology affected strategy and tactics and the scale and duration of the war. [**Analyze cause-and-effect relationships**]

7-12   Explaining ways in which colonial peoples contributed to the war effort of both the Allies and the Central Powers by providing military forces and supplies. [**Evaluate the implementation of a decision**]

7-12   Analyzing how the Russian Revolution and the entry of the United States affected the course and outcome of the war. [**Analyze cause-and-effect relationships**]

5-12   Assessing the short-term demographic, social, economic, and environmental consequences of the war's unprecedented violence and destruction. [**Formulate historical questions**]

Grades 5-6

Examples of student achievement of Standard 2B include:

▶ On a world map locate the areas in which fighting occurred during World War I and identify the countries that fought in each of these regions.

▶ Assume the persona of one of the people in a photograph depicting trench warfare and write a letter to a friend describing life in the trenches and your feelings regarding the war. *What might you see, taste, smell, and feel as you are writing this letter? What would you say to your family or friends in a letter that might be your last?*

▶ List the new and improved weapons of warfare and explain how technological advances made World War I an unusually brutal war. *How did weapons like "Big Bertha," poison gas, tanks, machine guns, airplanes, and submarines change warfare? How effective were these weapons of war?*

▶ Draw evidence from photographs and paintings of the war's devastation to determine the cost of the war in terms of environmental damage.

Grades 7-8

Examples of student achievement of Standard 2B include:

▶ Create a visual time line of the events of the war. *What do you think might have happened if the United States had not entered the war and Russia had not withdrawn from the conflict?*

♦ Research military units made up of colonial subjects who fought with the Allies during World War I. *Why did the Allies call upon people living in their colonial empires to fight? Were the colonial units integrated with European units? As a person living under colonial rule, how would you have responded to an appeal to fight? What would you have expected as a result of helping the colonial power in the conflict?*

♦ Graphically show on a map of the world the principal theaters of the conflict including Europe, Southeast Asia, Sub-Saharan Africa, East Asia, and the South Pacific. *What were the major turning points of the war? How did the physical geography of a region impact the war?*

♦ Design a propaganda poster that might have been used to mobilize civilians to support the war. *Why are they called "propaganda posters"?*

♦ Examine primary sources, including excerpts from Woodrow Wilson's war message, to determine the reasons why the United States entered the war.

♦ Draw evidence from literature, recruiting posters, popular graphics, and songs to examine the changing attitudes toward the war. *Why were men so eager to enlist at the beginning of the war? What caused a change in their attitudes as the war progressed?*

Grades 9-12

Examples of student achievement of Standard 2B include:

♦ Using historical and literary evidence, write letters or diary entries describing the feelings, experiences, and attitudes of soldiers from different areas of the world including Gurkhas, West Africans, and Chinese soon after one or more of the turning points of the war.

♦ Construct a flow chart comparing strategies of the Allies and Central Powers at the beginning of the war and identify at which point those strategies changed and why.

♦ Draw upon a variety of historical narratives to analyze the relative successes of the leading world powers in their propaganda campaigns to influence their colonial possessions and neutral nations during the war. *How effective was Allied propaganda in persuading neutral nations to enter the war? How effective was German propaganda?*

♦ Compare casualty figures from World War I with those of other wars. *Why was there such a heavy death toll in World War I?*

♦ Draw upon books such as Erich Maria Remarque's *All Quiet on the Western Front* to describe the physical and mental effects of trench warfare during World War I.

♦ Infer from a study of posters and cartoons in what ways and to what extent women's roles changed during the war. Evaluate the reliability of conclusions based on this evidence.

♦ Compare newspaper editorials, poster art, and cartoons from the perspective of the Allies and Central Powers, respectively, and discuss divergent views on how the Russian Revolution affected the war.

Students Should Be Able to:

2C **Demonstrate understanding of the causes and consequences of the Russian Revolution of 1917 by:**

`5-12` Explaining the causes of the Russian Revolution of 1917, and analyzing why the revolutionary government progressed from moderate to radical. [**Analyze multiple causation**]

`9-12` Explaining Leninist political ideology and how the Bolsheviks adapted Marxist ideas to conditions peculiar to Russia. [**Interrogate historical data**]

`7-12` Assessing the effects of the New Economic Policy on Soviet society, economy, and government. [**Analyze cause-and-effect relationships**]

`5-12` Describing the rise of Joseph Stalin to power in the Soviet Union and analyzing ways in which collectivization and the first Five-Year Plan disrupted and transformed Soviet society in the 1920s and 1930s. [**Evaluate the implementation of a decision**]

Grades 5-6

Examples of student achievement of Standard 2C include:

▶ Compile a list of the causes of the Communist Revolution. *If you had been a member of the republican government following the February Revolution of 1917, what actions would you have proposed to address these issues?*

▶ Research the lives of Russian leaders such as Tsar Nicholas II, Rasputin, and Lenin, and create biographical sketches or poems examining their importance in Russian history.

▶ Explain how Joseph Stalin rose to power in the Soviet Union. *How did he maintain power?*

▶ Draw evidence from stories about life in the Soviet Union under Stalin. Assume the role of a Russian student in the 1930s and write a secret letter to a friend in another country telling about life in the USSR. *What was life like in the Soviet Union during Stalin's rule?*

Grades 7-8

Examples of student achievement of Standard 2C include:

▶ Using biographies, examine Rasputin's role in determining Russian policy. *What influence did Rasputin have in the imperial court? How did Rasputin represent Russian mysticism?*

▶ Create epitaphs for the family of Tsar Nicholas II using information from the novel *Nicholas and Alexandra* by Robert Massie. *What is the mystery surrounding one of his daughters, Anastasia? What historical evidence, if any, supports the belief that Anastasia survived?*

▶ Draw from books such as Felice Holman's *The Wild Children* to describe how Russian life changed after the Bolshevik Revolution.

▶ Using excerpts from George Orwell's *Animal Farm*, investigate the discontent in Russia at the time of the revolution. *How do the farm animals represent characters in the Russian Revolution?*

▸ Using a Venn diagram or T-Chart, compare and contrast Lenin's New Economic Policy with Stalin's Five-Year Plan.

▸ Drawing from books such as Ephraim Sevela's *We Were Not Like Other People*, describe the means of survival for those persecuted during Stalin's purges.

▸ Research Stalin's policy of collectivization. *How did Stalin change Lenin's policy? How did the kulaks resist collectivization? What were the consequences of their resistance?*

<table>
<tr><td>

Grades 9-12

</td></tr>
</table>

Examples of student achievement of Standard 2C include:

▸ Compare and contrast the promises and platforms of Kerensky and Lenin in 1917. *What impact did the war have on Kerensky's program? How important was Lenin's promise of "land, bread, peace"?*

▸ Based on historical evidence, role-play a dialogue focusing on attitudes toward the revolution among a Red, a White, and a British, French, or Japanese soldier sent to intervene in the Russian civil war.

▸ Examine Lenin's program following the October Revolution and compare it with Marxist doctrines. *What accounts for the differences in Lenin's communist program? Why did Lenin fail to follow a doctrinaire Marxist economic policy?*

▸ Compare Lenin's statements concerning women's equality with statistics on women in the labor force and in education in the Soviet Union at that time.

▸ Having studied documentary and statistical evidence, assess the degree to which Stalin succeeded in his objective of bringing the USSR to industrial parity with the West. Compare Soviet industrialization to that of other nations. *How was the Soviet model different? What unique problems did Stalin encounter?*

▸ Drawing evidence from recently released documents, assess the human cost of Stalinist totalitarianism in the Soviet Union in the 1920s and 1930s. *How has our knowledge of Stalin's regime changed with the de-Stalinization programs initiated by Khrushchev? How have documents released by the Yeltsin government furthered our understanding of the Stalinist era?*

▸ Investigate the effects of industrial conversion from war to peace in Britain, France, Italy, and Germany and how the war impacted the international economy. *What effect did German inflation have on the Weimar Republic? How did the U.S. help to improve the economic situation in Europe? How strong was the economic recovery between 1924 and 1929? Did all European powers share in the relative prosperity of the era?*

Vladimir Ilich Ulyanov (Lenin)
Library of Congress

S T A N D A R D 3

Students Should Understand: *The search for peace and stability in the 1920s and 1930s.*

Students Should Be Able to:

3A **Demonstrate understanding of postwar efforts to achieve lasting peace and social and economic recovery by:**

5-12 Describing the conflicting aims and aspirations of the conferees at Versailles, and analyzing the responses of major powers to the terms of the settlement. [**Consider multiple perspectives**]

7-12 Explaining how the collapse of the German, Habsburg, and Ottoman empires and the creation of new states affected international relations in Europe and the Middle East. [**Analyze cause-and-effect relationships**]

5-12 Explaining how the League of Nations was founded, and assessing its promise and limitations as a vehicle for achieving lasting peace. [**Analyze cause-and-effect relationships**]

7-12 Analyzing the objectives and achievements of women's movements in the context of World War I and its aftermath. [**Analyze cause-and-effect relationships**]

9-12 Analyzing how the governments of Britain, France, Germany, and Italy responded to the economic and political challenges of the postwar decade [**Interrogate historical data**]

7-12 Assessing the effects of United States isolationist policies on world politics and international relations in the 1920s. [**Evaluate the implementation of a decision**]

| Grades 5-6 | **Examples of student achievement of Standard 3A include:** |

▶ On a map draw the boundaries of European nations after the peace treaties ending World War I. Compare this map with a prewar map of Europe. *Which countries were winners? Which were losers?*

▶ Assume the role of a representative of Britain, France, Japan, Italy, or the United States at Versailles and write an editorial expressing the hope your nation has for peace.

▶ Explain the goals of the League of Nations. Write a letter defending or opposing the League of Nations. *What countries became charter members of the League? What major countries were not members of the League? Why were they not members?*

▶ Write a poem or biographical sketch about one of the women who was active in the women's suffrage movement around the world. *What were her hopes and dreams? How did she work to achieve her goals?*

Grades 7-8

Examples of student achievement of Standard 3A include:

▶ Role-play discussions at the Versailles conference regarding reparation payments and Woodrow Wilson's Fourteen Points. *How would the representatives of the "Big Five Powers" stand on these issues? Why did China object to the settlement? What was Germany's response?*

▶ Write a protest ballad that captures the feeling of the women's suffrage movement. *Why is music such a strong medium for expressing issues?*

▶ Investigate United States foreign policy following the war. Stage a debate on the topic, "Should the United States isolate itself from European affairs?" Write an argument for or against U.S. involvement in the post-World War I era. *Why did the U.S. adopt an isolationist policy in the postwar era? How different was this policy from that of the prewar era?*

Grades 9-12

Examples of student achievement of Standard 3A include:

▶ Contrast the treaties ending World War I with Woodrow Wilson's Fourteen Points. *Why did France and Britain insist on reparations for all direct and indirect costs of the war? Why did Turkey refuse to accept the Treaty of Sèvres? Why was Italy dissatisfied with the provisions of the peace settlements? How did peoples in the colonial empires react to the failure of the settlements to address their concerns?*

▶ Identify major refugee populations created as a result of World War I and trace their movements and dispersion.

▶ Compare maps of southern Europe and the Middle East before and after World War I. *How closely did the new borders reflect the European powers' "spheres of interest" before the war? What long- and short-term interest influenced the decision-making process? To what extent did inhabitants of the region bring influence to bear upon the major powers?*

▶ Prepare a report on the methods and successes of Ataturk's program of modernization of Turkey. Write an interview with a "person on the street," assessing reaction to these cultural changes. *What effects did the succession of a modernized Turkey to the Ottoman Empire have on international relations?*

▶ Discuss the goals and failures of the "racial equality clause" in the preamble to the Covenant of the League of Nations.

▶ Investigate reactions in China to the provisions of the Versailles Peace Treaty. *Why were the demonstrations that followed the treaty regarded as the first expression of nationalism in China? What attracted Chinese intellectuals to Marxist-Leninist theory as they attempted to emulate the West, while simultaneously rejecting imperialist rights in China?*

Students Should Be Able to:

3B Demonstrate understanding of economic, social, and political transformations in Africa, Asia, and Latin America in the 1920s and 1930s period by:

7-12 Analyzing the struggle between the Guomindang and the Communist Party for dominance in China in the context of political fragmentation, economic transformation, and Japanese and European imperialism. [**Interrogate historical data**]

7-12 Analyzing how militarism and fascism succeeded in derailing parliamentary democracy in Japan. [**Interrogate historical data**]

5-12 Explaining how the mandate system altered patterns of European colonial rule in Africa and the Middle East. [**Evaluate the implementation of a decision**]

7-12 Explaining aims and policies of European colonial regimes in India, Africa, and Southeast Asia, and assessing the impact of colonial policies on indigenous societies and economies. [**Analyze cause-and-effect relationships**]

9-12 Analyzing how social and economic conditions of colonial rule, as well as ideals of liberal democracy and national autonomy, contributed to the rise of nationalist movements in India, Africa, and Southeast Asia. [**Analyze cause-and-effect relationships**]

5-12 Analyzing how the World War I settlement contributed to the rise of both Pan-Arabism and nationalist struggles for independence in the Middle East. [**Formulate historical questions**]

9-12 Assessing the successes and failures of democratic government in Latin America in the context of class divisions, economic dependency, and United States intervention. [**Analyze cause-and-effect relationships**]

| Grades 5-6 | Examples of student achievement of Standard 3B include: |

▶ Compare political maps of Africa before and after World War I. *What changes occurred? How did these changes affect peoples living in East and West Africa?*

▶ Explain what was meant by the League of Nations mandate system in the Middle East. *What areas became French mandates? British mandates? What countries became independent?*

| Grades 7-8 | Examples of student achievement of Standard 3B include: |

▶ Write an editorial either urging your government to establish colonies or to *not* set up colonies. Include reasons for your views as well as the benefits and drawbacks of the recommended course of action. *How did Westerners' views of other people influence the move toward imperialism?*

▶ Prepare a time line showing the important events in the growth of the Chinese Communist Party from 1927 to 1949. Map the areas controlled by the Guomindang and Chinese Communist Party after the Long March in 1934, and infer what social classes were the major supporters of each.

▶ Assume the role of either Jiang Jieshi or Mao Zedong and write an appeal either to Washington or Moscow for support.

▶ Research the career of Abd al-Qadir, the Moroccan resistance leader of the 1920s. *Why did he challenge Spanish rule in northern Morocco? What tactic did his fighting forces use? Why was he finally defeated? Was he a nationalist leader?*

▶ Construct a map of the Caribbean and indicate areas in which the United States intervened in the first two decades of the 20th century. *What factors led to intervention? What were the short-term and long-range consequences of the intervention?*

Grades 9-12

Examples of student achievement of Standard 3B include:

▶ Based on historical evidence, debate the following proposition: Japan's domestic democracy fell victim to the country's imperialist foreign policy.

▶ Debate issues from the perspective of the Guomindang and Chinese Communist Party before groups reflecting the interests of Chinese landlords, peasants, urban workers, and entrepreneurs, and attempt to persuade them to support your cause. *To whom did the Guomindang and Chinese Communist Party appeal? To what extent did the Japanese invasion of China in the 1930s change viewpoints regarding the two conflicting ideologies?*

▶ Read excerpts from Mao Zedong's *Report on an Investigation of the Peasant Movement in Hunan* (1927). Discuss Mao's understanding of the peasants as a revolutionary force. Compare Mao's analysis of the potential of the peasantry with classic Marxist theory. Discuss how Mao's adaptation of Marxism fits the Chinese situation. Analyze Mao's emergence as a major force in the Chinese Communist movement.

▶ Compare and contrast the Republican Revolution of 1911-12, the Nationalist Revolution of 1925-1928, and the Communist Revolution of 1949 in terms of the ongoing quest in China to establish a political and social system that could address the challenges of the 20th century.

▶ Compare maps of southern Europe and Southwest Asia before and after World War I. *How closely do the new borders reflect the Great Powers' "spheres of interest" before the war? What long- and short-term interests influence the decision-making process? To what extent did inhabitants of the region bring influence to bear on the major actors?*

▶ Develop a case study of a Latin American nation in the first quarter of the 20th century. Examine its political system, economic development, and class divisions. *How did foreign relations with the United States change during this period?*

▶ Compare the Hussein-McMahon correspondence and the Sykes-Picot agreement and contrast these with the settlements reached in the treaties of Versailles and San Remo with regard to Southwest Asia. *What purposes did these diplomatic efforts serve with respect to each party to the negotiations?*

Students Should Be Able to:

3C   Demonstrate understanding of how new departures in science and the arts altered human views of nature, the cosmos, and the psyche between 1900 and 1940 by:

[7–12] Evaluating the impact of World War I and its aftermath on literature, art, and intellectual life in Europe. [Draw upon visual, literary, and musical sources]

[9–12] Evaluating the meaning and social impact of innovative movements in art, architecture, and literature, such as Cubism, Surrealism, Expressionism, Futurism, and Socialist Realism. [Analyze cause-and-effect relationships]

[7–12] Evaluating the impact of innovative movements in Western art and literature on other regions of the world and the influence of African and Asian art forms on Europe. [Consider multiple perspectives]

[7–12] Assessing the impact of the work of Einstein, Freud, and other scientists on traditional views of nature and the universe. [Demonstrate and explain the importance of the individual]

[5–12] Analyzing how the new media — newspapers, magazines, commercial advertising, film, and radio — contributed to the rise of mass culture around the world. [Analyze cause-and-effect relationships]

| Grades 5-6 | Examples of student achievement of Standard 3C include: |

♦ View and discuss the art of Henri Matisse and Pablo Picasso. *How are their techniques different from previous artists? What are some of their new techniques?* Using one of their techniques create a picture that represents current cultural themes.

♦ Investigate how people spent their leisure time in the first half of the 20th century. *How did radio and motion pictures affect the way people spent their time? Did most people participate in sports or were they spectators? What were the popular sports of the period? How similar were leisure activities in the first half of the century to those of today?*

♦ Draw evidence from documentary photographs to examine changes in clothing and styles in the first half of the 20th century. Imagine you were in a "Rip Van Winkle sleep" for nearly a half century and, once awakened in 1940, describe the changes you observe. *How drastic were the changes in men and women's styles? What do these changes reveal about attitudes and values of the period?*

♦ Investigate the life of a scientist or inventor such as Thomas Alva Edison, Marie Sklodowska Curie, Albert Einstein, or Guglielmo Marconi. *How did the work of the person you selected change society?*

| Grades 7-8 | Examples of student achievement of Standard 3C include: |

♦ Research one of the media of the times: newspapers, magazines, commercial advertising, film, and radio. Develop a report on how it contributed to the rise of mass culture around the world. Use the same format for the report as the chosen media.

♦ Write parallel biographies or create a multimedia program of two artists, architects, musicians, or writers of the early 1900s and compare their styles and the impact of their works.

♦ Assemble a collection of examples of early 20th-century art from different parts of the world. Explain how the art styles and mediums of expressions were similar or different. *What mediums of art were used as methods of conveying support for a social, political, or economic philosophy? How effective were they in winning support for a cause?*

♦ Construct a time line of major discoveries in science and medicine in the first half of the 20th century. *Which were the most significant? Why? How did these discoveries affect the quality of life?*

Grades 9-12

Examples of student achievement of Standard 3C include:

♦ Explain the usage of the expression "Lost Generation" in the post-World War I era. *What were the themes of "Lost Generation" writers? How did postwar society influence their works? What was the impact of their works?*

♦ Select excerpts from the works of writers such as Spender, Remarque, Brooke, and Hemingway, and explain how the war affected their work.

♦ Research the Dada surrealist movements and establish their connections with the war.

♦ Research a leading musician and one or more of his or her works that were popular in the first half of the 20th century. *How did their music reflect cultural trends? What impact did the musical work have in different parts of the world?*

♦ Analyze excerpts from such texts as *Civilization and Its Discontents* by Sigmund Freud. *How did Freud's development of psychoanalytic method and his theories of the unconscious change the prevailing views of human motives and human nature?*

Albert Einstein
Library of Congress

Students Should Be Able to:

3D Demonstrate understanding of the causes and global consequences of the Great Depression by:

9–12 Analyzing the financial, economic, and social causes of the depression and why it spread to most parts of the world. [**Analyze multiple causation**]

5–12 Assessing the human costs of the depression, and comparing its impact on economy and society in such industrialized countries as Britain, France, Germany, the United States, the Soviet Union, and Japan. [**Compare and contrast differing values, behaviors, and institutions**]

9–12 Analyzing ways in which the depression affected colonial peoples of Africa and Asia and how it contributed to the growth of nationalist movements. [**Analyze cause-and-effect relationships**]

7–12 Analyzing how the depression contributed to the growth of socialist and communist movements and how it affected capitalist economic theory and practice in leading industrial powers in Western countries. [**Analyze cause-and-effect relationships**]

Grades 5-6

Examples of student achievement of Standard 3D include:

▶ Create a wall newspaper reflecting the worldwide economic crisis during the Great Depression. *How did the depression affect different countries in the world?*

▶ Assemble a collage of pictures showing the human side of the worldwide economic depression.

Grades 7-8

Examples of student achievement of Standard 3D include:

▶ Examine art works and photographs of hunger and poverty such as those by German artist Käthe Kollwitz, Mexican muralist José Clemente Orozco, and American photographer Dorothea Lange. *What emotions do these illustrations project? What impact did they have on society?*

▶ Create a model to explore the chain-reaction of a depression in a highly industrialized economy and how it impacted countries that relied on trade of commodities such as rubber, coffee, and sugar. *How were countries that depended on foreign markets and foreign capital investment affected by the depression?*

▶ Compare graphs of the changes in industrial production in different countries between 1920 and 1940. *What conclusions could be drawn from the statistical information?*

▶ Draw evidence from poster art to illustrate how economic depression contributed to the growth of fascist and communist movements in different parts of the world.

▶ Appraise the following quotation attributed to Hermann Göring: "Ore has always made an empire strong. Butter and lard have made people fat at best." *What is the meaning of the quotation? How would you respond to Göring?*

Grades 9-12

Examples of student achievement of Standard 3D include:

▸ Assess the effect of the Great Depression in the Middle East under British and French mandates by comparing statistical evidence with other types of historical material (letters, diplomatic dispatches, government reports, and journalistic accounts) from European and indigenous sources. *How did the hardship affect nationalists' struggles and political unrest?*

▸ Prepare a table showing ways in which the world depression affected the United States, Germany, and Japan. Show both the effects of the depression and how each country responded to them.

▸ Develop a case study examining the effects of the Great Depression on an industrial and an agrarian nation. *How severe was its impact in each of the selected countries? Did it have the same impact worldwide? Why or why not?*

▸ Research the impact of the depression on international trade. *What was the effect of the enactment of the Smoot-Hawley Tariff by the United States? How did other nations respond to the U.S. tariff? What effect did the tariff have on international trade? On economic recovery?*

▸ Examine statistics reflecting military production in the 1930s in nations such as Britain, Germany, Japan, the Soviet Union, and the United States. *To what extent was the military-industrial complex created as a means of stimulating recovery from the Great Depression?*

Queue in Berlin during the world-wide depression of the 1930s.
Ullstein Bilderdienst, Berlin

STANDARD 4

Students Should Understand: *Causes and global consequences of World War II.*

Students Should be Able to:

4A Demonstrate understanding of the multiple causes of World War II by:

[5-12] Explaining the ideologies of fascism and Nazism, and analyzing how fascist regimes succeeded in seizing power in Italy, Germany, and Spain. [**Analyze multiple causation**]

[7-12] Explaining the German, Italian, and Japanese drives for empire in the 1930s. [**Evaluate major debates among historians**]

[7-12] Analyzing the consequences of Britain, France, the United States, and other Western democracies' failure to oppose fascist aggression. [**Evaluate major debates among historians**]

[7-12] Analyzing the precipitating causes of the war and the reasons for early German and Japanese victories. [**Analyze multiple causation**]

[7-12] Analyzing the motives and consequences of the Soviet nonaggression pacts with Germany and Japan. [**Analyze cause-and-effect relationships**]

Grades 5-6

Examples of student achievement of Standard 4A include:

▶ Explain the characteristics of the different forms of government such as communism, democracy, fascism, and socialism. Create a poster of one of these ideologies.

▶ Describe Mussolini, Hitler, and Franco's rise to power in their respective countries. *How did Mussolini and Hitler come to control their governments? How was Franco's rise to power different?*

▶ Draw on books such as Helen Griffith's *The Last Summer: Spain 1936* to discuss the Spanish Civil War and the rise of fascism.

▶ Use books such as Judith Kerr's *When Hitler Stole Pink Rabbit* to describe Nazi oppression in Germany.

Grades 7-8

Examples of student achievement of Standard 4A include:

▶ Compare and contrast the steps that resulted in the ascendance in power of Mussolini and Hitler, and explain the statement, "Hitler's success grew out of the German people's despair."

▶ On a map of the post-World War I world indicate the territorial ambitions of Italy, Germany, and Japan. *How would the German concept of* lebensraum *affect Eastern Europe? Why would attempts to extend influence or annex new territories cause international problems? How would the major powers react to seizure of land?*

▶ Examine the reaction of Britain, France, the United States, and the Soviet Union to fascist aggression. Write a position paper from one of the major powers explaining policies that should be taken to stop aggression. *Why did the major powers fail to take forceful measures to stop aggression?*

▶ Construct a time line of international events from the Japanese seizure of Manchuria in 1931 to the Nazi-Soviet Non-Aggression Pact of August 1939. Explain how each of the major events lead to the outbreak of the war.

▶ On a world map illustrate the German, Italian, and Japanese advances between the invasion of Poland in 1939 and the fall of Singapore in 1942. *What accounts for Axis victories in the early years of the war?*

Grades 9-12

Examples of student achievement of Standard 4A include:

▶ Using historical evidence such as excerpts from *Mein Kampf* and Nazi Party platforms, identify the elements of Nazi ideology and the use of terror against perceived enemies of the state.

▶ Using excerpts from Leni Reifenstahl's films, identify what propaganda techniques were used to promote Nazi ideas.

▶ Draw evidence from speeches and writings from Italy or Germany in the 1920s and 1930s to examine the debates among political factions over the fate of the nation. *What role did nationalism play in the fascist drive for power? How did the economic situation in either Italy or Germany impact the political debate? What parties stood in opposition to Mussolini and Hitler? How effective was the Spartacus League in Germany?*

▶ Draw evidence from a variety of sources including George Orwell's *Homage to Catalonia* and novels or short stories by Ernest Hemingway to examine the human costs of the Spanish Civil War. *To what extent did foreign intervention affect the outcome of the Spanish Civil War?*

▶ Debate the *Diktat* thesis that the harshness of the Versailles agreement made revolt against its dictates and the nations that imposed them a necessity.

▶ Present arguments to support or reject Japan's "greater East Asia co-prosperity sphere." *As an individual under European colonial domination in East Asia, how would you react to the Japanese initiative? What reasons would you give to support or reject the greater East Asia co-prosperity sphere?*

▶ Examine newspaper and magazine reports on international issues from the Munich Conference to the declaration of war in September 1939. *What were the consequences of the Munich Agreement? What was Stalin's perception of the Munich Agreement? To what extent did this lead to the Non-Aggression Pact of August 1939?*

Students Should be Able to:

4B Demonstrate understanding of the global scope and human costs of the war by:

`5-12` Explaining the major turning points of the war, and describing the principal theaters of conflict in Western Europe, Eastern Europe, the Soviet Union, North Africa, Asia, and the Pacific. [**Interrogate historical data**]

`5-12` Analyzing how and why the Nazi regime perpetrated a "war against the Jews," and describing the devastation suffered by Jews and other groups in the Nazi Holocaust. [**Analyze cause-and-effect relationships**]

`7-12` Comparing World Wars I and II in terms of the impact of industrial production, national mobilization, technological innovations, and scientific research on strategies, tactics, and levels of destruction. [**Marshal evidence of antecedent circumstances**]

`7-12` Assessing the consequences of World War II as a total war. [**Formulate historical questions**]

Grades 5-6

Examples of student achievement of Standard 4B include:

▶ On a world map locate the turning points for the United Nations forces during World War II. *How important were these battles in changing the course of the war?*

▶ Drawing on books such as *Hear O Israel* by Terry Walton Treaseder, *Don't Say A Word* by Barbara Gehrts, *Gideon* by Chester Aaron, *Twenty and Ten* by Claire Hachet Bishop, and *Number of Stars* by Lois Lowry, describe the experiences of Jews living under the Nazi regime and the Holocaust.

▶ Review the treatment of children during the Holocaust and share poems from the book *I Never Saw Another Butterfly*. Illustrate one of the poems.

▶ As part of a group draw up a Declaration of Human Rights for Children. Discuss: *Would it be possible for the world to honor such a document? Is there such a document in existence today? Who wrote it? Would there ever be situations when human rights should not be honored?*

▶ Use books such as Monika Kotowska's *The Bridge to the Other Side* to discuss the human costs of war and the resulting social problems.

▶ Draw on books such as Eleanor Coerr's *Sadako* to discuss the costs of dropping nuclear bombs on Japan. Read *Sadako and the Thousand Paper Cranes*. Make origami cranes and write on them a personal message for world peace. Display in the classroom.

Grades 7-8

Examples of student achievement of Standard 4B include:

▶ Compare and contrast the roles of women and children in Allied and Axis countries.

▶ Drawing from books such as *The Journey from Prague Street* by Hana Demetz, *Cigarette Sellers of Three Crosses Square* by Joseph Ziemian, *My Enemy, My Brother* by James Foreman, and *Children of the Resistance* by Lore Cowan, describe the ways in which Jews and other Europeans resisted the Nazis and their policies.

▶ Use books such as Grigory Baklanov's *Forever Nineteen* to discuss the experiences of soldiers fighting in World War II.

▶ Compare Nazi public announcements concerning Jews during 1941-44 with Holocaust survivors' accounts of their experiences during this period.

▶ Conduct research as part of a group on the impact of World War II on science and technology, transportation and communication, or medicine. Create class projects illustrating research findings.

▶ Use *The Diary of a Young Girl* by Anne Frank to assess the personal impact of Nazi occupation of Europe. *How did Anne Frank's experiences differ from those of Jews living in other occupied countries of Europe?*

▶ Read the Potsdam Declaration and assess its importance in the Japanese decision to surrender.

Grades 9-12

Examples of student achievement of Standard 4B include:

▶ Develop an annotated time line of the history of the Nazi's "war on the Jews," and construct a map depicting the location and scale of Jewish deaths resulting from the implementation of Nazi policy.

▶ Use books such as Thomas Keneally's *Schindler's List* and James Foreman's *Ceremony of Innocence* to describe why some people were motivated to defy Nazi orders while other complied or failed to object to Hitler's "final solution."

▶ Drawing upon books such as Alexander Ramati's *And the Violins Stopped Playing: A Story of the Gypsy Holocaust,* Harry Muslich's *The Assault,* and Elie Wiesel's *Night,* examine the personal stories of Holocaust victims and the brutality of Nazi genocide.

▶ Identify the battles you consider turning points in both the Atlantic and Pacific theaters of the war, and explain why you consider them turning points.

▶ Debate the moral implications of the use of military technologies in World War II such as the bombing of civil populations in order to shorten the war.

▶ Construct a map showing the direction and scale of population displacements resulting from World War II.

▶ Debate the following two issues: (1) The United States was right to use the atomic bomb to end the war with Japan; (2) Japan should not have surrendered following the dropping of the bombs.

STANDARD 5

Students Should Understand: *How new international power relations took shape in the context of the Cold War and how colonial empires broke up.*

Students Should be Able to:

5A Demonstrate understanding of why global power shifts took place and the Cold War developed in the aftermath of World War II.

5-12 Analyzing how political and military conditions prevailing at the end of the war led to the Cold War and how the United States and the Soviet Union competed for power and influence in Europe in the postwar period. [**Analyze cause-and-effect relationships**]

5-12 Explaining how the Western European countries achieved rapid economic recovery after World War II under the Marshall Plan. [**Evaluate the implementation of a decision**]

7-12 Comparing the impact of Soviet domination on Eastern Europe with the transformations that occurred in Japanese society under American occupation. [**Compare and contrast differing values, behaviors, and institutions**]

7-12 Analyzing how the Communist Party rose to power in China between 1936 and 1949, and assessing the accomplishments and costs of Communist rule up to the Great Leap Forward of 1958. [**Analyze cause-and-effect relationships**]

5-12 Explaining why the United Nations was founded, and assessing its successes and failures up to the 1970s. [**Analyze cause-and-effect relationships**]

7-12 Analyzing the significance of international crises such as the Berlin blockade, the Korean War, the Hungarian revolt, and the Cuban missile crisis on international politics. [**Formulate historical questions**]

9-12 Analyzing causes and consequences of United States and Soviet competition for influence or dominance in such countries as Egypt, Iran, Chile, Vietnam, Nicaragua, Afghanistan, and Ethiopia. [**Analyze multiple causation**]

Grades 5-6	Examples of student achievement of Standard 5A include:

- Draw a simple cartoon illustrating the term Cold War. On a world map indicate the Cold War alliances of the postwar period. *How did the United States and the Soviet Union compete for power and influence in Europe in the postwar period?*

- Explain the reasons for the establishment of the United Nations. Make a list of the areas of the world in which the U.N. has played an active role. *How successful has the U.N. been as a peacekeeper?*

- Draw on books such as Margaret Rau's *Holding Up the Sky* to discuss social and political conflict in China.

- Using documentary photos of the destruction in Europe, explain the importance of reconstruction after the war. *What was the Marshall Plan? How did it promote the rebuilding of Western Europe?*

Grades 7-8

Examples of student achievement of Standard 5A include:

▶ Research the Marshall Plan and explain how it helped Western European countries achieve rapid economic recovery after the war. Contrast the recovery in the Eastern block to that of the West. *Why was the Nobel Peace Prize awarded to George Marshall in 1953?*

▶ Construct a map showing the new alliance systems that emerged as a part of the Cold War. On an accompanying chart, list the membership in each alliance and explain its purposes. *Why were these alliances formed after the war? Do they exist today?*

▶ Analyze the goals of the U.S. occupation of Japan. *How successful was the occupation in meeting them?*

▶ Research the Soviet Union's political influences on an Eastern European nation in the postwar era and contrast it with the role of the U.S. occupation of Japan. *To what extent did the USSR interfere in popular elections in Eastern European countries? How did the political development in Japan differ?*

▶ On a map of central Europe illustrate the division of Germany and Berlin. Assuming the role of an adviser to the British or French foreign office or the U.S. Department of State, write a position paper outlining problems that the partition may provoke. *What action would you have advised in the 1948 Berlin crisis?* Defend your position.

▶ Construct a time line tracing the major events that led to the Communist takeover in China from the Long March to the establishment of the People's Republic in 1949. *How did Mao's programs change China? What led to the Great Leap Forward? How successful was it? What factors contributed to the Cultural Revolution? What was its result in terms of economic development and human suffering?*

Grades 9-12

Examples of student achievement of Standard 5A include:

▶ List the characteristics of the U.S. and USSR that made them "superpowers," and explain how they acquired these characteristics. Construct a historical analysis on the role of the space race in defining the competition between the superpowers.

▶ Develop a case study examining a major Cold War conflict from the Berlin Blockade to the Soviet invasion of Afghanistan. Explain the developments that led to the conflict, how the competition between the superpowers inflamed the crisis, and the significance of the event in world affairs.

▶ Evaluate the strategic role of the Muslim countries in Southwest Asia during the Cold War. Compare the importance of geographic, economic, and political factors. *How has the role of the region changed since the breakup of the Soviet Union?*

▶ Debate the proposition: *Communist success in the Chinese civil war was the result of Jiang Jieshi's failure as an effective leader rather than a victory for Mao Zedong.*

▶ Write an essay analyzing why China made an alliance with the Soviet Union. *Considering that both countries had Communist governments, why did strains develop in the alliance?*

Students Should be Able to:

5B Demonstrate understanding of how African, Asian, and Caribbean peoples achieved independence from European colonial rule:

7-12 Assessing the impact of Indian nationalism on other movements in Africa and Asia, and analyzing why the subcontinent was partitioned into India and Pakistan. [**Analyze cause-and-effect relationships**]

7-12 Analyzing the impact of World War II and postwar global politics on the rise of mass nationalist movements in colonial Africa and Southeast Asia. [**Analyze cause-and-effect relationships**]

9-12 Analyzing connections between the rise of independence movements in Africa and Southeast Asia and social transformations such as accelerated population growth, urbanization, and the emergence of Western-educated elites. [**Analyze cause-and-effect relationships**]

7-12 Analyzing why some African and Asian countries achieved independence through constitutional devolution of power and others, as a result of armed revolution. [**Compare and contrast differing values, behaviors, and institutions**]

5-12 Explaining how international conditions affected the creation of Israel, and analyzing why persistent conflict developed between Israel and both Arab Palestinians and neighboring states. [**Interrogate historical data**]

9-12 Describing economic and social problems that new states faced in the 1960s and 1970s, and analyzing why military regimes or one-party states replaced parliamentary-style governments throughout much of Africa. [**Reconstruct patterns of historical succession and duration**]

| Grades 5-6 | Examples of student achievement of Standard 5B include: |

▸ Compare the position of women in developing countries with the position of women in industrialized countries. *How has change occurred in different societies?*

▸ Drawing on books such as Beverly Naidoo's *Cain of Fire*, describe the African experience under European colonial rule.

▸ Drawing on books such as Gloria Whelan's *Goodbye, Vietnam*, describe the political and economic conditions that drove many Vietnamese to seek refuge in other countries. *In what other countries did people experience similar conditions?*

| Grades 7-8 | Examples of student achievement of Standard 5B include: |

▸ Explain the role India played in World War II and assess the role of the war in the struggle for independence.

▸ Discuss the claim made by Mohandas Gandhi, "Through nonviolent means the Indian people could achieve independence from British rule." *Did the claim prove to be true?*

▸ Trace the rise of independent nations in Southeast Asia such as Burma, Malaysia, Singapore, Indonesia, Cambodia, Laos, and Vietnam.

- Construct a time line of important events in the struggle between Israelis and Palestinians since 1948. Debate the question of rights to the disputed land from an Israeli and Palestinian perspective.

- Use books such as Margaret Sacks's *Beyond Safe Boundaries* to discuss the moral, social, political, and economic implications of apartheid.

- Investigate the regime of Kwame Nkrumah in Ghana, Jomo Kenyatta in Kenya, or Idi Amin in Uganda. Decide under which regime you would have preferred to live and explain the reasons why.

Grades 9-12

Examples of student achievement of Standard 5B include:

- Examine the dispute over Kashmir resulting from the partition of the Indian subcontinent. *What interests were at stake for the disputants? What role did the United Nations play in mediating the dispute?*

- Research the role of the Buddhist-led priests against the Diem regime in South Vietnam and the Moslems against the Sukarno regime in Indonesia. Report the ways in which they were similar.

- Analyze the language of the Balfour Declaration and its relationship to the exercise of Britain's mandate in Palestine. Prepare a chart listing the goals of the Arab League and the Zionist Movement and report on how these goals conflicted with each other and were at odds with the mandate system.

- Prepare a map showing the distribution of Hindu and Moslem populations and devise a plan for the division of the subcontinent into Moslem and Hindu states. Investigate the actual partition and account for similarities or differences from the political boundaries you prescribed. *What conclusions can you make about the withdrawal of the British and the role of religion in the formation of the two new nations?*

- View the film *The Battle of Algiers* and place the events it describes within the chronological context of the Algerian Revolution of 1954-62. *How did the presence of a large group of French settlers in Algeria affect the course of the Algerian war? What tactics did the French and Algerian revolutionaries use against one another to win the battle of Algiers? Were these tactics justified on either side? Explain why the revolutionaries lost the battle of Algiers but nevertheless won the revolution?*

- Construct case studies of independence movements in two African or Asian countries; one through an evolutionary process and the other through revolution. Select from countries such as Ghana, Kenya, Algeria, Zaire, Angola, the Philippines, Indonesia, Burma, or Vietnam.

- Draw on books such as Alan Paton's *Cry the Beloved Country and* Mark Mathabane's *Kaffir Boy* to discuss Africans' survival and resistance under apartheid.

STANDARD 6

Students Should Understand: *Promises and paradoxes of the second half of the 20th century.*

Students Should be Able to:

6A Demonstrate understanding of how population explosion and environmental change have altered conditions of life around the world by:

`7-12` Analyzing causes of the world's accelerating population growth rate, and explaining why population growth has hindered economic and social development in many countries. [**Analyze multiple causation**]

`7-12` Describing the global proliferation of cities and the rise of the megalopolis, and assessing the impact of urbanization on family life, standards of living, class relations, and ethnic identity. [**Analyze cause-and-effect relationships**]

`5-12` Assessing why scientific, technological, and medical advances have improved living standards for many but have failed to eradicate hunger, poverty, and epidemic disease. [**Evaluate major debates among historians**]

`5-12` Analyzing how population growth, urbanization, industrialization, warfare, and the global market economy have contributed to environmental alterations. [**Analyze cause-and-effect relationships**]

`5-12` Assessing the effectiveness of efforts by governments and citizens' movements to protect the global natural environment. [**Obtain historical data**]

| Grades 5-6 | **Examples of student achievement of Standard 6A include:** |

▶ Use photographs and posters to examine the changes that took place with the proliferation of cities. *What was the impact of urbanization on family life and standards of living? How has industrialization contributed to changes in the environment?*

▶ Make a scrapbook of newspaper and magazine articles about the ongoing activities of groups trying to save the environment. *What can individuals do to help?* Organize a class project of recycling.

▶ Research United Nations programs to promote health and medical care and to improve the standard of living in developing nations. *How successful are these programs?*

| Grades 7-8 | **Examples of student achievement of Standard 6A include:** |

▶ Research in a group one of the following: population growth, urbanization, warfare, or the global market economy and the ways it has contributed to altering and degrading our environment. Create a large symbol representing the selected topic, such as an outline of a person for population or a cityscape for urbanization, and record your findings.

♦ Select readings from poems or articles about the environment from various countries around the world. Create a class Reader's Theater of meaningful passages.

♦ Debate the issues associated with the protection of the Brazilian rain forest from different perspectives such as that of an environmentalist, a landless peasant farmer, and a cattle rancher. *Is this a national or international issue? What proposals might be offered to address the issues raised by different interest groups? In what areas of the world are there similar issues? What should be the role of industrialized nations in meeting these challenges?*

Grades 9-12

Examples of student achievement of Standard 6A include:

♦ Trace population changes in selected countries, such as India, Egypt, Nigeria, Brazil, the United States, and Italy. *What assumptions can you make about population changes in relation to scientific, medical, and technological breakthroughs?* Test these assumptions with research and prepare a report with a bar graph on your conclusions.

♦ Research the impact of birth control in diverse areas of the world. Analyze why the impact was different in these areas.

♦ View the video *World Populations* by Zero Population Growth. *What is the frame of reference of the producer? What evidence is presented to support that organization's point of view? What arguments may be used to challenge their perspective?*

♦ Examine the issues raised by the 1994 Cairo Conference on World Population. *How did these issues address patterns of population growth? What were the objections raised regarding proposals restricting population growth? How difficult is it to arrive at a consensus document on population growth?*

♦ Prepare a graph illustrating China's population growth from the 1700s through 1990. Analyze the effects of China's "one-child" policy of the 1990s. *Why did China's population growth rate increase dramatically? How has China's population growth affected economic development from the 1800s onward?*

♦ Research United Nations efforts to promote programs to improve health and welfare, and assess the effectiveness of these programs. *Which major U.N. programs promote scientific and technical assistance? Does the U.N. provide adequate programs to avert catastrophes or does it simply react to events? How expensive are these programs? Who bears the cost of implementation?*

Population

	1900000	1950 0	2000 (est.) 0
Europe	401,000,000	559,000,000	1,000,000,000
North America	106,000,000	217,000,000	330,000,000
South America	38,000,000	111,000,000	650,000,000
Asia	937,000,000	1,302,000,000	4,300,000,000
Africa	120,000,000	198,000,000	660,000,000
Oceania	6,000,000	13,000,000	30,000,000

Students Should be Able to:

6B **Demonstrate understanding of how increasing economic interdependence has transformed human society by:**

5-12 Analyzing the effects of new transport and communications technology on patterns of world trade and finance. [**Analyze cause-and-effect relationships**]

5-12 Analyzing how global communications and changing international labor demands have shaped new patterns of world migration since World War II. [**Analyze cause-and-effect relationships**]

5-12 Describing major scientific, technological, and medical breakthroughs of the postwar decades, and assessing their impact on systems of production, global trade, and standards of living. [**Interrogate historical data**]

9-12 Comparing systems of economics management in communist and capitalist countries, and analyzing the global economic impact of multinational corporations. [**Compare and contrast differing institutions**]

7-12 Analyzing why economic disparities between industrialized and developing countries have persisted or increased. [**Formulate historical questions**]

7-12 Analyzing how the oil crisis and its aftermath in the early 1970s revealed the extent and complexity of the global economic interdependence. [**Interrogate historical data**]

Grades 5-6

Examples of student achievement of Standard 6B include:

▶ Construct a project examining either major scientific, technological, or medical breakthroughs of the postwar decades. *What would your life be like without these advances?*

▶ On a map show major patterns of migration since World War II. Assume the role of one of these migrants and write a letter explaining your reasons for moving. *What are the risks you are taking? What are your expectations?*

Grades 7-8

Examples of student achievement of Standard 6B include:

▶ Construct a case study of two developing countries. Compare and contrast your findings. *What has hindered industrialization in these regions? Are there similarities among the countries? Based on research, what generalizations can you make?*

▶ Assume the role of one of the following migrant workers: a Southeast Asian domestic worker in the Persian Gulf; an American oil executive in Dhahran, Saudi Arabia; a Moroccan factory worker in France; an Egyptian professor in the United States; or a Turkish Muslim religious teacher in Germany, and write a letter home. *What do you like and dislike about your new home? How difficult is it to adapt to a new culture?*

▶ Construct a time line or line graph of world oil price changes since 1950. Assess the reasons for these changes, both in the oil-producing and oil-consuming countries.

▶ Research important medical discoveries of the latter part of the 20th century and explain how these have enhanced the quality of life. *Have all nations shared in advanced medical research?*

▶ Explain the formation of the European Economic Community (EEC). *What are the advantages of the EEC? What similar economic partnerships have been formed in other parts of the world?*

Grades 9-12

Examples of student achievement of Standard 6B include:

▶ Assume the role of a representative to a world forum called to discuss the disparities between industrialized and developing countries. Examine statistical information regarding resources, production, capital investment, labor, and trade. *What accounts for the disparity? What measures should be taken by industrialized states to assist developing nations? What programs should developing nations undertake?*

▶ Identify the outward, inward, and internal flow of labor migration in the Middle East and North Africa. Identify the source countries, goal countries, and type of jobs involved. Assess the impact of income flowing into and out of the various economies.

▶ Assess the relationships between United States domestic energy policy and foreign policy in oil-producing regions since 1970.

▶ Research the development of multinational corporations and explain in what ways they have had an impact on the world economy. *What are the benefits of multinational corporations? Why are they moving production units into developing countries? How have multinational corporations contributed to the migration of people?*

▶ Write a report explaining why the countries of East Asia have experienced comparatively rapid economic development in the late 20th century. *What factors may explain why the economies of sub-Saharan Africa have on the whole developed much more slowly in recent decades?*

Women at a well, India
Photograph courtesy of Don Johnson

Students Should be Able to:

6C Demonstrate understanding of how liberal democracy, private enterprise, and human rights movements have reshaped political and social life by:

5-12 Assessing the progress of human and civil rights around the world since the 1948 U.N. Declaration of Human Rights. **[Formulate a position or course of action on an issue]**

5-12 Analyzing changes in the lives of women in both industrialized and developing countries since World War II and assessing the extent to which women have progressed toward social equality and economic opportunity. **[Analyze cause-and-effect relationships]**

9-12 Assessing the success of democratic reform movements in challenging authoritarian governments in Africa, Asia, and Latin America. **[Analyze cause-and-effect relationships]**

7-12 Analyzing why the Soviet and other communist governments collapsed and why the Soviet Union disintegrated in the 1980s and early 1990s. **[Marshal evidence of antecedent circumstances]**

5-12 Explaining the dismantling of the apartheid system in South Africa and the winning of political rights by the black majority. **[Explain historical continuity and change]**

7-12 Explaining why Cold War tensions eased in the 1970s and how the growing global influence of China, Japan, Western Europe, and the oil-producing states resulted in a world of multipolar power. **[Interrogate historical data]**

| Grades 5-6 | Examples of student achievement of Standard 6C include: |

▶ Interview women who lived before World War II. *How are women's lives different today in the areas of social equality and economic opportunity?*

▶ Write a diary of a young person caught in ethnic conflict in Europe, Africa, or Asia.

▶ Gather information from biographies and write character sketches of Nelson Mandela and Bishop Desmond Tutu. *How have these two men from different backgrounds fought against apartheid?*

▶ List the basic parts of the United Nations Declaration of Human Rights. *How are these rights similar to and different from the United States Bill of Rights? What other rights do you think should be added to the U.N. declaration? Why?*

| Grades 7-8 | Examples of student achievement of Standard 6C include: |

▶ Create an illustrated time line of the events leading up to the collapse of the Soviet Union. On a map of the old Soviet Union draw and label the independent countries formed from its boundaries. *Would changing any of the events on the time line have altered the collapse of the USSR? How were the borders of newly established states decided? What are some of the problems created by these new boundaries?*

▶ Research the United Nations Declaration on Human Rights of 1948. *Why was this document written?* Write an expository essay on the progress or lack of progress of human and civil rights around the world or in one country.

♦ In dyads, use newspaper articles to research and role-play an interview with the leader of a separatist movement in a country of your choice. *What moral issues are involved? What means are used by the separatist to achieve his or her goals? Why does he or she believe the struggle is necessary? What will be the effect on the people in that country?*

♦ Assemble a collection of documentary photographs or construct a collage to illustrate the system of apartheid in South Africa. Explain how the system was changed. *What pressure was placed on the South African government to end apartheid? How effective were the pressures?*

♦ Explain how Mikhail Gorbachev's policies of *perestroika* and *glasnost* changed the USSR and Soviet relations with Eastern European nations. *What impact did the United States military build-up have on Soviet willingness to negotiate with the West?*

Grades 9-12

Examples of student achievement of Standard 6C include:

♦ Use political and demographic maps showing the distribution of ethnic and religious groups in Africa to analyze the prevalence of ethnic and border conflicts since independence. Identify countries where several ethnic groups have come under one national roof as a result of colonial arrangements. *What are the implications for state-building?*

♦ Draw evidence from statements, speeches, and interviews with leaders of opposition groups in various countries to analyze the problems these movements identify and the solutions they offer. *Do these ideas conflict with or correspond to Western economic and strategic interests?*

♦ Assess the development and focus of nationalist movements in Eastern Europe from the pre-World War I to the post-Cold War periods. *What similarities and differences distinguish conflicts in Lithuania, Bosnia-Herzegovina, Armenian and Kurdish regions, and Czechoslovakia in terms of motivation, means of conflict resolution, and outcome?*

♦ Analyze the writings of male and female members of religious groups of various religions. *How do they differ in their views of women's roles?*

♦ Compare and contrast the legal status and social roles of Muslim women in various countries. *What changes have taken place for women of various classes in the past century?*

"Now, woman has always been man's dependent, if not his slave; the two sexes have never shared the world in equality. And even today woman is heavily handicapped, though her situation is beginning to change. Almost nowhere is her legal status the same as man's, and frequently it is much to her disadvantage...."

SIMONE DE BEAUVOIR, FROM *THE SECOND SEX*

Students Should Be Able to:

6D **Demonstrate understanding of major sources of tension and conflict in the contemporary world and efforts that have been made to address them by:**

`9-12` Analyzing the tensions and contradictions between globalizing trends of the world economy and dynamic assertions of traditional cultural identity and distinctiveness. [**Marshal evidence of antecedent circumstances**]

`5-12` Analyzing causes and consequences of continuing urban protest and reformist economic policies in post-Mao China in the context of state authoritarianism. [**Analyze cause-and-effect relationships**]

`7-12` Explaining political objectives of religious fundamentalist movements in various countries of the world, and analyzing social and economic factors contributing to the growth of these movements. [**Examine the influence of ideas**]

`5-12` Analyzing why terrorist movements have proliferated and the extent of their impact on politics and society in various countries. [**Evaluate the implementation of a decision**]

`7-12` Assessing the impact of population pressure, poverty, and environmental degradation on the breakdown of state authority in various countries in the 1980s and 1990s. [**Analyze multiple causation**]

`7-12` Assessing the progress that has been made since the 1970s in resolving conflict between Israel and neighboring states. [**Analyze multiple causation**]

| Grades 5-6 | Examples of student achievement of Standard 6D include: |

▶ Examine photographs of the student protest in Tiananmen Square. *What were the reasons for the protest?*

▶ Define "terrorism" and list several terrorist acts in the second half of the 20th century. *What methods can nations use to protect their citizens from terrorist acts? Is international cooperation necessary to stop terrorism?*

| Grades 7-8 | Examples of student achievement of Standard 6D include: |

▶ Develop criteria for defining a terrorist act. Analyze acts characterized as terrorism in news reports in terms of means, motivation, and victims. *What factors in modern society facilitate politically motivated terrorism and random forms of violence?*

▶ Define "fundamentalism" and trace its origin. *How does the modern connotation of the term differ from its historical use? How appropriate is the term to characterize 20th-century religious resurgence as applied to various world religions?*

▶ Research the opening of China and the impact of changes in the communist system in the post-Mao era. *How did world events help give rise to a reform movement in 1989? What actions did Deng Xiaoping take to crush the movement? How did world leaders react to the events in Tiananmen Square?*

▶ Compile a list of nations that have faced the breakdown of state central authority and anarchy in the last two decades of the 20th century. *What are the pressing problems facing these nations? Why have their respective governments been unable to cope with these problems? What has been the reaction of the international community?*

Examples of student achievement of Standard 6D include:

▶ Discuss the dichotomy between modernity and tradition with regard to the role of religion in contemporary society. Analyze both the secular and religious assumptions that place religious practice in one category or another.

▶ Research the application of economic and arms embargoes sponsored by United Nations resolutions, including the cases of Iran, Iraq, the former Yugoslavia, and Haiti. Assess the enforcement and political consequences for sanctioned countries. Evaluate criteria for applying and lifting various types of embargoes and on the exclusion of humanitarian aid.

▶ Define the meaning of *jihad* in Islamic belief. *What Islamic principles and laws are relevant to military activity? What rules apply to noncombatants and their property?* Compare these principles with the Geneva Accords. *How do these laws and principles apply to terrorist acts?* Evaluate events described as terrorist acts according to these criteria.

▶ Debate the question: *"Does the nation-state have a future in the 21st century?"*

Students working on the "Goddess of Democracy" which became a symbol of resistance during the demonstrations at Tienanmen Square
Bettman Archive

Students Should Be Able to:

6E Demonstrate understanding of major worldwide scientific, technological, social, and cultural trends of the late 20th century by:

7-12 Evaluating how modern art and literature have expressed and reflected social transformations and how they have been internationalized. [**Evaluate historical perspectives**]

5-12 Analyzing how revolutions in communication, information technology, and mass marketing techniques have contributed to the acceleration of social change and the rise of a "global culture." [**Analyze multiple causation**]

9-12 Assessing the impact of space exploration, biotechnology, the new physics, and medical advances on human society and ecology. [**Analyze multiple causation**]

5-12 Comparing the values and lifestyles characteristic of "consumer societies" in the industrialized world with those in predominantly agrarian countries. [**Compare and contrast differing values, behaviors, and institutions**]

5-12 Describing varieties of religious experience in the contemporary world and how the world's major faiths have responded to recent challenges and uncertainties. [**Demonstrate and explain the importance of ideas**]

Grades 5-6

Examples of student achievement of Standard 6E include:

◗ Chart the changes that have taken place in the 20th century in communication. *How have these changes affected life? To what extent have they helped bring people from different parts of the world together?*

◗ List the major challenges confronting contemporary society and explain the ways in which different religions have sought to help solve these problems.

◗ List 10 consumer items that you consider important today. *Would people in other parts of the world select the same items? Why or why not?*

◗ Construct a bulletin board display showing examples of contemporary art and architecture from around the world. *In what way do styles reflect local culture? In what way do they show evidence of a "global culture"?*

Grades 7-8

Examples of student achievement of Standard 6E include:

▶ Create, as a class, a large bulletin board picture and word collage of examples of "global culture." Include examples of global communications, information technology, and mass marketing. *How have these revolutions accelerated social change?*

▶ Research the global influence of CNN in the past ten years. *In how many countries of the world can CNN be viewed? What role did CNN play in the Gulf War?*

▶ Research artistic expression in the form of art, music, literature, architecture, dance, photography, and film in different areas of the world. Construct a time line of major political events and incorporate illustrations of artistic expression. *How have political changes impacted the arts? How do the arts reflect contemporary society?*

▶ Debate the proposition that the late 20th century is a time of religious ferment and vitality in the world.

▶ Construct a chart listing the differences in lifestyles in an industrial nation and an agrarian nation. *What consumer goods are valued in each society? How has modern communication created similar demands for consumer goods in different parts of the world?*

Grades 9-12

Examples of student achievement of Standard 6E include:

▶ Select several examples of art (within one artistic medium) in a given time period from different societies. Analyze how the examples reflect the cultural values of the period.

▶ Debate the advantages and disadvantages of participation in the world economy for a country eager to preserve its traditional cultural identity. Use evidence from specific countries to support your arguments.

▶ Evaluate the relationship between demands for democratic reform and the trend toward privatization and economic liberalization in developing economies and former communist states. Assess the influence of multilateral aid organizations and multinational corporations in supporting or challenging these trends.

▶ Read excerpts from autobiographies of teenage Red Guards during the Cultural Revolution of the late 1960s. *Why was China on a contingency quest for a "new culture" throughout most of the 20th century?*

▶ Use interviews, lectures, and articles to examine the views of a variety of contemporary Muslim intellectuals. *What models for family life, the economy, and social and political institutions do they put forth?*

▶ Research the innovations in scientific and medical research that have developed from the space program. *How has modern technology impacted our ability to deal with problems in health-related issues?*

▶ Define "liberation theology" and explain the ideological conflicts surrounding the philosophy.

Teachers Delfina Zermeno and Velda Patton with 5th grade students,
Art Haycox Elementary School, Oxnard, CA

Teaching Resources for World History

Introduction to Resources

While traditional printed sources are still invaluable, the revolution in information-processing technologies provides a new wealth of possibilities for studying the past. Today's teachers and students have a wide array of sophisticated resources and materials available for the improved study of history. The rapid advances in telecommunications and satellite technologies enable learners to engage in a variety of "distance learning experiences," including interactive field trips to historical sites and the use of modems and communications software to tap into distant data banks and sources. Making use of current technology, students have the opportunity to interview policy makers, conduct oral history projects, and explore different perspectives through links to individuals and students from throughout the world.

The evolution of CD-ROM and laserdisc technologies also provide access to an abundance of diverse printed, audio, and visual data. In addition, publishers increasingly incorporate such multimedia resources into their textbook packages. Finally, an extensive variety of public history resources and materials are available to enhance the study of history. Museums, art galleries, and folk art exhibits provide information and resources for studying history while local historical societies offer another avenue for exploring the impact of world events on local communities.

The following list is meant to be suggestive rather than inclusive and needs to be updated periodically.

Resources

Media
     Laserdiscs and video
     CD-ROM
     Computer software
     Audio-cassette

Printed Sources
     Primary documents
     Reference materials
     Journals and periodicals
     Visual resources

Teaching Materials
     Curricular units
     Primary source kits

MEDIA

Laserdiscs and videos

▶ **ABC Interactive Programs**
ABC, 1989-1991, interactive laserdisc (CAV) or Macintosh

These interactive laserdisc programs are part of the ABC Instant Replay of History series. The programs include interviews, speeches, and news footage. With Macintosh HyperCard programs students may print documents and use video clips to compile individual or group reports. The series includes programs such as "Lessons of War," "Communism and the Cold War," and "In the Holy Land." Recommended for grades 7-12.

▶ **Africa: A Voyage of Discovery with Basil Davidson**
RM Arts, 1984, VHS, video cassettes

A comprehensive overview of African history and culture produced in England in association with Nigerian Television. The four programs in the series examine the great civilizations of Africa, medieval trade and trading routes, imperialism, and nationalism. Recommended for grades 7-12.

▶ **Art With a Message: Protest and Propaganda, Satire and Social Comment**
Center for the Humanities, 1971, VHS video cassette from still photographs

A probing view of the power of art to sway minds. The program examines issues such as political corruption, legal injustices, wars, and contemporary issues. Recommended for grades 9-12; however the program may be adapted for grades 7-8.

▶ **The Buried Mirror: Reflections on Spain and the New World**
Films Incorporated, 1993

A series of five video tapes hosted by Carlos Fuentes available in both English and Spanish. The series explores the Indian and Spanish heritage of the Americas from the pre-Columbian era to the present and examines the impact of history on contemporary Latin American society. Recommended for teachers and grades 9-12.

▶ **Castle**
Unicorn, VHS, video cassette

David Macaulay guides students on a tour of a fictional castle. Live footage is combined with animation to explore the building and defense of a medieval English castle and the surrounding town. On separate videos, David Macaulay examines the building of a medieval cathedral in, "Cathedral: The Story of Its Construction," and an Egyptian pyramid in, "Pyramid." The videos are recommended for grades 5-8.

▶ **Civilization**
BBC, not dated, VHS video cassettes

These thirteen highly acclaimed 50-minute programs, narrated by Kenneth Clark, explore art, architecture, philosophy, music, and literature of Western Civilization from the Middle Ages. Recommended for grades 9-12.

◗ **The Diary of Anne Frank**
20th Century Fox, laserdiscs (CLV—"letterbox") or VHS video cassettes

The compelling story of Anne Frank and her family starring Shelly Winters and Millie Perkins. Recommended for grades 5-12.

◗ **Eyes: Images from the Art Institute of Chicago**
Voyager Co., interactive laserdisc, Macintosh

Over 200 works from the Chicago Institute with music, poetry, sound effects, and narration about each work. The program provides an introduction to the world of art for younger students. Recommended for grades K-6.

◗ **The First Emperor of China**
Voyager, 1993, interactive laserdisc (CAV) or Macintosh HyperCard stack

Original film footage of the excavation of the tomb of Qin Shi Huangdi with a bilingual soundtrack with narrative in English or Mandarin Chinese. Recommended for grades 5-12.

◗ **Global Filmstrips and Videos**
Upper Midwest Women's History Center
St. Louis Park, Missouri

Complete set of nine sound filmstrips and videos to introduce the subject of women's history in areas of world history including Africa, China, India, the Middle East, Japan, Ancient Greece and Rome, Medieval/Renaissance Europe, and Latin America. Each comes complete with a full script guide, discussion questions and picture credits. Recommended for grades 9-12.

◗ **History through Art and Architecture**
Alarion Press

World history as seen through art and architecture. Multiple video offerings for many regions and periods. All videos are accompanied by teaching manuals and class posters. Recommended for grades 5-9.

◗ **Japan: The Changing Tradition**
Great Plains National Television Library

A series of sixteen 30-minute documentary-style programs that cover the history of modern Japan from the first contacts with the West in the 1500s to the 1970s. Produced in cooperation with the Japan Broadcasting Corporation and other Japanese institutions. Recommended for grades 9-12.

◗ **Japanese Art and Architecture**
Alarion Press, 1992, VHS video cassettes

This series of five programs on three video cassettes examines the evolution of Japanese art and architecture from primitive bronze and clay objects to elaborate Buddhist shrines. Common themes such as inspiration drawn from nature, religious beliefs, and infusion from other cultures are emphasized. Recommended for grades 9-12.

◗ **Land of Demons**
ABC News, 1993, VHS video cassette

An examination of the crisis in Bosnia and the long-standing hatreds that fueled the dismemberment of Yugoslavia. The program is narrated by Peter Jennings. Recommended for grades 9-12

◗ **Legacy**
Maryland Public Television, 1991, VHS video cassettes

Host Michael Wood explores the core values and cross-cultural influences of ancient civilizations, including Egypt, Mesopotamia, India, China, and Mesoamerica. Short segments recommended for grades 7-12.

◗ **The Lost Kingdom of the Maya**
National Geographic Society, 1993, VHS video cassette

A study of the collapse of the highly developed Maya civilization using recently deciphered hieroglyphics. The video also uses reenactments to dramatize ancient rituals. Recommended for grades 7-12.

◗ **The Mighty Continent: A View of Europe in the Twentieth Century**
Time-Life

A video series written and narrated by John Terraine with commentaries by Peter Ustinov. The program uses documentary films and contemporary footage to examine the political and cultural history of Europe in the 20th century. Recommended for grades 9-12.

◗ **Motion Picture and Made-for-Television films**

"Gandhi," "Cromwell," "Shogun," "Lust for Life," "The Mission," "Last Emperor of China," "Great Expectations," "Gallipoli," and "Battle of Algiers" represent only a few of available videos. Foreign films such as "Danton" with English subtitles are also effective teaching tools. The length of major motion pictures may preclude using the entire work; however, selections are appropriate. Movies on laserdisc are especially useful as preselected sections are easily accessible. Various motion picture guides are available and should be consulted for additional titles. Each of the videos must be reviewed prior to showing to determine the appropriateness for grade levels and student maturity.

◗ **National Gallery of Art**
Laserdisc (CAV) or Macintosh HyperCard stack

The program consists of two documentaries, "The History of the National Gallery of Art" and "A Tour of the National Gallery of Art," which offer visual access to over 1,600 works of art from 8th-century Byzantine paintings to contemporary works of Pollock and Rothko. Recommended for grades 5-12.

◗ **The Pacific Century**
Pacific Basin Institute,
Annenberg/CPB Collection, 1992

Ten one-hour television programs that can be divided into half-hour segments for classroom use. The series features interviews, maps, charts, and archival footage on such topics as "Asia and the Challenge of the West" and "From a Barrel of a Gun: The Remaking of Asia." Recommended for grades 9-12.

◗ **Religions of the World**
Holt, Rinehart and Winston Video Series, 1989

A series introducing five of the world's main religions: Buddhism, Christianity, Hinduism, Islam, and Judaism. Tapes present the social, political, historical, and geographic impact of each religion on the past and present. Recommended for grades 7-12.

◗ **Schindler's List**
MCA, 1993, laserdisc or VHS, video cassette

The story of a German industrialist, Oskar Schindler, who risked his life and fortune to save over 1,000 Jewish workers from deportation and death. This award-winning film by Steven Spielberg contains graphic violence and should be previewed before showing. Recommended for mature students, grades 9-12.

◗ **Spain: The Moorish Influence**
Encyclopaedia Britannica Educational Corporation, 1989, laserdisc and video cassette

A complete and lavish history of Spain as the crossroads of two worlds. It shows the influence of Muslim scholars and translators, architects, and doctors on the development of Europe. Recommended for Grades 9-12.

◗ **Suleyman the Magnificent**
Metropolitan Museum and National Gallery of Art, VHS, video cassette

A biography of Suleyman using treasures from the Topkapi Palace, scenes from illuminated manuscripts, mosaics, and cityscapes of Istanbul to examine his reign and the power and influence of the Ottoman Empire. Recommended for grades 7-12.

◗ **20th-Century Art at the Metropolitan Museum**
Metropolitan Museum, 1987, VHS video cassette

A tour of the American and European art in the Lila Acheson Wallace Wing of the Metropolitan Museum examines the works of leading 20th-century artists such as Picasso, Matisse, Pollock, and de Kooning. Recommended for grades 7-12.

◗ **Videoletters from Japan**
The Asia Society

Units consist of a video cassette, teaching manual, and classroom poster. Six different video cassettes in all, including the "Living Arts," which introduces traditional dance, kabuki theater, the tea ceremony, and flower arrangement. Recommended for grades 5-7.

◗ **Witness of the Holocaust**
Anti-Defamation League, VHS video cassettes

The program begins with an overview of the Holocaust followed by segments which examine topics such as ghetto life, resistance, and liberation. Students must be prepared for the graphic scenes of atrocities. Recommended only after preview for mature students, grades 10-12.

♦ World History Videodisc
Instructional Resources Corporation, interactive laserdisc, IBM or Macintosh

Complete world history videodisc providing instant access to 2,400 images for use in world history, including more than 950 color images and 71 maps. A complete master guide accompanies the videodisc and each frame is described in depth. The addition of bar code selection makes frame access almost instant and easy for students as well as teachers to use. Recommended for grades 6-12.

CD-ROMs

♦ **History of the World: A Complete and Authoritative World History Reference on IBM or Macintosh**
Bureau Development, 1992

A storehouse of information on world history. The program includes short documents, complete books, and excerpts from seminal works. Students may compare legal codes of different civilizations, examine conflicting economic philosophies, or investigate leading historical figures.

♦ **The 1993 *Time* Magazine Compact Almanac**
Compact Publishing, 1993, CD-ROM for IBM, MPC compatibles, and Macintosh

A full text reference of every issue of *Time* for 1989 through the January 4, 1993 issue with CNN videos of major stories. The disk also includes a "*Time* Capsules" section with some articles dating to the first issue of the magazine in 1923, a "Compact Almanac," maps, and the CIA World Factbook with State Department notes. Recommended for grades 9-12.

♦ **Picture Atlas of the World**
National Geographic Society, 1992, CD-ROM for IBM

Photographs, motion pictures, maps, statistical graphs, and audio clips of music and voices from every continent are incorporated in this National Geography program. Students access areas of the globe or focus on individual countries. Recommended for grades 5-8.

♦ **Time Table of History, Science and Innovation**
Software Toolworks, 1991

A general historic survey of science from the origin of the universe to the present. Students scroll along a timeline which includes over 6,000 developments in all branches of science. Recommended for grades 5-8.

♦ **Time Traveler: A Multimedia Chronicle of History**
New Media Schoolhouse, 1992, CD-ROM for Macintosh

A historical record from 4000 BCE. Students may follow a topic through the centuries or investigate events around the globe for a given year. The program includes notes on the history and culture of a region and some entries include recorded speeches or period music. Recommended for grades 5-8.

▶ World History Illustrated
Queue/Clearvue, 1993-1994

Narrated tutorials on ancient cultures and different historical eras including key-word index and timeline feature. The five programs in the series are: "Ancient Egypt and the Mideast," "Ancient Greece," "Rome and the Celts," "Middle Ages," and "Renaissance and Reformation."

Computer Software

▶ The French Revolution
Appian Way, 1991, IBM

Short documents covering different aspects of the French Revolution. Teachers and students have the option of adding their own documents to the computer program. Recommended for grades 9-12.

▶ Hitler's Germany
Appian Way, 1991, IBM

The program incorporates primary and secondary source material including excerpts from diaries, speeches, poems, and historical appraisals of the period. Each disc contains short documents on all aspects of life in Nazi Germany. Teachers and students may add documents to the program. Recommended for grades 9-12.

▶ Mac TimeLiner and TimeLiner (IBM version)
Tom Snyder Productions, Inc., 1990, Macintosh, Apple, IBM

This timeline maker sorts the entered events into chronological order and arranges them proportionally. Recommended for grades 4-8.

▶ Non-Western Cultures
Focus Media, 1987, Apple discs

A computer game in a quiz format using high resolution graphics. The three programs are "Africa and the Middle East," "China and Japan," and "India and Latin America," the latter a contrast of the two regions. Recommended for grades 7-8.

▶ PC Globe, Inc.
Tempe, Arizona

PC Globe is an "electronic atlas" that provides users with instant profiles of 190 countries. Maps, graphics, facts and figures are available on all countries. Users can instantly compare countries for a wide variety of data, either on the maps themselves or with colorful bar charts and graphs. Pull-down menus and a clear, simple format for easy student use. Recommended for grades 6-12.

Audio cassettes

▶ The Lyrichord World Music Sampler, Audio Cassette

The recordings on this sampler represent seventeen varied examples of traditional world music. The sampler includes music from Bolivia, Costa Rica, Peru, Bali, China, India, Iran, Korea, Albania, Italy, Zimbabwe, ancient Egypt, and Japan.

PRINTED SOURCES

Primary Documents

▶ *African Civilization Revisited,* **edited by Basil Davidson**
Trenton, New Jersey: Africa World Press, 1991

The story of Africa from antiquity to modern times as told in chronicles and records. Recommended as a teacher reference and for grades 10-12.

▶ *The Africans: A Reader,* **edited by Ali A. Mazrui**
New York: Praeger Special Studies, 1986

A series of diverse readings to accompany the video series "The Africans." Selections are historical, political, and literary sources to coordinate with basic themes and questions in African history. Recommended as a teacher reference and for grades 9-12.

▶ *Chinese Civilization: A Sourcebook (2nd Edition),* **edited by Patricia Buckley Ebrey**
New York: The Free Press, 1993

A collection of primary source selections reflecting the social history of China. Recommended as a teacher reference and for grades 10-12.

▶ *Colonial Rule in Africa: Readings From Primary Sources,* **edited by Bruce Febber**
Madison, Wisconsin: University of Wisconsin Press, 1979

Colonial rule in Africa through the eyes of the principal actors, administrators, missionaries, and the colonized peoples themselves. Recommended as a teacher reference and for grades 10-12.

▶ *Eyewitness to History,* **edited by John Carey**
Cambridge: Harvard University Press, 1988

Short, readable eyewitness accounts of major events in world history. The selections include observations by both notable personalities and unfamiliar individuals of events such as the eruption of Vesuvius, Wat Tyler's revolt, Napoleon's entry into Moscow, the suppression of the Bulgarian revolt of 1876, the destruction of Guernica, and the fall of Philippine President Marcos. Recommended as a teacher reference and for grades 9-12.

▶ Greenhaven World History Program
Greenhaven Press, Inc. (originally published by George Harrap Publishers, London)

This series includes sixty-four different pamphlets covering the complete range of world history. Each pamphlet includes short primary source documents along with a historical survey of the period or issue under study. Recommended for grades 7-12.

▶ *Human Documents of the Industrial Revolution in Britain,* **edited by E. Royston Pike**
London: George Allen & Unwin, 1978

All documents are originals, prepared and written during the Industrial Revolution. The work emphasizes social history. Recommended as a teacher reference and for grades 9-12.

▶ **Primary Source Collections**

A number of publishers have produced source books as supplements to basic texts. Still others have taken thematic approaches with works such as readings on women in history, revolutions, wars, and contemporary problems. Primary source readings are appropriate at all grade levels; read-a-rounds and paraphrased documents offer two of many different approaches for younger students. Anthologies such as *The Democracy Reader* is one of many currently available source books which may be effectively used at grades 7-12.

▶ *Documents in World History*, Vols. I and II, edited by Peter N. Stearns
New York: Harper and Row, 1988

A complete collection of primary source readings for an entire world history course. Documents cover political, cultural, and social history and are amenable to cross-cultural comparison. Introductions to the documents are included along with questions to guide student reading. While designed for a college course, many readings can be adapted for high school use. Recommended for grades 10-12.

▶ *The Global Experience: Readings in World History*, Volumes I and II, edited by Philip F. Riley et al.
Englewood Cliffs, New Jersey: Prentice Hall, 1992

A brief, balanced collection of primary materials organized chronologically and focused on global themes. Materials represent global change and exchange as well as the distinct achievements of major civilizations. Introductory comments and questions to consider appear for each reading. Recommended for grades 10-12.

▶ *The Human Record: Sources of Global History*, Volumes I and II, edited by Alfred J. Andrea and James H. Overfield
Boston: Houghton Mifflin Company, 1990

A complete selection of primary sources for world history, including maps, charts, letters, and selections from literature. All sections have thorough introductions and leading questions to guide the reading. Many documents are used comparatively. Recommended for grades 10-12.

▶ Sources of Indian Tradition (2nd Edition), compoiled by Ainslie T. Embree and Stephen Hay
New York: Columbia University Press, 1988

A standard reference collection of primary source selections on India from ancient times through modern history. Similar sourcebooks published by Columbia University Press include: *Sources of Chinese Tradition* compiled by William Theodore de Bary, Wing-tsit Chan, and Burton Watson (1964) and *Sources of Japanese Tradition* compiled by Ryusaku Tsunoda, William Theodore de Bary, and Donald Keene (1964).

Reference Materials

▶ *The Cambridge Encyclopedia of Japan*, edited by Richard Bowring and Peter Kornicki
New York: Cambridge University Press, 1993

A one-volume reference providing a general survey of Japan's history, geography, politics, religion, and culture. Recommended for grades 8-12.

▶ Cambridge Introduction to World History Series
Cambridge University Press

A series of 18 well-illustrated topical books on Western Civilization. Books in the series include *Life in the Stone Age*, *Pompeii*, *Iron and the Industrial Revolution*, *Life in a Medieval Monastery*, *The Rebellion in India, 1857*, and *Railways*. Recommended for grades 7-8.

▶ Cultural Atlas of the World Series
Stonehenge Publications

A multivolume reference collection of the history and culture of different regions of the world and historical eras. Volumes in the series include: *Mesopotamia*, *The Jewish World*, *Medieval Europe*, *Islamic World*, *China*, *Japan*, and *Africa*. Recommended as a teacher reference and for grades 9-12.

▶ *An Encyclopedia of the Twentieth Century*
New York: Oxford University Press, 1989-1992

A set of well illustrated resource books which chronicle the 20th century. Volume titles are: *The Family: A Social History*; *The Arts: A History of Expression*; *Passing Parade: A History of Popular Culture*; *Science: A History of Discovery*; *Wealth and Poverty: An Economic History*; *Power: A Political History*; *Nations: A Survey of the Twentieth Century*; and, *Events, A Chronicle of the Twentieth Century*. Along with two companion volumes, *The Experiences of World War I* and *The Experiences of World War II*, this series provides an ideal reference for the 20th century. Recommended for grades 9-12.

▶ *Encyclopedia of World History*, edited by William Langer
Boston: Houghton Mifflin, 1980

A one-volume reference encyclopedia. Recommended for teachers and students, grades 9-12.

▶ Historical Maps on File
Facts on File, 1983

Three hundred reproducible maps which cover historical topics from early civilizations to the 1980s. Although one-third of the maps pertain to U.S. history topics, others include the Crusades, world religions, revolutions, trading routes, and colonial empires. Recommended for grades 5-12.

▶ *A History of Their Own: Women in Europe from Prehistory to the Present*, edited by Bonnie Anderson and Judith Zinsser
New York: Harper Perennial, 1989

A two-volume study of women in European history. Information is drawn from diaries, letters, wills, poems, plays, and art works. Recommended as a teacher reference.

▶ *Illustrated History of the World*
New York: Kingfisher Books, 1993

An illustrated dictionary of world history from ancient times to the present. The short descriptions of major events are enhanced by numerous illustrations and maps. Recommended for grades 4-8.

▶ Kwamena-Poh, Michael, John Tosh, Richard Waller, and Michael Tidy
African History in Maps
London: Longman, 1982

A visual treatment of African history in maps. Recommended for grades 5-12.

▶ *Lost Civilizations* Series
Time-Life Books

A series of well-illustrated books on ancient civilizations. The series includes *Sumer: Cities of Eden, Ramses II: Magnificence of the Nile, Africa's Glorious Legacy*, and *China's Buried Kingdoms*. Recommended for grades 5-8.

▶ *Makers of World History, Volumes 1 and II*, edited by J. Kelley Sowards
New York: St. Martin's Press, 1992

This is a collection of information and essays on 28 key individuals in world history including Akhenaton, Ashoka, Muhammad, Murasaki Shikibu, and Eleanor of Aquitaine. Typically, three selections are devoted to each figure, one selection usually autobiographical and the others commentary, either supporting, revising or rejecting each other. A series of review-and-study questions are included along with suggestions for further reading. Recommended for teachers; however, some documents may be used with students, grades 10-12.

▶ Miller, Donald E., and Lorna Touryan Miller
Survivors: An Oral History of the Armenian Genocide
Berkeley: University of California Press, 1993

A comprehensive study of the Armenian genocide based on oral histories, U.S. State Department files, missionary and ambassadorial accounts, and the Parliamentary Bryce-Toynbee Report. Recommended for grades 9-12.

▶ Philippe, Robert
Political Graphics: Art as a Weapon
New York: Abbeville Press, 1980

The work examines broadsides and leaflets from the Renaissance and Reformation to the wall posters of the late 20th century. Recommended for grades 9-12.

▶ *Readings in World Civilization, Volumes I and II*, edited by Kevin Reilly
New York: St. Martin's Press, 1992

Lengthy selections of both primary and secondary sources with brief introductions. Many interpretive pieces give teachers access to an analysis of a time period. Student questions are geared toward developing interpretive and critical thinking skills. Recommended for teachers.

▶ **Religions on File**
Facts on File, 1990

A collection of religious texts, chronologies of historical events, charts, maps, diagrams, and other information on the world's major religions. Approximately 200 reproducible pages are included. Recommended for grades 5-8.

▶ Rhodes, Anthony
Propaganda, The Art of Persuasion: World War II
Secaucus, NJ: Wellfleet Press, 1987

A well-illustrated book which demonstrates the power of visual images through art, architecture, motion pictures, poster art, cartoons, and caricatures. Recommended for grades 7-12.

▶ Roded, Ruth
Women in Islamic Biographical Collections
Boulder: Lynne Rienner Publishers, 1994

Roded offers a reassessment of the oft-disparaged role of women in Muslim society by examining the large number of female scholars, philanthropists, and other prominent contributors in the historical genre from early Islam to the 20th century. Recommended as a teacher resource.

▶ Silverblank, Fran
An Annotated Bibliography of Historical Fiction for the Social Studies, Grades 5 through 12
Dubuque, Iowa: Kendall/Hunt Publishing Co., 1992

A bibliography of historical fiction with grade level recommendations. Brief annotations of hundreds of children's trade books in world and United States history. Recommended for teachers.

▶ Szonyi, David M.
The Holocaust: An Annotated Bibliography and Resource Guide
New York: KTAV Publishing House, Inc., 1985

An annotated bibliography of nonfiction, fiction, media, curricular materials, oral histories, and music resources on the Holocaust. Recommended for teachers.

▶ *TimeFrame* Series
Time-Life Books

A series of 25 well illustrated books published by *Time-Life* books. The series is a re-conception of the popular Age of Man series. Titles in the series include *Light in the East, The Domestic World, Winds of Revolution, The Pulse of Enterprise*, and *The Nuclear Age*. Recommended for grades 7-12.

▶ Waddy, Charis,
Women in Muslim History
New York: Longman Group, Ltd., 1980

A comprehensive survey of Islamic views on women from a doctrinal and historical perspective. Recommended as a teacher resource.

▶ *Women in the Muslim World*
Edited by Nikki Keddie and Lois Beck
Boston: Harvard University Press, 1978

This collection of essays surveys an astonishing variety of topics from history, sociology, and anthropology, all anchored in studies of real women from various historical periods and regions. Recommended as a teacher reference.

▶ **Women in World Area Studies**
Glenhurst Publications

A series of books examining women's history and contemporary issues in various societies. The books include readings, statistical information, group exercises, and selected primary sources. This ongoing series includes *Women in Africa, Women in Latin America, Women in Traditional China*, and *Women in Japan*. Recommended for grades 9-12 with adaptations for grades 7-12.

Journals and Periodicals

▶ *Americas*

A magazine published bimonthly in English and Spanish by the Organization of American States. Articles cover a variety of topics from art and music to travel with historical articles published in virtually every issue. Recommended for grades 9-12.

▶ *Aramco World Magazine*

A free monthly magazine on all aspects of the Islamic world.

▶ *British Heritage*

A bimonthly magazine devoted to articles on British history and traditions. The magazine was formerly published as *British History Illustrated*. Recommended for grades 7-12.

▶ *Calliope, World History for Young People*

A magazine for students, grades 5-8, which focuses on a different in-depth topic or theme in world history in each issue. Usually includes plays, biographical articles, word games, archaeology, and history presented in practical and interesting ways. Published five times a year. Recommended for grades 5-8.

▶ *Cobblestone: A History Magazine for Young People*

A monthly history magazine for young people that often contains information that is valuable for research and for classroom debates. Recommended for grades 6-8.

▶ *Concord Review*

A quarterly journal devoted to student written articles on topics in United States and world history. An exceptional teaching tool offering outstanding essays researched and written by high school students. Class sets are available. Recommended for grades 9-12.

▶ *FACES*

A monthly magazine of world cultures. Published with the cooperation of the American Museum of Natural History, New York. Recommended for grades 5-8.

▶ *History Today*

An exceptional monthly magazine devoted primarily to British and European history with some articles dealing with topics in United States and world history. It is published in Britain. Recommended for grades 9-12.

▶ *Journal of World History*

The journal of the World History Association is published biannually. The scholarly articles and book reviews are a helpful resource for teachers.

▶ *Social Education*

Published periodically by the National Council for the Social Studies with articles of interest to educators. The magazine regularly features annotations of children's trade books, reviews of newly developed computer programs, and lessons using primary source documents. Recommended for teachers.

▶ *Social Studies and the Young Learner*

A quarterly magazine of the National Council for the Social Studies which includes articles of interest for K-6 teachers. Issues provide critiques of children's trade books. Recommended for teachers.

▶ *World Eagle*

Monthly publication of charts, maps, graphs, and general statistics for the social studies and world history. Excellent comparative maps (updates) and world data on many topics. Publications also include teaching units for world history. Recommended for grades 7-12.

Visual Resources

▶ **Art through the Ages**
Universal Color Slide Co.

A complete series of slides sets for world history through art. Recommended for grades 5-12.

▶ **Art resources**

Major art museums provide free or low cost rental of video cassettes and slide programs of historic themes such as The National Gallery of Art's "Treasures of Tutankhamen," "The Search for Alexander," "African Art," and "Ancient Moderns: Greek Island Art and Culture, 3000-2000 BC." Art prints are also available from galleries and publishing companies. Commercially produced series such as "Museum without Walls" and "The Grand Museums" offer detailed studies of artists and their works and tours of the world's most noted museums. Art resources may be used at different grade levels depending on student maturity.

● **Before Cortés: Sculpture of Middle America.**
Sandak Color Slides

A set of 50 slides which illustrate 3,000 years of sculpture from central Mexico to Panama and the Caribbean. Objects include works from the Olmec to the Aztec. Sandak offers a wide variety of slide collections including "Art Through the Centuries: The Americas," "Introductory Survey of Chinese Art," and "Global Art Slide Set." Recommended for grades 5-12.

● **Documentary Photographs**

A number of companies produce documentary photographs and posters which may be used as an integral part of instruction. Among the many documentary visuals are: "Talkabout Posters," which present photographs, paintings, or posters along with explanatory text on the reverse side and "Then and Now: The Wonders of the Ancient World," which use current photographs and acetate overlays to recreate architectural wonders of the world. Poster art of the world wars and sets of dramatic photographs of the Nazi Holocaust are also available from several publishers. Documentary photographs may be used across all grade levels.

TEACHING MATERIALS

Curricular Units

● **American Classical League**
Miami University, Oxford, Ohio 45056

Various books, pamphlets, posters, maps, slides, and teaching units on ancient Greece and Rome. Recommended for all grade levels.

● **Arab World and Islamic Resources (AWAIR)**
1865 Euclid Ave., Ste. 4
Berkeley, California 94709

A complete range of K-12 teaching materials about the Arab world, including a K-7 across-the-curriculum teaching manual, "The Arabs: Activities for the Elementary School Level," and a similar 7-12 manual, "The Arab World Notebook: For the Secondary School Level." Extensive materials and resources.

● **CITE Books**
New York, 1988

A series of books entitled *Through African Eyes, Through Chinese Eyes, Through Indian Eyes,* and *Through Japanese Eyes* which provide an introduction to culture and history. The books include multiple primary source readings and visual documents on traditional and contemporary history. The documents focus on a few major themes and present materials that try to recreate the reality of life. Recommend for Grades 8-12.

♦ Classroom Plays and Simulations

Numerous short classroom plays and simulation activities enhance the study of history. A number of companies have produced interactive activities in world history including classroom plays and readers' theater such as "Plays of Great Achievers" and "Children of the Holocaust." Simulations such as "Great Eras in History," "Civilization Game," and "World History Trials" are among many from which to select. A review of objectives for each of these activities is recommended. Grade level recommendations vary.

♦ CLIO Project
University of California, Berkeley
Berkeley, CA 94720

The CLIO Project publications contain overview essays and lesson plans covering a variety of topics from geography to changing gender roles in Asian cultures. Units include "Teaching and Learning About India" and "Teaching and Learning About Traditional China."

♦ East Asian Curriculum Project
Columbia University
420 West 118th Street, New York, NY 10027

Multiple resources and curriculum guides are available for teaching about Korea, Southeast Asia, South Asia, Japan, and China. These annotated guides for teachers present major recurring themes in areas under study. They include activities, lesson plans, art and cultural history resources in addition to teacher suggestions and pamphlets on developing central themes for each region. Recommended for grades 7-12.

♦ Echoes of China
Boston Children's Museum
300 Congress, Boston, MA 02210

Seven separate curriculum units developed by the Greater Chinese Cultural Association and the Boston Children's Museum. Titles for world history include "Jia: The Chinese Family," "Chinese American Families," "China and Her Land," "Travels with Marco Polo: Life in 13th-Century China," "Fine and Folk Arts of China," and "Chinese Architecture." Recommended for grades 7-12.

♦ National Center for History in the Schools
University of California, Los Angeles
10880 Wilshire Blvd., Suite 761, Los Angeles, CA 90024

A series of curriculum units based on primary source materials. The teaching units with lesson plans and teacher background information are recommended for various grade levels; however, they may be adapted for use in most classes, grades 5-12. The units include: "Wang Mang: Confucian Success or Failure?" "The Role of Women in Medieval Europe," "Mansa Musa: African King of Gold," "The Code of Hammurabi," "Timbuktu," "Early Chinese History: The Hundred Schools Period," and "The Scientific Revolution."

◆ **Stanford Project on International and Cross-cultural Education (SPICE)**
Stanford University
300 Lasuen St., Littlefield Center 14, Palo Alto, CA 94305

The Stanford Project offers over sixty titles which include curriculum units, resource guides, and research reports specifically designed for world history. Materials available include such units as "Two Visions of the Conquest," based on visual representations, primary and secondary documents, and maps for the period of the Spanish conquest of Mexico; and "The Modernization of Japan: Continuity and Change," analyzing life in Japan at the end of the feudal period and during the Meiji period (1868-1912). Recommended for grades 6-12.

◆ **Women in the World**
Curriculum Resource Project, Berkeley, California

Selected units in women's history including "A Message for the Sultan: Suleyman the Magnificent's Ottoman Turkey" and a series of "Spindle Stories," six units including "The Bird of Destiny: Ancient Egypt," "The Garney-Eyed Brooch: Anglo-Saxon England," plus others. Recommended for grades 5-9.

◆ **Women in World Area Studies**
Upper Midwest Women's History Center
Hamlin University, 1536 Hewitt Ave., St. Paul, MN 55104

Designed to integrate women's history into area world history courses. Complete set of thirteen books and teacher's guides includes *Women in Africa, Ancient Greece and Rome, Medieval and Renaissance Europe, Traditional China, Modern China, and Latin America* . Each book covers the diversity of female experience both within a given period and over time. Materials include essays, activities, and primary sources, both visual and written, plus selected bibliographies. Recommended for grades 9-12.

◆ **World History**
TAP Instructional Materials, Center for Learning, 1986

A series of books with self-contained lessons on topics in world history. Each lesson lists objectives, prerequisites, teacher notes, and recommended procedures. Student handout masters incorporate art, graphs, maps, poems, and short documents. Recommended for grades 9-12; however, some lessons may be adapted for grades 7-8.

◆ **World Literature**
Center for Learning

This two-volume teaching resource offers a variety of activities on world literature. Volume One examines great literature works including *The Odyssey, Don Quixote, One Day in the Life of Ivan Denisovich,* and *The Madwoman of Chaillot.* Volume Two looks at the works of great writers from four continents. Recommended for grades 9-12.

Primary Source Kits

▶ Jackdaws Portfolios of Historical Documents
Golden Owl Publishing

Jackdaws kits are available on a number of events in world history. Each portfolio contains primary source documents and essays by historians on the featured topic. Documentary photographs and political cartoons accompany the documents. Some of the case studies are: "Tutankhamen," "China: A Cultural Heritage," "The World of Islam," "Magna Carta," "The Spanish Inquisition," "The Russian Revolution," and "The Holocaust." Recommended for grades 7-12.

Students, Lakeview Junior High School, Santa Maria, CA

Contributors and Participating Organizations

Organizational Structure of the National History Standards Project

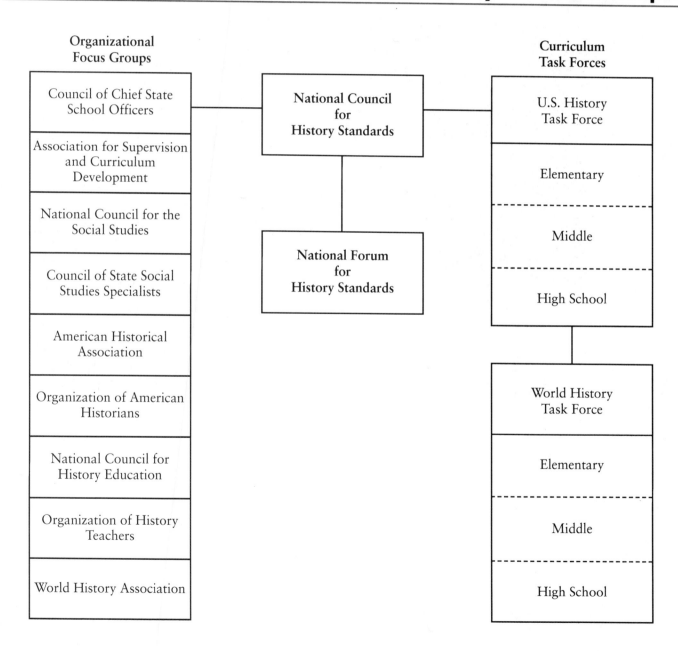

Organizational
Focus Groups

- Council of Chief State School Officers
- Association for Supervision and Curriculum Development
- National Council for the Social Studies
- Council of State Social Studies Specialists
- American Historical Association
- Organization of American Historians
- National Council for History Education
- Organization of History Teachers
- World History Association

National Council
for
History Standards

National Forum
for
History Standards

Curriculum
Task Forces

- U.S. History Task Force
- Elementary
- Middle
- High School

- World History Task Force
- Elementary
- Middle
- High School

Participating Organizations

American Association of School Librarians

American Association for State and Local History

American Federation of Teachers

American Historical Association

Association for the Study of Afro-American Life and History

Association for Supervision and Curriculum Development

The Atlantic Council of the United States

Center for Civic Education

Council for American Private Education

Council for Basic Education

Council for Islamic Education

Council of Chief State School Officers

Council of the Great City Schools

Council of State Social Studies Specialists

Educational Excellence Network

League of United Latin American Citizens

Lutheran Schools, The Lutheran Church-Missouri Synod

National Alliance of Black School Educators

National Association for Asian and Pacific American Education

National Association of Elementary School Principals

National Association of Secondary School Principals

National Association of State Boards of Education

National Catholic Educational Association

National Congress of Parents and Teachers

National Council for Geographic Education

National Council for History Education

The National Council for the Social Studies

National Council on Economic Education

National Education Association

Native American Heritage Commission

Organization of American Historians

Organization of History Teachers

Quality Education for Minorities Network

Social Science Education Consortium

World History Association

Organizational Rosters

National Council for History Standards

Officers

Charlotte Crabtree, Co-chair
Professor of Education Emeritus
University of California, Los Angeles

Gary B. Nash, Co-chair
Professor of History
University of California, Los Angeles

Linda Symcox, Coordinator
Associate Director, National Center for History in the Schools
University of California, Los Angeles

Members

Charlotte Anderson, President
National Council for Social Studies, 1992-93

Joyce Appleby, President
Organization of American Historians, 1992-1993
Professor of History
University of California, Los Angeles

Samuel Banks, Executive Director
Division of Compensatory and Funded Programs
Baltimore City Public Schools

David Battini, Teacher
Durham High School
Cairo, New York

David Baumbach, Teacher
Woolsair Elementary Gifted Center
Pittsburgh, Pennsylvania

Earl Bell, President
Organization of History Teachers
Teacher, Laboratory Schools
University of Chicago

Mary Bicouvaris, Teacher
Hampton Roads Academy
Newport News, Virginia

Diane Brooks, President,
Council of State Social Studies Specialists, 1993
Manager, California Department of Education

Pedro Castillo, Professor of History
University of California, Santa Cruz

Ainslie T. Embree, Professor of History Emeritus
Columbia University

Elizabeth Fox-Genovese, Professor of History
Emory University

Carol Gluck, Professor of History
Columbia University

Darlene Clark Hine, Professor of History
Michigan State University

Bill Honig, President,
Council of Chief State School Officers, 1992
Distinguished Visiting Professor of Education
San Francisco State University

Akira Iriye, Professor of History
Harvard University

Barbara Talbert Jackson, President
Association for Supervision and
Curriculum Development, 1993-94

Kenneth Jackson, Professor of History
Columbia University

Morton Keller, Professor of History
Brandeis University

Bernard Lewis, Professor of History
Princeton University

William McNeill, Professor of History Emeritus
University of Chicago

Alan D. Morgan, President,
Council of Chief State School Officers, 1993
State Superintendent of
Public Instruction, New Mexico

Stephanie Pace-Marshall, President
Association for Supervision and Curriculum
Development, 1992-93

John J. Patrick, Director, Social Studies Development
Center and Professor of Education
Indiana University

Theodore K. Rabb, Chairman,
National Council for History Education
Professor of History
Princeton University

Members (Continued)

C. Frederick Risinger, Associate Director, Social Studies
Development Center and Professor of Education
Indiana University

Denny Schillings, President
National Council for the Social Studies, 1993-94
Teacher, Homewood Flossmoor High School
Flossmoor, Illinois

Gilbert T. Sewall, Director
American Textbook Council

Warren Solomon, Curriculum Consultant for
Social Studies
Missouri Department of Elementary and
Secondary Education

Michael R. Winston, Vice President Emeritus
Howard University and
President, Alfred Harcourt Foundation

Organizational titles of all members were current at the
time of their first participation in the project.

World History Curriculum Committee

Joan Arno, Teacher
George Washington High School
Philadelphia, Pennsylvania

David Baumbach, Teacher
Woolsair Elementary Gifted Center
Pittsburgh, Pennsylvania

Richard Bulliet, Professor of History
Columbia University

Ainslee T. Embree, Professor of History Emeritus
Columbia University

Carol Gluck, Professor of History
Columbia University

Akira Iriye, Professor of History
Harvard University

Henry G. Kiernan, Director of Curriculum
West Morris Regional High School District
Chester, New Jersey

Colin Palmer, Professor of History
University of North Carolina, Chapel Hill

Theodore K. Rabb, Professor of History
Princeton University

Richard Saller, Professor of History
University of Chicago

Michael R. Winston, Vice President Emeritus
Howard University, and
President, Alfred Harcourt Foundation

World History Curriculum Task Force

Joann Alberghini, Teacher
Lake View Junior High School
Santa Maria, California

John Arevalo, Teacher
Harlandale High School
San Antonio, Texas

Joan Arno, Teacher,
George Washington High School
Philadelphia, Pennsylvania

David Baumbach, Teacher
Woolsair Elementary Gifted Center
Pittsburgh, Pennsylvania

Edward Berenson, Professor of History
University of California, Los Angeles

Margaret Binnaker, Teacher
St. Andrews-Swanee School
St. Andrews, Tennessee

Jacqueline Brown-Frierson, Teacher
Lemmel Middle School
Baltimore, Maryland

Richard Bulliet, Professor of History
Columbia University

Stanley Burstein, Professor of History
California State University, Los Angeles

Anne Chapman, Academic Dean
Western Reserve Academy
Hudson, Ohio

Peter Cheoros, Teacher
Lynwood High School
Lynwood, California

Charlotte Crabtree, Professor of Education Emeritus
University of California, Los Angeles

Sammy Crawford, Teacher
Soldotna High School
Soldotna, Arkansas

Ross Dunn, Professor of History
San Diego State University

World History Curriculum Task Force (Continued)

Benjamin Elman, Professor of History
University of California, Los Angeles

Jean Fleet, Teacher
Riverside University High School
Milwaukee, Wisconsin

Jana Flores, Teacher
Pine Grove Elementary School
Santa Maria, California

Michele Forman, Teacher
Middlebury High School
Middlebury, Vermont

Charles Frazee, Professor of History Emeritus
California State University, Fullerton

Marilynn Jo Hitchens, Teacher
Wheat Ridge High School
Wheat Ridge, Colorado

Jean Johnson
Friends Seminary
New York, New York

Henry G. Kiernan, Supervisor of Humanities
Southern Regional High School District
Manahawkin, New Jersey

Carrie McIver, Teacher
Santee Summit High School
Santee, California

Susan Meisler, Teacher
Vernon Center Middle School
Vernon, Connecticut

Gary B. Nash, Professor of History
University of California, Los Angeles

Joe Palumbo, Administrative Assistant
Long Beach Unified School District
Long Beach, California

Sue Rosenthal, Teacher
High School for Creative and Performing Arts
Philadelphia, Pennsylvnia

Heidi Roupp, Teacher
Aspen High School
Aspen, Colorado

Irene Segade, Teacher
San Diego High School
San Diego, California

Geoffrey Symcox, Professor of History
University of California, Los Angeles

Linda Symcox, Associate Director
National Center for History in the Schools
University of California, Los Angeles

David Vigilante, Teacher Emeritus
Gompers Secondary School
San Diego, California

Scott Waugh, Professor of History
University of California, Los Angeles

Julia Werner, Teacher
Nicolet High School
Glendale, Wisconsin

Donald Woodruff, Headmaster
Fredericksburg Academy
Fredericksburg, Virginia

National Forum for History Standards

Ronald Areglado
National Association of Elementary School Principals

Kathy Belter
National Congress of Parents and Teachers

Nguyen Minh Chau
National Association for Asian and
Pacific American Education

Cesar Collantes
League of United Latin American Citizens

Mark Curtis
The Atlantic Council of the United States

Glen Cutlip
National Education Association

Graham Down
Council for Basic Education

Chester E. Finn, Jr.
Educational Excellence Network

Mary Futrell
Quality Education for Minorities Network

Keith Geiger
National Education Association

Ivan Gluckman
National Association of Secondary School Principals

Ruth Granados
Council of the Great City Schools

Shabbir Mansuri
Council for Islamic Education

Joyce McCray
Council for American Private Education

Sr. Catherine T. McNamee
National Catholic Educational Association

Patricia Gordon Michael
American Association for State and Local History

Mabel Lake Murray
National Alliance of Black School Educators

Cynthia Neverdon-Morton
Association for the Study of Afro-American
Life and History

George Nielsen
Lutheran Schools,
The Lutheran Church-Missouri Synod

Charles N. Quigley
Center for Civic Education

Christopher Salter
National Council for Geographic Education

Adelaide Sanford
National Association of State Boards of Education

Ruth Toor
American Association of School Librarians

Clifford Trafzer
Native American Heritage Commission

Hai T. Tran
National Association for Asian and
Pacific American Education

Ruth Wattenberg
American Federation of Teachers

Council of Chief State School Officers
Focus Group

Sue Bennet
California Department of Education

Pasquale DeVito
Rhode Island Department of Education

Patricia Dye, History/Social Studies Consultant
Plymouth, Massachusetts

Mary Fortney
Indiana Department of Education

Connie Manter
Maine Department of Education

Alan D. Morgan
New Mexico State Superintendent of Public Instruction

Wayne Neuburger
Oregon Department of Education

Charles Peters
Oakland Schools, Waterford, Michigan

Thomas Sobol
New York Commissioner of Education

Robert H. Summerville
Alabama Department of Education

Staff

Fred Czarra, Consultant in International Education,
Social Studies and Interdisciplinary Learning

Ed Roeber, Director of the State Collaborative on
Assessment and Student Standards

Ramsay Selden, Director, State Education
Assessment Center

Association for Supervision and Curriculum Development
Focus Group

Glen Blankenship, Social Studies Coordinator
Georgia State Department of Education
Atlanta, Georgia

Joyce Coffey, Teacher
Dunbar Senior High School
District Heights, Maryland

Sherrill Curtiss, Teacher
Chairman, Dept. of History/Social Studies
Providence Senior High School
Charlotte, North Carolina

Geno Flores, Teacher
Arroyo Grande High School
Arroyo Grande, California

Alan Hall, Teacher
Chairman, Social Studies Department
Yarmouth High School
Yarmouth, Massachussetts

Erich Martel, Teacher
Wilson Senior High School
Washington, D.C.

Marilyn McKnight, Teacher
Milwaukee Public Schools
Milwaukee, Wisconsin

Mike Radow, Teacher
Tops Middle School
Seattle, Washington

Karen Steinbrink, Assistant Executive Director
Bucks County Intermediate Unit
Doylestown, Pennsylvania

Staff

Diane Berreth, Deputy Executive Director
Brian Curry, Policy Analyst

National Council for the Social Studies
Focus Group

Linda Levstick, Professor of Education
University of Kentucky

Janna Bremer, Teacher
King Philip Regional High School
Foxborough, Massachusetts

Jean Craven, District Coordinator/Curriculum Devel.
Albuquerque Public School District
Albuquerque, New Mexico

Mathew Downey, Professor of Education
University of California, Berkeley

Rachel Hicks, Teacher
Jefferson Jr. High School
Washington, D.C.

Jack Larner, Coordinator of Secondary
Social Studies, Department of History
Indiana University of Pennsylvania

Tarry Lindquist, Teacher
Lakeridge Elementary
Mercer Island, Washington

Denny Schillings, Teacher
Homewood-Flossmoor High School
Flossmoor, Illinois

Judith S. Wooster, Assistant Superintendent
Bethlehem Central Schools
Del Mar, New York

Ruben Zepeda, Teacher
Grant High School
Van Nuys, California

Council of State Social Studies Specialists
Focus Group

Norman Abramowitz, New York
Margaret (Peggy) Altoff, Maryland
Wendy Bonaiuto, South Dakota
Patricia Boyd, Nevada
Diane L. Brooks, California
Harvey R. Carmichael, Virginia
John M. Chapman, Michigan
Nijel Clayton, Kentucky
Pat Concannon, New Mexico
Edward T. Costa, Rhode Island
Thomas Dunthorn, Florida
Patricia J. Dye, Massachusetts
John D. Ellington, North Carolina
Curt Eriksmoen, North Dakota
Mary Fortney, Indiana
Rita Geiger, Oklahoma
Daniel W. Gregg, Connecticut
Carter B. Hart, Jr., New Hampshire
H. Michael Hartoonian, Wisconsin
Lewis E. Huffman, Delaware
Barbara Jones, West Virginia
Sharon Kaohi, Hawaii
Mary Jean Katz, Oregon
Marianne Kenney, Colorado
Judith Kishman, Wyoming

Frank Klajda, Arizona
John LeFeber, Nebraska
Richard Leighty, Kansas
Constance Miller Manter, Maine
Nancy N. Matthew, Utah
Nanette McGee, Georgia
Marjorie Menzi, Alaska
William Miller, Louisiana
Kent J. Minor, Ohio
John A. Nelson, Vermont
Bruce Opie, Tennessee
Linda Vrooman Peterson, Montana
Barbara Patty, Arkansas
Ann Pictor, Illinois
Joan Prewitt, Mississippi
Orville Reddington, Idaho
Michael Ryan, New Jersey
Warren Solomon, Missouri
Larry Strickland, Washington
Robert Summerville, Alabama
Cordell Svegalis, Iowa
Elvin E. Tyrone, Texas
Margaret B. Walden, South Carolina
Roger Wangen, Minnesota
James J. Wetzler, Pennsylvania

American Historical Association
World History Focus Group

Peter N. Stearns, Professor of History
Carnegie Mellon University

Robert A. Blackey, Professor of History
California State University, San Bernardino

John H. Coatsworth, Professor of History
Harvard University

Ross E. Dunn, Professor of History
San Diego State University

Robert Gutierrez, Teacher
Miami Sunset Senior High School

Joseph C. Miller, Professor of History
University of Virginia

Colin Palmer, Professor of History
University of North Carolina, Chapel Hill

Howard Spodek, Professor of History
Temple University

Julia Stewart Werner, Teacher
Nicolet High School
Glendale, Wisconsin

Judith P. Zinsser, Assistant Professor of History
Miami University

Staff

James B. Gardner, Acting Executive Director

Noralee Frankel, Assistant Director on Women and Minorities

Robert B. Townsend, Managing Editor

National Council for History Education
World History Focus Group

World History Association
Focus Group

John Mears, Chair
Professor of History
Southern Methodist University

Roger Beck, Professor of History
Eastern Illinois University

Jerry Bentley, Professor of History
University of Hawaii

Tim Connell, Teacher
Laurel School
Shaker Heights, Ohio

Darlene Fisher, Teacher
New Trier Township High School
Winnetka, Illinois

Steve Gosch, Professor of History
University of Wisconsin-Eau Claire

William B. Jones, Professor of History
Southwestern University

Donald Johnson, Professor of History
New York University

Jeannine Marston, Teacher
Castellaeja School
Palo Alto, California

Patricia O'Neill
Department of History
Central Oregon Community College
Bend, Oregon

Kevin Reilly
Department of History
Raritan Valley Community College

Sue Robertson, Teacher
Mills E. Godwin High School
Richmond, Virginia

Heidi Roupp, Teacher
Aspen High School
Aspen, Colorado

Lynda Shaffer, Professor of History
Tufts University

Organization of History Teachers
World History Focus Group

Susan Shapiro, Chair
The Laboratory Schools
University of Chicago

Mildred Alpern, Teacher
Spring Valley High School
Suffern, New York

Brant Abrahamson, Teacher
Riverside-Brookfield High School
Brookfield, Illinois

Geraldine Baader, Teacher
Bloom High School
Crete, Illinois

Robert Baader, Teacher
Brother Rice High School
Crete, Illinois

Bill Everdell, Teacher
St. Ann's School
Brooklyn, New York

Richard Hill, Teacher
Jordan High School
Durham, North Carolina

Ann Kazak, Teacher
Half Hollow Hills West High School
Dix Hills, New York

Ann Kashiwa, Teacher
Mariner Smith High School
Edmunds, Washington

Henry G. Kiernan, Supervisor of Humanities
West Morris Regional High School
Chester, New Jersey

Ronald Klene, Teacher
Lawrence North High School
Indianapolis, Indiana

Robert Lingow, Teacher
West Valley High School
Spokane, Washington

Alan Lucibello, Teacher
Montville High School
Montville, New Jersey

Tom Munkhall, Teacher
Spring Valley High School
Spring Valley, New York

Alan Proctor, Teacher
Hotchkiss School
Lakeville, Connecticut